WESTERN WAYS TO THE CENTER

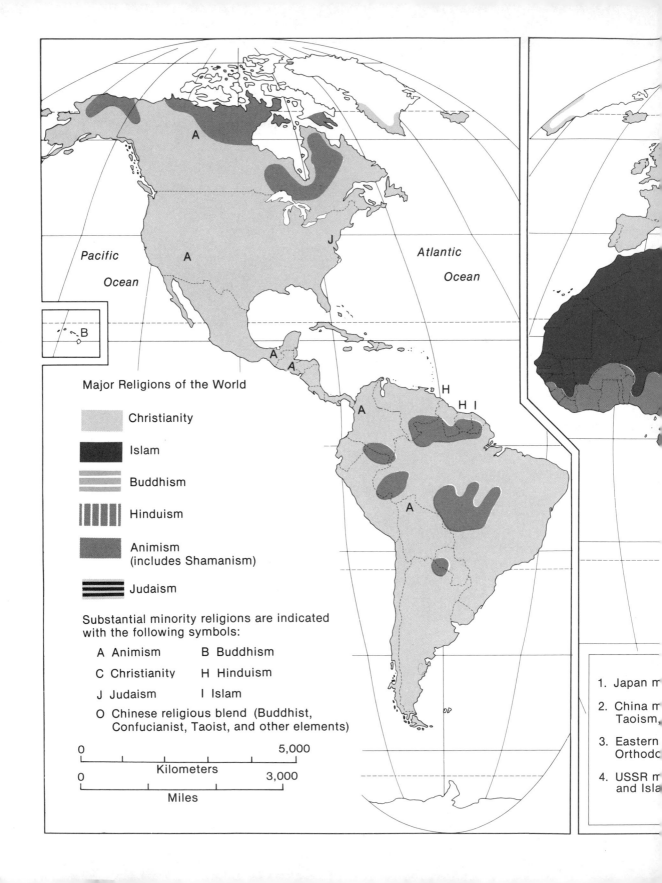

Pacific

Ocean

Atlantic

Ocean

A

A

J

B

A A

A

H

H I

A

Major Religions of the World

Christianity

Islam

Buddhism

Hinduism

Animism
(includes Shamanism)

Judaism

Substantial minority religions are indicated
with the following symbols:

A Animism   B Buddhism

C Christianity   H Hinduism

J Judaism   I Islam

O Chinese religious blend (Buddhist,
   Confucianist, Taoist, and other elements)

0   5,000
        Kilometers
0   3,000
          Miles

1. Japan m

2. China m
   Taoism,

3. Eastern
   Orthodo

4. USSR m
   and Isla

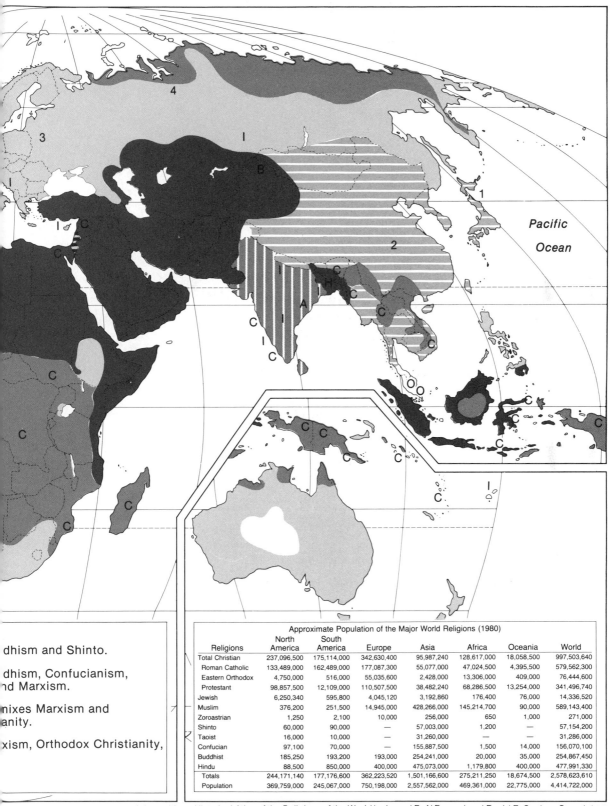

Pacific
Ocean

...dhism and Shinto.

...dhism, Confucianism,
...d Marxism.

...mixes Marxism and
...anity.

...xism, Orthodox Christianity,

	Approximate Population of the Major World Religions (1980)						
Religions	North America	South America	Europe	Asia	Africa	Oceania	World
Total Christian	237,096,500	175,114,000	342,630,400	95,987,240	128,617,000	18,058,500	997,503,640
Roman Catholic	133,489,000	162,489,000	177,087,300	55,077,000	47,024,500	4,395,500	579,562,300
Eastern Orthodox	4,750,000	516,000	55,035,600	2,428,000	13,306,000	409,000	76,444,600
Protestant	98,857,500	12,109,000	110,507,500	38,482,240	68,286,500	13,254,000	341,496,740
Jewish	6,250,340	595,800	4,045,120	3,192,860	176,400	76,000	14,336,520
Muslim	376,200	251,500	14,945,000	428,266,000	145,214,700	90,000	589,143,400
Zoroastrian	1,250	2,100	10,000	256,000	650	1,000	271,000
Shinto	60,000	90,000	—	57,003,000	1,200	—	57,154,200
Taoist	16,000	10,000	—	31,260,000	—	—	31,286,000
Confucian	97,100	70,000	—	155,887,500	1,500	14,000	156,070,100
Buddhist	185,250	193,200	193,000	254,241,000	20,000	35,000	254,867,450
Hindu	88,500	850,000	400,000	475,073,000	1,179,800	400,000	477,991,330
Totals	244,171,140	177,176,600	362,223,520	1,501,166,600	275,211,250	18,674,500	2,578,623,610
Population	369,759,000	245,067,000	750,198,000	2,557,562,000	469,361,000	22,775,000	4,414,722,000

Of related interest . . .

The Religious Life of Man Series   Frederick Streng, editor

WESTERN WAYS TO THE CENTER
AN INTRODUCTION TO WESTERN RELIGIONS

Denise Lardner Carmody
Wichita State University

John Tully Carmody
Wichita State University

Wadsworth Publishing Company
Belmont, California
A Division of Wadsworth, Inc.

Religious Studies editor: Sheryl Fullerton
Production editor: Judith McKibben
Managing and cover designer: Cynthia Bassett

Printed in the United States of America
1 2 3 4 5 6 7 8 9 10—87 86 85 84 83

ISBN 0-534-01328-7

Library of Congress Cataloging in Publication Data
Carmody, Denise Lardner, 1935–
    Western ways to the center.
    Bibliography: p.
    Includes index.
    1. Religions. I. Carmody, John, 1939–
II. Title.
BL80.2.C343   1982   291'.09182'1   82-15916
ISBN 0-534-01328-7

In Memory of

Catherine R. Carmody
Stephen J. Carmody
Denis Lardner
Martha Comen Lardner

Contents

Preface

This book derives from the numerous courses we have taught, singly and together, in the world religions. The following observations will indicate our intentions in writing it.

First, our main audience is college students. We do not assume prior courses in religion, and we have tried to use direct, clear prose.

Second, we have emphasized history and structural (philosophical and comparative) analysis, which seem to us the richest beginning approaches to the religions. The introduction explains our rationale, which we hope will give our work a distinctive character.

Third, a textbook has a secondary audience—the teachers who use it. For them (and the more adventurous students) we offer a sizable number of references, usually to recent sources. Because the journals *History of Religions* and *Journal of the American Academy of Religion* are easily available, we have frequently referred to articles in these journals, which we abbreviate in citations as *HR* and *JAAR*. The annotated bibliography at the back of the book, intended for students, emphasizes interesting works that are nontechnical.

Fourth, we explicitly discuss women's experiences with the Western religions, because most treatments give short shrift to the female population. Religion has been a major influence on women's cultural roles everywhere, so such neglect can impede liberation.

Fifth, the book revises and expands the materials on Western religions in our comprehensive world religions text, *Ways to the Center* (Wadsworth, 1981). The main blocks of new material are set in boxes, so that they may be used as enrichment studies.

Last, our deepest hope is that the book invites the reader to the mysterious center of human experience, where authentic religion offers all of us our best names.

We take pleasure in gratefully acknowledging help from the following persons and institutions: Robert L. Cohn, Thomas V. Peterson, John Pickering, the Institute for the Arts and Humanistic Studies of the Pennsylvania State University, the Institute for Ecumenical and Cultural Research (Collegeville, Minn.), the Mabelle McLeod Lewis Memorial Fund, the Office of Research and Sponsored Programs of Wichita State University, and the Research Office of the College of Liberal Arts of the Pennsylvania State University.

We are also indebted to the scholars who reviewed our manuscript at various stages and provided valuable suggestions: Willard Johnson, San Diego State University; M. Gerald Bradford, University of California at Santa Barbara; Gene R. Thursby, University of Florida; Robert F. Streetman, Montclair State College; Thomas V. Peterson, Alfred University; Nancy K. Frankenberry, Dartmouth College; Gary Davis, Northwest Missouri State University; W. Richard Comstock, University of California at Santa Barbara; Richard Paulson, Fresno City College; William B. Huntley, University of Redlands; R. Lanier Britsch, Brigham Young University; Robert S. Michaelsen, University of California at Santa Barbara; Glenn Yocum, Whittier College; Gerald Wilson, University of Georgia; J. Samuel Preus, Indiana University; and John Orr, University of Southern California.

Symbols Used on Chapter-Opening Pages

INTRODUCTION & CONCLUSION   *A contemporary sign for friendship between man and woman*

CHAPTER 1   *Egyptian symbol for divine wisdom*

CHAPTER 2   *Star of David*

CHAPTER 3   *Cross of Christ*

CHAPTER 4   *Crescent and star: Ancient Byzantine symbols taken over by victorious Islam*

Introduction

WESTERN WISDOM: TWENTY-FIVE KEY DATES

CA. 1360 B.C.E.	HYMNS OF AKHENATON
1000–500	REDACTIONS OF THE PENTATEUCH
CA. 750	HOMER'S *ILIAD* AND THE POETRY OF HESIOD
750–550	HEBREW PROPHETS
550	OLDEST PARTS OF ZOROASTRIAN *AVESTA*
525–406	AESCHYLUS, SOPHOCLES, EURIPIDES
469–322	SOCRATES, PLATO, ARISTOTLE
400–250	JOB; ECCLESIASTES
CA. 50–90 C.E.	NEW TESTAMENT WRITINGS
80–110	CANONIZATION OF HEBREW SCRIPTURES
325	FIRST COUNCIL OF NICAEA
413–426	AUGUSTINE'S *CITY OF GOD*

The religious life of humanity is a vast spectacle that is hard to keep in perspective. Therefore, we should make our goals and methods clear from the outset. Our primary goal is to make clear how the Western religious traditions have oriented billions of human lives. Our primary method is to place the study of religion in the context of the humanities and approach the traditions with a consistent format. Let us explain these notions in more detail.

THE NATURE OF RELIGION

Picture yourself in New Delhi. You are outside *Rajgat*, the memorial to Mahatma Gandhi, the politician and holy man who led India to freedom from British colonial rule. Before you, squatting on the broken sidewalk, are three small boys with wooden flutes. They are piping tunes directed toward round wicker baskets, and when they lift the baskets' covers, three silver cobras slowly weave their way out. You watch for several minutes, fearful but entranced. Then the boys shove the cobras back under their arms and approach you for their fee. A few rupees seem fair enough—you don't want to upset those cobras.

Does this picture shine a light on the exotic East? Is it a minor revelation of Indian culture? Yes, but only if you know a little background. In India, as in many other countries with ancient cultures, serpents have been potent symbols (think of the story in Genesis, chapter 3). Perhaps because they appear menacing or phallic (penislike), they have stood for something very basic, something very close to the life force. For centuries, groups of Indians have specialized in snake handling, and the skills have been passed along from father to son. Their profession has combined show business and a bit of crude religion. It has been both entertainment and an occasion to shiver about the implications of death and life.

Now picture yourself in medieval England. In 627 C.E. ("common era" = A.D.)

the monk Paulinus came to King Edwin in northern England and urged him to convert his people to Christianity. After some debate, one of Edwin's counselors stood up and said: "Your majesty, on a winter night like this, it sometimes happens that a little bird flies in that far window, to enjoy the warmth and light of our fire. After a short while it passes out again, returning to the dark and the cold. As I see it, our human life is much the same. We have but a brief time between two great darknesses. If this monk can show us warmth and light, we should follow him."[1]

For medieval Europe, the warmth and light that made life seem good radiated from Jesus Christ. At the core of Europe's complex and in many ways crude culture at that time, there was a faith that a personal father God so loved the world that he had given his son to heal and enlighten it. When they shared that faith, European monks, kings, and kings' counselors largely agreed on their conception of life. Monks, for instance, were willing to give up family life in order to bear witness to God's love. Kings tried to show that their rule derived from what God had done through Jesus, and counselors tried to show commoners how the kings' rule mediated God's will. Often, of course, monks and kings and counselors did things that we find hard to square with Jesus, pursuing wealth and power by means of guile. But their culture forced them all to confront Christian warmth and light, as Indian culture forced Indians to confront sex, death, and life.

Our two pictures are not quite compatible. The modern Indian scene stressed rather primitive sexual or vital energies, while the medieval English scene stressed lofty love and vision. Westerners have tended to view Indian and European life in that way, as the writings of early Christian missionaries to India suggest. However, the past century of scholarship in religious studies has shown the deficiencies of such an attitude, so we must add a few comments on the two scenes.

First, drawing a picture of medieval Europe that is raw and primitive would not

Figure 1   Head of Christ, attributed to Rembrandt (1606–1669). The Metropolitan Museum of Art, Mr. and Mrs. Isaac D. Fletcher Collection, bequest of Isaac D. Fletcher, 1917.

Spring sums up medieval primitiveness. Sex and death pour out in her blood, and only after her father has slain the rapists do we see hope for new life trickle forth in a fresh spring. Medieval Europe, Bergman suggests, was as raw as India has ever been.

Second, were we to go inside the memorial to Gandhi and look at the scene at his commemorative stone, the sublimity of Indian culture and its visions of warmth and light would rise up and parallel those of Christian Europe. *Rajgat* blends green grass, elegant black marble, and fresh flower petals of orange and pink. They symbolize the beautiful spirit of the Mahatma, the little man of great soul. Gandhi was a politician who moved people by *satyagraha*—the force of truth. Without military arms, much money, or even much respect from British leaders, he forced the whole world to take notice. When he vowed to take no food until India's just claims were met, the world held its breath. When he led groups of nonviolent *satyagrahis* into the midst of club-swinging soldiers, he upset the conscience of the world. By the simple rightness, the sheer justice, of his cause, Gandhi showed how his Hindu conception of God could be very powerful. His God was "Truth," and it finally shamed the British into withdrawal.

Snakes and scourges, love and truth—they have shot through India, Europe, and most other parts of the world. In contemporary America, they or their offspring live with us yet. For instance, our nuclear missiles are for many citizens and analysts eerie phallic symbols. Like cobras we are trying to get back in their baskets, the missiles give us shivers. Many people see the missiles' thrust, their destructive power, and the claims that they give us security or economic life as brutalizing and raping our culture. From Hiroshima to Three Mile Island, nuclear power muddles our wellsprings and hope.

So too with the ways that we whip ourselves for guilt, the ways that we still crave love, the ways that we search after light. Our guilt keeps psychiatrists in business. Our searches for light fill churches and

be hard. In Ingmar Bergman's movies of the medieval period, such as *The Seventh Seal* and *The Virgin Spring*, death and sex and life are jammed together like serpents in a basket. Because of the Black Death, the plague that killed about three-quarters of the late medieval European population, monks and commoners marched in processions while they beat themselves, scourging their flesh with whips to do penance for their sins and to keep death away. The harshness of medieval life also led to brutal wars and brutal rapes. The knight and the squire of *The Seventh Seal*, who watch the procession of penitents, have kept company with death since they went to war as Crusaders. The young girl who is raped and killed in *The Virgin* schools. Clearly we are sisters and brothers to religious Indians and Europeans. Clearly their snakes and saviors relate to our own.

Religion is the issue of ultimate meaning that this discussion of cobras and monks spotlights. It is the part of culture—Eastern, Western, or contemporary American—that we study when we ask about a people's deepest convictions. For instance, Hinduism is the animating spirit, the soul, the way of looking at the world, that has tied snake handling and *satyagraha* together for most Indians. Christianity is the way of looking at the world that has joined scourging to Jesus for most Europeans. Religion, then, is what you get when you investigate striking human phenomena to find the ultimate vision or set of convictions that gives them their sense. It is the cast of mind and the gravity of heart by which a people endures or enjoys its time between the two great darknesses.

STUDYING RELIGION

Certain attitudes should be cultivated in all study, but the study of religion demands more self-awareness and personal engagement with its materials than most other disciplines do. For instance, although reducing physical science to "objective" observing and testing is simplistic, since all knowledge is ultimately personal,[2] physical science does not make great demands on a student's inner experiences of suffering or love. The humanities (those disciplines that study our efforts at self-expression and self-understanding) involve more of such inner experiences, because suffering and love shape so much of history and literature, yet even the humanities seldom deal with direct claims about ultimate meaning. Only in philosophy and religion does one directly encounter systems about God, evil, and humanity's origin and end. Philosophy deals with such concepts principally in their rational forms, while religious studies meet them

more concretely in the myths, rituals, mysticisms, behavior patterns, and institutions through which most human beings have been both drawn to ultimate meaning and terrified of it.

More than in any other discipline, the student in a religious studies course is confronted with imperative claims. The religions are not normally warehouses where you pay your money and take your choice. Rather, they are impassioned heralds of ways of life. More than most people initially like, the religions speak of death, ignorance, and human viciousness. However, they also speak of peace and joy, forgiveness and harmony. Whatever they discuss, though, they are *mystagogic*, which etymologically means "mystery working." The religions work mystery. Their preoccupations, when they are healthy, are nature's wonder, life's strange play of physical death and spiritual resurrection, and the possibility of order in the midst of chaos. The religions say that the kingdom of God is in your midst, because you are a being who can pray, "Abba, Father." They say that the *Tao* ("the Way") that can be named is not the real *Tao*. Above all, they say that the person who lives divorced from the mysteries of rosy-fingered dawn and wintery death is less than fully human. So Sioux Indians revered the East, because dawn symbolizes the light of conscience. So Jewish scripture speaks of love as strong as death. So, finally, Islam speaks for all religions when it says that Allah—Muslim divinity—is as near as the pulse at our throats. Clearly, then, we cannot study the religions well if we are afraid of mystery or in flight from death and life.

We also cannot study the religions well if we insist on forcing them into the categories of our own faith. We must first take them on their own terms, giving their experiences and problems a sympathetic hearing. After we have listened to the wisdom of a scripture such as the Hindu *Bhagavad Gita*, we may and should compare it with the wisdom of our Western faiths. Unless we then say with the Christians' Saint Peter, "I see now how true it is that God has no favorites, but that in every nation the person who is God-fearing and does what is right is acceptable" (Acts 10:34), we risk acting with prejudice and condescension.

A second reason for remembering life's mystery, then, is that it helps us clear away prejudice. Talk of the New Testament superseding the Old or of revealed religion besting paganism—without strong qualifications— is self-serving and naive. Used as a word of God, Jewish scriptures open onto a divinity ever new, ever fresh, and ever free. Taken in its experiential vividness, a Zen Buddhist's enlightenment *(satori)* tears the veil of ignorance and comes as revelation and grace.[3] As Thomas Aquinas insisted, we do not know what God is. As John Calvin knew, the mind without mystery is a factory of idols. The most authoritative Western theologians have counseled against prejudice.

It is worth pointing out that the religious studies course offered here is not theology, at least not the theology of a church. Church theology tends to be a search for an understanding of one's own faith that is directed by the particular creed or commitment of an individual or group. Spontaneously the search spreads to a probing of all life's dimensions in terms of such a commitment. So, there develops a theology of art, a theology of history, and even a theology of the world religions.[4] In these theologies, however, a goal is to square data with one's own faith or religious group. Moreover, a church theology's ultimate goal is to promote its own faith. It studies art, history, or the world religions in order to beautify, advance, or defend its own vision of things, whether the church be Muslim, Buddhist, Jewish, or Christian. The understanding that theology seeks in such study is not necessarily distorted, but it is in the service of preaching, ministering, and counseling. When it is not in such service, church theology becomes divorced from the life of its community.[5]

In a university, however, neither students nor teachers are expected to confess their faith (or nonfaith). We, the authors, have argued elsewhere[6] that it is proper and healthy to make clear one's position on the *implications,* for thought and action alike, to which a course's studies lead. In other words, there is nothing wrong and much right with teachers and students becoming personal—dealing with concrete, practical implications. There is much wrong, however, in university courses that place their own values on other people's art, history, or religion and thereby distort them. One must listen with an open mind before judging and deciding.

So we urge you to get inside the religions' experiences and values and to compare them with your own. In fact, we very much hope that your study will enrich your appreciation of nature, increase your wonder about life's meaning, and increase your resources for resisting evil. But we do not set these hopes in the framework of any one faith. We are not, in other words, doing church theology. You may be Christian, Jewish, Buddhist, agnostic, atheistic, or anything else. To us such labels do not matter. What matters is that you be human: a man or woman trying to hear the Delphic oracle's "know thyself," a person humble with the Confucian virtue of sympathy or "fellow feeling" *(jen).*

What benefits will this effort to study humanistically bring you? At least two spring to mind. First, you will be able to grapple with some of the most influential and wisest personalities of the past. Second, you will better understand the world of the present, in which all peoples on the globe are much closer than they have ever been before.

To illustrate the first benefit, let us call on the Chinese sage Confucius. In his time (551–479 B.C.E.) people were advancing the dictum that it is better to pay court to the stove (to practicalities) than to heaven (to ideals) (see *Analects* 3:3). Confucius batted their dictum back. If you do not pay court to heaven, he said, you will have no recourse when practicalities fail to bring you good life. In other words, the mystery of life is more than food and drink, more than shelter and pleasure. Important as those things are, they do not make truly good life. Only moving in the Way *(Tao)* of heaven makes us humans what we ought to be and what we most deeply want to be. If we settle for the stove, we halve our potential riches.

To illustrate the second benefit of the humanistic study of religion, we must comment briefly on current history. Today it is a commonplace observation that the world is becoming one. That does not mean that all peoples are agreeing on a common government, economy, or philosophy. It does mean that communications, transportation, economics, and other forces are tying all nations together. Thus, commentators speak of a "global village" or a "planetary culture." They remind us of the novelty of the twentieth century, the only time when it could have happened that when Gandhi fasted, the world held its breath; that when Mao died, his funeral reached every capital. Further, in our nuclear age all curtains can be raised. In our age of escalating population and hunger, all the silos of Kansas cast shadows on East Africa.

All the implications of the current state of affairs are too numerous to detail. We may be on the verge of a new phase of evolution; the human sciences may just be approaching their maturity. Or the outer complexity of human affairs may just be developing a self-consciousness among humans so that they can cope with these affairs. In either case, religion acquires an added significance, because we cannot learn much about the evolution or self-consciousness of the global village unless we listen to its members' deepest perceptions and convictions. Religion shows a people's deepest perceptions and convictions. Hinduism, Buddhism, Christianity, and Islam form the souls of a majority of the world's population today. To live together in the future, humans will have to understand other religions very well.

THE SACRED

As a first step to understanding the Western religions, let us focus on an ancient notion that has been very important in all the Western traditions we shall study—the notion of the sacred. The *Oxford English Dictionary* defines *sacred* as "set apart for or dedicated to some religious purpose." For ancient peoples it meant the realm of the truly real, the realm of the gods or venerable powers.

This idea of the sacred was vital among the first humans. We believe this because nonliterate people today sense that one can live in passionate connection with what is most real and valuable or in disassociation from it. They sense that they ought to be in harmony with the power that courses through sky and earth and sea and that they often are not. Further, they, and no doubt the first humans, have seen the destruction that disharmony can bring— natural disasters, disease, slaughter, and death. So the realm of ultimacy, the realm of power and the truly real, has been both concrete and mysterious. It has been the massive given with which ancient people have had to contend. They may not have abstracted its powers into a "realm" or personified it as an expression of a primordial will, but they have completely turned their spirits toward its puzzles and sway.[7]

The experience of the sacred, in Rudolf Otto's celebrated description, involves the sense of a mystery that is both fearsome and fascinating.[8] It has been most vivid in nature's manifestations of power, but it might also occur in initiation rites, ceremonial ecstasy, or other intense experiences. With modifications, we can glimpse the experience of the sacred in the accounts of enlightenment and peak experiences from religious and psychological literature. The visions of Isaiah (6 : 1–13), Ezekiel (1 : 1–29), and Revelation (1 : 1–29) show some of the sacred's biblical expressions. In all these cases, we can see what is finally an ancient imagination dazzled by the pure power that makes everything that is. Perhaps this power, Van der Leeuw has argued, is religion's central object.[9]

As many scholars have shown, the sacred can touch any aspect of creation or life. Van der Leeuw himself deals with stones, trees, water, fire, sky, mother, father, demon, angel, king, life, death, preacher, priest, community, family, church, nation, soul, and more. The sacred may even focus on human hair and fingernails.[10] Clearly, ancient humanity felt the power of creation, the awesome force of life and being, everywhere. During a storm, the power could be manifested as thunder and lightning. More tranquilly, it could play on the waters.[11] Regularly it would rush in at birth and death. Hunting, planting, weaving, metalworking—all occupations felt power's touch. Thus, ancient peoples lived with a fact that the early Greek scientist Thales only glimpsed in a vision: "The world is full of gods." For them nothing that one saw or did was without its heavenly archetype.

This omnipresence of sacred power is perhaps our best thread through the labyrinth of the ancient religions. To dramatize the omnipresence, let us draw on some examples of sacredness that Mircea Eliade has assembled in his thematic sourcebook *From Primitives to Zen*.[12] For the Delaware Indians of North America, the four directions of the compass were sacred and merited prayers of thanksgiving. They thanked the east for the morning, when the light is bright and everyone feels good. They thanked the west for the end of day, when the sun goes down and everyone can again feel good. To the north they owed thanks for the wind, whose cold coming reminds us that we have lived to see the leaves fall again. To the south they owed thanks for the warm winds that make the grass turn green.

For the Naskapi Indians of Labrador, hunting was especially sacred, since it was their most important occupation. The Naskapi believed that the animals they hunted had emotions and purposes like their own, and that in the beginning animals could talk like humans. So the Naskapi would sing and drum to them as to friends. Similarly, they would take great care not to mutilate certain bones of the elk or beaver believed to enclose an inner soul, a spirit like the hunter's own. Indeed, at death the animals gathered in their animal realm, just as human spirits gathered in the human realm. Both realms were conceived as stages in a cycle of reincarnation (rebirth in a new form), and so both sets of spirits were bound together. If the hunters did not know the behavioral principles governing their sacred connections with the animals, all sorts of misfortune could ensue. The hunt would be fruitless, the people would be without food, or sickness and even death might descend.

As hunting peoples considered their pursuit of game sacred, so agricultural peoples considered farming sacred. Zoroastrians, for instance, taught that for the land to bear fruit, it had to be sown in the way that a husband lovingly fertilizes his wife. The Native Americans who raised corn (maize) reverenced it as the gift of the Corn Maiden and harvested it ceremonially.[13] Other Native Americans insisted on treating the earth especially gently in the spring, for then it was like a woman pregnant with new life. To plow it, even to walk or run on it without care, would have been to mistreat a full womb.

In a word, just about every aspect of human experience has at some time been held sacred. Thought and sex, trees and waters, stones and ancestors—all have been considered manifestations of power or holiness. We can say, therefore, that the sacred is the ultimate or deepest significance that anything, place, or person can manifest if seen at the right angle. For instance, the beggar can seem to wear a coat of holiness. Usually a marginal if not contemptible figure, he or she can, with a shift of vision, become a source of blessing. Then God is held to cherish the poor, and one hears stories of almsgivers meeting with angels or Christs in disguise. On the other end of the social scale, chieftains and kings have regularly been reverenced as sacred. In fact, the king has been not only a ruler by divine right but also a frequent sacrificial figure, killed for the sake of his people.[14]

More understandably, perhaps, the shamans, yogis, and medicine men who are prominent in ancient societies' dealings with the sacred take on auras of holiness. Because they are mediums for encountering the venerable powers, they themselves are venerated and feared. Normally ancient peoples feel that the sacred itself is a good or at least an indifferent force. If one is not in harmony with it, however, it can be destructive. Therefore, one has to approach sacred functionaries with some caution.

A story by the contemporary Native American storyteller Durango Mendoza captures this feeling of caution.[15] Two children make fun of an old man. He has a reputation for witchcraft—the ability to turn special powers against his enemies. When one of the children later becomes sick, the story suggests an almost palpable presence of evil. As studies of Navaho witchcraft have shown, this evil (power turned malevolent) is often a strong component of the American Indian world view.[16] In dealing with the holy, human beings risk being consumed in burning flames. If humans are not protected, the holy can destroy them.

Many ancient aversions and taboos (irrational or magical forbiddings of contact with items thought to be dangerous) can be explained by this belief that the sacred demands purity. Contact with the dead, for instance, is often a source of pollution. Because many peoples have considered contact with a menstruating woman to be polluting, ancient woman was a powerful figure.[17] In neither case is the pollution something moral—it is not a matter of bad will, bad choice, or sin. Rather, it is a matter of being out of phase with the sacred and so endangered.

It is difficult for us in modern technological societies to appreciate this ancient sense of the sacred. However, our own interests in the occult, astrology, demonology,

and parapsychology indicate that we still sense part of its world. Indeed, the ancient world portrayed so effectively by Carlos Castaneda forces us to realize how much our own reality is the product of social consensus and the inner dialogue that we constantly carry on.[18] If we lived in the midst of people who were awestruck by the sun, we, too, would likely reverence its rays.

Today simple vegetative forces remain quite tremendous, quite capable of humbling us. For instance, Annie Dillard reports that a single plant of winter rye grass can send forth 378 miles of roots with 14 billion root hairs. One cubic inch of its soil can contain 6,000 miles of root hairs.[19] The power coursing through the natural world is staggering, and when we are staggered, we are open to the sacred.

ORGANIZATION OF THE BOOK

In the pages that follow, we shall study Western peoples' dealings with the sacred. Throughout, the ancient veneration of holy forces will never be far away. Both prior to civilization (writing and town life) and through civilization to very recent times, the majority of Western people have lived fairly close to nature, participating deeply in the *cosmological myth* (the notion that all realities are part of a single living whole). Our book is organized to suggest the developments that went beyond the cosmological myth and gave rise to the civilizational religions of Egypt, Persia, and Greece, as well as to the Near Eastern prophetic religions, Judaism, Christianity, and Islam. In all of these cases, the sacred "differentiated" somewhat from the cosmological myth. That is, in all of these cases the differences among nature, society, the self, and divinity became more pronounced than they had been for nonliterate peoples.

Chapter 1 deals with Egypt, Persia, and Greece, stressing what religion looked like during humanity's development of agriculture, writing, early science, and fine art.

Chapters 2, 3, and 4 deal with Judaism, Christianity, and Islam. In Israelite (early Jewish) religion, we first focus on prophecy—people feeling called to speak God's "word." Using prophecy to characterize Judaism, Christianity, and Islam, we can say that Indian and East Asian religions, by contrast, are sapiential—concerned more with *wisdom*. Such a contrast is only partially true, but it is a useful way to first distinguish religions in Asia and the Near East.

Christians developed certain Israelite notions about prophecy, history, and messianism (the expectancy of an anointed leader), producing a rich culture of thought and institutions. Islam, perhaps the fullest prophetic religion, proceeded from Judaism and Christianity, and in its own eyes superseded them. Islam has experienced great waves of military triumph and culture, but also considerable stagnation. Today it is on the march, winning much of Africa and pressing on the West through its petrodollars.

These three Near Eastern religions, with their offshoots and cousins (for example, Sikhism and Baha'i), account for almost half the world's people. In the West, Judaism and Christianity, with Greek and Roman culture, remain our heritage.

The book concludes with reflections somewhat similar to those with which we began this introduction. Having surveyed the Western religious traditions, we shall at the end pause again to take stock. First, we will look back at the religions' unity and diversity. Second, we will have some thoughts on the uses of religion—on the services religion has tendered through the centuries. Third, we will reflect on being an American citizen of the religious world—a contemporary at least somewhat tutored by the mysterious humanity of the past. In that way, perhaps, our book will complete its circle and make a *mandala*—a symbol of wholeness.

Our material content is as comprehensive as our space allows. To organize all this information, though, we have employed a format that has three aspects. First, wherever possible, we will describe how the reli-

gion under consideration appears. In other words, we will try to describe what it looks like and its atmosphere. From travel and study, we will offer vignettes of Jewish temples, Christian churches, and Muslim art. Ideally, these vignettes will launch you into each religion briskly, engaging your interest and whetting your taste.

The second aspect of the format is history. Having dealt with the religion's appearance, we will tell its story—trace how it evolved. Historical explanation is now a staple in Western studies. You use its cause-effect reasoning every day. Therefore, the second aspect should present few problems.

The last aspect of our format is structural analysis: asking how a religion puts together its world view.[20] For example, how does it tend to think and feel about the physical world? As you will see, Egypt and Israel tended to think differently about the physical world. Similarly, if we investigate a religion's sense of society, self, or divinity, we will find illuminating likenesses and unlikenesses. Structural analysis and comparison, then, enable us to sharpen differences and discern similarities.

Finally, a few pedagogical comments. Our three-aspect format stems from what we have discovered about the mind's patterns of inquiry. In inquiry, the mind regularly moves from experience, through understanding and judgment, to decision.[21] That is, human knowing begins in wonder, from information that teases and beguiles. Then it works to grasp and affirm reality—to achieve an understanding of how the information makes sense, to achieve an insight or "click." Finally, this understanding leads to a decision: What am I going to do about this insight; what action does it command? Thus, our format moves from soliciting your interest in a religion, to explaining how it arose, to analyzing it structurally so that you can decide what it might mean for your own life.

Our job, finally, is to structure the material so that you may understand it and decide well. Your job is to be attentive, intelligent, reflective, and decisive. If you do so, you will make progress toward your center. If we do our job well, you will see how the religions themselves are but ways to the Center. The coincidence of your center and the Center is that peak experience which T. S. Eliot described as being "at the still point of the turning world." We human beings are so made that all our significant times, good and bad, take us into mystery. Mystery is more intimate to us than we are to ourselves. Mystery is closer than the pulse at our throats. Centering in mystery and recognizing that only ultimate reality can give us our lives, religious persons the world over have been paramount humanists. To follow their ways, even just in one's mind, is therefore a great chance for liberal—freeing—education. We will be happy if we increase your likelihood of seizing such a chance.

Study Questions

1. What would it mean for you to say, "Religious studies are integral to liberal education"?
2. Are the world religions more significant today than they were a generation ago?
3. How would you relate the history of religious traditions to their comparative analysis?
4. Can you describe your mind's movement from experience to understanding to judgment to decision?
5. How could the sacred be the center of ancient religion?
6. What was the American Indian notion of the sacred?

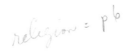

religion = p 6

Chapter One

RELIGIONS OF ANCIENT CIVILIZATIONS: TWENTY-FIVE KEY DATES

CA. 6500 B.C.E.   FIRST FARMING IN GREECE AND AEGEAN COUNTRIES

CA. 5000   AGRICULTURAL SETTLEMENTS IN EGYPT

CA. 3100   UNIFICATION OF EGYPT; MEMPHITE THEOLOGY

2700–2200   OLD KINGDOM IN EGYPT

2590   GREAT PYRAMIDS AT GIZA

2050–1800   MIDDLE KINGDOM IN EGYPT

2000   BEGINNING OF MINOAN CIVILIZATION IN CRETE

1570–1165   NEW KINGDOM IN EGYPT

CA. 1500   IRANIAN-SPEAKING PEOPLES RISE

1370   AKHENATON'S "MONOTHEISTIC" REFORM

1200   COLLAPSE OF MYCENAEAN CIVILIZATION IN GREECE

776   FIRST OLYMPIC GAMES

Religions of
Ancient Civilizations

The passage from oral, hunting societies to literate, urban civilizations was momentous. For oral Paleolithic peoples, the world was alive with animistic powers. For the civilized peoples who followed in the wake of the Sumerians' invention of writing (about 3100 B.C.E.), the world was still mysterious, but in a different way, in part because many plants and animals had been domesticated. Between Paleolithic and civilized peoples lay millennia of cultural evolution and significant technological and religious developments. Before dealing with three impressive religious civilizations—Egypt, Iran, and Greece—let us briefly consider those developments.

DEVELOPMENTS BEFORE CIVILIZATION

By now, you should realize that early humanity forged an impressive spiritual world. The pivotal discovery by prehistoric humanity was agriculture. Before we analyze the antecedents and consequents of that discovery, let us try to imagine how agricultural religion appeared.

Consider a prehistoric farmer. Most likely, the farmer is a woman. Centuries before, her forebears advanced from gathering seeds to planting them. Slowly they came to control a small number of crops and learned to make them thrive. So the farmer does her work confidently because she knows her craft. She still talks to the plants, as people did before agriculture, but many of her fellow farmers consider that outmoded. They know that the individual plants do not determine the harvest as much as the Great Mother, from whom all life issues. If she does not give, all fields will be barren. Our farmer knows this, too, but she still likes to talk to the plants.

It is a good time to be a woman. With a clearer understanding of the Mother has come a better appreciation of women's worth. Many tribes now have a matriarchal structure, and inheritance often passes along the female line. Further, the women's groups and temples form strong bonds among the women. Serving the Mother, many women are deeply content. In rites of praise or holy sex, they affirm their own woman power and need a man only briefly. The important work proceeds secretly, as it does under the earth.

Patiently the farmer cares for her field. Soon the child she is carrying may be helping. She hopes it will be another maker of life, another daughter for the Mother. The warm sun soothes the farmer's neck, and her strained muscles unknot. She wipes her brow and speaks again toward the Mother. "Care for my child, holy Mother. See that my field grows well. I am your daughter, consecrated to you. Give my days full measure. The first fruits I gather have always been yours. They will always be. When you help me, all my work is easy. Help me, then, all days."

Before Agriculture

For the more prosaic, and more certain, aspects of the history of religion before civilization, a useful guide is the first volume of Mircea Eliade's history of religious ideas.[1] In it, Eliade, a very influential historian of religion, summarizes the major religious advances from prehistory to the time of the city-state. At the beginning, more than 2 million years ago, our ancestors pondered life's mysteriousness—largely in terms of the implications of hunting. Living off animal flesh, they both established a mystical bond with the animal world and made a significant change in their own evolution: "Hunting determined the division of labor in accordance with sex, thus reinforcing 'hominization'; for among the carnivora, and in the entire animal world, no such difference exists."[2] Thus, well before 600,000 B.C.E. (the date of the first documented use of fire), humans had moved into a world of self-generated meanings by developing tools for hunting and home use.

The earliest remains believed to be used for religious purposes are bones, and those from the Mousterian period (70,000–50,000 B.C.E.) indicate the practice of burial, probably with hopes for an afterlife. The problem in interpreting ancient artifacts (many of them much older than the Mousterian), though, is that they are "opaque": Their meanings are uncertain. Without written texts or at least semididactic ("teaching") art, we can only imagine how Paleolithic people used such artifacts—what the people thought, why they sang and danced, and so on. The situation is somewhat better in the Paleolithic period (30,000–9000 B.C.E.), since many cave paintings reflect the theme of animal life. They make it clear that Paleolithic peoples were bonded to animals out of need, reverence, and fear.

Some of the motifs in the cave paintings correspond to what we know from shamanist hunting peoples of modern times. For instance, many paintings combine animal and human forms (the shaman often identifies with a bird or wolf), and the "X-ray" paintings manifest an interest in skeletal structures (many shamans meditate on skulls and bones, which they consider the crucial animal elements).

If the apparent similarities between certain Paleolithic remains and the arts of ancient peoples living today are valid, we can infer that Mesolithic tribes had a complex world of signs and symbols—a cosmos (ordered whole) with many sacred layers. We know that shamanist ecstasy is a prehistoric phenomenon. We can guess that a more enduring wonder about the human language lent great imaginative power to such ecstasy, as it did to ritual and myth. From at least Mesolithic times, then, human beings have tried to coordinate sex, sacrifice, death, animals, the moon, and the stars—all the striking, impressive phenomena of their lives.

Moreover, the end of the Ice Age seems to have marked a division between prehistoric peoples and their ancestors. From Mesolithic times there is mention of a golden era, a paradise when human relations with heaven and the animals were more harmonious. Probably this idea represents the culmination of hunting peoples' myths and reflection—an early form of mythic speculation on the ways things ought to be. In any case, when the glaciers melted, the flood brought the world's periodicity into sharper focus. Also, questions arose of moral responsibility and guilt: What caused the flood? How did we lose paradise? Ancestors, believed to linger on as ghosts or spiritual presences, also stimulated such questions: What is our relationship to our predecessors who knew better times? To increase their chances of living in a good age, ancient hunters likely developed a code of behavior and a cluster of taboos that they attributed to their ancestors: "Live this way and you will prosper."

After Agriculture

The great practical advances of the Mesolithic period were settled communities and the domestication of plants and animals. In the Near East, especially in Palestine, these advances created a period of strong cultural activity, as people strove to understand and express the far-reaching changes in their life-styles. The remains of the Natufian culture at Wadi en-Natuf, for instance, show a people who built a village of circular huts, harvested wild cereals with stone sickles, and ground seeds with mortar and pestle. (There is evidence that cereals were a dietary staple in the valley of the upper Nile as early as 13,000 B.C.E.) By 6500 B.C.E. different Near Eastern communities had domesticated sheep, goats, and pigs. The Mesolithic period also produced numerous important inventions, among them the bow, cords, nets, hooks, and boats.

In Eliade's view, such inventions have more than just practical or economic effects. When people work with different materials imaginatively and creatively, they develop a sophisticated sense of the many possibilities in matter—the many analogies between tools and artifacts, human work and natural processes. Thus, they easily create rich symbolisms or mystiques. Many ancient peoples gave mining, harvesting, or sewing a sort of densely symbolic value. A fairly direct line runs from their prehistoric world to that of the medieval alchemist and even that of the modern engineer.

Before the Mesolithic turn to agriculture and a more settled life, nomadic cultures depended on hunting, blood sacrifices, and a close identification with animals. In later times, these Paleolithic themes continued to play in the background. Through military groups, myths of the days of nomadic life, hunting for sport, and occasional orgies (with frenzied tearing of animals and eating of raw flesh), agricultural peoples kept contact with their past. Nonetheless, after village life came "vegeculture" (the cultivation of roots, tubers, and rhizomes), and then agriculture (the cultivation of cereals and grasses). The religious impact of these cultures was revolutionary.

For instance, as producers of food, human beings had to calculate the seasons much more accurately. This led to astronomical calculations, astrology, and the worship of planets and stars. Further, agriculture meant a more intimate knowledge of the regular cycle of death and rebirth. In the typical myth of Hainuwele, from New Guinea, we can see the ancient struggle to comprehend this new set of mysteries.[3] By her murder and dismemberment, the semidivine Hainuwele allowed tuberous plants to spring forth. In other words, vegeculture depended on a primordial murder. More deliberately than hunters, who find available animals, cultivators bury life in order to secure their food. Summarizing the psychic impact of this new situation, Eliade says, "All responsible activities (puberty ceremonies, animal or human sacrifices, cannibalism, funerary ceremonies, etc.) properly speaking constitute a recalling, a 'remembrance,' of the primordial murder. It is significant that the cultivator associates with a murder the essentially peaceful labor that insures his existence, whereas in societies of hunters the responsibility for slaughter is attributed to *another*, to a 'stranger.'"[4]

Succeeding the mystical solidarity between hunters and animals, then, is a mystical solidarity between cultivators and plants. Whereas in earliest times blood and bone were the essential, most sacred elements of life, in agricultural times the generative elements—masculine sperm and feminine blood—became most sacred. Above all, women dominated agricultural life, and "mother earth" was the prime focus. Through the millennia, before the biology of reproduction became clear, the earth was believed to give birth independently, without need of any male. Because women developed agriculture and controlled it, and because women issued all human life, Mesolithic culture valued women as it did mother earth and gave women great religious and political power. Thus, from this period the best-known great goddesses came; during this period matriarchy thrived. Sexuality became a sacred drive and process, because all nature—the whole cosmos—moved through a religious cycle of conception, gestation, birth, nurturance, growth, decline, and then death (which may be a new conception).

Houses, villages, shrines, and burial vaults all reflected the womb architecturally. The earth itself is uterine: From it we come, to it we return. Accordingly, myths of human creation speak of first ancestors crawling forth from mines or caves, and funerary rituals consign the dead offspring back to the Great Mother. During this initial period of agriculture, there was an increased stress on polarities—earth and sky, dirt and rain, yin and yang (the Chinese dual elements).

This stress on the earth of the Mesolithic continued into Neolithic times, when village life developed into city life, agriculture became more extensive and secure, and arts and crafts such as pottery, weaving, and tool manufacturing were established. Also, in the Neolithic period, cults of fertility and death assumed even greater prominence. From sanctuaries excavated in Anatolia (modern Turkey), we know that around 7000 B.C.E. worship involved skulls and various gifts, such as jewels, weapons, and textiles. The principal divinity was a goddess, who was manifested in three forms: a young woman, a mother, and a crone (old woman). Figurines represent her giving birth, breasts adorn her cave sites, and drawings portray her among animals, especially bulls and leopards. In many caves the double ax, symbol of the storm god, underscores the fertility theme (stormy rain fecundates mother earth).

Representations of bees and butterflies relate this fertility theme to the burial skulls and gifts, since both bees and butterflies pass through distinct stages in their life cycles. Worshipers likely tried to fit death into such a scheme—to see it as another transformation of the life force, another stage. Subordinate to the goddess was a male god, a boy or youth, who seems to be her child and lover and who has some correlations with the bull.

With the discovery of bronze about 3500 B.C.E. in the Middle East, new weapons and tools came into use. Also, more specialized work developed, such as mining, smelting, and casting metal. In turn, this work created more efficient farming implements, which led to the production of surplus food. Surplus food allowed a new class of religious specialists (who were agriculturally unproductive) to arise, while the metals "industry" stimulated the exploration and colonization of new territories for raw materials.

From 1900 to 1400 B.C.E., following the Hittite invention of tempering, iron came into widespread use, and the production of bronze and iron further stimulated the human imagination and increased the symbolic content of mother earth. Whereas the earliest iron was a gift from the sky (coming in the form of meteorites), mined iron came from the womb of the earth. Indeed, miners developed regimes of fasting, meditation, and purification, since they had to go into sacred depths and extract a new form of life. Their mythology spoke of elves, fairies, genies, and spirits who inhabited the underground, assisting or witnessing the slow gestation of mother earth's strangest children, the ores. Metallurgists, like blacksmiths and

potters, had to be "masters of fire," which associated them with the shamans, who were masters of inner, magical heat. Also, metallurgists took on some of the paradoxical nature of metal itself. Coming from mother earth and a boon to humanity, metal was sacred. However, being invulnerable and easily an instrument of death, metal was too close to evil for humans to handle comfortably. Thus, the smith entered the mythology of the gods, fashioning weapons for their heavenly battles and tools for their heavenly enterprises. In India, Tvastr made Indra's weapons for the fight against Vrtra; in Greece Hephaestus forged the thunderbolt that enabled Zeus to triumph over Typhon.

Megaliths

The Bronze and Iron Ages begot the first great civilizations, and their religions will be our major interest. Before discussing them, however, we should survey one last prehistoric phenomenon, the megaliths. *Megalith* means "great stone," and it brings to mind the prehistoric European cultures that left remains such as the famous cromlech (circle of huge stones) at Stonehenge in England. Actually, prehistorians speak of a megalithic cultural complex, centered at Los Millares in southeastern Spain and covering Portugal, half of France, western England, and parts of Ireland, Denmark, and Sweden. In some cases, prehistoric peoples in these areas arranged either cromlechs or *dolmens* ("immense capstone[s] supported by several upright stones arranged to form a sort of enclosure or chamber")[5] from slabs weighing as much as 300 tons.

What was the point to all this labor? Apparently the megalith was the major symbol for a cult of the dead. For Neolithic peasants of the fifth and fourth millennia B.C.E., stone was the symbol of permanence—of resistance to change, decay, or death. Unlike peoples in central Europe and the Near East, who strictly separated themselves from the dead, megalithic tribes sought close communion with the deceased, probably because they regarded death as a state of security and strength. To these people, ancestors could be powerful helpers and great allies. With the discovery of agriculture, human life probably seemed even more frail than it had before. Like that of the plant, it was ephemeral, bound to a cycle of birth, life, and death. By associating with "ancestral" stones—the bones of mother earth—humans might overcome their frailty and impermanence.

The megaliths represent burial vaults or ritual areas where this faith was practiced. At Stonehenge, for instance, the cromlech was in the middle of a field of funeral mounds. (Stonehenge was also a sophisticated instrument that could be used for making astronomical calculations.) At Carnac in Brittany, there was an avenue large enough for thousands to parade. Both sites were likely ceremonial centers or unenclosed temples—both were likely areas of sacred space for communing with ancestral stones.

Practically the whole island of Neolithic Malta was a megalithic sanctuary system. There a great goddess presided as the guardian divinity of a cult of the dead. One necropolis, now called the Hypogeum, has yielded bones of more than 7,000 people. Previously, scholars thought that this cultural complex, like the European ones, derived from a cultural basin around the Aegean Sea. However, radiocarbon datings show that the megaliths are older than the remains from the prehistoric Aegean, so western Europeans apparently developed their megalithic death cult independently.

Moreover, megaliths later cropped up in a vast geographic area extending from Algeria to Korea and North America. Thus, huge stones probably prompted certain ideas about death, ancestors, permanence, and escape from time and decay to all peoples. If most prehistoric peoples were moved to ponder their mortality more deeply because of agriculture, perhaps they tended to use stone to assist in this contemplation. Indeed, studies of megalithic societies that continued into the twentieth century confirm this hypothesis. In Indonesia and Melanesia, stone monuments defended the soul during

its journey to the beyond, ensured an eternal existence after death, linked the living and the dead, and fertilized the crops and animals through their sacred durability. Certain customs of European peasants in megalithic areas further confirm this hypothesis. As late as the early twentieth century, peasant women in parts of France slid along stones or rubbed themselves against stones to stimulate conception. For them as for women who lived in their locales 5,000 years earlier, stone was powerful and fertilizing.

The New Religious Mentality

Clearly, then, the ancient religious mind of prehistoric oral peoples produced a variety of cultures well worth our study and appreciation. The majority of them depended on hunting and gathering or relatively simple agriculture and thus tended to be nomadic and loosely organized. In anthropological terminology, they tended to be societies of small scale. The rest of this chapter addresses settled societies of larger scale—cultures that evolutionists classify as "higher" or "more developed." Extensive agriculture, estimable art and technology, city life, and complex government are some of the characteristics of societies so classified.

Equally important, though, is the development of writing, which led to history, literature, and other forms of communication that radically altered how human beings thought about themselves and the world. Written records enabled people to control trade, administer a large realm, and chart the movements of the stars. Therefore, our main interest in most of this chapter is the new religious mentality that arose when humanity became literate and superseded the ancient religious mentality.

In examining that new religious mentality, we shall study the rich, complex cultures of three ancient civilizations: Egypt, Iran, and Greece. These civilizations merit special attention because of the elaborateness of their religious systems and their influence on the modern world. They exhibit quite different orientations, so by the end of this chapter the term *ancient civilization* should be a complex, broadly defined term. Also by the end of this chapter we hope to have clarified Eric Voegelin's pregnant concept, "the cosmological myth," which explains much about ancient religious consciousness, particularly the pervading ancient notion that the world is a single living whole.[6] No ancient civilization ever broke the cosmological myth completely, but the differing attempts by the Egyptian Akhenaton, the Iranian Zoroaster, and the Greek Plato are key moments in their respective peoples' cultural histories and in humanity's religious march.

Many other cultures might have been studied in this chapter had space allowed. Ancient Mesopotamia, for instance, was probably the birthplace of writing, and its anxiety-ridden, very human religious culture contrasts instructively with Egypt's stability and optimism.[7] Both the Mesopotamian creation account *(Enuma Elish)* and the heroic *Epic of Gilgamesh* deserve their renown as masterpieces of ancient thought, and an ideal, leisurely introduction would surely review them carefully. Similarly, Roman religion would be a valuable subject. As perhaps the paramount empire of Western antiquity, Rome is a striking instance of civil religion. All ancient civilizations combined religion and politics, but Rome developed a legal and military efficiency that makes its blend especially striking.[8] Since civil religion has become a rallying point in recent analyses of bicentennial American religion,[9] studying the imperial Roman product could be quite timely.

Ideally we would also take up the religions of ancient Europe and the New World. Though these peoples did not develop full writing systems, they did produce estimable technologies and arts fully informed by their religious notions. In pre-Christian Europe, Germanic, Celtic, and Slavic peoples lived close to a wild, hearty nature and were shamanist, priestly, kingly, and folkloric. They had matriarchal societies, practiced some human sacrifice, and were vigorously concerned with magic and fertility. Because the

ideas of these people have entered our own cultural blood, often less obviously than those from Israel, Greece, Rome, and Christianity, they could have the special fascination of mysteries ingredient in our own psyches.[10]

In the New World, the great cultures of ancient Mexico and Peru beg for comparison with North American ancient cultures. Why, for instance, did the Aztecs develop such a rich system of myths and sacraments concerning gods who traded with human beings? Why did that trade balance slip toward the end of the pre-European period and human sacrifice arise? The ancient Incan civilization of Peru, which predated European contact by more than 2,000 years, integrated the human life cycle with nature's fertility rhythms almost classically. The Peruvian *huaca*, like the Sioux *wakan*, was a divine force present in all holy things. Yet, archeological excavations have shown traces of both an early creator god and later animal divinities, such as snakes, condors, and cats. Thus, a full account of Western religiosity would discuss old America.[11]

EGYPT

Today Egypt is a powerful center of Arab and Muslim culture. Taxi drivers career through Cairo with a Qur'an on the dashboard to protect them; common people lay rugs in the train station and kneel at the call to prayer. Yet the treasures of Tutankhamen, the Giza pyramids, and above all the Nile tie modern Cairo to the pre-Islamic Egypt of more than 5,000 years ago. Merely follow the Nile by train to Alexandria and you will see in its delta *fellah* (peasants) drawing water with buffalo much as they did in the Old Kingdom.

The Nile itself is a principal player in Egyptian history. Its moods, both varying and constant,[12] reflect the Egyptian soul. Historically, the Egyptian soul appears ageless. For the best part of 2,500 years Egyptian life remained the same. At the Great Pyramids near the Sphinx, the desert seems to

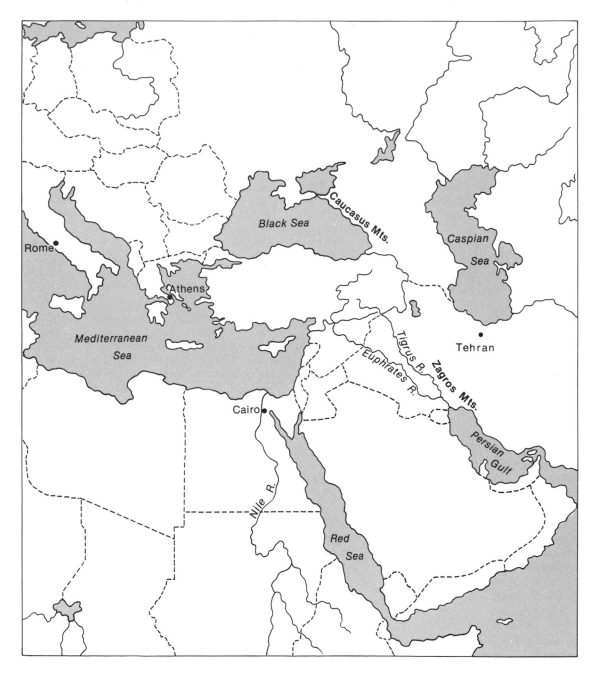

Figure 2   Egypt, Iran, and Greece.

have mimicked the Nile's behavior. The endless sand, like the river water, changes with the wind. Actually, though, little changes. Sky, sun, sand, and water—they all endure. Like stable props, they are set on every stage.

On the Egyptian stage, pharaohs and *fellah* enacted a mortality play. As the pyramids show, death kept adamant hold on this people's soul. Beyond life under the sun, life in the flesh, lay deathlessness. The tomb then was an archway through which everybody passed. Sanity was preparing to pass well.

Standing before the Sphinx, an Egyptian might offer this prayer: "O god of the puzzle, well do you symbolize our situation. Strong as a lion, winged like thought, you beguile us like a woman. In this flesh, we mainly know contradiction. Body and thought, we go diverse ways. Clearly, though, all ways end in the underworld. Help us stand judgment there before Osiris. Help us enter Re's course through the sky. May our time in the sun go smoothly. May our afterlife be content. Help us solve our riddle."

Religious History

Scholars debate the history of Egyptian religion, but the major events are clear. Unification of Upper (southern) and Lower (northern) Egypt occurred about 3100 B.C.E., and with it began the central Egyptian religious dogma—divine kingship.[13] In the prehistoric years before unification, Neolithic culture gradually developed small-town life, characterized by domestic animals, significant crafts (especially pottery), and probably

Figure 3   Great Sphinx near Giza pyramids, outside Cairo, Egypt. Photo by J. T. Carmody.

the burial of the dead with hopes of an after-life. From the beginnings of Egyptian history, local gods had great influence, and throughout the long dynasties they comprised a pantheon (assembly of divinities). It is well established that ancient Egypt was amazingly stable culturally. Divine kingship, concern with an afterlife, and a rather unorganized complex of gods exemplify that stability, for they characterized the entire 2,000 years of the native dynasties.

Egyptian splendor began vigorously in the period 3100–2200 B.C.E., which historians divide into the Early Dynasties (3100–2700 B.C.E.) and the Old Kingdom (2700–2200 B.C.E.). A famous product of Old Kingdom religion is the Memphite theology, developed to justify the new, unified kingdom centered at Memphis. Central to the justification is that the god of Memphis, Ptah, is the foremost creator god. Ptah originated Atum, the supreme god of the older cosmogony, and the other gods by an idea in his heart and a command on his tongue. Scholars are fascinated by this notion, because it suggests that 2,000 years before the Hebrews or Greeks came up with the notion of a first spiritual cause, an Egyptian had more than suspected it.[14]

From about 2200 to 2050 B.C.E., there was an intermediate period of disorder. The social order rooted in the permanence of nature and the gods gave way to chaos. We catch overtones of that upheaval in the famous "Dispute over Suicide," a remarkable text from the end of the third millennium. A man says to his soul, "To whom can I speak today? My fellows are evil, my friends do not love, . . . the land is left to those who do wrong." So, he considers suicide: "Death faces me today like the recovery of a sick man, like going out into the open after a confinement, . . . like the longing of a man to see his home again, after many years in captivity."[15] Clearly the prehistoric Egyptian hope of a happy afterlife with the gods functioned for this desolate writer as a way to justice—a way to symbolize the friendship and social order that life must have if it is not to seem absurd.

The Middle Kingdom (2050–1800 B.C.E.) was centered at Thebes. It nurtured several trends that brought important changes, although they worked below the surface constancy of Egyptian life. The most important of these trends was a democratization of certain religious rights, as the distance between the pharaoh and the common people narrowed. Also, there was an effort to elevate the more important gods and an increasing inclination to worship gods who were in the form of animals,[16] two phenomena that we shall observe below when we analyze the complex Egyptian sense of divinity. The most important religious rights that democratization brought the middle classes were privileges in the afterlife and a chance to participate in ceremonies that had been confined to the king and a few priests.

A second intermediate period (1800–1570 B.C.E.) dissolved the Middle Kingdom and included a century or so of rule by the Hyksos (shepherd kings), who were probably Syrians. The New Kingdom (1570–1165 B.C.E.) began with the famous XVIII dynasty, which made Egypt a true empire that stretched to the Euphrates. For our limited review of the high points in later Egyptian religious history, the New Kingdom's speculation on monotheism and a purer divinity is important. In the XIX dynasty under Akhenaton (1369–1353 B.C.E.), there was a move to make Aton, previously just the sun disk, the sole deity. Apparently Akhenaton himself bullied through this change (Egypt quickly reverted to polytheism after his death) because of his own spiritual perceptions.

Eric Voegelin calls Akhenaton " a new voice in history, the voice of a man intimately sympathetic with nature, sensitive to the splendor of light and its life-spending force, praising the god and his creature."[17] In a joyful climax, one of Akhenaton's hymns cries out: "The Aton is the creator-god: O sole god, like whom there is no other! Thou didst create the world according to thy desire, while thou wert alone."[18] Moreover, Aton was not the god of Egypt alone. Akhenaton saw that a true creator god must have established all peoples, whatever their country, speech, culture, or skin. This was truly a remarkable leap toward universalism, especially coming from the leader of a resolutely ethnocentric people, and it was the centerpiece in the so-called Armarna Revolution that gave the New Kingdom a great charge of cultural energy.

Another high point of New Kingdom theology was the Amon hymns, which probably date from the reign of Ramses II (1290–1224 B.C.E.). They illustrate a return to Amon and the demise of Aton, as well as a deep sense that the first creator god must be mysterious. Amon is "far from heaven, he is absent from the underworld, so that no gods know his true form. His image is not displayed in writings. No one bears witness to him. . . . He is too mysterious that his majesty might be disclosed, he is too great that men should ask about him, too powerful that he might be known."[19] Along with the hymns of Akhenaton, these praises of Amon represent the greatest advance in Egyptian theology.

For the most part, the Egyptians were not a speculative, intellectually probing people. They easily tolerated many gods and relied almost unquestioningly on ethical maxims and proverbs. In the Amon hymns, however, we see traces of a negative theology—a rising of the mind to the true nature of divinity by denying that creatures can represent it adequately. Because negative theology is a paramount way of breaking the cosmological myth, the Amon hymns show how close Egypt came to the revolutions that Israel and Greece accomplished.

In the centuries after the New Kingdom, the capital moved to Tanis, Bubastis, and Saïs—a good indication of the political turmoil of that era. Persians ruled Egypt from 525 to 405 B.C.E., and the last native dynasties (405–332 B.C.E.) ended with the conquest of Alexander. In the period from Alexander to about 30 B.C.E., the Hellenistic Ptolemies ruled, and the city of Alexandria was the luminary of the eastern Mediterranean. Christian influence rose in the Roman and Byzantine periods (30 B.C.E.–641 C.E.),

bequeathing Egypt the Coptic church. Since 641, Egyptian culture has been largely Muslim, but its native orientations have never completely died.

World View

In analyzing the Egyptian religious mentality, we quickly realize that studying any single portion of such a long-lived culture is bound to be inadequate. Therefore, the remarks below about the basic attitudes of Egyptians are just generalizations.

With regards to divinity, the proliferation of gods and symbols is overwhelming. The basic hieroglyph for God was a pole with a flag—the emblem flying in front of major temples, which designated purity and the creative life force. Since the Egyptians sensed purity and creativity in many places, they split divinity into many gods. The gods most important in the old cosmogony were four male-female pairs. The males bore the head of a frog, and the females the head of a snake—symbols, apparently, of self-renewal (the frog begins as a tadpole, while the snake sheds its skin). The belief (before the Memphite theology established Ptah as the creator) was that an invisible wind moved over primal waters and used these four pairs of gods to make life.

Throughout Egyptian history, the most important gods were associated with the sun and death-resurrection. Their names and images varied from cultural center to cultural center, but the most common name for the sun-god was Re, symbolized by either the sun's disk or the falcon. Another name was Khepri, represented by a scarab pushing the sun disk; a third name was Atum, whom people at Heliopolis worshiped and represented by the setting sun. In the mythology of Heliopolis, Atum generated himself on the primordial hill of creation (the great pyramids of the Old Kingdom represented this hill). He conquered chaos, took charge of the world, and established *maat*, the eternal cosmic order. The *Book of the Dead* (17 : 3–5), from the New Kingdom, says that Re became king of the gods in the earliest times by defeating all his opponents. Maat is his daughter but also his mother, because in his course through the sky, the sun-god follows her cosmic order.

That course determined Egyptian reality. The west was the land of the dead, and the east was where the daily miracle of the sun's return from the dead occurred.[20] On the walls of royal tombs near Luxor, twelve sections divide the night realm, or underworld, through which the sun-god's boat travels. Although the sun-god is dead during this time, he still possesses the power of resurrection. Middle night is the realm of Sokaris, who appears in human form with the head of a falcon. His area is a desert through which Re's boat has to be dragged before the sun can reemerge into the light.

It was Osiris, however, around whom the funerary cult developed that made the underworld almost an Egyptian obsession. Nowhere is the myth of his descent to the underworld detailed, but it probably had the following plot. Osiris and Seth were brothers, and Isis was Osiris' sister and wife. Osiris ruled the world as a good regent, but Seth hated him and killed him by guile. He got Osiris into a coffin and sent it down the Nile. Isis recovered Osiris' corpse and uttered a soulful dirge (which inspired litanies used in Osiris' worship). This dirge had a magic power that revived Osiris. Once again Seth moved against Osiris, this time hacking Osiris' body into fourteen pieces and then scattering them. Isis recovered them all and buried each piece properly wherever she found it (this explained the many Osirian sanctuaries). Further, Isis conceived a son Horus by the dead Osiris and brought Horus up in the marshes to hide him from Seth.

When Horus reached manhood, Isis arranged for a trial at which Seth was condemned for murdering Osiris and Horus was recognized as Osiris' heir. Osiris himself remained in the underworld, accepting the roles of lord of the nether realm and judge of the dead. Osiris seems to represent the growing power of vegetation, which roots in the earth, and he relates to all buildings that are set on the earth, to the moon, and to the dead. Isis represents the throne, the sacred seat of the king. As such, she "makes" the king and is his mother. For instance, on a relief in a temple at Abydos, the pharaoh sits in Isis' lap. Thus, Horus and the pharaoh are correlated. As Horus owed his throne to his mother Isis, so did the pharaoh.

Horus had many appearances, but most frequently he wore the head of a falcon. He was the model son but shows traces of an older sky god. In the Osiris myth, Horus fought Seth and lost an eye, while depriving Seth of his testicles. They reconciled, however, to suggest that life and death, too, can agree. Thoth, originally a moon god, was the agent of their reconciliation. Usually Thoth was represented as a baboon or ibis. He was also a god of the dead and is thought to have found Horus' lost eye and have returned it to him. This eye became a token of life returned from the dead.

The prime attribute of Egyptian divinity, then, was life. It shone in the sun, who daily accomplished the miracle of being resurrected from darkness, bestowing life-giving light and warmth. Life flowed in the Nile, whose annual flooding was necessary for crops to grow. Even the underworld became a realm of life. Osiris ruled there, judgment took place there, and vegetation rooted there.

Nature and Society

From this association of divinity with life, it follows that nature itself had a potent sacredness. Henri Frankfort, in fact, has analyzed Egyptian divinity in terms of the sun's power of creation, the power of procreation in cattle, and the power of resurrection in the earth.[21] We have seen a little of the sun and the Osirian earth. Apis, the bull god, was a focus of procreative power, as was Min, a mummy with a huge projecting phallus.

By the "cosmological myth," we mean the tendency to run these various sacred forces together so that nature and divinity are coextensive. Apart from the brief ventures behind the hymns to Aton and Amon, Egypt little doubted the cosmological myth. It could support so many gods because, like oral ancient peoples, Egyptians sensed sacredness everywhere. Unlike Jews, Christians, and Muslims, however, they did not fashion a popular, effective negative theology that said, "True divinity is actually in no one place—it is beyond all place, all time, all this worldly containment." As a result, nature's cycles and changes all represented aspects of the basic Egyptian divinity, which was the world itself. This cosmos of rocks and trees, water and land, living things and dying things—this was the ultimate reality.

The Egyptian people participated in the sacred cosmos through their king, who to them was quite literally divine. The king represented Horus, Re, or Osiris. In the analytic terms of Western scholars, he mediated between nature's divine order and his people. Society and politics were part of one natural circuit; the *maat* (goddess of order) that gave the world its law or reason ran from heaven through the pharaoh to the people. Thus, the pharaoh was under *maat* and yet, for the common people, the source of *maat*. Psychologically, this order was a major reason for the stability of the Egyptian culture. With divinity in their midst, what need the people fear?

Through many agricultural ceremonies and many regal rituals, these beliefs took dramatic form.[22] At first the common people had limited access to most kingly ceremonies, but in the later centuries their participation increased. The greatest threat to social stability, understandably, was the king's death. Consequently, the most influential mythic cycle was that of Osiris and Isis, which explained where the king (identified with Osiris) had gone at death. Relatedly, the most important ceremonies were the old king's burial and the new king's accession. For a hint of how effective this mythic-ritualistic faith was, consider the pyramids. The common people supplied the immense, brutal labor needed to build the pyramids, which assured the kings' happy afterlife and the state's continuance.

Ancient Egypt had a powerful caste of priests, and at times, despite the dogma of the king's divinity, it clashed with the crown. The conflict between Akhenaton and the priests of the old god Amon was a vivid instance of such friction, but conflict was almost always on the verge of breaking out. When Akhenaton moved the capital from Thebes to Amarna, he bruised theological, class, and local sensitivities all at once. The local priesthood, fighting for its own gods and people, consistently defended those sensitivities. As a result, the priesthood was a powerful sociological force.

Women were quite subordinate in Egyptian society, but not without influence and religious importance. The goddesses Hathor, Nut, Neith, Maat, and Isis represented the feminine aspects of divinity, while the queen had vital roles in the political theology.[23] Hathor, Nut, and Neith were forms of the mother goddess—both sacred representations of fertility and figures of comfort. Maat ruled cosmic justice, while Isis was sister and wife of the god as king. On rare occasions a queen could rule (Hatshepsut, 1486–1468 B.C.E., is the most famous instance), and as the source of the divine king, the queen mother was much more than just another harem wife.

Egyptian proverbs encouraged husbands to treat their wives well so that their property would prosper, but they also pictured women as "frivolous, flirtatious, and unreliable, incapable of keeping a secret, untruthful and spiteful as well as naturally unfaithful. To the storytellers and moralists [women were] the epitome of all sin and an endless source of mischief."[24] Women of the New Kingdom served in the temples and as popular entertainers, but in both cases they risked reputations as prostitutes. In both formal and popular religion, Isis was a focal point for women's own religion, especially in Hellenistic times. Related to Osiris, she was the ideal wife (and a potent exemplar of grief); related to Horus, she was the ideal mother. Through Isis, then, women in ordinary roles participated in divinity.

Perhaps due to this divinity, legal documents from about 500 B.C.E. suggest that

Egyptian women had the right to own property, buy or sell goods, and testify in court.
They were taxpayers and could sue; they
could inherit from parents or husbands.[25] On
the other hand, husbands could dismiss
wives at their pleasure (but not vice versa),
and concubinage, adultery, and prostitution
were widespread. Because many Egyptian
women worked the fields or had other
important economic roles, their lot was better than that of women in other ancient civilizations (Mesopotamia, for instance). Still,
women were not equal to men, in part
because of a prevailing male suspicion of
woman: "She is a deep water whose twisting
men know not."[26]

The Self

The religious conception of the self
relates intimately to the Egyptian concern
with death, burial, and the afterlife. That
concern, John Wilson insists,[27] was a result
not of gloom but of optimism. The ancient
Egyptians loved life, despite its dependence
on such uncertain phenomena as the Nile's
proper rising, and they looked forward to
another, better chapter after death. The
remains of many burial sites, well preserved
because of the desert sand and dry climate,
show that the departed took with them
favorite utensils and even favorite servants.
The *ba* was that aspect of a person that continued after death, which contrasts with the
ka, or vital force, the impersonal power animating the living. A third concept, the *akh*,
was the shining, glorious aspect of the dead
in heaven. With these three notions, the
Egyptians had a sense of what moves the living and what continues on after death.

As indicated in our outline of the
myth, Osiris judged the dead in the underworld. The pyramid texts of the Old Kingdom, coffin texts of the Middle Kingdom,
and *Book of the Dead* from the New Kingdom show a constant concern with judgment and hence a certain awareness of
personal responsibility. The *Book of the
Dead* contains a famous "negative confession" that illustrates both the posthumous

trial Egyptians imagined and some of their
principal ethical concerns. The deceased
claims before Osiris: "I have not committed
evil against men. . . . I have not mistreated
cattle. . . . I have not blasphemed a god. . . . I
have not done violence to a poor man. . . . I
have not made anyone weep. . . . I have not
killed. . . . I have not defamed a slave to his
superior. . . . I have not had sexual relations
with a boy." In all, thirty-six declarations of
innocence are made.[28] Then, to complete his
show of religious virtuosity, he gives each of
the forty-two divine jurors, by name, a specific assurance. For example, "O Embracer-
of-Fire, who comes forth from Babylon, I
have not stolen. O Eater-of-Entrails, who
comes forth from the thirty [judges in the
world of the living], I have not practised usu-
ry. O Eater-of-Blood, who comes forth from
the execution block, I have not slain the cattle of the god."[29]

In ancient Egypt, then, the gods were
everywhere. Economics, politics, the arts,
nature—all aspects of life were religious. In
symbolically mythic ways, nobles and peasants alike looked to the king, tried to discern
maat, and hoped for mercy before Osiris.
The sun, the river, and the land all witnessed
the interplay of death and resurrection with
comfort. Each dawn, each annual flood, each
spring sprouting was a pledge of hope. Therefore, one could live optimistically and even
with good humor; on most days, life was
good.

IRAN

Contemporary Iran is a nation in the
throes of choosing its identity and direction.
On first view, the principal factors are Western secularism (almost unavoidable because
of Iran's massive petroleum industry) and a
volatile form of traditional Islam. These factors alone are more than enough to bewilder
analysts, but the snowcapped mountains
rimming Tehran suggest there is much
more—the long history of culture that
crossed the Iranian plain. When one sees Ira-

nian women draped in black, showing only a panel of dark eyes, something flickers more ancient than Islam.

That something is the spirit of Zoroaster, priest and prophet. In the mind's eye, it burns toward Truth. Picture Zoroaster as being fiery, choleric, fierce of face. He is angry that some Iranians do not accept his Wise Lord. In their dimness, they stick to the old vital forces. Zoroaster, though, knows better—he knows the battle between Evil and Good.

The battle between Evil and Good absorbs Zoroaster completely, and in every conflict he sees its mark. His vision brings forth symbols of judgment. The wicked, who reject the Wise Lord, will never cross Paradise Bridge. Paradise Bridge is sharp as a razor and cuts all deceit to the quick. But the Evil Spirit is a powerful enemy, and his handiwork, the Lie, is everywhere. Thus, Zoroaster redoubles his insistence on Truth. Rugged as the Elburz Mountains in the distance, he is highly disciplined. This is a man who has discovered the utter clarity of conscience's call to the light. Expect from him no compromise, no accommodation. Thus spake Zarathustra (the Greek form of the name), who formed ancient Iran.

Ask about Zoroaster on the streets of Tehran today, however, and you will likely be rebuked: "We are Muslims!" the typical residents will say. True enough, less than 10,000 Zoroastrians remain in Iran (perhaps 100,000 remain in India). Nonetheless, Zoroaster was the greatest religious influence in the epochal Persian Empire, the strongest molder of the Iranian spirit. As well, he was the first son of Asia adopted by the West.[30]

Zoroaster first intrigued the Greeks, whose explorers encountered his culture 400 years before Christ. Much later he impressed Western historians, philosophers, and artists as a cultural hero—a founder of civilization and conscience.

The Founding of Zoroastrianism

The historical influence of Zoroaster stretches from the tenth century C.E., when the Arab military conquest of the seventh century began to affect Iranian culture, back beyond 1500 B.C.E., when speakers of Indo-Iranian filtered through the Caucasus Mountains to the Iranian plateau. Before that date, "cave man," as Ghirshman calls him, lived around that plateau in holes dug into wooded mountainsides.[31] Indeed, archeological remains suggest that humans have inhabited Iran since the beginning of a dry period, twelve to seventeen thousand years ago.

According to Ghirshman, in primitive agricultural societies that developed on alluvial deposits, such as on the Iranian plateau, women had an economic, political, and religious superiority. Indo-European conquerors probably adopted their matriarchal social structure from these first inhabitants of present-day Iran.

Those first inhabitants were great potters, and archeologists have found among their relics designs and figurines of a naked goddess, whose mate was likely a god who was her son. This belief would be the most direct explanation for the early Iranian customs of marriage between blood relations, descent through the female line, and, in certain tribes (for example, the Guti of Kurdistan), female army commanders. Later archeological remains, dating back to 2000 B.C.E., suggest a people both artistic and hopeful, for impressive pendants, earrings, bracelets, and the like found in gravesites imply a strong belief in an afterlife.

In the second millennium B.C.E., Indo-Europeans, pressured by population shifts in the areas around them, left their homelands in the plains of southern Russia and migrated southeast across Iran. Some of them eventually ended up as far south as India.[32] In the west they established the Hittite Empire, sacked Babylon, and confronted the Egyptians. From the east, tribes called the Mittani conquered northern Mesopotamia and allied themselves with Egypt in about 1450 B.C.E. Linguistic, religious, and social parallels suggest that pre-Zoroastrian Iranian culture, as well as the culture of the peoples who conquered the Indus Valley in India and produced the Vedic culture, derived from the

Mittani, Hittite, and other Indo-European "Aryans" (from an Indo-European word meaning "noble"). In particular, the Iranian and Indian Aryans had similar gods and similar social structures. (French scholar Georges Dumezil has argued that the Aryan gods correlated with a three-part social structure—priests, warriors, and agriculturalists—in which each social class had both a legal and a magical aspect.)[33]

The native Iranian religion that Zoroaster challenged was probably controlled by Median priests (the Medes were a later Aryan tribe) from western Iran called *magi.* Apparently that religion was an animistic polytheism (devotion to many divine spirits) similar to that of early Aryan India. After Zoroaster's death, the magi fused their old ideas onto his new notions, making Zoroastrianism a hodgepodge of conflicting gods and practices.

Zoroaster is estimated to have lived from 628 to 551 B.C.E., but the only direct source for his message is a fragment of the sacred Zoroastrian liturgical text, the *Avesta.* That portion, called the *Gathas,* along with later Greek and Persian traditions, suggests that Zoroaster's enemies (magi and men's societies of the old religion) forced him to flee from his native western Iran eastward into ancient Chorasmia (the area today of Khurasan, western Afghanistan, and the Turkmen Republic of the Soviet Union). There, when about forty years old, he found a patron in King Vishtapa and his message began to have social effect.

R. C. Zaehner has suggested the following summary of Zoroaster's main doctrines:[34] (1) There is a supreme God, the Wise Lord (Ahura Mazdah), who has thought all things into existence by his Holy Spirit. The Wise Lord is holy, righteous, and generous, and he expresses himself through the Holy Spirit, Good Mind, and Truth—three entities inseparable from his essence. Wholeness, Immortality, and Right-Mindedness are his attributes. (2) The world is divided between Truth and the Lie. Ahura Mazdah made Truth, but Zoroaster does not say who made the Lie. (3) Creatures of the Wise Lord (spiritual beings and humans) are free to choose between Truth and the Lie. Angra Mainyu (the Destructive Spirit), twin brother of the Holy Spirit, chooses to do evil. "This he does of his own free will as do the *daevas,* the ancient gods whom, on account of the violence associated with their worship, Zarathustra considered to be evil powers." (4) Because human beings are free, they are responsible for their ultimate fates. By good deeds they win the eternal reward of possessing Wholeness and Immortality; by evil deeds they merit eternal pain in hell. (5) The great outward symbol of Truth is fire, and the center of the Zoroastrian cult is the fire altar.

When we set these doctrines in the context of Zoroaster's times, they are striking for their interiority. Before this prophet, little in Indo-European, Mesopotamian, or Egyptian religion focused on the mental concepts of truth and lie, the spiritually intuitive concepts of immortality and right-mindedness. In a way that prefigures the Greek philosophers' more radical discovery of reason, Zoroaster generates his images of divinity and human destiny from the operations of his own spirit. He turns away almost completely from nature toward the inner light of human conscience. In so doing he steps at least halfway out of the cosmological myth.

Two verses from perhaps the most autobiographical of Zoroaster's hymns suggest the religious experience at the core of his preaching:

As the holy one I recognized thee, O Wise Lord,
When I saw thee at the beginning, at the birth of existence,
Appoint a recompense for deed and word:

> *Evil reward to the evil, good to the good,*
> *Through thy wisdom, at the last turning-point of creation [43 : 5].*[35]

> *As the holy one I recognized thee, O Wise Lord,*
> *When he came to me as Good Mind.*
> *To his question: "To whom wilt thou address thy worship?"*
> *I made reply: "To thy fire! While I offer up my veneration to it,*
> *I will think of the Right to the utmost of my power" [43 : 9].*[36]

In Iran in the early sixth century B.C.E., only an exceptional personality could have cut through the welter of Aryan gods, spells, and semimagical practices and discerned a clear religious call to identify divinity with justice. Similarly, only an exceptional personality could have lingered over abstractions such as Good Mind and the Right and made these terms God's best names.

It is true, as most scholars remind us, that Zoroaster's revelations had a social background and significance;[37] for instance, he championed the farmer over the nomad. Nonetheless, the deeper explanation of Zoroaster's religious power is the interior, spiritual experiences indicated by the *Gathas*. Like Jesus and Muhammad, Zoroaster met a holy, compelling divinity or ultimate reality. His mission was simply to spread the truth of this divinity far and wide. The origins of Zoroastrian history, then, are the visions and the religious insights of a founding genius. Through all its later changes, Zoroastrianism and the world religions that it influenced kept some aspect of Zoroaster's Wise Lord.

Zoroastrianism after Zoroaster

The great leaders of the Achaemenid empire who followed Zoroaster were the Persians Cyrus II (559–530 B.C.E.), Cambyses II (530–522 B.C.E.), and Darius I (522–486 B.C.E.). They conquered eastern Iran, the prophet's initial sphere of influence, and we can read in inscriptions that they left something of Zoroastrianism's function as the religious rationale for a new, energetic empire. Eric Voegelin cites these inscriptions as products of what he calls the "ecumenic age," when the new, transnational kingdoms precipitated the problem of how many peoples could be equally human.[38]

Spiritually, the new kings were neither fish nor fowl. On the one hand, they could not quite see themselves in the role of an Egyptian pharaoh or a Babylonian king. Both the ethnic complexity of the new Persian Empire, which contained several peoples, and Zoroaster's insights into God's universality went against Egyptian and Babylonian beliefs that Egypt and Babylon were the center of all creation. On the other hand, the Achaemenids still tended to think of the *ecumene*, the inhabited world, in terms of the countries that they had conquered. That is, they still failed to see that the true *ecumene*, the more profound "inhabited world," is not a matter of territories but of reason and spirit. Thus, they did not develop Zoroaster's spadework on the human soul's openness to a universal God by adopting a political philosophy in which no people are closer to divinity than any other, and no functionary (king, clerk, or peasant) is closer to God than any other.

However, as the inscriptions of Darius at Behistun and Naqsh-i-Rustam indicate, the Achaemenids did make Ahura Mazdah the source of their success, sensing the universal outreach of Ahura Mazdah's kingdom of truth. (Unfortunately, they also identified their opponents with the realm of the Lie.) For example, a Naqsh-i-Rustam inscription says of Darius' work:

A great god is Ahuramazda [Ahura Mazdah]
who has created this all-surpassing work,
that has become visible,
who has created the peace for men,
who has endowed with wisdom and good-being Darius the King.[39]

In Voegelin's view, this inscription represents a definite, if incomplete, step away from the political theology of the cosmological myth: "The substance of order that fills the far-flung empire through the conquering and administrative action of the king is no longer cosmic but the spiritual and moral substance of Ahura Mazda."[40] Xerxes, Darius' successor, building on this order, opposed his rule to that of certain rebels in terms of a clash between his Zoroastrian divine commission and their demonic worship of pre-Zoroastrian *daevas*, or lower gods. Unlike Egyptian political theology, the Persian political theology of the Achaemenids made the king the mediator of a divine truth that came from beyond the natural world. The pharaoh was the conduit of *maat*—cosmic order. The Persian king was the champion of Ahura Mazdah's Truth, which was precosmic and transcosmic, the enemy of the Destructive Spirit's realm of the Lie.

If the advance or decline in clarifying reality marks the importance of a given epoch, the Achaemenid empire represented a very significant time. In it humanity advanced toward definitions of nature, divinity, and society that stem from wise judgment. We today have yet to secure those definitions, but we would be even less advanced had there been no Zoroaster or Persian culture.

Following Alexander's victory over Darius III in 331 B.C.E., the Achaemenids gave way to the Greek Seleucids. Under the Seleucids, for almost a century, Hellenistic cultural ideals blended with Persian. Zoroastrian influence probably declined, being overshadowed by a Greek-Iranian syncretism (combination of two forms of belief). While the practice of pure Zoroastrianism seems to have remained in Fars (the southern province called Persis), the old Iranian goddess Anahita, fused with the Mesopotamian goddess Nanai, complicated the religious picture in other provinces. *syncretism*

Also complicating the picture was the Greek hero Heracles, who joined with local gods. Heracles was the patron of the gymnasium, the place of physical exercise, an important feature of Hellenistic culture. Also, he was one of several "savior" gods (gods who made life whole) whose influence grew apace with the disintegration of the previously secure city-state religions. The *Avesta* was probably still evolving at this time, incorporating hymns to the god Mithra, who had existed before Zoroaster and later became an important savior god for the Romans. In the *Avesta*, Mithra's main functions are to preserve cattle, sanctify contracts, and render judgment on human actions.[41]

The Era of Many Religions

The Greek Seleucids yielded to the Parthians, who entered Iran from the area southwest of the Caspian Sea. The Parthians dominated Iran, bit by bit, from the first conquest by Arsaces in about 238 B.C.E. until about 226 C.E. While sources are scanty, Zoroastrianism apparently made some gains against syncretism under the Parthians, achieving a privileged status. Richard Frye relates this to the influence of the magi: "We may suspect that Magi, in various parts of Iran, upheld the worship of Ahura Mazda and/or other old Aryan gods in varying forms and degrees of piety."[42] Nonetheless, in Parthian times the cultures of the different geographic areas varied considerably. Coins, art, and other remains indicate different local preferences for a variety of gods. Ahura Mazdah and Mithra certainly were influential, but the cult of the goddess Anahita was probably the most important.[43] The northern magis' custom of exposing the bodies of the dead on mountains (burial would pollute the earth) spread as far south as Susa, capital of the old Elamite kingdom. We also know that the Parthians were tolerant of religious minorities, so much so that Jews regarded them as great protectors.

The history of Zoroastrianism under the Parthians remains rather vague. Under the Sassanians (ca. 226–637 C.E.), it is more definite, as is the story of Persian culture generally. The early Sassanian king Papak probably was the director of the shrine to Anahita at Istakhr in Persis (south central Iran), and his successor Shapur had quite liberal religious policies. That soon changed, however, largely due to the influence of Kartir, a zealous Zoroastrian priest. By the last third of the third century, he had made Zoroastrianism the established Persian "church." Kartir favored proselytizing, establishing fire temples for worship and instruction, purging Zoroastrian heretics, and attacking all non-Zoroastrian religions. Consequently, he persecuted Jews, Buddhists, Hindus, Christians, and Manichaeans, destroying their centers and proscribing their faiths. From his time marriage between blood relations became a common Zoroastrian practice, and the Zoroastrian clergy were a political power.

The Manichaeans—followers of the native Iranian prophet Mani—were the chief heretics. Under Shapur I, Mani had been free to travel and preach, but soon after Shapur's death the Zoroastrians martyred him. Nonetheless, his ideas gained considerable acceptance, both in Iran and throughout the Roman Empire. They stressed a dualism of good and evil, equating good with the spirit and evil with matter. Consequently, Manichaeans denigrated the body, sex, marriage, women, and food—anything perceived as carnal. As we shall see, Manichaeanism had an exciting effect on Christians, influencing Augustine and spawning several medieval heresies. At the end of the fifth century C.E.,

Persian Manichaeans led a socioeconomic movement called Mazdakism (after its leader Mazdak), which preached a sort of communism that included the division of wealth and the sharing of wives and concubines. Many poor people embraced this movement, but Prince Chosroes Anosharvan massacred the Mazdakite leaders about 528 C.E.[44]

By the last decades of Sassanian rule, the Zoroastrian church sanctioned a rigid caste system based, somewhat like that of India, on an ideal division of society into priests, warriors, scribes, and commoners. Ritual tended toward a sterile formalism, and a number of speculative or gnostic (relating to secret knowledge) tendencies emerged. At the beginning of the Sassanian period, Zurvanism had become the dominant Zoroastrian theology, in good part because of an increasing interest in the problem of evil. Zurvan is Infinite Time. Slowly, he displaced Ahura Mazdah (now called Ohrmazd) as the first principle. Ohrmazd then became identical with Holy Spirit, and Zurvan became his father, as well as the father of Holy Spirit's twin, Destructive Spirit. Thus, Zurvanism begot a dualism: Holy Spirit and Destructive Spirit. However, unlike Mani's dualism, Zurvanism did not make matter evil. For Zurvanite Zoroastrians, nature remained God's good creation.

After Muslims conquered Persia in the seventh century, Zoroastrianism lingered on for some time. The province of Fars, for instance, remained Zoroastrian into the tenth century. Gradually, however, the Zoroastrians retreated into ghettoes, and by 945, when Shiite Muslims took Baghdad, the end was near. Zoroastrian elements remained culturally important through the tenth-century renaissance of Persian letters, but thenceforth Islam was Iran's religion. Today perhaps 10,000 Zoroastrians remain in Iran around Gizd and Kerman. In the eighth century significant numbers emigrated to India to avoid Muslim rule. Their descendants have survived, retaining the original scriptures and much of the traditional doctrine. Known as Parsis, they now number about 150,000, with the largest concentration in Bombay. They keep the fire sacrifice, expose the dead in "towers of silence" where vultures may strip their flesh, and are one of India's best educated and most prosperous groups.

Zoroastrian World View

Before Zoroaster, Iran acknowledged a number of *ahuras*—good celestial spirits. The most prominent were lucidity (the brightness that glances off the waters or that leaps from fire); the sacred liquor *haoma*, used in the old Aryan cult; and plain water, symbol of purity and motherliness. Zoroaster pushed one wise Ahura to the fore, whose special qualities, such as Wholeness and Good Mind, were expressions of divine being. In later Zoroastrianism, these qualities became angelic beings who served Ohrmazd and influenced humans.

Opposing the good angels were powerful, antidivine forces led by the evil one, Ahriman. According to speculation after Zoroaster, Ohrmazd realized that to destroy Ahriman, he would have to lure him out of eternal time (Zurvan) into finite time. Zoroastrian theology thus became highly eschatological (interested in the last events of humanity) and developed imaginative doctrines of judgment, heaven, and hell. Ultimately Ohrmazd and goodness would triumph, and hell would cease after the wicked had been purged of their sins.[45]

If Ohrmazd and Zurvan represent the most refined aspects of Zoroastrian divinity, Mithra and Anahita express aspects no less influential. Both relate divinity to nature— Mithra to the sky and sun, Anahita to water. On the folk level, Anahita was very powerful, in effect giving Iran a great goddess. For instance, in one *Avestan* text (*Yasht* 5:17), Ahura Mazdah asks Anahita to make Zoroaster think, speak, and act according to good religion. Clearly, then, there was considerable confusion in developed Zoroastrian theology. Pressed by pre-Zoroastrian traditions and by outside cultural influences, Zoroastrianism tried to accommodate a variety of divinities within its monotheistic stress on

Wise Lord. As a result, the goddess of plenty, the god of wind, the star Sirius, the Fravashis (the preexistent souls of good men and women), and more were objects of veneration. Thus, we might call Zoroastrianism an impure monotheism.

Though Zoroaster's theology turned away from nature and toward mental processes, the physical elements continued to shape Iranian religion. Mental processes and physical elements conspired in practical living, since the basic ethical imperative was to maintain goodness and life by fighting against evil and death.[46] As a result, Zoroastrianism frowned on fasting, asceticism, and celibacy. Rather, humans were to foster the powers of generation in nature and humanity alike. One basis for this view was Zoroaster's own stress on the holiness of agriculture, which to him was a cooperation with Ahura Mazdah. The farmer who sows corn, he said, "feeds the religion" of the Wise Lord.

Ancient Iran established a pronounced caste system, but most of its cultic practices cut across class distinctions. Some common people were quite interested in magic, but the orthodox leaders feared the occult, treating sorcerers and witches as criminals. Superstitions and totemic practices (for example, rubbing oneself with the wing of a falcon to ward off an evil spell) flourished, in part because of contact with Mesopotamia. Both divination and astrology were common, and other nations considered Persian magis to be specialists in dream interpretation. Finally, to add a little excitement now and then, there was trial by fire or molten lead (if the person survived, he or she was deemed innocent).

Zoroaster himself seems to have disapproved of blood sacrifices, going out of his way to try to protect cattle. Blood sacrifices survived in later Zoroastrianism, though, the most important being the bull sacrifice. Also important to later Zoroastrians was the preparation and offering of *haoma*, the sacred liquor, which until recently served as a sort of sacrament for the dying. The most important sacrifice and cultic focus, however, was the fire sacrifice. The flame had to be "pure," (obtained by burning "pure" materials such as sandalwood), and it had to pass to another flame before its fuel became embers. The fire sacrifice has overtones of an ancient wonder at the source of light and heat, but its major emphasis has always been to symbolize the divine.

Through their several sacrifices, Zoroastrians kept a sense of righteousness before Ahura Mazdah. For individuals, rites of passage at maturity, marriage, and death were important, as were various purifications. At maturity, both men and women apparently received a sacred thread and shirt. The thread was a compound symbol: cosmically, it stood for the Milky Way, the thread of the stars through the heavens; mythologically, it recalled Ahura Mazdah's gift of *haoma*; personally, it symbolized taking up adult responsibilities. The shirt was white, to symbolize purity and the garment that the soul dons after death.

Death and bloodshed were prime occasions for purification, because they were prime pollutants. As noted, Zoroastrians exposed the dead so as not to defile other persons, the earth, fire, or water. In some periods of Zoroastrianism, blood from a cut, extracted tooth, or even menstrual flow could render one ritually unclean. Emily Culpepper, who has surveyed Zoroastrian menstrual taboos, suggests a strong ancient element in this concern with purity.[47] (Complicated rites in which bodily impurities were passed through bull's urine, sand, and water also evidence this concern.)[48] In general, women played only a small part in the Zoroastrian world. Their part in redemption was to furnish males to fight against Ahriman. Most of the tradition held that in the beginning women defected to the Destructive Spirit. Theologically, then, Zoroastrianism viewed the female nature as unholy.

Conclusion

Zoroastrianism is important beyond its own confines. Because its eschatology attracted Jews, Christians, and Muslims, it has influenced perhaps half the world's believers. That is its historical prestige. In terms of philosophical prestige, where the issue is wisdom—the clarification of reality—Zoroaster is a prime religious figure because he made a strong contribution to the discovery of order. Order is the proper perspective on reality that only comes when we determine the relations among nature, society, self, and divinity.[49]

In cosmological civilizations, such as Egypt, the spirituality or reason of the human self remained unclear. As a result, Akhenaton's view of Aton and the Amon hymns to the unknown God were historical dead ends. Zoroaster, however, impressed upon Iranian culture a permanent sense of human and divine spirituality—a glimpse of a reality independent of matter, sense, or imagination. His insight was only partial, and it never dominated Iranian life. Nonetheless, it makes Zoroastrianism a significant, history-changing step. For if order is our goal, Zoroaster is a hero, and Iran is a country of wonders.

GREECE

Egypt amazes the world historian by the stability of its civilization. Iran-Persia impresses the historian of religion by Zoroastrianism's contribution to the clarification of order and its influence on Judaism, Christianity, and Islam. Greece, the third land of ancient religious civilization that we study, dazzles both world historians and historians of religion with its cultural diversity and splendor. Like classical Egyptian and classical Iranian religious culture, classical Greek religious culture has passed from the scene. Its influence in modern Greece lies under the surface of Eastern Orthodox Christianity, much as classical Egyptian religion lies under present-day Egyptian Islam and classical Zoroastrianism lies under present-day Iranian Islam. It is dead, but not without its influence.

Moreover, the influence of classical Greek religion is active in a different sense

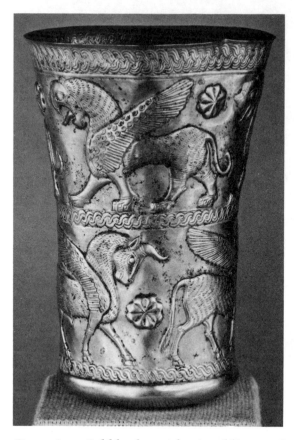

Figure 4   Gold beaker with winged lions and bulls, Persian, about eighth century, B.C.E. Nelson Gallery-Atkins Museum (Nelson Fund).

than that of its Egyptian or Iranian counterparts. Through the philosophy, science, literature, politics, and art that it nurtured, classical Greece became tutor to the West. For example, it furnished Christianity and Islam with many of their intellectual categories. Insofar as those categories have been developed in modern science and technology, classical Greece has been absolutely instrumental in shaping the present global society.

In addition, the Greek love of wisdom clarified the nature of human reason, prompting a momentous step toward right order—far greater than Zoroaster's. Classical Greece was the climax of ancient efforts to discern how human spirit is consubstantial ("of the same stuff") with God. Since the Greek dramatists, the wisdom to manage human spirit has been closely associated with suffering. Since Socrates, Plato, and Aristotle, human thought has reached into the mind of God.

The cultural splendor of Greece blazed forth in a land of great beauty. If the Athens of today suffers disturbing pollution, the Athens of yesterday still glimmers on the Acropolis and bustles in the streets of its port, Piraeus. Indeed, leave Piraeus by boat, or Athens by bus, and in less than two hours pre-Christian Greece is upon you. What do you feel? That it is, above all, a place of vision—of incredibly clear light and unbounded blue sea. On Cape Sounion or one of the islands, this beautiful clarity remains today. John Fowles describes the scene:

It was a Sunday in late May, blue as a bird's wing. I climbed up the goat-paths to the island's ridge-back, from where the green froth of the pine-tops rolled two miles down to the coast. The sea stretched like a silk carpet across the shadowy wall of mountains on the mainland to the west, a wall that reverberated away south, fifty or sixty miles to the horizon, under the vast bell of the empyrean. It was an azure world, stupendously pure, and as always when I stood on the central ridge of the island and saw it before me, I forgot most of my troubles.[50]

The natural beauty of classical Greece, above all in Athens, stimulated poets, artists, philosophers, and politicians to make a human counterpart—a beautiful society. Perhaps the clearest way to sketch the history of Greek religion is to show its ascent to the pinnacle of fourth century B.C.E. Athens and its descent to the Hellenistic syncretism of the early centuries C.E.

Religion of Minoan Crete   *History*

In his world history, Arnold Toynbee locates the beginnings of Greek culture about the middle of the third millennium B.C.E., when Sumerian and Egyptian influences apparently stimulated civilization in Crete.[51] Sir Arthur Evans, the foremost archeologist of ancient Crete, called the Bronze Age culture that had developed by 2000 B.C.E. "Minoan" after Minos, the legendary king of Crete. By about 1700 B.C.E. the Minoans had a linear script, and in the period 1580–1450 B.C.E. a splendid civilization flourished. The first true Greeks, called Minyans, were Aryan-speaking Indo-Europeans. They established relations with Minoan Crete, and between 1450 and 1400 B.C.E., at which time they were known as Mycenaeans, the Greeks had settled at the capital city of Knossos. The Mycenaean period (1400–1150 B.C.E.) constituted Crete's last glory; the Dorians invaded from northern Greece and cast a "dark age" over the Aegean from 1100 to 650 B.C.E.

During that period, literacy largely passed from the Greek scene. Consequently, much of our knowledge of Minoan religious culture comes from archeological excavations. These reveal that caves were great cultural centers from Neolithic times, serving as dwellings, cemeteries, and churches all in one. (Insofar as they gave rise to the mythic labyrinth, Cretan caves influenced the Greek religious psyche permanently.)[52] As the archeological excavations show quite clearly, the foremost deity of Cretan cave religion was a goddess, whose primary features were fertility and mastery of animals.

This corresponds with remains found on Cretan mountains, where Minoans also celebrated fertility.

However, the goddess cult probably did more than simply venerate natural life. The many burial remains, symbols of butterflies and bees (change-of-state beings), and other artifacts suggest a complex veneration of life, death, and rebirth. Probably participants underwent initiation into these mysteries, much as ancient Africans or Australians have long done. The remains or artistic representations of bull horns, double axes, trees, animals, cosmic pillars, and blood sacrifices testify to a particularly rich Neolithic agricultural goddess religion like that described on pages 18–19.

In light of later Greek initiations—for example, those of the Eleusinian and Orphic mysteries—it is likely that the Minoan goddess cult aimed at insuring a happy afterlife.[53] If so, it probably had conceptions of immortality that continued through the dark age and served as a counterpoint to Zeus and the Olympian gods. In the Olympian scheme, the afterlife was only a shadowy, dismal existence. The mystery religions that offered a more hopeful view may well have derived from the Cretan earth goddess.

At any rate, as the script that archeologists have discovered and called Linear B shows, people spoke Greek on Crete from 1400 B.C.E. By that time, Minoan and Mycenaean cultural forces were interacting. One important effect was that later Greek religious culture appropriated Minoan Crete as its golden age. For instance, according to Olympian legend, Zeus was born on Crete, and Apollo, Heracles, and Demeter (and even the non-Olympian Dionysus) performed prodigies or had high adventures in Crete. Crete thus became the *omphalos*, the navel or birth center, of the classical Hellenic world. At the end of his life and literary career, when he composed his masterpiece the *Laws*, Plato placed his characters on Crete, walking from Knossos into the hills to the temple cave of Zeus.

Sky-oriented

Olympian Religion

The Cretan or Minoan strand of Greek religious history wove itself deep into the Hellenic fiber. The Mycenaean strand, however, was throughout more predominant. Linear B shows that the people who invaded Crete were Indo-Europeans—the people that shaped both Iran and India. One of the outstanding characteristics of Indo-European religion was its interest in sky phenomena—storms, wind, lightning, the sun, and stars. Zeus, the prime Greek Olympian god, is a close relative of both Vedic and Iranian sky gods. (In proto-Indo-European religion, Mother Earth was polar to Father Sky but less powerful.) Further, the Indo-Europeans were much concerned with the human word—in sacrifices, chanting, spells, and sagas. Their traditions were largely oral, and they opposed writing when they first encountered it among Near Eastern peoples. It is worth underscoring that they had a powerful, double sense of the sacred—the sacred was both charged with divine presence and forbidden to human touch. Throughout its later development, Greek religion never lost this sense of awe-filled untouchability. Lastly, as we noted in connection with Iran, Indo-Europeans divided their society and gods into three groups. As a result, Vedic India, Aryan Iran, and preclassical Greece all thought in terms of priests, warriors, and commoners (though in Greece the priestly class was underdeveloped), as did Celts and Romans.

If both Crete and mainland Greece maintained earlier traditions during the dark age,[54] we can assume that the emergence of Homeric, Olympian religion was quite slow. By the time of Homer, however, the Indo-European religion had a distinctively Greek flavor. For instance, Zeus had acquired a mythological lineage. According to Hesiod's *Theogony*, he was born in the third generation of gods, after the original period of Earth and Heaven and the second period of the Titans. When Zeus overthrew his father Kronos, the present world resulted. (Eliade sees in the rather violent mythology of the *Theogony* a Greek account of creation. Heaven and earth separate; nature's forces assume their present order.)[55]

Zeus came to preeminence slowly. Most likely, his many liaisons with local goddesses represent a religious and political takeover, as a unified Greek culture emerged out of local traditions. These local traditions did not disappear, but instead entered the larger complex of Greek religious notions, enriching both Greek mythology and religious practices. For instance, the local Cretan dances of armed youths during their initiation ceremonies became part of the colorful story of the infant Zeus' birth in Crete. The noise of the youths' clashing shields drowned out the infant's cries, and so saved him from Kronos, who wanted to devour him. Further, the Cretan Zeus merged with the child and lover of the Cretan goddess, linking him to the island's Neolithic past.

In classical Greece, Zeus was first among the gods dwelling on Mount Olympus, as Homer portrayed him. He was the father of humans, the ruler of their destinies, and, despite his own moral waywardness, the ultimate upholder of justice. In addition to Zeus, the roster of the foremost Olympian gods includes Hera, Zeus' wife; Poseidon, god of the sea; Hephaestus, the divine blacksmith; Apollo, god of law and order; Hermes, the divine messenger; Artemis, mistress of wild beasts; Athena, patroness of feminine and practical arts; and Aphrodite, goddess of love.

Apollo and Dionysus

Of these gods and goddesses, Apollo deserves special mention, because he came to symbolize many virtues that seem typically Greek, such as serenity, harmony, balance, and order.[56] Through his oracle at Delphi, Apollo gave counsel on matters of liturgical propriety and ritual purification. For example, Apollo had charge of purifying homicides, who had to cleanse themselves of their "pollution." One would take serious matters needing counsel to Apollo's pythia (priestess) at Delphi. In trance, she would exclaim the wisdom with which Apollo filled her. The origins of the pythia's exclamation may lie in shamanism, but by classical times Apollonian wisdom had distanced itself from the emotional and irrational, becoming primarily intellectual *theoria*—relatively serene religious contemplation. As epitomized in the Delphic oracle's command "Know thyself," Apollonian religion deified thought and spirit. For that reason, it encouraged science, art, philosophy, and music.

Somewhat the antithesis of Apollo was Dionysus, an eccentric among the gods of the Olympian period. A son of Zeus by a mortal woman, Dionysus apparently always remained an outsider. His cult was not native to central Greece, while psychologically its concern with the irrational and emotional made many fear it. In his well-known study *The Greeks and the Irrational*, E. R. Dodds associates Dionysus with "the blessings of madness."[57] Unlike the ecstasy of the Apollonian pythia, that of the followers of Dionysus (for example, of the women called maenads)[58] was wild, frenzied, and orgiastic. Such ecstasy represented the enthusiasm (being filled with divine force) that could come from dancing and wine drinking.

For Eliade, Dionysus conjures up "the totality of life, as is shown by his relations with water and germination, blood or sperm, and by the excess of vitality manifested in his animal epiphanies (bull, lion, goat)."[59] Finally, Dionysus was a god of vegetation who would disappear to the underworld and then spring back to life. The most influential literary source on the Dionysian cult, Euripides' play the *Bacchae*, portrays the god's followers as wildly joyous. If the play is accurate, their mountain revels culminated in tearing apart live animals and then eating their flesh raw (so as to commune with the god of animal life).

Strangely enough, the Greeks recognized something essential in Dionysus. Call it the need for madness, reverence for the life force, or the value of temporarily escaping one's mortal bonds—they blessed it and called it good. As a result, Apollo vacated Delphi during the three winter months and allowed Dionysus to reign.

Heroes

The Olympian religion had another category of influential figures called heroes, who include Heracles, Achilles, Theseus, Odysseus, and Orestes. These heroes were the subjects of much mythology and folklore. In the hands of Homer and the playwrights, their stories became the most profound reflections of classical literature. Aeschylus' *Oresteia*, for instance, has become a literary classic.

Eliade notes that the heroes tended to be active in the time of human beginnings, when things were unsettled. They had superhuman capacities and illustrated the heights and depths of achievement that history usually levels. Further, heroes typically suffered dramatic deaths, were great warriors or athletes, were expert at visions or the healing arts, or founded cities and clans. They created many of humanity's greatest achievements, such as city laws, writing, metallurgy, songs, and military tactics.

Indeed, as popular religion developed initiation rites and various mysteries, heroes became the mythological founders or patrons. For example, Theseus, prime hero of the Athenians, was the paradigm of the ritually initiated warrior because of his exploits in the labyrinth with the Minotaur. So, using history and their striking imagination, the Greeks made a world of fascinating characters who were larger than life. As exemplars of human potential, the heroes excited a will to excel, to push bone and spirit to the limits, that made *arete* (excellence) a Greek watchword.

Mortality

Excellence, like justice, raises the issue of anthropology—the conception of human nature. Olympian religion generally regarded humans rather bleakly. The prime attribute of an Olympian god is immortality, so according to Olympian religion human nature is from the outset defective. Gods are different from humans because they do not know death, the most striking aspect of the human condition. As Homer says, humans are but leaves scattered by the wind. They suffer many pains, abuses, and injustices. Because of this heavy burden, it would be a mercy not to be born or not to live in such an uncertain, mysterious, unjust world. Human life lies in the hands of the gods or of a less personalized fate.[60] Therefore, one can only hope that the gods are just. As the Homeric tales show only too clearly, however, divine justice is far from certain. Consequently, a theological purification set in. By the time of Euripides, Socrates, and Plato, justice was virtually identified with divinity. As a fragment from Euripides puts it, "If the gods do anything base, they are not the gods."

Whether divine justice is perfect or imperfect, though, humans have to submit to it. A major belief of official Greek religion supported the maxim "Nothing to excess"— no wild leaps of Dionysian enthusiasm, no hubris (overweening pride) that forgets human fallibility, no striving for immortality. Rather, we should accept our mortality and try to live nobly the brief span that fate has spun for us. Paradoxically, perhaps, this attitude led to affirming, even sanctifying, mortal life. In fact, it led to a *joie de vivre*: a delight in the human body, in festivals, sports, song, and dance.

Socrates, the restless prober of traditions, came to his calm before death by pressing Greek joy to the hilt. His sole tutor in wisdom, he claimed, was the great god Eros. However, Eros takes much of his flame from our certitude of dying. He urges us toward the perishing beauty of this work, that lovely person. Right now they have fine, precious life. Right now we can celebrate their wondrous luster. If the afterlife is but a place of shades, the here and now—the glorious sea, the dazzling sun—is all the more precious, all the more holy.

Earthly Religion — to balance sky-oriented Olympian religion

However, the sky-oriented Olympian religion never was the whole story. From the Minoans and the psyche came an earthly religion to balance the sky. Certainly the Dionysian cult was a major manifestation. So, too, were the many mother goddesses. Hera, Artemis, and Aphrodite, for example, all relate to fertility and mother earth. In Hesiod's *Theogony*, Gaea (earth) actually precedes and produces heaven. In popular religion, Demeter and Persephone were very influential. In fact, Demeter's search for Persephone in the underworld was a major theme of the Eleusinian mysteries, which are described below.

The result of this earth-oriented counterweight to the somewhat overbearing Olympians was a view that humans should aim to become, in Plato's phrase, "as much like God as possible." Through contact with the forces of life and fertility (in the Eleusinians' case) and with the forces of intellectual light (in the philosophers' case), the limits of mortality were challenged. "No," many Greeks said, "we are made for more than a few days in the sun. If we truly know ourselves, we can find undying life."

The Eleusinian mysteries were practiced in Athens from about 600 B.C.E. on, though they clearly originated much earlier. They evolved from the myth of Demeter's search for Persephone in the underworld,[61] which included a subplot about Demeter's unsuccessful (because of human folly) attempt to make Demophoon, the infant prince of Eleusis, an immortal. Thus, the mysteries consisted of rites and revelations that gave initiates precious knowledge in this life and bliss in the world to come.

We do not know the particulars of the mysteries, which were strictly secret, but the mysteries probably grafted Neolithic agricultural ideas onto the Olympian theme that the gods are immortal. If so, the mysteries moved beyond the myths of the Hainuwele type, in which agriculture entailed ritual murder and gods that die. The result was a new, powerful synthesis of sexuality and death (as reflected in Persephone being carried to the underworld by Pluto) and of agriculture and a happy existence beyond the grave (as in Demeter representing mother earth). This religious synthesis made Eleusis an important cultic center for almost 2,000 years. Adherents to the Eleusinian mysteries lived in all parts of the Greek world and came from all social classes. Anyone who spoke Greek and had "clean hands" (including women, children, and slaves) could take part. Poets of the stature of Pindar and Sophocles praised the mysteries, and they were a powerful force in Greek life.

The background of the Orphic rites was a mythology somewhat like that of Demeter and Persephone.[62] Orpheus was a prominent Thracian hero, the son of Calliope by Apollo. His great gift was for music—when he played the lyre wild beasts grew calm, trees danced, and rivers stood still. Orpheus married the nymph Eurydice, who died from snakebite while fleeing Aristaeus, another son of Apollo. Orpheus could have regained Eurydice from the underworld if he had been able to resist looking at her. But he had to wander inconsolably until followers of Dionysus tore him apart (because of his devotion to Apollo). From this background Guthrie concludes: "The story throws light upon the Orphic religion because that is exactly what, in its main features, it stood for, a blend of the Thracian belief in immortality with Apolline ideas of *katharsis* [purification]. From the one it took *ekstasis*, enthusiasm, and a deep spiritual hope; from the other a formalizing influence, an almost legal atmosphere of rules and regulations."[63]

The direct basis for the doctrines elaborated in the Orphic rites, however, was another myth, that of Dionysus Zagreus, the son of Zeus and Persephone. Zeus proposed to make Dionysus ruler of the universe, but the Titans were so enraged that they dismembered and devoured him. Athena saved Dionysus' heart and gave it to Zeus, who swallowed it and then destroyed the Titans with lightning. Dionysus Zagreus was born anew from that heart, while from the ashes

of the Titans came the human race, which was thus part divine (from Dionysus) and part evil (from the Titans). Consequently, the Orphics believed in the divine origin of the human soul but also in the need to leave behind the soul's Titanic inheritance through ritual initiation and reincarnation.

For eternal blessedness, Orphics preached, one had to follow a strict moral code, abstain from the flesh of living creatures, and cultivate the Dionysian part of human nature. When fully pure, the soul would be reincarnated no more. No more would it drink of the spring of Lethe (forgetfulness), but, light as air, it would live in union with the divine mind. The Orphics appealed to persons of refinement, and Orphism certainly influenced Plato, the natural philosopher Empedocles, and the Roman epic poet Vergil.

Both the Eleusinian mysteries and the Orphic rites sought immortality, the one by a profound ritualization of the life force, the other by purifying the divine soul. Together, they were a strong counterforce to the pessimism fostered by heaven-oriented Olympianism. Another counterforce to the sky was the *chthonioi*, the spirits who lived in the dark recesses of the earth.[64] Though they were hardly mentioned in Homer, in popular religion they tended to spell out the twofold function of mother earth: fertility and rule of the dead. For the most part, the *chthonioi* were local spirits, concerned with a particular town's crops or deceased. Sometimes their cult blended with the cult of a local hero. Other times sacrifices to the *chthonioi* had overtones of devotion to Gaea, Demeter, Pluto, or Trophonious—divinities of fertility or Hades. Whether the *chthonioi* were gods or shady figures imagined to populate the afterlife is not clear. Regardless, they elicited considerable fear, and the common people tried not to offend them.

Popular Religion — *the emotional relig. of ordinary ancient Greek*

Our last topic before we consider philosophy is the emotional religion of the ordinary ancient Greek.[65] If we confine our study to the literary sources of the classical period we get a false picture of Greek religion. By that time, the intellectuals were quite refined. Homer, Hesiod, and the early poets and philosophers had moved from gods who were simple nature forces, to gods who were anthropomorphic (personified), to a divinity that had to be pure—more just, more intelligent, and less limited than what the traditional myths described. The great playwrights (Aeschylus, Sophocles, and Euripides) and the great philosophers (Socrates, Plato, and Aristotle) completed this movement.

However, from prehistoric times well into the Christian era, over a span of perhaps 4,000 years, the nonintellectuals—the poor, ordinarily illiterate Greek peasantry—lived with a lively, emotional, hopelessly complicated blend of hopes and fears. Of the Olympians, they favored Hermes, whose Trickster quality, concern for travelers, closeness to shepherds, sexuality, and fondness for human beings made him unthreatening. Indeed, he was even the companion and patron of thieves. The other Olympians seem to have become less and less impressive, finally giving way to the *chthonioi*. Certainly local patron gods continued to be important; all Athenians, high and low, reached out to Athena. But the fertility forces, heroes (such as Asclepius the healer), and Apollo and Dionysus in their most popular aspects dominated the religion of most ordinary Greeks.

Most ordinary Greeks also believed in other, often malevolent, forces:[66] *keres*, whose function was to harm; *erinyes*, whose function was to punish; and *daimones*, spirits of the dead or inner voices who populated the world of intuition, suspicion, and dread. Committing any of several offenses might make one polluted, which would require ritual cleansing. Magic, personal prayer, and sacrifice were employed for various reasons.

These beliefs and practices were maintained throughout pre-Christian Greek history. Indeed, when Christianity became popular, this prevailing Greek religion largely looked upon it as just a new set of instruments: saints, blessings, and ceremonies. To the present day, peasants relate Christ to their old fertility religion. At Easter vigil, they have been heard to say, "If Christ does not rise tomorrow, we shall have no harvest this year."[67] Among the Greek people, then, divinity has remained close to the earth.

Philosophy

The common people did not build Athenian culture or make the breakthrough called philosophy. Rather, an aristocratic elite, working for several centuries, slowly distinguished the realms of myth and reason and in so doing wrote a pivotal chapter in the history of human consciousness. Before philosophy, the concept of reason was vague. We have seen the prehistoric suspicion that something can travel in dreams, rise in shamanist flight, and survive the grave. In Egypt, the Amon hymns exhibited a strong sense of transcendence—of the human mind pressing beyond materiality to divine mystery itself. In Iran, Zoroaster's interior dualism (the battle between Truth and the Lie) revealed a striking grasp of the abstract spirit.

Although many cultures thus showed some awareness of reason and spirit, the culture of the Greek city-state identified reason and controlled it. Only the line of pre-Socratic thinkers—most prominently, Pythagoras, Xenophanes, Parmenides, and Heraclitus—so disciplined their dissatisfaction with Olympian culture that they saw human mind (*nous*) itself as being divine and real. India approached this belief but never came away with Greece's balancing belief in the material world.

The story of the pre-Socratics, which weaves into that of the dramatists and Sophists (teachers of shallow philosophy), is a fascinating chapter in religion.[68] Partly from interior experimentation and partly from an empirical study of nature, the early philosophers moved beyond what most previous peoples had meant by the word *god*. As we have seen, peoples believing in the cosmo-

*Figure 5   The Parthenon, remains of a prime symbol of Athens' golden age.
Photo by J. T. Carmody.*

logical myth considered the world to be a living whole. With the rise of civilized religion, Mesopotamians, Egyptians, Iranians, and others focused on the political aspect of the cosmos. In other words, divinity to them was in good part a symbolic representation of their own society. Even Ahura Mazdah had a strong political function. For Darius I, Ahura Mazdah sanctioned the building of an empire of Truth.

Out of its dark age, Greek creativity produced a pantheon—a roster of gods—that was neither natural nor political. The Olympians were anthropomorphic, evidencing human aspects. To be sure, Zeus was a sky god and Athena fought for Athens. But although nature and politics played important roles, they did not make the Olympians distinctive. What made the Olympians distinctive was the rich, anthropomorphic mythology surrounding them. In these divine characters or personalities, human passions were blown up to divine stature. Contemplating such divinity, ruminating on the Olympian mythology, the Greek geniuses clarified where and how *mythos* shatters on *logos*—where story must yield to analytic reason.

Of course, this realization was prompted by historical events. It did not spawn at a seaside resort. Looking around them, the Greek geniuses of the fifth and fourth centuries B.C.E. saw a succession of empires. The decline of Babylon, Egypt, and Persia evoked the question, "What is the meaning of history's process?" As a result, historians such as Herodotus and Thucydides wanted a break with myth, an explanation of the flux in political affairs.[69] As a result, Socrates, Plato, and Aristotle labored heroically to produce such a break.

When the Athenians sentenced Socrates to death for impiety, they shocked Plato to the depths of his soul. If Athens could reject the one wise person who might save it, what chance did truth have?[70] Eventually Plato correlated the Athenian city-state experience with the flux of empires and came to wonder about the possibility for human order. The *Republic* and *Laws*, which constitute about 40 percent of Plato's writings, testify to how long and deeply problems of political order absorbed him. His great problem, in fact, was the disorder of most humanity—citizens, empire builders, the great and small alike. Grappling with this problem, Plato saw that all order—personal, sociopolitical, and historical—depends on a truth only luminous from God. Since Plato's great problem remains our own, we do well to attend to his insight.

From instinct, observation, and reflection, Plato decided that history means more than wars and power struggles. Restricted to that level, history is literally absurd—a cause for despair—and yields no ordering truth (except negatively as an analysis of cultural destruction).

Rather, we must become aware of a reality that is not distorted by our lusts; divine mystery must shine forth an ordering light. Where warmongers and powerbrokers close themselves, philosophers must be receptive and willing to change. Where politicians restrict reality to money and influence, philosophers must go to the center of things—to the soul's passion for justice and love. Like a new Prometheus firing humanity's soul, the Platonic lover of wisdom made justice and love humanity's great passion. The presence or absence of that passion makes health or disease. Plato minces no words: One either admits divine mystery or faces disaster.

The fire and order of the Platonic soul clarified human reality. From Plato's time, some persons have realized that the meaning of their existence was to move through experience toward the intellectual light of God. Thus, the process of human questioning— human searching for flashes of insight and then sustained visions—has been a primary task for those seriously religious since Plato. The Western development of science, philosophy, and the humanities was made possible by the Greek consecration of this task.

Plato himself used myth and symbols to suggest the psychology, politics, and natural philosophy of the newly clarified human consciousness. These uses were deliberate, calculated attempts to keep touch with the whole field of human awareness, to keep from getting lost in abstraction. Aristotle, more prosaic, commonsensical, and scientific than Plato, analyzed the new clarification of consciousness in drier, more technical terms.[71] As he saw it, a person first experiences ignorance about the meaning of human existence. This ignorance, however, is peculiar: It is knowing that one does not know—being aware that one is in the dark. Instinctively we seek release from the tension that this realization produces. Aware of our confusion, upset that we do not know how our lives make sense, we are moved to clarify things. If distractions, whether personal or social, do not interfere, we will pursue enlightenment, and our search will become inner directed. We will grope forward by an intuition or foreknowledge of what we seek, just as we work a math problem by a knowing ignorance that enables us to recognize when our answer is correct.

Likewise, in the profound problem of human understanding that Aristotle was working on, there is a sense of the answer or goal from the beginning. Looking for the reality that will order both ourselves and our world, questioning and following the thoughts of our mind, we slowly advance toward the divine light, the divine mind, the divine being. Indeed, divinity itself, Aristotle finally realized, had been attracting him from the beginning. From the first, his glimmerings of light, of intellectual understanding, had been sharings in God. Developing this Platonic and Aristotelian insight, the Christian theologians Augustine and Aquinas wrote a new treatise on the image of God, stating that our intellectual light is a share in the activities of the Father, the Son, and the Holy Spirit.[72]

This is not the place to review all the other changes resulting from the classical philosophers' achievement. We must underscore, though, that classical Greek philosophy made a quantum leap in the search for divinity. With the philosophers' new tools of self-awareness and analysis, immortality and becoming godlike became more than symbols from the mystery religions. Rather, they became substantial themes of the contemplative life *(bios theoretikos).*[73] Aristotle placed the contemplative life at the pinnacle of human achievement, for in such a life he saw human beings most directly cooperating with God. Seeking the explanation for all things, humans would sometimes be drawn into an overwhelming fullness of life. For Aristotle, God was the explanation for all things, and God's life was "thought thinking itself." After Aristotle, human beings could rejoice or groan at the calling to participate in divine self-thinking. After Aristotle, the contemplative life was a potent symbol of human perfection.

The Hellenistic Religions

Following the cultural flowering of Greek religion in drama and philosophy, the Hellenistic religions dominated. This period resulted from Alexander the Great's conquests (*Hellenism* is the term for his vision of an ecumenical, transnational culture). The Hellenistic era extended from Alexander (who died in 323 B.C.E.) well into the Roman and Christian periods. According to historians who love classical Greek culture, it was not a time of glory. Gilbert Murray, for instance, speaks of a "failure of nerve," while E. R. Dodds speaks of a "fear of freedom."[74] From our standpoint, perhaps the most significant feature of Hellenistic religion was its syncretism. In an imperial area populated by numerous ethnic groups, many different gods, beliefs, and rituals all became alike. We can conclude our historical survey of Greek religion by describing the most important aspects of this syncretism.

Alexander himself was something of a visionary, for what lured him to empire building was the idea of an ideal realm in which conquered peoples "were to be treated not as uncivilized and barbarous members of subject races but as equals with whom one must live in concord."[75] Prior to Alexander, the Greeks had some knowledge of foreign religions through travel and trade, but, in general, oriental deities had made little impact on their own piety. (One exception might be Cybele, a mother goddess imported from Phrygia [central Turkey], who was identified with Rhea, the mother of Zeus.) However, from the time of the Diadochi, Alexander's successor rulers, oriental cults began to spread. By the beginning of the second century B.C.E., they were predominant. The most popular gods were Cybele, Isis, and Serapis. In the later Roman period, Mithra also flourished.

As noted, Cybele was a mother goddess (and mistress of the animals). Usually she was accompanied by her young lover, Attis. (We may hypothesize that to the Greeks Cybele and Attis echoed the Minoan cave goddess and her consort.) She was severe and vengeful, and accompanied by lions. When Attis was unfaithful, she drove him insane. Eventually Cybele became a maternal deity such as Demeter, Hera, and Aphrodite—a patroness of life, protectress of particular cities, and defender of women.

In her ceremonies devotees reenacted Attis' insanity and consequent self-castration. They would take the pine tree (Attis' symbol), bury it, mourn for the dead god, and then observe his resurrection. Resurrected, Attis would rejoin Cybele, which was cause for great feasting. The cult seems to have promoted fertility, and its rituals have overtones of the vegetative cycle and sexuality. Celebrants went to emotional extremes, dancing, scourging themselves, and even on occasion imitating Attis' castration. We could say that the worship of Cybele attracted Dionysian energies.

In ancient Egypt, Isis was the wife of Osiris and the mother of Horus. In the Hellenistic period she achieved a wider influence, often in the company of Serapis. Serapis was an artificial creation, the result of the Greeks' aversion to the Egyptian tendency of worshiping gods in animal form. Fusing Osiris with his symbol (Apis, the bull), the Greeks made a new god: Serapis. He was bearded and seated on a throne, like Zeus, Hades, and Asclepius, some of whose functions he shared (such as rule of the sky, rule of the underworld, and healing). Joined with Isis, Serapis was primarily a fertility god, bedecked with branches and fruit.

Isis rather overshadowed Serapis, for she became a full-fledged, several-sided deity. As the consort of Osiris-Serapis, she was the heavenly queen of the elements, the ruler of stars and planets. Because of such power, she could enter the underworld to help her devotees or to stimulate the crops. Indeed, as a vegetative goddess she blended with Demeter and also the moon goddess Selene. Perhaps her most important role, though, was to represent feminine virtues. In distress, she had sought the slain Osiris and brought him back to life. Sensitive and compassionate, she would do the same for her followers. As the mother of Horus (she was often represented as suckling him), she would help women in childbirth and child raising. Unlike Cybele, the Hellenistic Isis was soft and tender. Yet, as recent scholarship has shown,[76] her devotees assumed a code of high ethics and her cult was strikingly upright.

Like those for Cybele and Attis, the ceremonies for Isis and Osiris-Serapis amounted to a cycle of mourning and rejoicing. Mourning, followers reenacted Isis' search for Osiris and her discovery of his dismembered parts. Rejoicing, they celebrated Osiris' resurrection and the return of Isis' joy. Apuleius' famous account gives some of the details of the rituals, which included bathings, ten days of abstinence from sex, "approaching the gates of death," and entering the presence of the gods.[77] Clearly, the ceremonies were elaborate and effective, much as the Eleusinian mysteries must have been. Through the cycle of Osiris' death and resurrection, followers would gain confi-

dence that their own lives were in good hands. Through the dramatic symbolization of the afterlife, they could anticipate security and bliss.

Mithra, whom we know from Iran, never took strong hold among the Hellenistic Greeks, but he did become important among the Romans influenced by Hellenism, especially the Roman soldiers. Indeed, his transformation illustrates almost perfectly the religious hodgepodge that cross-cultural contact produced at this time. In Mithra's Romanization, Jupiter (Zeus) took on attributes of Ahura Mazdah and became a great champion of Truth. Mithra, in turn, became Jupiter-Ahura Mazdah's faithful helper in the battle against the Lie. In this later mythology, Mithra was born of a rock (symbol of the celestial vault), and from birth carried a bow, arrows, and dagger (much like a Persian noble). He shot the arrows into the heavens from time to time to produce a heavenly spring of pure rain water. Very important was his sacrifice of the bull, from whose blood sprouted the corn (symbol of vegetation).

Thus, Mithra was both a celestial deity (later associated particularly with the sun) and a fertility god. His followers would trace his circuit through the sky, reenact the mythology of his birth, and celebrate a bull sacrifice in his name. After the sacrifice they would feast together, believing that the bull's meat and blood contained the substance of eternity. As the Mithraic doctrine developed, it generated a complicated astrology, by which the progress of initiates' souls through the heavens was shown. At its peak, Mithraism ran underground "churches" and schools. Today excavations under Christian churches, including St. Clement's in Rome, reveal statuary, classrooms, and altars used by Mithraists.

In summary, the Hellenistic period was a time of profuse religious activity. Onto Greek and then Roman religious culture, a cosmopolitan era grafted elements from the Egyptians, Persians, Phrygians, and others. (We have not even mentioned the Syrian cults of the mother goddess Adonis and of various baals [Canaanite and Phoenician local deities], which constituted another strand of Hellenistic fertility religion.)[78] Beyond doubt, a certain cultural confusion underlay all this excitement. Thrown into close contact with foreigners, all persons in the new empires had to face new divinities and beliefs. Partly as a result, many persons felt great need for signs of salvation or assurances of a happy afterlife. The upshot was a frenzy of mysteries through which devotees could feel stirring emotions or see marvelous sights. With a rush of sorrow, sexual excitement, or hope for rebirth, an initiate would feel passionately alive. In a time of disarray and ceaseless warfare, when the city-state or clan no longer offered security or guidance, such a sense of vitality was more than welcome.

Structural Analysis

Nature and divinity run together in Greek religion. Throughout its history, the Greek religious mind associated all major natural phenomena with particular gods. As noted, the sky, sea, and earth were powerful deities. The major stress was on fertility (which was the focus of most local festivals), perhaps due to the poor quality of the rocky Greek soil. The Homeric hymns, for instance, sing praise to mother earth, who feeds all creatures and blesses humans with good crops. Relatedly, they make the man with good crops a symbol of prosperity. The earth, mother of the gods and wife of the starry heavens, has blessed him—his children can play merrily.[79] As a result of its prehistoric roots, then, Greece saw much divinity in natural growth.

In social terms, Greek religious culture reflects the ethical ideas that bound first the early clanspeople and then the citizens of the city-state. The ethics of the early historical period evolved from the extended family. There was no money, and banditry was rife, so a man's great virtue was to provide food, shelter, and defense—whether by just means or otherwise. Consequently, most men (it was a patriarchal culture) petitioned the gods for material prosperity and success in arms. They called one of their number good *(agathos)* and praised him for excellence *(arete)* if he was a survivor. The more elevated notions of justice later developed by philosophers clashed with this less moral tradition. Since early Greek religion did not associate godliness with justice, the philosophers called for its overthrow.

Another primitive concept that died hard was "pollution." This was the dangerous state of being unclean, or at odds with the natural powers because of some dread deed. Homicide was especially polluting, but incest, contact with a dead person, or even a bad dream or childbirth could also be polluting, each in varying degrees. Washing in a spring would cleanse away a bad dream; purification by fire and the offering of pig's blood cleansed a homicide. The concept of pollution seems to have been a way for the Greeks to deal with dreadful, amoral happenings that might bring destructive contact with the sacred, even though they were unintentional. Since polluted persons could contaminate others, they were often banished.

Greek cults used magical formulas, prayers, sacrifices, dances, and dramatic scenes—a wealth of creative expressions. Magical formulas probably were most prominent in agricultural festivals, where peasants mixed models of snakes and phalluses with decomposing, organic materials, such as pine branches and remains of pigs, to excite powers of fertility. Greek prayers would recall a god's favors and the sacrifices that the praying person had offered previously. This implied a sort of barter: We will honor you and offer a sacrifice if you give us success in crops (or war, or family life, or whatever). Occasionally texts indicate pure admiration for divine power or beauty, but the ordinary attitude was quite practical. Since the gods were not necessarily rational or holy, they had to be cajoled. Indeed, a Greek tended to pray and sacrifice rather parochially, addressing the family Apollo or Athena, who might remember fat sacrifices offered in the past. Each family or city-state had its own traditions, customs, myths, and gods, which served both to bind the members together and to maintain the splintering among the different tribes.

Sacrifice was a primary way to keep local religion in good health. By giving the local god good things, one could expect prosperity in return. (Significantly, this implied that the gods blessed those who were wealthy and had good things to sacrifice and that those who sacrificed and met bad luck had secret sins or wicked ancestors. Either way, human success and goodness were rather arbitrary.) In a sacrifice, usually parts of an animal were offered and the rest was consumed. According to a Homeric account, for instance, a pig was cut up, pieces of each limb were wrapped in fat and thrown on the fire, and barley grains were sprinkled on the fire. The meal that followed was a mode of communion with the deities.

Greek cults produced many priests, but their status and functions were limited. In principle, any person could pray and sacrifice to any god, so priests had no monopoly. They tended to be limited to particular temples and were seldom organized into bands or hierarchies. A large clan might have its own officiating priest, and the priest of a prosperous temple might make a good living from sacrifice fees. Otherwise, priesthood was not a road to status or wealth. Priests seldom gave instruction or performed divinations, though some priests in the mystery rites did both.

Many Greek religious authors were rather harsh on women. Hesiod, for instance, reported the myth of Pandora and the box of evils, which made woman the source of human woes. In other places he called woman "that beautiful evil," the "snare from which there is no escaping," and "that terrible plague."[80] Socrates, when asked about the advisibility of marriage, balanced the boon of heirs against the woes of a wife: "One quarrel after another, her dower cast in your face, the haughty disdain of her family, the garrulous tongue of your mother-in-law, the lurking paramour."[81] In Plato's *Repub-*

lic, women were to be equal to men socially and sexually, having rights to education and rule. Nonetheless, Plato tended to consider women less independent than men, in good part because of their physique: "The womb is an animal that longs to generate children." Aristotle, however, was the most unequivocal misogynist. To him women were simply inferior, both intellectually and morally. In his matter-and-form theory, women supplied only the matter for human reproduction, men supplying everything effective and active.

Women did have legal rights in Athenian society, but their lives were largely circumscribed by male control. Their basic function was to bear children. The playwright Euripides summarized the impact of this socialization, putting into the mouths of the women of his *Andromache* such self-evaluations as: "There's a touch of jealousy in the female psyche"; "For nature tempers the souls of women so they may find a pleasure in voicing their afflictions as they come"; "A woman even when married to a cad, ought to be deferential, not a squabbler"; and "And just because we women are prone to evil, what's to be gained from perverting men to match?"

On the other hand, we have seen that Greek divinity frequently was powerfully feminine. In the Minoan-Mycenaean period, a great goddess was the prime deity. In the Olympian period, Demeter, Hera, Athena, Artemis, and Aphrodite all exerted great influence. In the Hellenistic religions, Cybele and Isis more than equaled Mithra. Psychologically, then, Greek culture never doubted the divinity of the feminine. More than Israelite, Christian, or Muslim culture, Greek divinity was androgynous. Further, certain religious groups offered women escape from social oppression, such as the Eleusinian and Dionysian sects. There, in a sort of utopian free zone, women could experience equality and dignity. Although these cults never compensated for women's lack of dignity or status in ordinary life, it was an implicit admission that ordinary life was quite imperfect.

The personal side of Greek religion is perhaps most manifest in myths dealing with human creation. In the most famous collection of myths, Hesiod's *Works and Days*, ancient Greeks read that they were the last and lowest in a series of human generations. During the first ages, races of gold, silver, and bronze flourished, but they came to various bad ends. A flood intervened, followed by the age of the heroes. Finally the present iron people arose. In other words, Hesiod's myth put into Greek form the widespread belief in a golden age or a previous paradise, with the accompanying message that the present age was a low point.

Partly from this religious heritage, the prevailing mood of many Greek writers was pessimistic. As Sermonides, a writer of the seventh century B.C.E. put it, "There is no wit in man. Creatures of a day, we live like cattle, knowing nothing of how the god will bring each one to his end."[82] Others echoed Sermonides: Human beings have only a short time under the sun. Their powers fade quickly, their fortunes are uncertain. By comparison, Delphic wisdom was more positive: Gain self-knowledge and moderation. Self-knowledge, above all, was accepting one's mortality. By moderation, one could avoid hubris and tragedy. There were overtones of jealousy in this advice from Apollo, however, as though the god feared humans' yearning for immortality or resented their craving a life of passion.

Indeed, passion was ever a danger, for the Greeks were competitive and lusty. In the end, they would not give up their dreams of immortality. So becoming godlike became a central theme of philosophy and mystery religion. Empedocles, for instance, thought that his wisdom made him a god among mortals. Plato taught that the soul is divine and deathless. The common person would more likely find divinity in one of the mystery rites, through a union with Demeter or a knowledge from Isis, either of which could bring victory over death.

The personal implications of Greek religion were greatest in the philosophers' clarification of reason, universal humanity, and the participation of divinity in human thought. As we have noted, the poets, dramatists, and early philosophers slowly clarified the nature of human reason, separating it from myth. By focusing on mind *(nous)* and its relations with being *(ousia)*, the pre-Socratics prepared the way for Plato and Aristotle, who realized how mind and being coincide. Moreover, this work did not take the Greek intellectuals away from either religion or politics. Rather, it introduced them to an order that set all the fundamentals—nature, society, self, and divinity—in harmony. In other words, it took them to the heart of what it means to be human.

Finally, the philosophers' order meant a new perspective on death. In early times, death was shadowy. For Homer, the dead had only a vague existence around their graves or in the underworld. There was no judgment or punishment for injustice towards one's fellows. Only those who had directly affronted the gods had to suffer. The mystery cults said one could conquer death by union with an immortal divinity, and their great popularity indicates the hold that death had on Greece starting in the sixth century B.C.E. The philosophers spoke of judgment and punishment because they were acutely aware that justice rules few human situations. In quite deliberate myths, Plato symbolized the inherent need we have for a final accounting. Without it, he suggested, reason would lose balance.

There is no need to review the side of divinity in the Greek world view, since we have traced its development in our history. In the eyes of many scholars, the Greeks were among the most religious of ancient peoples. From heaven to under the earth, from crude emotion to the most refined spirituality, their great culture put a religious shine on everything. Today, if we find the world "sacred" (deeply meaningful) through science or art, if we find the human being "sacred" (deeply valuable) through medicine or philosophy, if we find the political order alive with counsels both good and bad—if we ever think in these ways, it is largely because of the Greeks. They made the "transcendental" qualities—unity, truth, goodness, and beauty—part of Western religion.

SUMMARY

We have surveyed the antecedents and consequences of the rise of civilized religion. We should now reflect at least briefly on the main patterns that our survey reveals.

First, civilization—culture and social organization at a scale larger than that of the tribal village—developed on the foundations of agriculture. The increase in population, the sedentary life, and the economic and cultural specialization that farming allowed made cities and their cultural advances possible. Not surprisingly, then, many agricultural or earth-related motifs continued on in the religions of the first great civilizations. For all their moments of spiritual achievement, Egypt, Iran, and Greece all remained immersed in peasant views.

Second, the discovery of writing was essential in the advances of civilized religion. Through writing—even the hieroglyphic writing of the Egyptians—came the record that both the early civilizations themselves used and we, their latter-day students, have used to retrieve what they thought and felt. Within the early peoples' own religious horizon, the sense of history that came with writing was a significant development. Of course, oral peoples have memory and tradition, but writing makes both more precise.

Writing also raises the possibility of a new attitude toward the realities of the traditional religious world. For writing makes the realities of the traditional world *mediated*, as they previously were not. Spoken language has a holistic quality, conveying its message immediately, in a rather imperative or at least soliciting way. Written language is more detached and indirect. To the benefit of science, and perhaps the detriment of religion, it tends toward scholarship. For example, once the biblical legends were written down, scholars could dissect them at leisure. In the development of the early civilizations,

we catch sizable traditions at their very revealing transition from oral to written religion.

Third, this chapter has mainly dealt with religious traditions that lasted for long stretches of time. Of course, Egypt, Iran, and Greece all changed significantly during the times that we studied. Also, Paleolithic religion probably retained its basic forms at least a dozen times longer than the religions of our three civilizations did. Nonetheless, Egypt had a quite coherent religious culture that lasted longer than Christianity has so far, and Iran and Greece both provide impressive instances of an enduring religion. Because of their duration, the world view of these religions can be reconstructed. These religions are also precious because they produced culture complex enough—theologies, arts, justifications for war, major social institutions—for us to find it familiar. Thereby, we can empathize with these civilizations more than we can with oral peoples.

Finally, we should compare the three religions here briefly. Concerning nature, they all preserved close ties with a living cosmos. In rites, myths, and popular religion, for instance, they all had strong agricultural influences. On the other hand, each separated itself from the cosmological myth somewhat. Akhenaton's reform was Egypt's most dramatic separation, but the Amon hymns and the man's dispute with his soul about suicide provide additional evidence.

Zoroaster made Iran break with the cosmological myth more sharply than Egypt did, but later Zoroastrianism retreated on this point. Greece took the only full step toward the realization of spirit. The philosophers discovered the mind; for Plato and Aristotle, what is and what can be thought coincided.

Still, none of the early civilizations broke the cosmological myth entirely. None conceived of a personal creator God. All their divinities were world forces, and all their ultimate world views tended to follow nature's rhythms.

Socially, Egypt appears as the most

hierarchical and rigid civilization; its culture is remarkably static. Iran appears as a welter of ethnic influences and a welter of religious trends. It was in great turmoil, but few personalities, other than military kings, stand out. Personalities stand out most dramatically in Greece, despite its large patches of social conservatism. Especially in the Athenian golden age, tradition seemed just flexible enough. Thus, Greece fostered geniuses. In art and philosophy, we study them still. We probably know ancient Greek religion better than the other two and find it richer.

Study Questions

1. What major religious innovations did the rise of agriculture produce?

2. What was the paramount symbolization in the religion of Megalithic peoples?

3. Why was the sun so prominent in Egyptian religion?

4. Does the myth of Osiris illumine the religious significance of the pyramids? How?

5. In what sense did Zoroaster differentiate Iranian religious consciousness?

6. What significance do you see when you compare Ahura Mazdah and the Egyptian Amon-Re?

7. What do you make of the statement "Greek love of wisdom definitively clarified the nature of human reason"?

8. Do Dionysus and Apollo together compose a complete symbolization of divinity? Why?

9. Is it fair to summarize the Hellenistic religions as a return to a prephilosophical emphasis on fertility, or did their "salvation" entail considerably more?

Chapter Two

JUDAISM: TWENTY-FIVE KEY DATES

CA. 1200 B.C.E.   EXODUS FROM EGYPT

CA. 1013–973   DAVID

722   FALL OF NORTHERN KINGDOM TO ASSYRIA

586   FALL OF SOUTHERN KINGDOM TO BABYLON

331   ALEXANDER CONQUERS PALESTINE

168   MACCABEAN REVOLT

63   ROMANS CONQUER JERUSALEM

70 C.E.   ROMANS DESTROY JERUSALEM

80–110   CANONIZATION OF HEBREW SCRIPTURES

CA. 200   PROMULGATION OF MISHNAH

CA. 500   BABYLONIAN TALMUD COMPLETE IN ROUGH FORM

640   MUSLIM CONQUEST OF MIDDLE EAST

Judaism

Judaism is the oldest of the three major prophetic religions. The founding and development of Christianity and Islam could not have occurred without the preexistence of Judaism. (Zoroastrianism can claim some prophetic equality with Judaism, but its prophecies never became dominant in Near Eastern and Western beliefs. Zoroastrianism's major influence in the West was its eschatology—its ideas of death, judgment, resurrection, punishment, the warfare between good and evil, and so on.) Abraham, Moses, David, Elijah, Isaiah—they are the personalities that dominated the Near Eastern beginning.

APPEARANCE

In recent times, to arrive at Ben-Gurion Airport outside Tel Aviv has been to enter a climate of tension. Because of terrorist incidents the whole airport is fraught with caution. Security measures for departing passengers are the most severe in the world. As if to downplay the dangers, though, the authorities expedite the entry of new arrivals, rushing them through to the money changers and taxis. That rush adds a touch of Europe to the normally languid Middle East, as do the fields made green through irrigation. The land has bloomed, the trees, once destroyed, have returned. Just the hour's drive from the airport to Jerusalem tells the new arrival that in contemporary Israel the Middle East has a Western will and a technological mind.

Jerusalem is the spiritual heart of modern Israel, as it has been the Jews' spiritual center through nineteen centuries of Diaspora (dispersal).[1] Christians and Muslims revere it as a holy city, but it is absolutely pivotal for Jews. The new city blares with taxis, gleams with white high rises. From any of its several hills you see overgrown lots and new constructions juxtaposed—an aggressively expanding city. The old city bustles with tourists and is more multilingual. Jews share it with Muslims and Christians of various denominations. It is a blend of churches and bazaars, piety and merchandising.

Often, in fact, it merchandises piety, for the traffic is heavy in pieces of the "true" cross, tours of the tomb of David, slides of the Dome of the Rock. You can walk along walls that go back to the time of Herod, if not to David himself, yet on either side of the Western Wall modernity intrudes. To the west is the showplace of new Jerusalem, the modern apartments of which the mayor is so proud. To the east, in the precinct of the mosques, are soldiers dressed in olive drab who check all parcels and handbags. Their authority derives from their small machine guns.

At the Western Wall, Judaism's most revered memorial, men don prayer shawls and join women in weeping. The wall is steeped in history. Its sheer presence occasions great joy: For centuries Jews had little access to this remnant of the Temple. To approach it and pray, then, fulfills the dreams of generations. On the other hand, those dreams were so often nightmares that the wall is also a pillar of sorrow. Those praying may feel, "Why should we be so fortunate? What of the centuries when 'next year in Jerusalem' was but an illusion? What of the millions who perished without a sign of God's care?" The prayers at the wall, like Jewish prayer generally, are more for the collectivity than for the individual. They praise God for his steadfastness, ask God for his protection, and wonder why human history involves so much suffering.

Complementary to the ancient memorial of the Western Wall is a new memorial at Yad Vashem. Yad Vashem lies outside Jerusalem, on a high hill from which the land stretches forth. It has a pillar, a museum, and an undying flame—all to commemorate the Holocaust. The Holocaust, of course, is the "burnt offering" of six million Jews in the concentration camps of World War II. The Holocaust gave Zionism—the movement to return to the ancient land—much greater impetus than it had before the war.[2] Opposite Yad Vashem, on Mount

Herzl, lie buried the founder of Zionism, Theodor Herzl, and other Zionist heroes.

Outside Munich, at the remains of the Dachau death camp, is confirmation of the documentation found in the Yad Vashem museum. Though not everyone who died in the Nazi concentration camps was a Jew, the desire to achieve a "final solution" to the "Jewish question" was a major reason for building the camps. When the cantor sings his haunting song before the undying flame at Yad Vashem, the shivers run to Dachau. They touch the Western Wall, the garrisons on the West Bank, even the menorahs (Jewish candelabra) in the Jewish Museum. The past life on the holy land, the present militarism, and the traditional faith—they all pour into the lament.

These psychic currents run in other national waters, too. As of 1970, about 44 percent of the world's 14 million Jews lived in the United States.[3] Only 24 percent lived in Israel, so the United States had almost twice as many Jews as Judaism's own nation. Eighteen percent resided in the Soviet Union, which gives weight to Soviet Jews' struggle for the right to emigrate. Because of its internationalism, then, Judaism is a religious and historical question for all the Western world. Its history in Europe, as well as its current situation in the world's economic trouble spot, gives Judaism a far more international presence than its tiny population would indicate. Whether and how Israel survives are questions that make the Western Wall a major symbol of humanity's current spiritual drama.

HISTORY

The Biblical Period

"From the point of view of the Jew, Judaism and the Religion of Israel are the same, and what is called the religion of [biblical] Israel is but one chapter of a long and variegated historical continuum."[4] We accept this point of view, avoiding the Christian tendency to distinguish biblical Judaism

from Judaism in the common era. In the beginning, the Jews were most likely a loose collection of seminomadic tribes that wandered in what is today Israel, Jordan, Lebanon, and Syria. They may have cultivated some crops, but their self-designation was "wandering Aramaeans" (Deut. 26 : 5). Thus, when scouts returned from Canaan (present-day Western Israel) with grapes, pomegranates, and figs (products of settled cultivators), they caused quite a stir.[5]

Members of an extended family tended to worship their particular "god of the father," defining themselves largely in terms of their patriarch and his god. The cult therefore centered on clan remembrance of this god, who wandered with the tribe in its nomadic life. The common name for such a clan divinity was *el*. Before their settlement in Canaan, the people seem to have worshipped a variety of *els*: the god of the mountain, the god of seeing, the god of eternity, and so on. Usually they worshiped at altars constructed of unhewn stones, which they considered the god's house. In addition to the *els* were household deities and minor divinities and demons of the desert. In later orthodox Jewish interpretation, Abraham drew on whatever sense there was of a unity among these *els* or of a supreme *el* over the others to dedicate himself to a God who was beyond nature. That God, the creator of the world, Abraham called Yahweh.[6]

For later orthodoxy, Abraham became the "Father" of the Jews and his God Yahweh became their God. In that sense, Judaism began with Abraham. Abraham lived around 1800 B.C.E. From about 1650 to 1280, the people of Abraham, then known as Hebrews, were in Egypt, subjects of the Egyptian kingdom.[7] Their leader at the end of their stay in Egypt was Moses. In later Jewish theology, Moses functioned as the founder of the Jewish people, because God revealed through Moses his will to strike a covenant and fashion himself a people. In the incident at the burning bush, Jewish faith said, Moses experienced God's self-revelation. God commissioned Moses to lead the people out of Egypt, giving as his

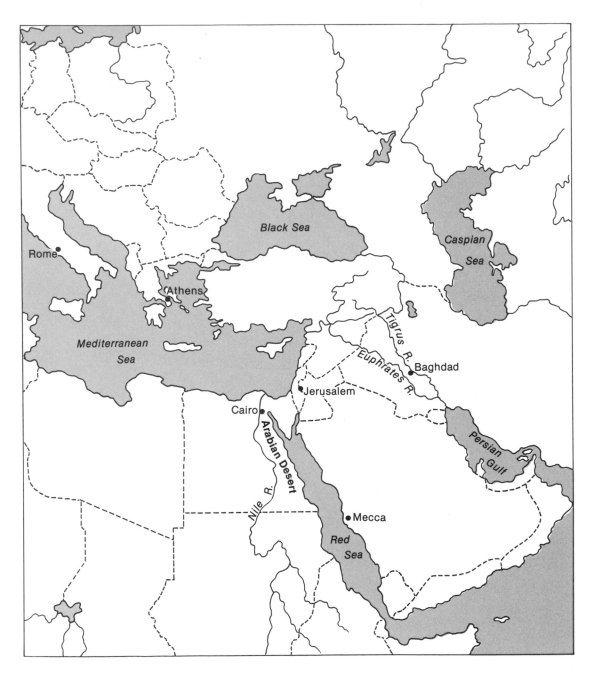

Figure 6   *The Near East.*

authoritative name only "I am who I am" (or "I am whatever I want to be").

Moses then led an exodus from Egypt; in the most significant episode in that exodus, Egyptian pursuers drowned in the sea. Free of them, the Israelites (the descendants of Jacob, Abraham's grandson) wandered in the desert until they entered the homeland that God had promised them. The deliverance from Egypt through the unexpected event at the Reed Sea (not the present-day Red Sea) marked all subsequent Jewish faith. Looking back to this event, later generations clung to the belief that their God ruled history and would continue to liberate them from oppression.

In the desert, Moses and the people tested the meaning of their exodus experience. They came to believe, through what the Bible pictures as God's miraculous speaking to them, that they were bound to God by a covenant.[8] In this compact, based on the relation between an overlord and a vassal, God pledged care and the people pledged fidelity. The commandments accompanying this covenant gave the binding relationship (which the Bible saw as prefigured in Adam, Noah, and Abraham) an ethics. They became the basis of the Law and the revelation that bound the people together.

When the Israelites finally settled in Canaan (in the latter half of the thirteenth century B.C.E. under Moses' successor Joshua),[9] they changed from a nomadic to an agricultural people. They were still a group of confederated tribes, but in settlement their bonds tended to loosen, as each group kept to its own area and developed its own ways. Only in times of common danger would the groups weld together. Settlement also meant religious changes, as local sanctuaries replaced the wandering ark of the covenant as the house of God. A somewhat professional priesthood apparently developed around these sanctuaries, and as the Israelites conquered Canaanite temples, they took over the scribal schools attached to the temples. These schools were probably the first sources of written Hebrew religious literature. In addition, the Canaanite religion itself was a great influence on the Israelites. Before long it produced a conflict between Israelites who favored the older God Yahweh—the God of Abraham, Moses, and the covenant—and those who favored the agricultural gods (baals) of the Canaanites.

Kings and Prophets

From about 1200 to 1000 B.C.E., the Israelites had a government by "judges"—charismatic leaders who took command in times of common danger. However, they eventually adopted monarchical rule, organizing a sturdy little kingdom under David at a new capital: Jerusalem. This kingdom unified the tribes of both north and south, and under Solomon, David's son, it had a brief but golden age of culture and empire. Some of the most striking narratives of the Hebrew Bible (Old Testament) derive from this period, including the brilliant memoir we find in 2 Samuel, chapters 13–20.[10]

In these narratives, David is portrayed as the ideal king and yet a man undeniably human—lustful for Bathsheba, tragically at odds with his son Absalom. Much later, David's achievements in war and his fashioning a kingdom for peace made him the focus of messianic hopes—hopes for a king anointed by God who would usher in a new age of prosperity and peace. David, then, was the Jewish prototype for sacred kingship. Similarly, David's son Solomon became the prototype for wisdom; just as many pious Jews attributed the Psalms to David, so they attributed much of the Bible's wisdom literature to Solomon.

Following Solomon's death, the northern and southern portions of the kingdom split apart. The north (Israel) lasted from 922 to 722 B.C.E, when it fell to Assyria. The south (Judah) lasted until 586, when it fell to Babylon. (Both Assyria and Babylon lay to the northeast.) These were centuries of great political strife. They also spawned a series of important religious "prophets," who dominate the next phase of biblical history. Greatest of the early prophets was Elijah, who preached in the north against the corrupt kings Ahab and Ahaziah and the queen Jezebel. The legendary stories about Elijah portray him as a champion of Yahweh and of true prophecy against the false prophets of the Canaanite baals. What is clear from these stories is the influence at that time of charismatic personalities who felt that God inspired them to stand up for the old religious ways—even if doing so infuriated the establishment.

Around 750 B.C.E. the northern prophet Amos, who was the first of the writing prophets, issued a clarion call for justice. Changing the notion that Yahweh was simply Israel's protector, Amos made his divine blessings dependent on repentance from sin. His God was clearly in charge of nature, but the key access to him was social justice. In other words, he was a God of people and history, especially concerned that humans deal with one another fairly.

Hosea, another northern prophet, also spoke up for mercy and justice (and for nonidolatrous cult), but he expressed God's attitude as that of a spouse willing to suffer infidelity, unable to cast off his beloved (the people covenanted to him). In the south, the successors to these northern prophets were Isaiah, Jeremiah, and "Second Isaiah" (the source of Isaiah, chapters 40–55). They made the same demands, but with greater stress on punishment by foreign powers. Reading the signs of the times, they thought that God would subject his people to captivity because they had not relied upon him in pure faith. However, both Jeremiah and Second Isaiah held out hope for a new beginning, assuring Judah that a remnant of the people would keep faith.

During the reign of the southern king Josiah (640–609 B.C.E.), there was a religious reform that scripture scholars see as the source of the "Deuteronomic" recasting of the early Jewish tradition. It shaped not only the book of Deuteronomy but other historical writings as well. Among the influential ideas were that Yahweh had elected Israel to be his people; that observing the covenant laws was necessary for religious prosperity; that Jews ought to repudiate contacts with foreigners and foreign gods; that the cult should be consolidated in Jerusalem; and that Israel ought to rely only on Yahweh, since he controls history and oversees nature.

JEREMIAH

It will be useful to consider the personality, career, and message of Jeremiah, for Jeremiah is a striking example of the prophetic vocation. Born in the middle of the seventh century B.C.E. (in 645, according to some scholars), and coming from a priestly family, Jeremiah preached during the reigns of kings Josiah, Jehoiakim, and Zedekiah, until he was deported in 582 to Egypt, where he died. We know more about Jeremiah's personal life than that of the other prophets, and Jeremiah's personal life shows a man completely dominated by God's call. He did not marry, because he wanted to symbolize that most children would not survive the troubles coming because of Israel's infidelities (Jer. 16 : 1–4). He would not take part in mourning ceremonies or festivals, because soon there would be none left to mourn and nothing good to celebrate (16 : 5–8).

As one might expect, these dire forecasts made Jeremiah very unpopular. Enemies conspired against his life (11 : 18–23), he was confined in the stocks (19 : 14–20 : 6), and for announcing the coming destruction of the Jerusalem Temple he was tried for blasphemy. King Jehoiakim considered Jeremiah his deadly enemy and had him flogged. Jeremiah reciprocated Jehoiakim's enmity, flogging the king verbally. Indeed, his indictment of King Jehoiakim reveals so much about Jeremiah's character that the verses are worth reproducing:

Woe to him who builds his house by unrighteousness, and his upper rooms by injustice;
who makes his neighbor serve him for nothing, and does not give him his wages;
Who says, "I will build myself a great house with spacious upper rooms,"
and cuts out windows for it, paneling it with cedar, and painting it with vermillion.
Do you think you are a king because you compete in cedar?
Did not your father eat and drink and do justice and righteousness?
Then it was well with him.
He judged the cause of the poor and needy; then it was well.
Is this not to know me? says the Lord.
But you have eyes and heart only for your dishonest gain,
for shedding innocent blood, and for practicing oppression and violence."
Therefore thus says the Lord concerning Jehoi'akim the son of Josi'ah, king of Judah:
"They shall not lament for him, saying, 'Ah my brother!' or 'Ah sister!'
They shall not lament for him, saying 'Ah lord!' or 'Ah his majesty!'
With the burial of an ass he shall be buried,
dragged and cast forth beyond the gates of Jerusalem" (22 : 13–19 RSV).

Whence came this lashing tongue, this need to accuse the mighty to their faces? Jeremiah felt his painful vocation had been laid upon him by God, who had chosen him to be a prophet from the moment of his conception (1 : 5–10). His mission would extend beyond Israel, bringing the Lord's message to all the nations.

Jeremiah apparently came to this understanding of his vocation while still a teenager, and the responsibility it imposed overwhelmed him. But the Lord would hear none of Jeremiah's protests, assuring him that if he spoke divine words he would receive divine support: "Behold I have put my words in your mouth" (1 : 9). "Be not afraid of them, for I am with you to deliver you" (1 : 8). So a prophet was formed, a man dominated by "the word of the Lord," the message his God impelled him to deliver.

Along with Jeremiah's calling came two visions (1 : 11–19). The first vision was of an almond tree. Punning on the similarity of the Hebrew words for *almond tree* and *to watch*, God told Jeremiah that his vision of the almond tree was accurate: The Lord would watch over his word to perform it. The second vision was of a boiling pot, facing away from the north. Just as boiling water spilled out of the pot and swept away twigs and pebbles, so foes would sweep out of the north and inflict evil on Jeremiah's countrymen. Jeremiah himself would face strong opposition for delivering these oracles, but his enemies would not prevail. The Lord would be with him, to deliver him.

From the outset, therefore, Jeremiah was a troubled man. He felt a charge to bring before his people the unpleasant news that hard times were coming, as the just deserts of their irreligion. From the outset Jeremiah was also a poetic man, brimming with powerful imagery. In a few lines he could sketch the whole career of a dishonest king, withering him by contrast with his righteous father. In a few phrases he could etch the king's coming demise, depicting the funeral that none would mourn. The word of the Lord pouring from the mouth of this troubled man riveted his people's imagination and lashed their soul. Jeremiah's passion for justice, his almost obsessive sense that the people had abandoned the very basis of their existence by falling away from the true God, gave him the courage to flay kings and leaders publicly. Thus he asks the people, in the name of God, "What wrong did your fathers find in me, that they went far from me, and went after worthlessness, and became worthless?" (2 : 5).

As Jeremiah read the political situation, God would punish this worthless people, using Babylon as his instrument. King Zedekiah consulted with Jeremiah about the political situation, but the king's advisers were bitterly opposed to the prophet, feeling that his predictions of woe were destroying the people's will to resist the Babylonians. Babylon did lay siege to Jerusalem, and when in 588 or 587 Jeremiah used a brief break in the siege to leave Jerusalem, his enemies arrested him for desertion. Zedekiah soon released him from the dungeon but had him kept in confinement. Undeterred, Jeremiah continued to proclaim that the Babylonians would defeat the Jews, and for this stubbornness his enemies threw him into a cistern, with the intention that he should starve there. When Jerusalem finally fell in 586, the victorious Babylonians treated Jeremiah well, offering him the choice of living either in Babylon or Judah. Jeremiah chose Judah, and he urged his countrymen left in Judah to try to live in peace.

Peace was not to be, however, for some discontented Jewish fugitives from the army killed Gedaliah, the governor appointed by the Babylonian ruler Nebuchadnezzar. Most of the Jewish community feared Babylonian vengeance for this murder, but when the community appealed to Jeremiah for a divine oracle on whether they should flee to Egypt or stay where they were, Jeremiah told them to stay in their own country. The people would not accept this oracle, however, so they took Jeremiah and his scribe Baruch with them to Egypt. In Egypt Jeremiah continued his unpopular ways, predicting that the Babylonians would defeat the Egyptians and castigating Jews who fell to worshiping a heavenly queen. The Jews in Egypt rejected this rebuke, and according to later legend they stoned Jeremiah to death.

Overall, most of Jeremiah's warnings, visions, symbolic actions, and oracles were gloomy. Thinking that his people had enmeshed themselves in secular politics to the neglect of their religion, the prophet saw Judah becoming crushed by the much larger foreign powers surrounding it, and saw this fate as a fitting punishment for Judah's defections. Still, not all Jeremiah's prophecies were gloomy. Like the other great prophets, his message balanced judgment with consolation. If God was judging the people harshly, because of their wanton irreligion, God was also assuring the people that the future would bring better times. Jeremiah's most consoling assurances occur in chapters 30–32, which are a high point of biblical poetry and theology.

Chapter 30 begins with the formulaic introductory phrase, "The word that came to Jeremiah from the Lord." This word was positive:

The days were coming when God would restore his people's fortunes. He would bring them back to their land, lost when the northern kingdom fell in 722 to Assyria. No matter how great the present pains grew, God would save the people from them. He would break the yoke of their foreign rulers, lead them back to serve him, the Lord their God, and serve a king like David.

With great poetic skill, the prophet plays variations on this theme. Behind the people's present sufferings is the hand of the Lord, punishing them for their transgressions. But that same hand will punish Israel's enemies: "Therefore all who devour you shall be devoured, and all your foes, every one of them, shall go into captivity, those who despoil you shall become a spoil, and all who prey on you I will make a prey" (30 : 16).

Similar poetry sings of what the restored people will enjoy: good fortune for the tents of Jacob, compassion on all Jacob's offspring's dwellings, songs of thanksgiving throughout the city and the palace, many voices making merry. "And you shall be my people, and I will be your God" (30 : 22). Harkening back to the Exodus from Egypt, the prophet has God say that the people who survived the sword, and found grace in the wilderness, would come to know God most intimately. Why? Because "I have loved you with an everlasting love; therefore I have continued my faithfulness to you" (31 : 3).

So in the future weeping would be for joy rather than sorrow, walking would be along lovely brooks of water and straight paths of virtue. God would gather his scattered people, like a shepherd gathering his flocks. Maidens would join in the dance, young and old alike would make merry. And the voice of Rachel, lamenting the exile of the northern kingdom, would cease. In the future, voices would not be for mourning, eyes would not be for tears. After the present time of painful chastening, the people would realize that God had never forgotten them, never stopped feeling merciful toward them.

In the good future, no longer would it be said, "The fathers have eaten sour grapes, and the children's teeth are set on edge." Rather, each person would be responsible for his own good or evil. Indeed, there would be an entirely new covenant, better than the covenant the people had entered upon after God led them out of Egypt. The people broke that covenant, though God was their husband. "But this is the covenant which I will make with the house of Israel after those days, says the Lord: I will put my law within them, and I will write it upon their hearts; and I will be their God, and they shall be my people. And no longer shall each man teach his neighbor and teach his broth- er, saying, 'Know the Lord,' for they shall all know me, from the least of them to the greatest, says the Lord; for I will forgive their iniquity, and I will remember their sin no more" (31 : 33–34 RSV). In all the literature of the world religions, few passages express the divine love more beauti- fully.

Both the prophets and the Deutero- nomic historian-theologians, therefore, tes- tify to the dangers to survival that Jews of that time felt. Political subjugation by the much larger neighboring powers was ever a possibility, but it was less ominous than cul- tural assimilation. To preserve their identi- ty Jews would have to keep clear of their neighbors' fertility religion. Only an adher- ence to a quite different god—Yahweh, the God of Moses and Abraham—could keep the people true to themselves.

Thus, the stress on nonidolatrous cult and on detailed religious law was most likely a reaction to the threat of adopting non-Hebrew influences. For instance, both adopting kingship and holding agricultural celebrations could be false steps, because they could take the Israelites away from Yahweh. When the Israelites were dispersed into Babylon, Jews of the southern kingdom tested the prophets' theology. A few realized what they had lost by playing power politics and relying on new gods. When the Persians gained control of the region from the Babylo- nians, Artaxerxes (464–424 B.C.E.) allowed Jews to return to Jerusalem. The relatively small number who did return under Nehe- miah and Ezra chose to rebuild the Temple and reestablish themselves on the basis of a strict adherence to the covenant law. Mar- riage to foreigners was interdicted, and priests strictly controlled the new Temple.

Covenantal Theology

From their exile to Babylon, Jews thought they had learned a capital lesson. They now viewed their history as one of wavering fidelity to the covenant, and this view suggested to them that infidelity to religious law led to national disaster. God had chosen them by covenanting with them in a special way, and unless they responded with signal fidelity, they would reap not blessing but judgment. Consequently, the returnees stressed their isolation and uniqueness. Still, historical experience also suggested, at least to some prophets and religious thinkers, that God himself was uni- versal, Lord of all peoples. His dominion included the foreign nations, for they had obviously served as his instruments for chas- tening Israel. He had punished through the Babylonians and freed through the Per- sians.

As a result, exile and return made Jews focus more and more on Jerusalem and its cult as the source of their identity. At the same time, they clarified their ideas about God's worldwide outreach, finally realizing that God had to be the creator of all things. Views of the covenant changed somewhat, but the predominant view was that God would punish Israel for infidelity and reward it for standing firm. However, God was not bound to be merciful. Mercy, rather, was an outflow of his unpredictable, unmeasurable goodness. Somehow, despite all human weakness, God would give a new future. Often the Jews envisioned this future as messianic—coming through a holy ruler anointed by God.

The stress on covenant by the Deuter- onomic and postexilic leaders exalted Moses as the religious figure par excellence. However much David stood for kingly success, indeed for the very establishment of Jerusalem, Moses stood for the Torah—revelation, teaching, law. The Torah was a much more solid foundation than either kingship or Jerusalem. By the words of God's mouth, the heavens were made. By the words God spoke through Moses' mouth, the Jews were made a people. If the people kept to those words, they would choose life. If they forgot them or put them aside, they would choose death. Thus, Moses said: "I call heaven and earth to witness against you this day, that I have set before you life and death, blessing and curse; therefore, choose life, that you and your descendants may live, loving the Lord your God, obeying his voice, and clinging to him" (Deut. 30 : 19–20). In the sober climate that followed the return from exile, the wise way for Jews seemed to be to keep to themselves and their own special laws.

Wisdom and Apocalypse

Two other movements marked the Jewish biblical period. The first is found in the wisdom literature of the Hebrew Bible. As many commentators point out,[11] Ecclesiastes and Proverbs bear the marks of the prudential, reflective thought expressed in maxims that was available from Egypt. Somewhat incongruously, it grafted itself onto Jewish speculation about God's action, which suggests that postexilic Judaism found its times rather trying. At least, the wisdom literature is dour and sober compared with the historical and prophetic sections of the Bible. It retains a faith that God still has his hand on the tiller but it finds the seas gray and choppy. The fire in the Jewish soul for poetry and prophecy had been tempered.

The Book of Job, however, is an exception. Job probes the problem of suffering, which surely is a wisdom concern, but it reaches poetic depths. Job reveals that the innocent do suffer mysteriously—that we cannot understand our fate, because all human life unfolds by the plan of a God whose mind we cannot know. This God set the boundaries of the seas, made the different species of all living things. He is not someone we can take to court, not someone who has to account to us. Rather, we can only cling to him in darkness and in trust. Because Job does not profess the older theology, in which punishment was in response to sin, instead proposing a mystery beyond legalistic logic, it brings the postexilic centuries some religious distinction. Against the tendency to a rather arid adherence to the covenant code, Job indicated a contemplative mind that knew how all law falls away when the spirit faces God directly.

By the end of the third century B.C.E., however, the constraints on Jewish national life brought about another reaction to the problems of suffering and providence. Job refers to Satan, a force of evil that opposes God (though God controls him), and, perhaps due to Iranian influences, in the last years of the pre–common era a dualistic concern with good and evil came to the fore. God and his supporting angels fought against Satan and his minions. The world, in fact, was conceived of as a cosmic battlefield, with God and the forces of light against the forces of darkness. For the first time, Jewish religion started to focus on an afterlife. Pressed by the problem that the good do not necessarily meet with reward nor the evil with punishment, Jewish religion raised the notion that a divine judgment would mete out proper justice. Correspondingly, it started to imagine heavenly places for the good who pass judgment and infernal places for the wicked who fail.

The Book of Daniel expresses these concerns through what scholars call "apocalyptic" imagination.[12] This imagination purports to be a revelation *(apocalypsis)* from God about how the future will unfold. Psychologically, it is an effort to comfort people who are under stress with promises that they will find vindication. Theologically, it puts a sharp edge on the question of whether God controls history. Daniel joins apocalyptic concern with the older prophetic concern with a messiah, casting the future vindication of the Jews in terms of a supernal being (the "Son of man") who will come on the clouds. His coming is the dramatic climax in the eschatological scenario that Jews developed in postexilic times. Thus, the Son of man came to figure in many apocalyptic writings (most of them not included in the Bible), and among apocalyptic believers he was the preferred version of the messianic king. (Christians seized on this figure as a principal explanation of Jesus.)

Hellenism

From the end of the fourth century B.C.E., the political fate of the Jews lay in the hands first of the Greeks and then of the Romans. Thus, Greek and Roman influences mixed with Israel's wisdom and apocalyptic concerns. The ideals that the Jews derived from Alexander the Great are commonly labeled "Hellenistic." They included the notion that all persons have a basis for community *(koinonia)* in human reason and so can share an inhabited world *(ecumene)*.[13] Contact with Hellenism divided the Jewish community. Some priests and intellectuals took to the notion of a common humanity, as well as to Greek science, philosophy, and drama, but the majority of the people, sensing a threat to their identity, reacted adversely. By the time that Antiochus IV tried to enforce pagan Hellenism and destroy traditional Judaism, most Jews supported the (successful) revolt that the Maccabees led in 168 B.C.E.[14]

Nonetheless, Hellenism influenced the Jewish conception of law, and it sparked the first strictly philosophical efforts to make the Torah appear reasonable to any clear-thinking person. Philo, a contemporary of Jesus, and Maimonides, a thinker of the twelfth century C.E., were the great expositors of this sort of philosophy. In the final decades of the biblical period, however, political and religious differences (largely about how to respond to Roman rule and to Greek intellectualism) divided the Jewish communities. Some people, called the Zealots, urged political action, in the spirit of the Maccabean rebellion. These Zealots opposed those (such as the Essenes of the Qumran community around the Dead Sea) who urged a withdrawal from political life and a purification for the coming of the Messiah. The Pharisees and Sadducees, lay and priestly groups, adopted centrist positions, urging both a political accommodation and a reliance on the Torah.

Rabbinic Judaism

The forces who urged revolt against the Romans suffered a crushing defeat in 70 C.E., when Titus destroyed the Temple in Jerusalem and cast out most of the Jews into the Diaspora (in this context, *Diaspora* refers to the settlement of Jews outside of Palestine). The Pharisees and their successors, the doctors of the law, picked up the pieces. They originated with the lay scribes (lawyers) who arose in the postexilic Hellenistic period, but they did not organize themselves as a distinct party until the Maccabean revolt.[15] The Pharisees stood for a close observance of the covenant law, applying it in all aspects of daily life. This belief had come to dominate the scribes who preceded the Pharisees, and it dominated the rabbis (teachers) who came after them.

In the Diaspora these rabbis became the center of communal life. The Temple had fallen and with it the cultic priesthood. So the alternative to cultic sacrifice—an alternative that had begun in Babylonian exile, when Jerusalem and the Temple were far away—filled the religious void. This alternative was the synagogue—the gathering place where the community could pray and hear expositions of the Torah. The synagogue became the central institution of Judaism in exile, and the study necessary to expose the Torah well made Judaism an intellectual powerhouse.

What we call rabbinic Judaism focuses on the synagogue, legal exposition, and study that emphasize the teacher (the rabbi). Increasingly, the teachers wanted to base their expositions on the teachings of their eminent predecessors, so they gathered a great collection of commentaries. Eventually, this collection became the Talmud ("the Learning"), a vast collection of the oral law that was composed of the Mishnah (itself a collection of interpretations of biblical legal materials) and the Gemara (commentaries on the Mishnah).[16]

The Mishnah arose at the end of the first century B.C.E. from the new practice of settling legal disputes by a systematized appeal to recognized authorities. This practice prompted a conflict between the Sadducees and the Pharisees. The Mishnah represented a Pharisaic effort to outflank the Sadducees, who denied the binding character of the oral law and relied on the literal biblical text alone. After the Temple fell in 70 C.E. and times became tumultuous, a written record of all the great teachers' legal opinions became highly desirable. The recording took place in Jabneh, a town on the coast west of Jerusalem. Many teachers moved to Jabneh, among them the great Rabbi Akiba (50–135), who later set up his own influential academy at Bene-Berak to the north. They began the real systematization of the Mishnah (the word implies repetition). The Mishnah continued and even intensified the scrutiny of every scriptural jot and tittle, but it went hand in hand with more pastoral activities.

Under the emperor Hadrian, Jews felt so oppressed, especially by his decision to build a temple to Jupiter on the site of the great Jewish Temple in Jerusalem, that they mounted the short-lived revolt led by Bar Kokhba. The Romans crushed it in 135 C.E., and thenceforth Jews could enter Jerusalem only on the anniversary of the destruction of the Temple, when they might weep at the wall (Figure 7).

In Babylon, to which many of the teachers fled, the talmudic work went on. When Hadrian died in 138, Palestinian Jews' fortunes rose, and a new intellectual center soon was established in Galilee. There, under Rabbi Judah, the Mishnah was elaborated to the point where it could be both a code and a digest of the oral law. It consisted of six parts, whose subject matter reveals a great deal about the rabbis' conception of

religious life.[17] The first Order (part) deals with the biblical precepts concerning the rights of the poor, the rights of priests, the fruits of the harvest, and other agricultural matters. The second Order deals with the Sabbath, festivals, fasts, and the calendar. The third Order (entitled "Women") contains laws of marriage and divorce and other laws governing the relations between the sexes. The section entitled "Damages" addresses civil and criminal law. The fifth Order deals with cultic matters and the slaughtering of animals, and the final Order concerns ritual cleanliness.

Law and Lore

Perhaps the best-known portion of the Talmud is the *Pirke Avot* ("Sayings of the Fathers"), the last tractate of the fourth Order.[18] It contains opinions of some of the oldest and most influential rabbis, but it is especially valuable for the spirit, the animating love, with which it infuses both the study of the Torah and the ethical life that the Torah should inspire. Often commentators on Judaism state that the Talmud represents a psychology of defense. It is a "fence" for Torah—a protective device to keep people from violating the Law on which their identity and survival depend.

But the religious spirit of the Fathers forces us to analyze this interpretation. The Fathers built an ethics and religion that are, if not offensive, at least positive and constructive. On first reading, the *Pirke Avot* suggests the thought of sober, disciplined, studious minds—minds not unlike that of Ecclesiastes and the other wisdom writers. However, further study shows that the Fathers' sobriety encourages a study that reaches the heart. This is explicit in Johanan ben Zacchai (2:13), but surely it is implicit in Hillel (1:12), Simeon the Just (1:2), and many others.

The rabbis called the legal portion of the Talmud *halakah*. Through reason, analogies, and deep thought, it made the most minute applications of the Torah. For instance, halakah concerned itself with the

Figure 7   Jerusalem: the Western Wall, with the Dome of the Rock in the background. Photo by J. T. Carmody.

dietary laws intended to keep the Jews' eating practices clean or fitting *(kosher)*. It also went deeply into the laws for the observance of the Sabbath. For centuries such laws, in their biblical forms (for example, Leviticus and Numbers), had kept the Jews separate from their neighbors. As the scribes, Pharisees, and then the Diaspora rabbis concentrated their legal expertise, however, halakah became very complex. Certainly in the Roman Empire, non-Jews strongly associated the Jews with their laws. Thus, halakah partly contributed to anti-Semitism, insofar as it stressed the sense of "otherness" that often is used to justify bigotry.

Balancing the strictly legal teaching and lore, however, was the looser, more folkloric *haggadah.* This was a treasury of exegetical and homiletic (preaching) stories that applied biblical passages to a congregation's present circumstances.[19] Where halakah reasoned closely, haggadah was apt to employ mythic devices, including paradigmatic figures and symbols. Haggadah drew much of its authority from the fact that Jewish theology had always held (at least in the ultimately dominant Pharisaic opinion) that an oral Torah accompanied the written Law of Moses (the Pentateuch, or first five books of the Bible) and the other books of the Hebrew Bible. Haggadah shows unscientific but pious reflection over traditional passages, especially those of scripture, that pictured God in his holy freedom—God at work creating this world in which we live.

Thus, tradition relates Rabbi Hanina bar Pappa's teaching on how God guides conception: "The name of the angel appointed over conception is Night. He takes the seed and lays it before the Holy One, blessed be he, and says to him: Master of the universe, what is this seed to be—mighty or weak, wise or foolish, rich or poor? But he does not say 'wicked' or 'righteous.' So according to Rabbi Hanina. For Rabbi Hanina said: 'All is in the hands of heaven, except the fear of heaven.' " In other words, the haggadah tried to explain how a phenomenon (such as conception) was under God's control. It also urged certain attitudes (such as fear of heaven) to make faith consonant with such control. This method probably began with Ezra in the postexilic period, and it dominated what Jewish historians call the Soferic period, when the scribes came to dominate the reassembled community's spiritual life. Haggadah continued to develop side by side with halakah for at least a millennium, ministering to the needs that common folk had for a teaching that was vivid and exemplary.

In Babylon, under the rule of the Exilarch (as the head of the Diaspora community was known in the common era), scholars collected the fruits resulting from discussions of Rabbi Judah's Mishnah which were conducted at various academies. In addition, they immersed themselves in the ideas and *responsa* (masters' answers to questions about the Law's application) that flowed between Babylon and Palestine. Both halakah and haggadah contributed to this broad collection of legal materials, and the final redaction of the Babylonian Talmud, written early in the fifth century, amounted to an encyclopedia of scholarly opinion not only on the law but also on much of the learning of the day, including biology, medicine, and astronomy, that formed the background for many of the discussions.

Talmudic Religion

In terms of theology proper, the Talmud (whether the Palestinian or the more influential Babylonian version) clung to scriptural faith.[20] Its central pillar was the Shema (Deut. 6 : 4): "Hear, O Israel: The Lord Our God is one Lord." (A second pillar was the biblical notion of election.) The Talmudic view of the Shema was practical rather than speculative. That is, the rabbis did not spend much energy probing the unity of God, the confluence of the divine attributes, or the like. The oneness of God meant to them God's sole dominion over life. He was the Lord of all peoples, the world's only source and guide.[21] The most practical of God's attributes were his justice and his mercy, but how they correlated was not obvious. Clear enough, though, were the implications for ethics and piety: A person ought to reckon with God's justice by acting righteously and avoiding condemnation. A person also ought to rely on God's mercy, remembering that he is slow to anger and quick to forgive.

Through such righteous living, a person could look forward to God's kingdom, which would come through the Messiah. The Messiah would rejuvenate or transform this earthly realm, which is so often a source of suffering. Of the Messiah Isadore Epstein says, "At the highest the Messiah is but a moral leader who will be instrumental in fully rehabilitating Israel in its ancient homeland, and through a restored Israel bring about the moral and spiritual regeneration of the whole of humanity, making all mankind fit citizens of the Kingdom."[22] This description rejects the Christian tendency to equate the Messiah with a divine son and also provides a foundation for the Zionistic fervor to return to the land. The concept of God's kingdom eventually included a supernatural dimension (heaven), but Judaism rather distinctively emphasizes that personal fulfillment comes through daily life.

The thrust of the Talmud, therefore, is not so much theological as ethical. The rabbis were more interested in what one did than in how one spoke or thought. So they balanced considerable theological leeway with detailed expectations of behavior. One could hold any opinion about the subtleties of God's nature, but how one observed the Sabbath was clearly specified.[23] A major effect of this ethical concern was the refinement of the already quite sensitive morality of the Hebrew Bible. For instance, the rabbis wanted to safeguard the body against even the threat of mortal injury, so they called wicked the mere raising of a hand against a person.

Similarly, since the right to life entailed the right to a livelihood, the rabbis concerned themselves with economic justice, proscribing once accepted business practices such as cornering a market, misrepresenting a product, trading on a customer's ignorance, and so on. In the same spirit, they pondered a person's rights to honor and reputation. To slander another obviously was forbidden, but they reprehended even putting another to shame, likening the blush of the shamed to the red of bloodshed.

Despite the caricature that they were concerned only with legalistic niceties, their writings show that the rabbis were very sensitive to social interaction. Lying, hatred, infringement on others' liberty—all these were targets of their teachings. The rabbis held that the goods of the earth, which prompt so much human contentiousness, were to be for all persons. Thus, after a harvest, the owner should leave his field open for the public to glean; the wealthy are obligated to help the poor; and no bread should ever go to waste. Moreover, the rabbis did not limit their lofty social ideals to the Jewish community. Glossing the injunction of Lev. 19 : 34 to love the stranger "who sojourns with you . . . as yourself," the Talmudists made little political or social distinction between Jew and non-Jew. Human rights applied to all.

The spirit of talmudic ethics, thus, is both precise and broad. The Talmud goes to extreme detail, but it applies to all humanity. According to the Talmud, the great vices are envy, greed, and pride, for they destroy the social fabric. Anger is also socially destructive, so the rabbis lay great stress on self-control. On the other hand, self-control should not become gloomy asceticism. Generally speaking, the Talmud views the goods of the earth as being for our enjoyment. We should fear neither the body nor the world. In fact, God, who gives us both the body and the world, obliges us to keep them healthy and fruitful. To spurn bodily or material goods without great reason, then, would be to show ingratitude to God—to withdraw from the order God has chosen to create. Wealth and marriage, for instance, should be viewed as great blessings that should be accepted with simple thankfulness. For the truest wealth, finally, is to be content with one's lot. In faith, the pious Jew tried to raise his sights beyond everyday worries to the master of the universe, from whom so many good things flow. The ultimate purpose of religious life was to sanctify this master's name—to live in such love of God that his praise was always on one's lips.

Hallowing Time

Through religious observances the Talmudists set the social program for inculcating their ethical ideals. In practice, every day was to be hallowed from its beginning. At rising the faithful Jew would thank God for the night's rest, affirm God's unity, and dedicate the coming hours to God's praise. He was supposed to pray at least three times each day: upon rising, in mid-afternoon, and in the evening. Ritual washings, as well as the kosher diet, reminded the faithful of the cleanliness that dedication to God required. Prayer garments such as the fringed prayer shawl; the phylacteries, or *tefellin* (scriptural texts worn on the head and the arm); and the head covering reinforced this cleanliness. The mezuzah (container of scriptural texts urging wholehearted love of God) over the door was a reminder to the entire home to adopt this attitude. Home was to be a place of law-abiding love. When possible, Jews would say their daily prayers together in the synagogue.

The synagogue, of course, was also the site of congregational worship on the Sabbath and on the great feasts that punctuated the year. Primary among them were (and still are) Passover, a spring festival that celebrates the exodus of Israelites from Egypt;

Shavuot, a wheat harvest festival occurring seven weeks after Passover; Booths (Sukkoth), a fall harvest festival whose special feature is the erection of branch or straw booths that commemorate God's care of the Israelites while they were in the wilderness; New Year's; and the Day of Atonement *(Yom Kippur)*.

The last is the most somber and solemn of the celebrations: the day on which one fasts and prays forgiveness of sins. It is a time when estranged members of the community should make efforts to reconcile their differences, and when all persons should rededicate themselves to the holiness that God's covenant demands. There are other holidays through the year, most of them joyous, and collectively they serve the several purposes of a theistic cult: recalling God's great favors (anamnesis), binding the community in common faith, and expiating offenses and restoring hopes.

In the home, celebration of the Sabbath did for the week what the annual feasts did for the year. It gave time a cycle with a peak that had special meaning. From midweek all looked forward to the Sabbath joy, preparing the house and the food for God's bride. When the mother lit the candles and the Sabbath drew near, even the poorest Jew could feel that life was good. Special hospitality was the Sabbath rule; rest and spiritual regeneration were the Sabbath order. Regretful as all were to see the Sabbath end, a glow lingered that strengthened them so that they could return to the workaday world.[24]

The principal rites of passage were circumcision, through which males entered the covenant community on their eighth day; bar mitzvah, to celebrate the coming of age; marriage; and burial. Through communal celebration, these rites reenforced the faith that life is good, the Torah is life's crown, marriage is a human's natural estate, and death is not the final word.

The Medieval Period

From the seventh century on, this talmudic religious program structured the lives of Jews who were mainly under Muslim rule.[25] Muhammad himself took rather kindly to Judaism, because he thought that his own revelation was rooted in biblical thought. "Hence his uncompromising monotheistic doctrine, his insistence on formal prayers, fasting and almsgiving, his adoption of the Day of Atonement, his introduction of dietary laws (such as the prohibition of swine's flesh), and his requirement that his followers turn towards Jerusalem in prayer."[26] However, things grew more complicated when the Jews refused to convert to Islam, and under Muhammad and his successors the Jews had to endure not a little trouble. Nonetheless, Muslims frequently found Jews useful as translators or businessmen, and Muslim countries were generally tolerant. So long as non-Muslim religious groups posed no threat to security or orthodoxy, they could have a decent, if secondrate, civil status.[27]

During the first centuries of Muslim power, the Jewish community's prestigious center of learning was at the heart of its Diaspora in Baghdad (in Babylonia). According to talmudic tradition, the leaders of the Baghdad schools gave *responsa* to points of law and held sway over community religion. They also fixed the pattern of communal worship, which hitherto had been a source of confusion and controversy. During the ninth and tenth centuries, the scholars of the Babylonian schools also standardized the pronunciation for the Hebrew Bible. These scholars (Masoretes) supplied the vowel points, accents, and other signs necessary to make readable a text that had consisted only of consonants. (Pronunciation, consequently, had been a matter of oral tradition.) The same work went on in Palestine, and eventually the version of a Palestinian author named Ben Asher won acceptance as the canonical text.

At the end of the first millennium of the common era, Jews emigrated to Europe, North Africa, and Egypt, taking with them the scholarship of the talmudic school to which they felt the closest ties. The Babylonian traditions were more popular, but in countries such as Italy, which had close ties with Palestine, Palestinian influence was great. In Europe, of course, the Jews were largely under Christian rule, although southern Spain and southern France were under Muslim rule.

The two great Jewish traditions, the Sephardic (Spanish) and the Ashkenazic (German), can be characterized by their subjugation under either Muslim or Christian rule, respectively. The two traditions shared more than they held separately because of the Talmudists, and their different styles in intellectual matters and in piety largely derive from the different cultures in which they evolved. In the tenth and eleventh centuries, the Sephardim in Spain developed a golden culture, with philosophy, exegesis, poetry, and scientific learning at their peak. Toledo and Cordoba were great centers of learning, but so were Cairo, Avila, and Lisbon.

The major internal problem during this period was the Karaite heresy, which began under the leadership of Anan ben David in the eighth century. This movement rejected the Talmud and based its beliefs on a literal reading of the scriptures. For instance, Karaite Sabbath law forbade washing, leaving the house, carrying anything from one room to another, wearing anything except a shirt, making a bed, or any other activity construed as work. Karaites interpreted the injunction of Exod. 35 : 3, to kindle no fires on the Sabbath, to mean that one had to spend Friday night and Saturday in darkness and cold. They were so scrupulous about incest laws that finding an acceptable marriage partner was difficult.

Because Karaism appealed to individual conscience and had some master propagandists, it mustered considerable support. Anan withdrew from Babylonia to Jerusalem, where he set up a community, and he pushed for a complete break with talmudic Jews (called Rabbanites). In the ninth and tenth centuries Karaism spread to Persia, Egypt, Spain, and parts of Asia and seemed to be on the verge of replacing Judaism. When we add to its appeal the confusion that the

Muslim recovery of Greek learning was producing in scholarly circles, we can understand the complexity of the Jewish religious situation and why it came close to crisis. With literalist Karaites on their right and rationalistic Hellenists on their left, the Talmudists felt besieged.

The Talmudists responded to the Karaites with an intensive campaign of biblical study, which included exegesis, Hebrew grammar, philology, and the other learning necessary to defend their own interpretations of the sacred text. Against the rationalists they took up the tools of philosophy, logic, and physical science in an effort to show the compatibility of reason and faith. The great champion in this talmudic or Rabbanite counterattack was Saadya ben Joseph (892–942), who lived in upper Egypt. He combined Hebrew and Arabic learning, biblical scholarship, and philosophical erudition. In addition, he wrote halakic *responsa*, codified rules of talmudic logic, resolved problems with the calendar, and composed an order for public worship.[28] The counterattack that he spearheaded was successful, and when the Jews fled from Babylonia at the breakup of the Muslim Empire into the eastern and western caliphates, they took with them at least the beginnings of a renewed talmudic tradition. The golden age in Spain was in no small measure possible because of this renewal.

Philosophy

The early medieval period thus saw a ferment in talmudic learning. As well, a Jewish philosophical theology arose.[29] While Philo, in the first century of the common era, worked at what could be called philosophical theology, trying to reconcile Hellenistic thought with biblical thought, the medieval thinkers, especially Maimonides, brought philosophy into the Jewish mainstream.

Philo, whose strong point had been what he called *allegoresis* (a reading of scripture on several levels, so as to remove the problems that the philosophical mind might have with anthropomorphism), never exerted a decisive influence on his contemporaries. Maimonides did. He was the response that made Judaism competitive in the new arena opened by the Muslim retrieval of Aristotelian logic and science. As such, his work was apologetic, making Judaism a strong contender in the debates that were being conducted by the Western religions on the supposedly common ground of rational analysis. However, Maimonides' work was also constructive, setting talmudic and traditional learning in the context of a philosophical system. Finally, the philosophical services of thinkers such as Maimonides were very useful in internal fights with literalists such as the Karaites, who (despite their literalism about points of biblical law) mocked both biblical anthropomorphism and much of haggadah (because it was poetic and symbolic).

The great questions of this period of philosophical debate were the criteria of biblical exegesis, the relation of faith to reason, the nature of the human personality and its relation to God, God's existence and attributes, the creation of the world, and providence and theodicy (God's justice). In debating these questions, the philosophers based their work on the Greek view that contemplation *(theoria)* is the most noble human work. Thus, the Jewish philosophers made rationality the source of human imaging of God. From that they derived an obligation (they would have called it a religious obligation) to develop one's reason—to explore God and his world.

Whereas for the Talmudist study of the Torah was the highest activity, many of the medieval philosophers considered the contemplation of God's eternal forms (through which he had created the world) as such. Maimonides became the prince of Jewish philosophers largely because he was also learned in the talmudic tradition and so could reconcile the old with the new. For him philosophical contemplation did not take one away from the Torah, because the proper object of philosophical contemplation is the one Law we find in both scripture and nature.

A key teaching in Maimonides' system was divine incorporeality. God had to be one, which he could not be if he occupied a body, since matter is a principle of multiplicity. To rationalize the anthropomorphic biblical descriptions of God, where he has bodily emotions if not form, Maimonides allegorized as Philo had done. The dynamic to his system, however, was the conviction that philosophical reason can provide the key to scripture. As his own *Guide for the Perplexed* puts it, "This book will then be a key admitting to places the gates of which would otherwise be closed. When the gates are opened and men enter, their souls will enjoy repose, their eyes will be gratified, and even their bodies, after all toil and labor, will be refreshed."[30]

Maimonides has probably been most influential through the thirteen articles in which he summarized Jewish faith, and which even today are listed in the standard prayer book. They are: (1) the existence of God, (2) God's unity, (3) God's incorporeality, (4) God's eternity, (5) the obligation to worship God alone, (6) prophecy, (7) the superiority of the prophecy of Moses, (8) the Torah as God's revelation to Moses, (9) the Torah's immutability, (10) God's omniscience, (11) reward and punishment, (12) the coming of the Messiah, and (13) the resurrection of the dead.[31] In this summary a philosopher gave the key headings under which reason and biblical revelation could be reconciled.

However, Jewish philosophy before Maimonides expressed a somewhat contrary position. The lyrical writer Judah Halevi (ca. 1086–1145), for instance, insisted that the God of Aristotle is not the God of Abraham and the biblical Fathers. Halevi's position is reminiscent of the later Christian philosopher Blaise Pascal, and it draws on the same sort of religious experience that made Pascal visualize God as a consuming fire—no Aristotelian "prime mover" but a vortex of personal love. Halevi did not despise reason, but he insisted that it is less than full religious experience, faith, or love. Moreover, he was concerned that Judaism remember where it had found God in the past—that it not lose itself in supposedly timeless philosophical truths. Concrete historical acts had furnished the Jews their election and destiny as God's covenanted people, not eternal forms ever available for human contemplation.

Mysticism

The devotional current in influential philosophers shows that the appropriation of Greek rationality did not extinguish Jewish mystical life, any more than it extinguished talmudic preoccupation with law. Law, in the sense of guidance for a daily practice of faith and ethics, certainly predominated over philosophy in the popular religious mind, but both philosophy and mysticism colored its interpretation. Gershom Scholem has treated the major trends in Jewish mysticism admirably,[32] tracing them back to biblical origins. The major influence, discernible even in Maimonides' doctrine of God, was Ezekiel's vision of the divine chariot *(merkabah)*. Philosophers and mystics alike agreed that under this symbolism lay the most profound mysteries of the divine nature. The Talmudists tended to stay away from the subject, lest they fall into impious speculation, but the mystics, even though they cautioned about dangers, repeatedly went back to it.

In medieval Germany a movement arose among people called the Hasidim, who upheld a relatively new spiritual ideal. Biblical religion had spoken of the poor of God *(anawim)*, and from early times a *hasid* was one who piously devoted himself to God. The medieval expression of this piety, in which intellectualism was subordinate to devotion, contested rabbinic learning. What characterized the truly pious person, this movement argued, was serenity of mind, altruism, and renunciation of worldly things. The asceticism, especially, ran counter to traditional Judaism, for it seemed to entail turning away from the world. Indeed, Hasidic speech relates to the reality that has always drawn mystics and caused them to neglect the world—the reality of glimpsing the divine being itself, of experiencing the biblical "goodness of the Lord."

This divine love exalts the soul and seems far more precious than anything the world can offer.

Hasidism in its medieval, Germanic form is not the direct ancestor of the modern pietism that goes by this name. Intervening between Hasidism's two phases was a most influential Jewish mysticism, that of the Cabala. *Cabala* means "tradition," and the Cabalists sought to legitimize their movement by tracing it back to secret teachings of the patriarchs and Moses.

Such secret or esoteric overtones stamp Cabalism as a sort of Jewish Gnosticism (secret knowledge); indeed, several Cabalistic doctrines smack of the Gnostic concerns with the divine *pleroma* (fullness), the emanations of different divine aspects, and secret doctrines explaining how divinity intends to redeem the wicked fallen world.[33] Thus, R.J.Z. Werblowsky characterizes Cabalism as a "theosophical" (concerning wisdom about God) movement especially concerned with the *pleroma*.[34] This fullness, which the prophets glimpsed in their ecstatic visions, humans can only conceive symbolically. Hence, Cabalists engaged in their own brand of allegorical exegesis of scripture, trying to decode secret symbols about divinity that the Hebrew Bible couched in deceptively simple language.

For Cabalistic thought, the divine and the human spheres are interdependent. The fallen state of the world (most acutely manifested in the suffering of the Jews, God's chosen people) signals a disruption within the divine essence itself. Human sinfulness, it follows, reflects this divine wounding. On the other hand, human holiness contributes to God's repair, and so every human act takes on cosmic significance. In fact, human life can become a sort of mystery play or theurgy (divine work), in which the significant aspect of its actions is their wounding or repairing of the divine life.

When the Spaniards expelled the Jews from the Iberian Peninsula at the end of the fifteenth century, the Cabalists had the perfect crisis on which to focus their somewhat fevered imaginations. Isaac Luria, who taught in Jerusalem in the sixteenth century, and Sabbatai Zevi, the "false messiah" of the seventeenth century, interpreted the expulsion as an effect of a cosmic disaster that actually occurred before Adam's fall. They had great popular impact.

The paramount book of the Cabalistic movement, and the most representative of its symbolism, was the *Zohar*—the "Book of Splendor." From 1500 to 1800, the *Zohar* exerted an influence equal to that of the Bible and the Talmud. Analysis of the work suggests that it was written in Spain at the end of the thirteenth century, most likely by Moses de León.[35] The *Zohar* is similar to haggadic materials in that it interprets scriptural texts symbolically and in pietistic fashion rather than in the legal manner of halakah. What distinguishes the *Zohar* from traditional haggadah is its suffusion with the Gnostic ideas mentioned above. For instance, its commentary on the first verse of the Hebrew Bible, Gen. 1:1, goes immediately to what the divine nature was really like "in the beginning": Within the most hidden recess of the infinite *eyn sof*, the divine essence, a dark flame went forth, issuing in the *sefiroth*. The *sefiroth* were what the philosophers called the realm of divine attributes, but the mystics saw them as the emanations of God's own being. Such a view makes the world alive with divinity. It gives history and human experience eternal implications, because the emanations move through our time, our flesh, our blood.

The *Zohar* turns over each word of Genesis, searching for hidden clues to the divine plan. It concerns itself with the numerical value of the words' letters (for example, a = 1) and correlates clues in Genesis with clues from other visionary parts of the Hebrew Bible, such as Ezekiel, chapter 1, and Isaiah, chapter 6. To align its interpretation with respectable past commentary, it cites traditional rabbis, but the *Zohar*'s immediate concern is not the rabbis' interest in ethics but an imaginative contemplation of divinity and the divine plan.

In other words, the *Zohar* draws persons with the splendor of its vision, its graphic display of divinity. With its beauty, the *Zohar* can move the spirit to ecstatic joy. No doubt the Cabalists devoutly hoped that such an imaginative and contemplative experience would build up faith and inspire good works. However, they differed from the Talmudists (some of whom had secret sympathy for Cabalism) in their predilection for visionary appreciation of the Law's source rather than a sober perusal of the Law's applications.

The Modern Period

If the mark of modernity is a turn from rather mythical religious authority to human authority and self-reliance, modernity did not begin for Judaism until the end of the eighteenth century. In fact, thorough exposure to a secularized, technological culture did not come to most of the rural population of the eastern European *shtetls* (villages) until close to World War II. Until that time enlightenment and reform made little impact, for talmudic and Hasidic orthodoxy kept the traditions basically unchanged.[36]

Cecil Roth[37] and Leon Poliakov[38] have described the constant repression and persecution that Jews endured in medieval and early modern times. What Roth calls "the crowning tragedy" was the Jews' expulsion from the Iberian Peninsula in 1492, since that devastated what had been Jewry's greatest cultural achievement. In its aftermath, the eastern European ghetto became home to most Jews, and the false messiah Sabbatai Zevi, who finally apostatized to Islam, shows the intensity that Jewish messianic yearning reached by the mid-seventeenth century. Part of the success of Israel Baal-Shem-Tov (1700–1760), the father of modern Hasidism, resulted from the effects of Sabbatai Zevi. There was a void into which apostasy, nihilism, and antinomianism (lawlessness) threatened to rush.

Baal-Shem-Tov and his followers taught a religious inwardness, a joyous communion with God.[39] They sought to restore the traditional faith, which they saw as endangered by false messianism, arid intellectualism, and talmudic legalism. Hasidism did not attack the Law and traditional practice itself. Rather, it shifted Jewish religious focus from the "scientific" rabbinic leader to the gifted Hasid or holy person, who manifested divine wisdom and joy. The movement quickly caught fire in eastern Europe, and thousands rushed to the Hasidic "courts." In their vivid portrait of *shtetl* life, Zborowski and Herzog[40] have shown the attraction that the Hasidim exerted in the typical village. Many of the villagers (usually men) yearned to go off to the courts for spiritual refreshment, and many would leave their families for substantial periods of time.

HASIDIC TALES

The Hasidic masters made a deep impression on the Jewish imagination, and some of the tales about them are wonderfully entertaining, as well as deeply instructive. For example, there is the story of the burning of the Torah, which deals with "the terrific struggle between the Baal-Shem-Tov and the Enemy, who by foul trickery sought to have the Torah taken away from the Jews."[41]

Satan was tormented by the good he saw the Baal-Shem-Tov doing on earth, so he schemed to overcome the Master. Calling all his servants of darkness together, he disclosed to them a wicked plan. He would station devils on all the roads that led to heaven. Whenever a prayer rose upward, toward heaven's gates, the devils would be able to throttle it, and so keep it from getting through. Thus no prayers would come before God's throne. After some days without prayers getting through, Satan would be able to go to God and say, "Look, your people have deserted you. They no longer send you prayers. Even your favorite puppet, Rabbi Israel Baal-Shem-Tov, has ceased to pray. Take back his wisdom, then. Take away his people's Torah."

The soldiers of the Evil One listened attentively, and then slunk out to execute the foul scheme. Leaving no bypath unguarded, they lurked silently in wait of any prayer. When a prayer came, they leaped upon it, pummeling and kicking it. They could not kill the prayers, but they flung them sideways into chaos. Thus all of space became filled with wounded prayers, whimpering and moaning, lost from their way. On Fridays the flux of prayers was so great that many got through to heaven's gate, but there a great army of devils saw to it that the prayers were rebuffed.

Three weeks passed in this fashion, and Satan thought it time to confront God.

Going before the divine throne, Satan said, "Take away the Torah from the Jews." But God said, "Give them until the Day of Atonement." Satan struck a hard bargain: "Give the command today, but hold back on its execution until the Day of Atonement." So God gave the terrible edict, and the Jews were to lose the Torah. On earth, the archbishop issued a proclamation. In ten days, the bishops were to have all the Hebrew books of learning confiscated. Men were to be sent into the synagogues to seize the Torah, and into all the Jews' homes. Then they were to heap all the Hebrew books into a great pile and set fire to them. The bishop of Kamenitz-Podolsky in Russia was the most zealous in obeying, sending his servants into all the Jews' homes. On the Day of Atonement, a great fire would destroy all the books of God's Law.

When the Baal-Shem-Tov saw these things happening, he knew Satan was mounting a terrible attack. Yet he did not know how Satan was accomplishing this great evil, nor how to counteract it. Each day the horror mounted, as Jews were stripped of the Torah. In home after home cries of anguish rended the night. Fasting and sleepless, the Baal-Shem-Tov struggled on behalf of his people, sending mighty prayers toward heaven day and night. They rose on colossal wings at incredible speed, but the Enemy himself caught them outside heaven's gate and cast them aside. So the heart of the Baal-Shem-Tov emptied, becoming a great cave of grief.

At last the Day of Atonement dawned. Rabbi Israel went into the synagogue to hold the service, and the people saw the fever of his struggle on his face. Hope rose in their hearts. "He will save us today," they said. When the time came to sing the *Kol Nidre* ("All Vows"), Rabbi Israel's voice poured out the pain of his heart, freezing all who listened.

It was the custom for Rabbi Yacob to read each verse of the lamentations aloud and then for Rabbi Israel to repeat it. But when Rabbi Yacob read out the verse, "Open the Portals of Heaven!" Rabbi Israel did not utter a word. The people first were confused, and then waited in growing fear. Once again Rabbi Yacob repeated, "Open the Portals of Heaven!" but still Rabbi Israel did not utter a word.

Then, in monumental silence, Rabbi Israel threw himself upon the ground, beat his head, and roared like a dying lion. For two hours he remained doubled over, his body shaking with the force of his struggle. Those watching in the synagogue dared not approach him. They could only worry and wait.

At last, the Baal-Shem-Tov raised himself from the ground, his face shining with wonders. "The Portals of Heaven are open," he said, and then he ended the service.

Years afterwards, it became known how Rabbi Israel had passed those terrible two hours. He had gone to the Palace of the Eternal, traveling by the road that goes directly to the throne. There he had found hundreds and hundreds of prayers huddled before the gate. Some were wounded, some lay gasping as though they had just ended a terrible struggle, some were emaciated and old, and some were blind from having wandered so long in darkness. "Why are you waiting here?" the Baal-Shem-Tov asked them. "Why don't you go in and approach the throne?"

The prayers told Rabbi Israel that only his approach had scattered the dark angels. Before he came, no prayer could pass through the gate. "I will take you in," the Baal-Shem-Tov told them.

But just as he started to pass the gate, the Baal-Shem-Tov saw the army of evil spirits rush forth to close it. Then Satan himself came forward and hung a great lock, as big as a city, upon the heavenly gate. The Baal-Shem-Tov walked all around the lock, looking for a crack through which to enter. It was made of solid iron, however, so there seemed no way he could pass through. Still, Rabbi Israel did not despair.

For each of us living on earth, there is an exact duplicate living in heaven. So, Rabbi Israel called across the gate to his heavenly counterpart. "What shall I do," he asked, "to bring the prayers before the Name?" Rabbi Israel of heaven told him, "Let us go to the Palace of the Messiah."

They went to the palace, where the Messiah sits waiting for the day when he may go down to earth. As soon as they entered, the Messiah told them, "Be joyous! I will help you," and he gave the Baal-Shem-Tov a token. The Baal-Shem-Tov took the token back to the heavenly gate. When he brandished the token, the heavenly portals swung open, as wide as the earth is large. So all the prayers entered, going straight to the Throne of the Name. Heaven fell to ecstatic rejoicing, and all the angels sang hymns of praise. But the dark angels fled back to their hellish dungeons, routed and fearful again.

On earth, the bishop of Kamenitz-Podolsky was lighting a great fire. Beside him was a mountain of Hebrew books, which his minions had readied for the flames. He took a tractate of the Talmud and hurled it into the fire. He hurled another and another, until the flames leaped high as the clouds. But then his hand began shaking, and he fell down in an epileptic fit. The crowd was seized with terror, and ran out of the central square. The fire soon died down, and most of the books were saved. When the news of this happening spread to other towns, they abandoned their plans to burn the Torahs. Fearing they too would be struck by seizures, their bishops gave back all the stolen volumes. That was how the Baal-Shem-Tov saved the Torah for the Jews, on the Day of Atonement.

When we reflect on this little story, it reveals volumes about premodern Jewish belief. The Baal-Shem-Tov is the central hero, but there are many other actors in the drama. The evil genius threatening Jewish life was Satan, the angel of power and light who had turned bad. Hating God and everything good, Satan was constantly plotting against God's people. If the Jews had not had saints like Rabbi Israel, there is no telling how their misfortunes might have grown. Bad as life was in the midst of unsympathetic Christians, it would have been much worse without the sainted rabbis.

The central treasure of premodern Jewish life was the Torah. Enclosed in the holy pages of the treasured books lay the only wisdom worth pursuing. Without the Torah, the Jews would not have been God's people. Without the Bible and the Talmud, there would have been no faith, joy, or hope. For the common person, the volumes of Torah were both pledges and holy presences. To destroy a book of Torah therefore was to slash at a central artery, to snuff out the breath of life.

The theater for the drama of Satan against the Torah was not limited to earthly cities. For the popular Jewish mind, heaven was a central factor in the play. Before the throne of God, all parts of Jewish life passed review. God's ways were terribly inscrutable, but no pious Jew doubted the efficacy of prayer. If the people would pour out their hearts to the Master of the Universe, he would find them a way to survive. The Torah spoke of many past acts of salvation and of the coming of the Messiah, the one who would bring lasting peace. Prayer and strict observance therefore became the people's armor. Helpless in earthly terms, the Jews looked to their learned rabbis as to spiritual generals. By the holy power they generated, the rabbis might storm heaven's gates and keep Satan's dark forces at bay.

Of course, it is hard to say how literally the average person took imagery like that of our story. Whether heaven had a big gate, whether there were roads to heaven, whether prayers could be kicked and wounded—all that is hard to tell. Most likely, all that was quite secondary. Lost in a good, gripping story, most Jews probably indulged their imaginations. To picture prayers like little people, or like swift birds winging up to God, made the act of praying more dramatic. Most people knew they could never picture God accurately. They knew heaven was beyond any tongue's ability to describe. So they let their imaginations paint whatever settings most helped them in their prayers and inner struggles. There had to be close connections between this world and heaven, for otherwise God would not be involved in what his people were doing. But it was the essence of convenantal theology that God was always deeply involved in what his people were doing, were suffering, and were hoping. So the life of the Jewish home and the services of the Jewish synagogue encouraged many vivid pictures of heaven. Indeed, the worse earthly life became the more heaven gleamed in contrast.

Hasidism tended toward irrationalism and an intolerance of anything modern, but for discerning contemporary Jews such as Martin Buber[42] and Abraham Heschel,[43] it became a valuable resource. Although large portions of the educated, who were desirous of a Jewish enlightenment and emancipation from Christian discrimination, strongly opposed Hasidic piety, it remained vigorous in the villages well into the twentieth century. There it tended to commingle with talmudic faith, blending legal observance with emotional fervor. Jewish village life hinged on the Sabbath (in the time-organizing way described above) and on three blessings: the Torah, marriage, and good deeds.

The Torah meant God's revelation and Law. In practice, it meant the exaltation of learning. *Shtetl* parents hoped that they would have learned sons, well versed in the Law, who would bring glory to the family.

Thus, the ideal son was thin and pale, a martyr to his books. From age five or so he marched off to a long day of study, beginning his education by memorizing a Hebrew that he did not understand and then progressing to subtle talmudic commentaries. The Torah shaped the economic and family lives of *shtetl* Jews, because men tried to free themselves for study, placing the financial burdens on women. The poor scholar, revered in the *shul* (synagogue school) but master of a threadbare family, exemplified the choices and values that the Torah inspired.

Many men did work in trades (the state usually prevented Jews from owning land and farming), but even they would try to gain dignity by devoting their spare time to learning. Glory for women came from caring for the home, the children, and often a little shop. So much were those responsibilities part of religion for women that no commandments prescribed for them exact times for prayer, fasting, synagogue attendance, charitable works, or the like. Women's 3 principal *mitzvah* (duties) out of the traditional 613 were to bake the Sabbath bread, light the Sabbath candles, and visit the ritual bath *(mikvah)* after menstruation.

In the *shtetl*, marriage was the natural human situation and children were its crown. Father and mother were obligated to create a home steeped in Torah and good deeds (fulfillment of the *mitzvah* and acts of charity). In semiserious popular humor, nothing was worse than an old maid, while an unmarried man was pitied as being incomplete. Of course, kosher rules and keen legal observance marked the devout home, which was but a cell of the organic community. That community supported needy individual members with material goods, sympathy in times of trouble, and unanimity in religious ideals. One had to share one's wealth there, whether wealth of money or wealth of mind, and the seats of honor in the synagogue went to the learned and to the community's financial benefactors.

Tribulations

The community exacted quite a toll through the pressure it exerted to conform with its ideals and through the gossip and judgment that ever circulated. Nevertheless, most Jews gladly accepted being bound by the common laws and custom, and few Jews could avoid being bound by the equally overt and common suffering. The urban populations in the Russian and Polish ghettos shared an almost paranoid spiritual life, with pogroms (persecutions) a constant specter, while the rural populations of eastern Europe never knew when some new discrimination or purge would break out. In both situations, Jews' mainstay was their solidarity in faith. Consequently, we can understand how threatening movements to change the faith, such as the Reform or Enlightenment (described below), must have been. The old ways had been the foundation of Jewish san-

ity. New conditions, as in Germany and the United States, seemed much less solid than long familiar suffering and endurance.

The bulk of the Jewish population in the late 1700s was in eastern Europe: the pale of the Russian Empire, Austria, and Prussia. Their life was rather precarious, and attacks by Russians and Ukranians produced a stream of emigrants to the New World. Yet European Jews contributed to the formation of the notion of the modern, secular state, probably because they hoped that it would offer them greater religious freedom. The Jewish philosopher Spinoza (1632–1672) suggested such a political arrangement, and Moses Mendelssohn (1729–1786), a German man of letters, plumped for a secular state prior to the French Revolution. Generally, Jews' civil status seemed to prosper in countries or under regimes that were open to the new, liberal ideas of equality. However, when nationalism prevailed, the Jews tended to experience more anti-Semitism, since non-Jews considered them outsiders at such times.

Jacob A. Argus has noted three principal Jewish reactions to modern nationalism.[44] First, many Jews identified themselves with the people among whom they lived. For instance, German Jews became great supporters of German culture, which was enjoying a golden age in music and philosophy. Second, some of the Jewish intelligentsia embraced the new universalist philosophies that downplayed race or ethnicity and that stressed the common humanity all persons share through their reason. Third, some Jews incorporated nationalistic feelings into their own group consciousness by thinking of the cohesiveness of the "nation" of Israel. Argus sees these reactions working, respectively, in the time of Emancipation in France (see below), the socialist movements in Europe and Russia (which led to the formation of the *Bund* [party], influential in Poland during the two world wars, and also to the Reform movements in Germany and the Anglo-American world), and the Zionist movement, which he conceives of as a Jewish nationalistic renaissance.

Dissolution of Traditional Judaism

Jacob Neusner attributes the breakup of traditional Judaism in the modern period to two factors, the Enlightenment and Hasidism.[45] The Enlightenment, whose main feature according to Kant was the realization that humanity should be guided by its own reason and not by institutional authorities, in effect attacked the legal and philosophical underpinnings of traditional Judaism. By extending political rights to Jews ("Emancipation"), the Gentile thinkers of the Enlightenment took away the basis of the Jewish community—it was no longer a ghetto or a world set apart from the national mainstream.

By its philosophical turn to individual reason, the Enlightenment attacked the talmudic assumption that traditional law and its interpretation by the Fathers are the best guides for life. Thus, intellectual Jews who accepted the ideals of the Enlightenment tended to abandon talmudic scholarship (or at least deny that it was the most important learning) and devote themselves to secular learning. This movement spawned the distinguished line of Jewish scientists, social thinkers, and humanists, but it meant that the Jewish community lost some of its best talent. It also meant intellectual warfare between the advocates of the new learning and the defenders of the old.

The relation of Hasidism to traditional, talmudic Judaism is more complex. On the one hand, as we have seen, Hasidism accepted traditional assumptions about the Law, the specialness of the people, the coming of the Messiah, and the reality of God's reign over the world. On the other hand, Hasidism set the charismatic holy man rather than the learned rabbi at the center of the community.[46] This new figure, the *tzaddik* (righteous one), Hasidim revered for his intimacy with God, his ability to pray evocatively, and his gifts as a storyteller. (As a storyteller he was an updated version of the ancient haggadist.) But the simple faithful held the *tzaddik* to be a wonder worker.

Thus, the Hasidim abound with stories of God's coming to the aid of his oppressed people through the special interventions of the *tzaddik*.[47] The story with which Elie Wiesel prefaces his novel *The Gates of the Forest* epitomizes the impact of Hasidic faith in the masters' powers:

When the great Rabbi Israel Ba'al Shem-Tov saw misfortune threatening the Jews it was his custom to go into a certain part of the forest to meditate. There he would light a fire, say a special prayer, and the miracle would be accomplished and the misfortune averted. Later, when his disciple, the celebrated Magid of Mezritch, had occasion, for the same reason, to intercede with heaven, he would go to the same place in the forest and say: "Master of the Universe, listen! I do not know how to light the fire, but I am still able to say the prayer" and again the miracle would be accomplished. . . . Then it fell to Rabbi Israel of Rizhyn to overcome misfortune. Sitting in his armchair, his head in his hands, he spoke to God: "I am unable to light the fire and I do not know the prayer; I cannot even find the place in the forest. All I can do is to tell the story, and this must be sufficient." And it was sufficient. God made man because he loves stories.[48]

Reform

Thus, the traditional legal authority crumbled because of the new secular learning. From within, Judaism succumbed to a desire for more emotionally or spiritually satisfying evidence of God's helpfulness. In response to this crisis of the tradition came a "Reform" of orthodox conceptions. On a popular level (though we are still speaking of the relatively educated), Reform meant an effort to accept modern culture and still remain a Jew. In other words, it meant searching for new definitions of Jewishness that would not necessitate alienation from the intellectual and political life of Gentile fellow nationalists.

Among the "virtuosi," as Neusner calls the important personalities of the Reform movement, the effort was not just accommodation but rethinking the tradition to bring it up-to-date with integrity. A good part of the virtuosi's effort emphasized the Jewish philosophical and ethical beliefs that seemed eminently rational (and so applicable to all persons). In effect, emphasis shifted from what was distinctive in Judaism, what gave Jews their unique status as God's chosen ones, to what Judaism could offer to all humanity.

The stress of Reform was ethical. Reform Jews saw their tradition as offering all peoples a moral sensitivity, a concern for the rights of conscience and social justice, which derived from the prophets and the great rabbis but that could serve the dawning future age of equality, political freedom, and mutual respect. In part, this ethical stress was the result of wishful thinking. Reform Jews tended to be talented people who were either formally or informally excluded from national and university life. As a result, their visions of a new day led them to stress what in their own religious past might abet equal opportunity.

A response to Reform within Judaism was a self-conscious "Orthodoxy." It tended to recruit those who shared many of the Reformers' perceptions but who disagreed with their reinterpretation of the tradition.

Instead, Orthodoxy insisted that the Torah be the judge of modernity and not vice versa. Positively, however, the Orthodox conceded the possibility that living with Gentiles might be a good, God-intended arrangement. No doubt, the breakup of Christian control over culture that marked the Western shift from medieval to modern times played a strong role in this reevaluation. That is, the Orthodox realized that, despite its evident dangers to faith, living among Gentiles might free Jews of the prejudice endemic in medieval Christian faith. (In its most virulent form, that prejudice branded all Jews as "Christ killers.")

In their contests with the Reformers, the Orthodox could draw on factors that tradition had driven deep into the Jewish psyche. First, there was the conservatism that was almost intrinsic to a faith built on teaching "fathers" and the father-figure of the family. Such conservatism made it difficult for the younger generation to convince the older. Second, the Orthodox could claim, much more plausibly than the Reformed, that they represented the wisdom and experience of the past by which the people had survived. Third, the Orthodox were more genuinely religious than the Reformed; although the virtuosi wanted to develop faith, the majority of reformers were secularly minded, drawn by goods outside the traditional culture. Last, the combination of these factors gave Orthodoxy the advantage of appearing safer and surer than Reform.[49]

Conservative Judaism represented an effort to find a centrist position, between Reform and Orthodoxy. Its founder was Rabbi Zecharias Frankel (1801–1875), chief rabbi of Dresden and later head of the Breslau Theological Seminary in Germany. Frankel's position was that Judaism should change slowly, remaining true to its traditional character and only allowing slight modifications of traditional practice. In the United States, Solomon Schechter of the Jewish Theological Seminary of America was the central promoter of Conservative Judaism.

Presently Conservative Judaism is the

largest of the three main groups of American Jews. Its intellectual center is the Jewish Theological Seminary in New York, its rabbinical assembly numbers more than one thousand members, and its league of synagogues (the United Synagogue) numbers more than one thousand congregations. The Conservative worship service has introduced family pews, developed a modernized liturgy in the vernacular, and allows women a fuller role in the congregation's ritual life.

Zionism

The movement most responsible for the establishment of the state of Israel is Zionism. Most of the medieval piety movements anticipated Zionism insofar as their messianism regularly involved the notion of returning to the ancestral land (and to the holiest of cities, Jerusalem). Thus, the Karaites of eighth-century Iraq (Babylonia) emigrated to Israel, and some of the Cabalists took up residence in Galilee. In the eighteenth and nineteenth centuries, Hasidim in Poland sent many people to the holy land, with the result that there were circles of devout Jews in Jerusalem, Tiberias, and Safed.[50] The upsurge of nationalism in modern Europe tended to make Jews consider their own national roots, while new movements of social thought, including those led by Marx and Tolstoy, caused many Jews to dream about a new society based on the *kibbutz* (collective).

The greatest impetus to Zionism, however, was the persecutions that convinced European Jews they were in peril on the Continent: pogroms in Russia from 1880

Figure 8   Infamous gate at Dachau concentration camp, outside Munich, Germany, reading "Work Frees." Photo by J. T. Carmody.

to 1905, Ukranian massacres from 1917 to 1922, persecutions in Poland between 1922 and 1939, and, above all, the Nazi persecution that began in 1933. By 1948 about 650,000 Jews lived within the British mandate of Palestine, and at the birth of Israel many hundreds of thousands more emigrated from Europe and from Arab lands (where, after the 1948 war, conditions were difficult). The main ideologist for the movement was a Viennese named Theodor Herzl. His witness of anti-Semitism during the Dreyfus case in France at the end of the nineteenth century convinced him and many other Jews that only by having their own nation could Jews be free of constant persecution.

Today Judaism is most vital in Israel and the United States, and in both places the battles over what it means to be a Jew in the modern world continue unabated. Israel has become the spiritual center of Judaism, and what faith can mean after Auschwitz and the Holocaust has become the prime topic of theological discussion.[51] Because of its vigorous intellectual tradition, Judaism disproportionately contributes to the debates about the value of modernity, and its voice is now influencing many Christian thinkers.[52]

STRUCTURAL ANALYSIS

Nature

Generally speaking, nature has not been an important concept in Judaism. For example, Maimonides did not refer to it in his thirteen articles of faith, and scholars dealing with the biblical period,[53] a historical perspective,[54] or even Jewish values[55] do not focus on nature. That does not mean, of course, that Jews had no consciousness of their land or that the physical world played no part in their religion.

In the biblical period nature was quite important, because the earliest "Jews" were shepherds or farmers. The earliest theology appears to have been a veneration of differ-

ent *els* (gods) related to natural powers, and the constant lament of the prophets and other biblical theologians that the gods of the neighboring peoples (the Canaanites especially) were seducing the people away from true religion is testimony that the cosmological myth held considerable attraction.

Still, contesting the cosmological myth (in which divinity is immanent to the world and natural processes are divinity's most intimate operations) were the "great acts" of Yahweh in his people's time. Eric Voegelin has argued that "history" itself (our human conception of time) is substantially the product of Israelite theology.[56] For Voegelin, history gets periodicity from the revelations of a God outside the world, and it is those revelations that decisively shaped the Jewish people. So Yahweh, the most transcendent of Gods, was also the most interactive. He was the God of the Fathers, Abraham, Isaac, and Jacob. He was the one who led the ancestors out of Egypt, struck the covenant on Sinai, and ushered the people into the promised land.

From the beginning, the Jewish conception of God, coupled with the Jewish ethnic memory and sense of identification through religious history, combined to deemphasize nature as a religious focus. As the Psalms show, Yahweh was the lord of nature as well as of time. He was the creator of the physical world, the benefactor of good harvests, a God who could appear with clouds and lightning. What made him special in Jewish eyes, though, was his redemptive activity and covenanting—actions in which he stepped out of natural phenomena and acted on a personal basis.

For instance, the liturgical feasts, though they began as nature festivals, ran through the agricultural year, and were expressions of gratitude for harvests, reached their peak at Passover and Yom Kippur—celebrations of historical events and of a moral requirement based on the covenant. Further, the sacrificial aspect of early Jewish worship was replaced by the sermonizing and Bible reading of the synagogue. In fact, as the Torah grew in influence, the human qualities of law, reason, study, and ethics came to the fore. Celebrations still involved food, drink, and dance, but they were probably due more to a social sense, from a desire to affirm a common identity, than from a close connection with Mother Earth or Father Sky. (Interestingly, though, in their elaboration of the Torah, the rabbis were remarkably sensitive to animals' welfare. They glossed the biblical injunction not to muzzle the grinding ox, and they demanded that ritual slaughtering be as painless as possible.)

Urban Values

Many of the countries in which Jews lived, as a distinct and often inhibited minority, forbade them ownership of land, while their tradition of study tended to lead them into intellectual occupations and business. The tensions between *shtetl* Jews and *goyim* (Gentiles) in eastern Europe, for instance, were due as much to different occupations as to different theologies. The Gentile peasants worked the land and valued rather brutish strength. The *shtetl* Jews did not farm, engaging themselves in small businesses and study.

As a result, the qualities valued by the Jews were not the goyish qualities of strength and violence. Jews were not to fight, engage in hard labor, drink, or carouse. They were to be disciplined, cultured, and family and community oriented. Because few Jews lived on farms, they had to concentrate on living in densely populated areas. The Gentile peasants needed customers for their goods, middlemen for their trades, craftsmen, and doctors, and Jews tended to fill these roles. Thus, they clearly stood at some remove from nature.

Women's Status

The Jews, then, focused more on culture than on nature.[57] Anthropologists sometimes use these two concepts as opposing points on a spectrum to determine a people's attitudes toward itself and cosmological processes. For instance, anthropologists have used this spectrum to study sex roles.[58] Women have generally been associated with nature, because of menstruation, childbirth, nursing, and—to male eyes—more instinctive, less cerebral behavior. Men have been associated with culture: craft, art, literature, and politics. It does not take a great deal of research to dispute this construct, but many societies have used it, more or less consciously, to characterize sex roles. Therefore, the construct is useful in analyzing how societies view the play of physical nature in human nature.

This sexual stereotype is somewhat applicable among Jews. As we noted, during many periods of Jewish history women worked or ran the home while the men studied. The biblical portrait of women,[59] and the portrait of women in the Talmud[60] and in the *responsa*,[61] reflect a traditional view that placed women away from law and the mind and towards nature and the body. Separating the patriarchal structure of Middle Eastern society, the Jewish religious conception of God (usually as a husband or father, seldom as a wife or mother), and the Jewish perception of nature is almost impossible. The facts, however, are that women and nature went together and that they were subordinate to men and culture.

For instance, women did not read the Torah in the synagogue (usually they could not read Hebrew), did not have many legal obligations (only three *mitzvah* pertaining only to them), could not be priests or rabbis, were tabooed during menstruation, and were both indulged and criticized for their "flightiness." Under biblical law, Jewish women were essentially considered as property—akin to animals and goods. For instance, the laws concerning adultery and rape were principally intended to protect the rights of the male—the injured husband or father. The principal value of women throughout Jewish history was motherhood—a quite "natural" function. They seldom could have careers and had difficulty obtaining the education that would have enabled them to be their husbands' best friends. They were the source of the family line and of emotional support, not leaders. In good measure because he enjoyed being less natural, the male Jew prayed thanks to God for not having created him a woman.[62]

Zionism

With Zionism and the return to the holy land, Judaism has brought back to center stage a theme that was prominent in premodern times—the predilection for Israel and Jerusalem as the most religious places, favoring the prosperity of Jewish faith. In the centuries of Diaspora, the typical Jew felt something of what the first biblical exiles lamented—the inability to sing and rejoice in a foreign land. No doubt that feeling did not afflict the descendants of the actual exiles as intensely, for few of them returned from Babylon when they had the opportunity, but it mixed a certain nature orientation with Jews' desire to have a place of their own. Consequently, Israel became not just a venerable place but also a beautiful, fruitful, arable, desirable land. Thus, the biblical theme of a promised land joined with messianic hopes to link the new age that the Messiah would usher in and the people's return to a place flowing with milk and honey. Zionism drew on these traditional themes, joining them to socialistic (if not utopian) theories of working the land and living together in close cooperation.

Though few American Jews farm or do their religious thinking along cosmological lines, quite a few Israelis live in a kibbutz and work the land (and quite a few American Jewish youths join them for a summer or a year). The land, if not nature, is most important to kibbutzniks. Because of Israel's ancient history and Jews' present need to have their own place in the sun, the Israelis are more agrarian than their recent predecessors were. How that affects their religious consciousness is hard to determine. Many do not consider themselves religious, and they often view their life on the land, even though it brings them close to nature, in sociological

terms. Frequently, then, they resemble other idealistic groups who form communes and farm in order to augment their freedom (and often to "purify" their lives). On the other hand, those who do form kibbutzim out of religious motivations are often fundamentalists who are trying to regain their biblical heritage. That heritage is not so much harvesting God's earth as living where God made the Jews his special people.

Thus, Judaism views nature rather prosaically. To be sure, some Jews have farmed, and some non-farming Jews have found religious significance in seasons, sunsets, flowers, and stocks of grain. However, the Hebrew Bible, the Talmud, and other products of the mind have been more central to the tradition.

Society

Few religions are as community minded as Judaism. Even when we consider that modern individualism is a historical novelty, the fact remains that the Jews were the chosen *people*—chosen as a group or line rather than as individuals. From tribal beginnings, through kingdom, Diaspora, and ethnic diversification, Jewish religion has always been a group affair. Of course, the Torah is inseparable from this phenomenon, for it is a special law designed expressly for the chosen, covenanted people. It sprang from a group sense that life must flow to "our" God, who led us out of captivity to be his own people. The Torah also specified the theological direction of Jews by giving election and covenant the forms by which they shaped social life.

Thus, the synagogue has been a popular gathering place, uniting the action of the people. The Christian *ecclesia* ("church") has a similar etymological meaning, but the building it names has been almost as much a place for private prayer as for public. Perhaps the relative smallness of the Jewish population has helped it to gain a more worldwide sense of community than Christians have. Perhaps, as well, the relative mildness of its sectarian divisions has helped to keep Judaism a family affair. In any event, Muslims, despite their democratic worship and pilgrimage, have been less united than Jews have been, and Christians, despite their lofty theology of the Church, have been more individual oriented and divided. Finally, nothing in Hinduism or Buddhism prompts a different judgment: Judaism is unified and social to an incomparable degree.

JEWISH RITUALS

Traditionally, Jewish social life involved many rituals. To begin with, there was circumcision, the ritual through which males entered the covenant community. Herman Wouk, the celebrated novelist, has tried to explain circumcision and other Jewish rituals to sympathetic Gentiles.[63] He begins by noting the scorn that often has been directed at circumcision and similar Jewish customs. Thus Voltaire mocked a God who could care whether or not people cut off their sons' foreskins. On the other hand, Spinoza, the rationalistic Jewish philosopher, thought that circumcision alone was sufficient to keep the Jews a separate people. However, whether mocked or made a subject of philosophy, circumcision can be a key to Jewish faith.

In the perspective of Jewish faith, circumcision is not a matter of hygiene. It is a sign of the pledge made between Abraham and God, a sign in the very organ of life. For the rest of his life, the man signed this way stands out from the rest of unsigned humanity. Naked, the Jewish man is clearly a Jew. In Wouk's interpretation, the swing of modern medicine to circumcision was but a ratification of the sound policy Jews have always expected God's laws to entail. With or without such a ratification, however, Jews would continue to circumcise their males on the eighth day after birth, the time when Abraham circumcised Isaac.

The circumcision ritual is called a *bris*, the Hebrew word for covenant. When most children were born at home, the bris meant a family feast, with crowds of relatives and friends, learned speeches, and general merrymaking. Each step of the ceremony was something to be stored in the memory for later meditation. Contemporary ceremonies retain what they can of this tradition, gathering relatives and friends to celebrate the new birth. The bris intensifies the ordinary joy

parents feel at the gift of a child, by emphasizing that the convenant community is being extended another generation.

So the father of the child pronounces a joyous blessing: "Blessed are you, Lord our God, Master of the Universe, who have made us holy with your commands, and have commanded us to bring this boy into the covenant of Abraham our father." Ideally the father would do the circumcision himself, as Abraham did, but the accepted practice has become to employ a *mohel* or ritual circumciser to perform it. The mohel may or may not be a medical doctor, but he has been well trained in medical safeguards and antisepsis. In Wouk's view the mohel is preferable to an ordinary doctor, both because the mohel likely has fuller technical training and because he understands the full meaning of the ritual. Thus, he can stand in for the father more adequately.

Following circumcision, the next rite of passage for the Jewish child is the *bar mitzva* or ceremonial accession to adulthood. Recently American Jewish feelings about this ceremony have become quite sensitive, and Wouk reports having received many bitter, even violent complaints about his somewhat humorous depiction of a bar mitzva in his novel *Marjorie Morningstar*. Where he thought he had portrayed the bar mitzva accurately and affectionately, many of his fellow Jews thought he had been satirical, even disrespectful. His reply is that when people lose their sense of humor, becoming unable to see the foibles of their tribe, it is time they take themselves to the mirror.

Sticking to his humorous guns, Wouk likens the American bar mitzva to a Christmas feast orchestrated by Charles Dickens. The lengthy preparations, the incredible eating, the enormous wassailing, and the swirl of family emotions seem parallel in both cases. In both cases, a great deal of purely human gusto dances on top of a religious rationale. In the case of American Jews, the bar mitzva seems to have become an occasion to celebrate a relative freedom from discrimination. While Wouk applauds this freedom, he wonders whether American Jews aren't in danger of losing the religious significance of the bar mitzva, much as American Christians are in danger of losing the religious significance of Christmas, through all their buying and partying.

The religious tradition behind the bar mitzva assumes that a child does not develop the capacity to grasp the concepts of Judaism, nor to fulfill Judaism's disciplines, until the age of thirteen. Prior to that time, the father is responsible for the child. The bar mitzva marks the child's transition to personal responsibility. Donning the phylacteries that an adult wears when he prays, the boy bar mitzvahed can now receive an *aliya*, a call to speak the blessing over a part of the weekly reading of the Torah.

The most honorific aliya is the last one, the call concerning the weekly piece from the prophets. In European Jewish communities the custom arose of giving this special aliya (called the *maftir*) to a boy on his bar mitzva Sabbath, and this custom has been retained in the United States. Often, however, the solid preparation in Hebrew that the European tradition assumed has been lacking. Thus, in Wouk's view, the American bar mitzva frequently became a time of crisis, the young person feeling that his blitz of preparations was a sham. In a number of communities, this has led to a renewal of Hebrew studies, so that the ceremony can express a genuine mastery of Judaism's foundations.

With the rise of a Jewish feminist consciousness have come rituals for bringing girls into the covenant and adulthood. Thus Judith Plaskow, a prominent Jewish feminist and theologian, has written a bris ceremonial for a girl. It begins with the song Hannah sang on the occasion of the birth of her son Samuel (I Sam. 2 : 2–8), including the words: "The bows of the mighty are broken, but the feeble gird on strength. Those who were full have hired themselves out for bread, but those who were hungry have ceased to hunger. The barren has borne seven, but she who has many children is forlorn. God creates and destroys; She brings down to Sheol and raises up."[64] With similar adaptations of other scriptural passages, Plaskow weaves together a celebration of a baby girl's entrance into the community's life parallel to that for a baby boy.

Concerning a girl's coming of age, Wouk indicates some of the reasons there was no special ceremony in the past and why present times have led to coming-of-age ceremonies for girls. Traditionally, women were exempted from most Jewish rituals, that they might be free for family tasks. When the bar mitzva was a rather minor ceremony, for which boys began intensive studies at the age of five, "a girl would have been out of her head to agitate for the burdens of scholarship." But when the preparation for the bar mitzva dwindled, and the event came to occasion a great party, there were good reasons for girls to want an equal celebration. Thus, there has arisen the "bas mitzva" ceremony for girls, an improvised way to ritualize girls' graduation from Sunday-school training and recognize their new status as adults. (Wouk seems insensitive to the traditional correlation between learning and religious status in Judaism, as well as to the deeper hopes of feminists for full sexual equality.)

In most religions' ritualization of the life cycle, the third recurring ceremony has been marriage. Judaism has been no exception, giving marriage a great deal of ritual attention. *The Jewish Catalogue*, a high-spirited collection of lore and advice that tries to make Judaism attractive to contemporary Americans, begins its section on marriage with a story from the talmudic tradition.[65] Once a Roman matron asked Rabbi Jose bar Halafta how long it took God to create the world. The rabbi replied that it took six days. The woman then asked, "What has God been doing from then until now?" The rabbi answered, "The Holy One, blessed be He, is occupied in making marriages." The matron scoffed at this, saying that marriage should only take a short time. Indeed, she went home and in one night married off a thousand of her male slaves to a thousand of her female slaves. The next day the slaves came before her, broken, wounded, and bruised. Each slave said, "I do not want the one you gave me." So the woman went back to the rabbi and apologized: "I see now that your Torah is beautiful—

praiseworthy and true." The rabbi replied, "Yes. God considers making a suitable match as difficult as dividing the Red Sea."

Difficult or not, Jews, like all other peoples, have persisted in marrying, generation after generation, for better or worse, for richer or poorer. Traditionally, their marriages have taken place under a canopy *(huppah)* supported by four poles, the original purpose of which was to provide the ceremony a sacred space. The day itself usually entailed a fast, and other similarities to the Day of Atonement, in the belief that on their wedding day God forgives a couple all their past sins, so that they may begin their life together afresh. Another custom was for the bride and groom to wear white as a symbol of purity.

Jewish betrothal occurred by writing a legal document binding on both parties. The rabbi asked the groom if he was prepared to fulfill his obligations as stated in the contract *(ketubbah)*, and the groom answered affirmatively by taking hold of a handkerchief or some other object given him by the rabbi. After the groom signed the contract, the men present surrounded the groom and danced with him over to the bride, who sat regally on a throne. The groom lifted the veil from the bride's face, while the rabbi recited the phrase, "O sister! May you become the mother of thousands of myriads" (Gen. 24:60). The bride and groom then processed to the huppah, the bride circled the groom seven times (entering all seven spheres of her beloved's soul), there were psalms, hymns, a blessing of wine, and then the essential act occurred.

The essential act was the groom putting a ring on the index finger of the bride's right hand and saying, "Behold you are consecrated to me with this ring according to the Law of Moses and Israel." After this the marriage contract was read, seven blessings were recited, and the groom smashed a glass by stamping on it, to conclude the ceremony. Traditionally, the bride and groom then retired to consummate the marriage. Nowadays they retire to break their fast. When they emerge, their families and friends greet them with music, dancing, and celebration.

Figure 9   Judith with the Head of Holofernes, by Simon Vouet (1590–1649). Nelson Gallery-Atkins Museum (Nelson Fund).

Funeral rites, the last stage on life's way, involved Jews in a final confession of faith. Ideally the dying person said, "Understand, O Israel, the Lord our God is One. I acknowledge before Thee, my God, God of my fathers, that my recovery and death are in your hand. May it be your will to heal me completely, but if I should die, may my death be an atonement for all sins that I have committed." After death there was a ritual washing of the body, a funeral dominated by the recitation of psalms, a ritualized burial, a meal for the mourners, and then the *shivah*, a seven day period of mourning, during which friends were expected to visit and a *minyan* (quorum of ten) was to gather each day. The mourning period concluded with visiting the synagogue the first Sabbath after the shivah.

A Jew has always prayed in the plural, for the sake of the many. When a student or scholar devoted himself to Torah, it was usually in common. In the *shtetl*, one clearly lived very much with people—at times oppressively so. As we noted, wealth was for the common good and study had teaching as its goal. Unlike Christian society, Jewish society had no monastic alternative (neither solitary nor communitarian) to marriage and family life.[66] (The Essene community at Qumran, if it was an exception to this rule, was short-lived.)

The rabbinic mind uncompromisingly intended that all the people live socially. The scholar pondered a law incumbent on all; the working person normally was in business rather than in the solitude of the fields or the forests; in the home, which was largely the woman's province, feelings were gotten "out," almost compulsively expressed. In fact, silence was considered antisocial and even cruel behavior. The two things that a child could do to punish its mother were not to eat and not to speak. Finally, community conversation buzzed with a detailed analysis of each member's learning, wealth, and family lineage. Small wonder, then, that being called forth to read the Torah before the community was an honor, placing one among the *sheyneh yidn*, the "beautiful Jews."

As we have seen, this communitarian consciousness is rooted in patriarchal times. Jews first identified themselves by their tribal origins, which they tied together under the concept of "the twelve tribes." They attributed their sense of commonness to fatherly figures: Abraham, Moses, and David. Abraham was the source of the seed. To him had been the promise of a progeny as numerous as the stars in the heavens or the grains of sand along the sea. Moses was the founding father, in the sense of being the lawgiver. David was the sacred king, the mediator between heaven and earth, the top of the human pyramid. From his line would spring the Messiah. In a special way, the capital city of Jerusalem was the city of David.

Prophecy and the Chosen People

Of the three key figures, Moses predominated, because the Law that came through him was the backbone of Jewish religious life. As different cultures were assimilated by Judaism, Abraham's lineage became less important than his exemplary faith. Similarly, as political sovereignty became a dim memory, David's kingship became more metaphorical, propping future hopes rather than guiding present living. Moses, however, stayed wholly relevant: He authored the code that kept Jews united; he was the mediator of the covenant into which the community circumcised each male. When prophecy had become central to Jewish religion, Moses became the prophet par excellence.

Prophecy, which often distinguishes Western religion from Eastern wisdom religion, is not so much the predictions that appear in today's tabloids as a discernment of what the divine spirit is saying to the people of God. The great biblical prophets analyzed the state of faith and, from that analysis, shrewdly estimated political or military fortunes. A goodly portion of such recorded prophecy was, of course, written after the fact. No portion of respectable prophecy, though, pries into the divine mystery. God remains God; the prophet has only the word that God deigns to speak. The establishment of Moses as the supreme prophet testifies to the social utility that Jews have expected communication with God to bear. They expected such communication to result in communal renovation, strengthening, and redirection. Prophecy was not a display of individual virtuosity or a matter involving crystal balls.

As prophecy intimates, the ultimate bonding agent of Jewish society has been God; only the atypical, modern secular Jew would dispute this. Through history the master of the universe, the Adonai that all prayers bless, has bound Jews together as his people. Physically and legally one is a Jew if one is born of a Jewish mother; spiritually one is a Jew if one identifies oneself with the people fashioned at Sinai, framed by the Torah, and covenanted to God. To be sure, many problems attend election as God's people, and Jews have not been unmindful of them. Indeed, the relation between the chosen people and the Gentile nations has been a constant topic for Jewish meditation. In good times, such meditation has turned over history's mysteries gratefully: Why were we chosen when we show no special merits? What are our obligations to the nations?

Indubitably, the Gentile nations were under God's direction, too. It could not be that God had no fulfillment in store for them. So Jewish thinkers worked out the notion of the Noachian covenant: God made a pact with the Gentile nations modeled after the promise he made to Noah, in which he stressed the need for human beings to respect life, especially by avoiding bloodshed. The Bible sees the rainbow as a symbol of God's fidelity to this pact: He will never destroy humanity, never again allow it to suffer as it did in the flood. Yet God could well have more in store for the nations than this Noachian covenant, and Israel's vocation was to be a light unto the nations—to provide them with a greater knowledge of God. In that way, being the chosen people became less a matter of honor than of responsibility.

In bad times, however, reflection on being chosen by God had to probe darker mysteries. For instance, the prophets almost fixated on the horror that Israelites refused their election. Such people wanted kings like the nations had, cults like those to Baal, fertility from the land rather than from the covenant. With some deliberateness, many Jews turned their backs on God because they could not endure living in faith; "I am whatever I want to be" was too much for them. For the prophets, this was the deepest sickness of the soul, the most debilitating sin, as well as a rejection of Israel's better self. The worst of biblical times, then, occurred when people left the covenantal faith.

At such times, the prophets brought the whole question of what the Jewish people at core were into paradox. They spoke of a remnant, of an Israel within Israel that was composed of the few who did keep faith. A major Jewish-Christian controversy has hung on this point, for Christians have claimed to succeed Israel by accepting God's later revelation (specifically, his revelation in Jesus the Christ). Within the Jewish community, prophetic religious leaders have worried about the correlation between bad faith and loss of membership.

The Law

For rabbinic Judaism, the Law helped to ease the problem of bad faith. Without abandoning their ideal of the perfect faith outlined in Maimonides' thirteen articles, the rabbis focused more on performance than on motivation or thought. What one believed about God, within broad limits, was less important than keeping the Sabbath and fulfilling one's communal obligations. This attitude encouraged considerable intellectual freedom, including lively debate, tolerance, and theological ambiguity. As well, it prevented the establishment of a clear-cut religious authority and dogma, such as that encountered by Roman Catholicism in the magisterium of its councils and popes. The Law, which seemed so specific, had dozens of interpreters. On and on the Talmud grew, because most interpreters had insights worth preserving.

The result was a subtle but significant shift in the notion of the faith requisite for community membership. It was expressed in action, not in speculation or confession. How one used one's body, money, and time was more important than how one used one's mind or tongue. Such a practical view of faith meant that the community could bind itself through rituals, ethics, and laws without excessive concern about their meaning (although the rabbis did not ignore their meaning or the proper motivation behind actions).

This emphasis on action relates to the

Jewish refusal to separate mind and body and to the Jewish commitment to hallowing life. One obeyed the Law to express and learn that God, who is holy, wants holy people. Through the quite overt keeping of the Law, Jews reminded themselves that they were the people called to sanctify God's name. A Jew knew that his neighbor accepted this identity because he could see that his neighbor obeyed the Law. Not accidentally, withdrawal from the Law and from the traditional God whom the Law hallowed have gone hand in hand in modern times.

The Holocaust

Lastly, contemporary Jewish identity has been annealed as a result of the Holocaust. While exodus and entry into the promised land characterized Jews in biblical times, suffering and persecution have characterized Jews recently. Jewish commentators have no consensus on what recent history means. For Richard Rubenstein, it means the death of the traditional God.[67] For Emil Fackenheim, it means a call to hold together both evil and divine providence.[68] For Hanna Arendt, it shows that history can make evil utterly commonplace or banal.[69] Such commentators do agree that we must not ignore, deny, or explain away the evil of the Holocaust. As Elie Wiesel has said, it is better to keep silent than to depreciate the suffering of so many innocent victims with "explanations."[70] Thus, Jewish identity, the theme of so many American novels, has yet to be fully resolved.

Self

An intense community, such as Judaism's, can heighten individualism. One can prize the individual because the richer the individual, the richer the group. Judaism appears to have appreciated this proposition.

For example, after the prophets (such as Ezekiel and Jeremiah), individual responsibility separated from collective responsibility. No longer could one hold, rather magically, that the fathers had eaten sour grapes and so set the children's teeth on edge. Further, both Hellenization and internal legal development set apart individual reason. For instance, Jewish thinkers in Alexandria reflected Platonic, Aristotelian, Epicurean, and Stoic interests in mind and reason. Philo, the luminary of these thinkers, tried to correlate Mosaic teaching with a cosmic law. In the medieval period, Maimonides, Halevi, and others tried to square the Torah with rational demands for a less mythic, more analytic explanation of faith. Since the individual soul is the site of reason, such concerns inevitably clarified the personality's partial independence of group thought. That is, it underscored that any particular person might grasp or miss the divine Law.

Moreover, the Torah and the Talmud themselves inculcated something of this sensitivity. As a scriptural religion, Judaism demanded literacy and encouraged learning. But, literature and learning are obviously cultural developments deriving from a common human nature that tend to distinguish people according to their talent. Thus, the bright little boy may distinguish himself by the age of ten. Through his unique gifts he may stand out from the crowd, and even increase regard for his family. If he develops into a sage, he will join the line of masters whose commentaries on the Law are the classics. So, by stressing personal insight, legal study encouraged individuation.

To a lesser degree, Jewish mysticism and Jewish attitudes toward wealth also encouraged individuation. Mysticism, like study, is a personal inward phenomenon. Despite its debt to tradition and its occurrence within a community of faith, mysticism is a solitary pursuit involving an "I-Thou" relation. When mysticism flowered in Judaism, it produced revered personalities, such as the Baal-Shem-Tov and the Maggid of Mezritch. To their disciples, these *tzaddikim* were stunning demonstrations of the ardor which divinity could inspire. Their personalities were special, set apart, distinguished. Despite the threats that mysticism posed for the traditional rabbinic authority, the mystics were precious for strengthening the common people's faith. Thus, one could aspire to Hasidic distinction, as one could aspire to rabbinic distinction. Because mystical prowess edified the community, it was a worthy ambition.

Analogously, one could aspire to the (lesser) distinction that came with wealth. Judaism is not, comparatively speaking, an ascetic religion. As much as Hinduism, it views wealth or prosperity as a legitimate life goal. For his good fortune and financial talent, as well as for his philanthropy, a successful Jew could win recognition. True, with success he was sure to gain a host of petitioners, but their attestation to his generosity somewhat offset the burden that they imposed.

This description of the self must be qualified in discussing women. Since their vocation was marriage and practicality, their distinction was basically reflected—that of being a rich man's wife or a scholar's mother. Nevertheless, women had rights to self-expression, at least regarding nonscriptural matters. The tradition that a woman had no soul did not mean that she had no say. In matters of the home or the shop, she probably had the dominant say. In matters of affection or emotion, she surely did. Thus, few distinguished Jews were not first signalized by women, and most *shtetl* neighborhoods recognized certain girls as being especially nubile and certain mothers as being especially benevolent.

Mind-Body Unity

Judaism stressed the unity of mind and body, eschewing a body-soul or matter-spirit duality. Scholars usually contrast biblical Jewish notions of personhood and contemporary Greek notions. This contrast can illumine the tendency of Judaism towards an existential concreteness that most of Western culture has been struggling for centuries to recapture.

For instance, Descartes, the father of modern European philosophy, worked hard to reconcile the opposition within the human being between its *res cogitans* (thinking part) and its *res extensa* (material part). In contrast, the "soul" *(nepes)* of Hebrew biblical thought was a unity of mind and body that could not be divided into thinking and material parts. So the heart rather than the head stood for the center of thought and emotion. Out of the fullness of the heart the mouth would speak. This conviction fought against the Hellenization of Jewish theology, which would have made the mouth speak what reason dictated. It fought against the aridity latent in rabbinic theology, keeping space for haggadic tales whose appeal was more than mental. The earthiness that one finds in Hebrew literature, from biblical times to the present,[71] reflects these convictions about the heart and body.

Further, through his or her body, the Jewish personality maintained contact with the natural world. In the beginning, God had formed human beings from the earth, breathing into them a living spirit. Various biblical figures, such as Job, acknowledge this connection with the earth when they humble themselves before God and say, "We are but dust and ashes." The connection with the earth is more intense in the command to be fruitful and multiply, for the command implies that living things have an inbuilt drive to survive and grow. Biblical notions of stewardship over the earth found an evolutionary aspect in the command to be fruitful and multiply. (They also subordinated nature to human need.)

The command to be fruitful and multiply also influenced Jewish attitudes toward marriage. The fulfillment of the spouses was a value, at least in talmudic times, but a strong focus was always kept on procreation. As many commentators point out, the late development of the notion of personal immortality in Judaism is due not only to the lack of a clear sense of a spiritual (immaterial) soul, but also to the tendency to think that one continued to exist through one's offspring. In other words, the family line was a sort of concrete immortality.

Thus, marriage was a treasure of Jewish faith in part because it prevented the individual from being totally lost in the abyss of death. From this and other benefits attributed to marriage, sexual activity derived a certain dignity, even a certain obligation. It is true that in rabbinic Judaism prudery seemed to offset the high evaluation of sexual love. The rabbis counseled against raising one's eyes to a woman's face, and they desired that the sexes be segregated as much as possible. They laid on women the heavy burden of the temptress that one can see in other religions. Indeed, in Judaism, unchastity was not only sinful but also deplorable because it drew the mind down from the (masculine) heights of the Torah and prayer.

In most Orthodox homes (which for the poor often had only one or two rooms), husband and wife did not sleep in the same bed. Tradition encouraged them to have relations except during the menstrual flow but to keep the sexual appetite in check. One of the nice customs of the Sabbath, however, was that in its leisure spouses should make love. As the Cabalists stressed, the Sabbath was the bride of God. Consequently, they found in the coexistence of man and woman a supplement to the notion that human reason is an image of God. Humanity also images God through sexual love, acting in accordance with the Genesis line "male and female he created them."

The Human Spirit

In prophecy Jewish religion found understandings of God's relationship to the human spirit new to human history. That is, the ecstatic experience of the prophets, who seem to have begun as wandering bands of exultants *(nebi'im)*, evolved into something other than ordinary shamanism (which we may take as the typical model of ancient ecstasy). For where shamanism usually kept the world divine and usually confused the relations between imagination and reason in the ecstatic experience (though some shamans were well aware of the divine incomprehensibility), the prophets had experiences that burned below imagination to the base of the spirit. The burning bush, for instance, occasioned the realization that we only know of God what the divine mystery shows in time. Elijah's small, still voice suggested that God comes more through spiritual recollection than through natural storms. Jeremiah, finally, went to the core of the matter: Divine creativity best expresses itself by writing its law upon the human heart.

That does not mean that the prophetic, or later the mystical, Jews did not mix myth, symbol, and imagination. The *merkabah* (chariot) imagery, as we mentioned, dominated even the philosophers' ruminations about God, while the Cabalists' bliss was to imagine the divine emanations. Still, the union of the entire numinous experience (the entire experience of divinity) with ethical demands refined what it means to be religious by communion with a transcendent God. Implicit in the prophetic and talmudic program is that true religion is doing justice and worshiping purely. It is the twofold commandment of loving God (who is one) and loving one's neighbor (who is another self). This maxim developed into the powerful concept of individual conscience: One only is the mystery that dominates and constitutes the human person in its being and its morality alike. Realizing such monotheism was a deathblow to all idolatry, an emancipation of the Jewish spirit. History continues to unfold the implications of this ethical monotheism. From biblical times, then, the Jews have cast the self, as well as the people, in partnership with a single God.

Divinity

The question of the place of divinity in Judaism is difficult for Westerners, because the Jewish God is inseparable from

Western culture. We can no more filter out Israelite ethical monotheism from the Western world view than we can filter out Greek reason. It requires considerable imaginative energy, therefore, to grasp the origins of Jewish divinity and trace how those beginnings developed into theological conceptualizations.

The biblical beginnings were extremely novel, constituting a "leap in being" rivaled only by the Greek clarification of reason. The biblical beginnings were deep spiritual experiences: irruptions of divinity that seized and formed the soul (more than they clarified reason). The God who was revealed was lively, personal, and free.

Perhaps because the genius of Israelite religion was not reason but spirit, the biblical Jews expressed this God's character as the world's origin and destiny in myths. That is, they expressed the truth of order, of humanity's proper place in and with nature and God, symbolically, from the "dead spot," the bottom of the soul, which revelation seizes. Moreover, having expressed its order mythologically, the Israelite religious genius hardly criticized its symbols, making little effort to interpret them in clearer, if less complete, conceptual terms. In other words, it did not attack the problems of inner coherence that today's analytic philosophy associates with meaning.[72] So the God of Moses "is" only what time shows him to be; the God of Genesis makes the world "in the beginning" from primal chaos, the status of which is quite unclear; and the God of Isaiah is placed beyond the world by a dazzling cluster of symbols.

THE GOD OF JEWISH PRAYER[73]

Through more than 2,500 years of liturgical experience, Jews have developed the biblical notion of God. Probably the prime characteristic of the Jewish God that has emerged is his unity. As a summary of Jewish belief and prayer, the Shema has said it all: "Hear, O Israel: The Lord our God is One Lord." Thus the daily prayers of the individual Jew, as well as the communal prayers of the synagogue, have always lauded the divine unity. Nonetheless, the divine unity is not the only word in Jewish theology. The God of the Fathers has not only been One, he has also been the Creator, the revealer, and the redeemer. In his actions toward the world and his people, he has made new things, disclosed his will, again and again saved the people from dead ends.

All these motifs are manifest in the prayers that we shall describe. One should picture the community assembled in the synagogue as abuzz with these prayers, since the basic form of the Orthodox liturgy has been for each person present to say such prayers aloud. That is what the basic Jewish word for prayer *(daven)* has meant: to say the liturgy aloud yet quietly and privately.

In the *Jewish Prayer Book* one finds praise for the One God who is King of the Universe: "Praised are you, O Lord our God, King of the Universe." This prayer then itemizes the great things the King of the Universe does. He fixes the cycles of light and darkness. He ordains the order of all creation. He is the source of the light that shines over all the earth. His mercy radiates over all the earth's inhabitants. Because he is so good, he recreates the world day by day. His manifold works reveal his great bounty. Their beauty and order reveal his great wisdom.

And what does the devout Jew ask of the King of the Universe? That he continue to love his people. He, the only One exalted from of old, the One praised and glorified since the world began, has been all Jews' shield and protection. He has been the Lord of our strength, the rock of our defense. In his infinite mercy, may he continue to love us. His goodness is for all time, so we may hope for this mercy. Daily he renews the work of creation, so daily he may be our reliance. The Psalmist knew this and sang, "Give thanks to Him who made the great lights, for His loving kindness is everlasting." O God, make a new light to shine on Zion. Make us worthy to behold its radiance. All praise to you, O Lord, maker of the stars.

The One God is also the revealer of the

Torah. The *Prayer Book* expresses this conviction in connection with God's compassion. Out of tender regard for his people's needs, the Lord has taught our Fathers the laws of life. For their sakes, may he continue to teach us. May we, too, learn the divine Laws, more and more trust in the divine guidance. May we observe all the precepts of the divine Law, fulfill all its teachings. If we are to do this, God must enlighten our eyes and open our hearts. He must gather together our scattered thoughts, uniting our whole beings in reverence and love. This reverence and love will keep us from shame, and help us to feel God's aid. If we trust in God's holiness, we will come safely from the corners of the earth to the dignity of our own holy land. It is you, God, who are our deliverance, you who have chosen us from all peoples and tongues. We praise and thank you for having drawn us close to you. "We praise You and thank You in truth. With love do we thankfully proclaim Your unity, and praise You who chose Your people Israel in love."

When the *Prayer Book* reproduces the Shema, it includes much of the Shema's original biblical gloss. Thus after expressing the call to love God with whole mind, soul, and strength, the *Prayer Book* reminds the people that the words of the Shema should ever be in their hearts. They should teach these words diligently to their children. They should talk about the Shema at home and abroad, day and night. The words of the Shema ought to be a sign upon the hand, or as frontlets (browbands) between the eyes. They should be inscribed on the doorposts of the home and on every gate. If the people fulfill these injunctions, they will find God favoring. He will give them rain in the autumn and rain in the spring, that their harvests may flourish. He will provide them grain, wine, and oil. Their grass will grow thick in the fields for their cattle. They will have food enough to eat in contentment.

The way away from God is the way to disaster, so the people must take care not to wander after false gods. If they forsake the true God, they will find the heavens closed, unwilling to provide them rain. They will find the earth barren, unable to provide them food. Before long, there will be no good land for the people to enjoy. The good land will disappear, and with it the once good people. So all Jews should stay mindful of

God's words of the Shema, keeping them in their hearts and souls. The words should sign the hand, to guide all that the hand works. They should be stamped between the eyes, to guide all that the eye sees, all that the mind conceives.

In speaking of God as redeemer, Jewish prayer spotlights his intervention on his people's behalf. God has been the king of each generation, the people's only sovereign guide. He has been the redeemer of each generation, the One to whom all Jews must go in time of need. Creator, he has been a victorious stronghold, a fort no enemy could overrun. Through his redemptive interventions, he has shown there is no God but he.

Though God dwells in the heights of heaven, his decrees reach all of creation. The very ends of the earth stand or fall by God's Laws. Happy is the person who takes these Laws to heart, obeying the commands of God's Torah. Such a person experiences what it really means to have a Lord, a defender and mighty king. The true God is the first and the last. The true people have no king or redeemer but him.

Addressing God directly, the weekly *Prayer Book* prays: "You, O Lord our God, rescued us from Egypt; You redeemed us from the house of bondage." As though retreating to a favorite haunt of memory, Jewish prayer again and again goes back to the Exodus. God slew the firstborn of the Egyptians, and saved his people's firstborn. He split the waters of the Red Sea, rescuing his faithful and drowning the wicked. When the waters engulfed the enemies of Israel, not one of the arrogant remained.

God the redeemer is therefore God the powerful, God the One not to be trifled with. In the Exodus episode, Israel received its greatest lesson in redemption. Ever since, Jews have sung great hymns of thanksgiving to God. Ever since, they have extolled God with psalms of praise. For ever since they have known that the Lord their God is a mighty king, overseeing everything from his high heaven. Great and awesome, he is the source of all blessing, the ever-living divinity exalted in majesty.

As the Exodus episode revealed, the God of Israel humbles the proud and raises the lowly. He frees the captive and redeems the meek. Helping the needy and answering the people's call, he shows himself no respecter of earthly persons, a respecter only of what is right. So let all voices ring out with praise for the supreme God: ever praised be he! As Moses and the children of Israel sang, "Who is like You, O Lord, among the mighty?" Who is like God in holiness, wonderful deeds, worthiness of praise? There is none like he, because there is only One God. The people God saved in the Exodus sensed this stunning uniqueness. They sang a chorus of praises by the sea. The Lord will reign forever. Rock of Israel, may he ever rise to his people's defense. "Our Redeemer is the Holy One of Israel." Lord of Hosts is our God's name. May the Lord by praised, the Redeemer of Israel.

Such prayer combines a remembrance of God's past deeds with a meditation on God's constant nature. Its regular accent is thankful and praising. God has made everything that exists. He has revealed his will to Israel. And he has saved Israel from its enemies. For these and all his other splendors, he deserves his people's full worship and confidence. Though king, Lord, ruler of heaven, he has deigned to concern himself with his people's needs. Though holy and righteous, he has manifested mercy and steadfast love.

When a person or a group prays in this mood, its words and images fall into an easy rhythm. One image sparks another, one memory brings another memory to mind. Phrases tend to repeat themselves, for the point is not innovation. The point is moving one's soul back to the dispositions of one's forebears in faith, who forged the canonical expressions. In their time, God was manifest in nature and was a fellow-warrior, with

them against their foes. In their time, good harvests and military victories derived directly from God's hand, while bad harvests and military defeats suggested the people had faltered in their religion.

What has predominated in the Jewish liturgy, however, is the memory of God's saving deeds. In times past God has shown himself the people's redeemer. Times present and times future will reveal God to have remained faithful and true. Reviving their faith by journeying back to the biblical experiences, generations of Jews have been able to open their spirits to the God who lay ahead of them, in the mystery of the future. God has given his people a way to walk into the future with confidence. Not only has he promised he would reveal himself to Israel through time, he has given his Torah, to detail what holy living with him requires.

So Jews prayed for God's help to fulfill God's Torah. They wanted to be good, to do what was right, and they sensed that for this they needed God's help. Unless God gave them light for their minds and purity for their hearts, they would miss the path of Torah. Unless they did justice to their neighbors and worshiped God day and night, they would lose their heavenly protector. One can see how modern experiences of persecution could put this faith in God's redemptive activity to a severe test. Nonetheless, the *Prayer Book* has continued to promote the biblical phrases, confident that Jews of today need to worship God wholeheartedly no less than Jews of the past.

Christian Contrast

The development from these biblical beginnings followed a somewhat different course in Jewish theology than in Christian theology. Christian theology, Eastern and Western alike, structured itself through Hellenistic philosophy. Origen, Arius, Athanasius, the Cappadocians, Augustine—these great speculators utilized the Greek discovery of mind. No less, the architects of doctrinal theology that succeeded them (Nestorius, Cyril, Boethius, Anselm, and

Aquinas) designed with Greek intellectual tools. Jewish theology for the most part bypassed Hellenism. As we have seen, Philo and Maimonides appropriated Greek logic, Greek epistemology (theory of knowledge), and Greek metaphysics. The mainline, talmudic development of the Torah, though, contained Hellenism's impact.

The overall result was a theological predominance of law over philosophy. The infrastructure of Jewish belief appears less, or at least quite differently, defined than the Christian. It did not try to ground itself in reflective reason as Christian scholasticism did. At its core, Jewish theology was a symbolic, ethical, and mystical movement, if not flux. It was more imaginative and less controlled and clarified by philosophy than Christian theology was. As well, it was more historical—more concerned with honoring the covenantal mystery and keeping the teachers' traditions.

Christians could reply that they tried hard to honor the new covenant and that their doctrine of apostolic succession was an effort to keep their teachers' traditions. True enough, but the increasingly speculative emphasis of Christian theology made its consciousness of history less effective and tangible than that of Jewish theology. As well, Christianity spread to many ethnic groups, among whom unity was hard to maintain. Last, in Jewish theology one did not have a metaphysics of God developed from the psychology of his human image, as one did in Augustine and Aquinas. Rather, one had amazing refinements of the behavior that living with God demanded.

The impact of this difference is perhaps clearest in the two religions' doctrines of God's relation to the world. Working from a similar literature (the Hebrew Bible was the Christians' Old Testament), the two theologies went quite different ways. Christian scholasticism developed the position that God has no "real" relations with the world or with human beings. Rather, all God's relations with the world are simply "rational" *(entia rationis* ["clarifications that have no foundation in the divine being itself"]).

The consequence of this Hellenistically based conceptualization is that God does not change, suffer, move, or develop in his relations with creatures. This makes for a theology that is at variance with the biblical picture (and, according to contemporary "process theology," at variance with intuitions of "perfection" that challenge the intuitions of Hellenistic thought).[74] Except perhaps for the Jewish philosophers, Jewish theology kept God "really" related to the world—the God of refined Jewish reflection

was held accountable for history and thought capable of change and movement.

The differences in this aspect of God's conception in popular Judaism and Christianity are less pronounced, because popular Christian faith seems to have imagined God more on the model of biblical anthropomorphism than on the model of the philosophical theologians' "Pure Act" of being. In terms of prayer (which Friedrich Heiler has suggested is the most central religious activity),[75] the average Jew and Christian likely thought about God in the same way: God is interested in us, loves us, listens to our petitions, and controls the world in such a way that our prayers can make a difference. If this popular equivalence is valid, Jewish "professional" theology kept closer ties to its faithful than Christian "professional" theology did.

Thus far, our comparison of Christian and Jewish conceptions of divinity has bracketed the question of Jesus' divinity. Clearly, however, the Christian development of Jesus as the Messiah into the union of his humanity with God differentiates Christian theology from Jewish. In fact, it even separates Christians from those Jews who view Jesus as a remarkable expression of Jewish religion. Moreover, when Jesus' divinity produces the Christian conception of God as the Trinity (Father, Son, and Spirit), the difference becomes extreme. At that point, the two prophetic religions become different faiths.

The case is different with Islam, because (largely through borrowings from biblical thought) Allah is personal, one, and in charge of the world. Conceptually, therefore, Islamic theology changed less of what it received from Jewish tradition about God than Christian theology did. In popular religion, however, Islam appears more fatalistic than Judaism. Consequently, its God appears less involved, less changeable than the Jewish God. Alternatively, Muslims so stressed Allah's power that they somewhat suppressed human freedom (though officially they affirmed it). Nonetheless, Allah is as near as the pulse at one's throat, and he is merciful, compassionate, willing to forgive the sinner, and an intervener for Muslims in holy war. Thus, the Muslim God can make a difference in a believer's life.

Because of its strict monotheism, Islam probably has a doctrine of God that is closest to that of Judaism. Thus, Islam has multiplied the effects of Jewish revelation. However, the ripple of monotheism through Islamic cultures produced quite a different law, tradition of scholarship, and piety. In terms of practice, then, the two theologies are quite distinct.

Study Questions

1. Why was David's kingship an ambiguous symbol?
2. What is the main theme of the history that the Hebrew Bible writes?
3. In what ways does rabbinic or talmudic religion differ from biblical religion?
4. How would you summarize the religious mentality expressed in Maimonides' thirteen articles of faith?
5. In what ways has Judaism focused more on culture than on nature?
6. Discuss the significance of celebrating a Sabbath each week.
7. Define exactly the senses in which the Jewish God is *creator* and *redeemer*.
8. Describe the faith of the prophet Jeremiah.
9. What is your impression of Jewish rituals?

Chapter Three

CHRISTIANITY: TWENTY-FIVE KEY DATES

CA. 30 C.E.	DEATH OF JESUS OF NAZARETH
CA. 65	DEATH OF APOSTLE PAUL
CA. 95	LAST OF NEW TESTAMENT WRITINGS
CA. 100–165	JUSTIN MARTYR, LEADING APOLOGIST
CA. 185–254	ORIGEN, LEADING THEOLOGIAN
313	CHRISTIANS FREED OF LEGAL PERSECUTION
325	FIRST COUNCIL OF NICAEA
354–430	AUGUSTINE, LEADING THEOLOGIAN
451	COUNCIL OF CHALCEDON
CA. 480–550	BENEDICT, FOUNDER OF WESTERN MONASTICISM
CA. 540–604	POPE GREGORY I, FOUNDER OF MEDIEVAL PAPACY
787	SECOND COUNCIL OF NICAEA (LAST ONE THAT THE ORTHODOX CHURCH CONSIDERS ECUMENICAL)

Christianity

If we gather all its parts, Christianity is the largest religion in the world. What began as a Jewish sect has carried its version of the Torah and prophecy around the globe.[1] We begin our study of Christianity by describing its appearance in several different countries.

APPEARANCE

We have tried to indicate something of what Jerusalem means to Jews. To a lesser but still significant extent, Jerusalem is for Christians as well as Muslims the "Holy City." Christians venerate Jerusalem because of its significance for Jesus and the early Church. It is the place where Jesus died and the Church was born. Today the different groups of Jesus' followers preserve, even hawk, this memory. Franciscan priests in brown robes lead pilgrims through the narrow streets of the Old City, along the *via dolorosa*—the path down which Jesus carried the cross according to tradition. Behind high walls are numerous churches dedicated to events in Jesus' life. For instance, a church lies near a grove of olive trees where the Gospels say Jesus prayed after the Last Supper.

In Bethlehem, a few miles south of Jerusalem, a church sits at the spot where tradition says Jesus was born. One corner of it belongs to Eastern Orthodox Christians, who celebrate their solemn liturgy in flowing robes and conical hats and with clouds of incense. In another corner Catholics stand watch at a grotto they venerate as the birthplace.

Christianity is simpler—theologically and culturally—in Rome than in Jerusalem. Despite its historical riches of a pre-Christian culture, Rome clearly is a Catholic capital today. Even many Italian Communists marry, baptize their children, and are buried in Catholic ceremonies. St. Peter's and the Vatican, as well as the art of Florence and Venice, are unthinkable apart from Italy's Catholic history.

St. Peter's disappoints few visitors. Its sheer size is impressive, but it is more than a giant. Michelangelo's *Pietà*, for instance, is exquisite. Bernini's columns around the main altar also deserve their fame. The whole basilica, in fact, recalls the age when Christ's vicars patronized art to make Catholic religion stream forth in crimson, azure, ermine, and gold.

Eastern Orthodoxy has no capital, but you can feel its pulse in Athens. The humble cathedral, for example, shows some of the differences between Eastern Christendom and Western. First, its layout is not the long rectangle of St. Peter's but a more intimate square. People stand close together before the icons. Second, Orthodox devotion to Mary is different from what the *Pietà* suggests. For the East, Mary is the *theotokos* (the God-bearer). Portraits of her show a queen of heaven with crown and mantle. Her infant is a princely teacher, his hand raised for blessing. In the cathedral people pause before an icon or Bible, cross themselves from right to left, and end their prayers with a kiss. On the Greek islands are tiny churches, whitewashed and onion spired. Their people project a tough, deep-burning faith that dresses widows in black for the rest of their lives and disciplines the flesh. The Orthodox priests, too, seem fierce. Their full beards, bushy brows, and black robes pay the world and the body little homage.

Dourness winds through the streets of Geneva, where John Calvin's spirit lives. Though Lake Leman (Geneva) sparkles with Gallic charm, the stony streets are all Protestant discipline. Geneva is the peak of Swiss neutrality, and the World Council of Churches there tries to keep the Christian peace. It is open to Catholics and Orthodox, but their participation has been limited. In recent years the World Council has supported third world movements, calling for a new economic order. That has not sat well with conservative brethren, who used to hesitate to mix religion and politics. For progressives, the World Council's internationalism has made Geneva the center of a new reformation. While the old Reformation was a matter of returning to scripture, the new reform would increase bread for the world.

The art, spirit, and politics of Christianity clearly vary among the three major traditions, yet their common heritage still shapes the West. Even though Western culture proclaims itself secular, it originates from a Christian past. Without its Christian heritage, Western secularism would have few of its analytic tools—and fewer of its enemies. If this state of affairs seems asleep in the frame churches of rural America, it is fully alert in the centers of culture. Detroit and Wall Street, for instance, are brazen in their contempt of biblical justice. If it is easier for a camel to pass through the eye of the needle than for a rich person to enter the Kingdom of God, Detroit, Wall Street, Madison Avenue, and America's centers of affluence are home to many who stand outside the kingdom.

HISTORY

Jesus

Christianity developed from the life and work of Jesus of Nazareth,[2] as Buddhism developed from the life and work of Gautama. Jesus (whose historical reality is attested to by such non-Christian authors as Josephus, Tacitus, Suetonius, and Pliny the Younger) was born about 4 B.C.E. (by current calendars) in Palestine. We know little about his youth except through Gospel stories, such as those of his circumcision and his dialogues with religious teachers. (The stories of his birth are legendary, in the service of the various New Testament authors' theologies.)[3] We assume that he grew up as a Jewish youth of his times. About the year 27 C.E. he started from his native Galilee on a career as an itinerant preacher. Geza Vermes has described the contemporary political and religious context, suggesting that Jesus was a preacher and healer on the model of the *hasid* (pious one) familiar to his time and locale.[4]

While Jesus' message has been inter-preted in very different ways, certain essentials seem quite clear. Joachim Jeremias's careful study argues that Jesus' own voice echoes in the New Testament parables, riddles, discussions of the reign of God, the peculiar use of *amen,* and the peculiar use of *Abba* (Father) for God.[5] On etymological and historical grounds, these are the safest leads to how Jesus himself preached (with concrete, lively language) and to what he had to say (that a new time was dawning and that God is intimately parental). In their admirable digest of Christian theology, Rahner and Vorgrimler state that Jesus' main theme was an announcement that the reign of God was at hand in his (Jesus') own person.[6] That reign or kingdom was a new beginning, a time of justice and holiness.

According to the New Testament writers, this theme meant that Jesus had fulfilled Jewish religion and superseded it. Jesus himself solicited a radical commitment to the new opportunities that God's reign offered, which included intimacy with God and friendship with other persons. The morality that Jesus anticipated in the kingdom[7] is most graphic in his Sermon on the Mount. There the evangelists have him bless those who are poor, gentle, mourning, hungry and thirsty for what is right, merciful, pure in heart, peacemaking, and suffering for the cause of justice. They are the citizens of the kingdom; dispositions or circumstances like theirs render human beings open to divine love. The gist of Jesus' own life, according to the New Testament, was just such love.

Information on Jesus' public life and ministry remains imprecise (because of the limited sources). Apparently he linked his work with that of John the Baptist, his message raised opposition from the religious establishment, he worked out only some of the particulars for living in the kingdom, and he predicted woe to those who rejected his program. Further, he planted at least the seeds of the Christian Church by gathering disciples and co-workers, and he gained a reputation as a healer. His death came by order of the Roman procurator Pontius Pilate on the dubious grounds that he threatened the peace.

Interpretations

Beyond this bare outline, historical and theological interpretations diverge. According to the New Testament and the orthodox faith of later centuries, the old reign of Satan and sin died with Jesus. Further, after death Jesus was raised (resurrected) and was disclosed to be "Lord" or ruler of humanity. More tersely, Jesus was the divine Son whose dying and rising brought the world salvation. This interpretation thus stresses a twofold quality in Jesus: He was both human and divine. The councils that specifically discussed and defined Jesus' being found this interpretation to be the intent of the Gospel and Epistle writers.

Another interpretation of the New Testament is that Jesus was the Messiah—the anointed king of the age of grace, where *grace* came to mean not just peace and material plenty but intimacy with God and sharing in divine life. From the titles that the New Testament gives to Jesus, his own reported claims, and the miracles (healings, raisings from the dead, and so on) that the New Testament attributes to Jesus, we can conclude that the New Testament writers found him most remarkable—so remarkable that he had to be more than human. For them he was the bringer of salvation,[8] God's Word incarnate, the Christ (Messiah), and the divine Son.

In the earliest portions of the New Testament, the Epistles, Jesus is a living spiritual reality. The assumption behind Paul's directions for Church life, for instance, is that "the Lord" lives in Christians' midst. After Jesus' death, his followers apparently thought that his movement was finished, but the events of the resurrection convinced them that he had assumed a new form of existence. They stayed together in Jerusalem; at Pentecost (seven weeks after Passover, when Jesus had died), they experienced what they called the Holy Spirit,

whom they thought Jesus and the Father had sent. The Spirit charged them to go out and preach about Jesus. Thus, the early Christians proclaimed that Jesus' life and death were the definitive act of salvation. The disciples also preached that Jesus was the Messiah. As such he was in accordance with Jewish tradition and yet responsible for its transformation. From a historical perspective, then, the first Christians appear as sectarian Jews—Jews with a new interpretation of messianism.

It took some time for the first interpretations of Jesus to sift out and clarify, and a principal catalyst in that process was Paul. From the accounts in Acts and his own writings, Paul was a Pharisaic Jew whose conversion on the road to Damascus (Acts 9 : 3–9) was quite dramatic. After his conversion he tried to show his fellow Jews that Jesus was their Messiah, but their opposition to his preaching, plus his own further reflection on Jesus' life and death, led Paul to think that in Jesus God had opened the covenant to all persons—Gentiles as well as Jews.

Consequently, Paul made the Gospel (good news) about Jesus a transformation of the Torah. Because God had fulfilled in Jesus the intent of the Law, the Law's many detailed prescriptions were passé. Adherence to an external code could not make one righteous (on even terms with God). Only by opening to God's love and healing could one stand before him acceptably. Paul called that opening "faith." For him Jesus was the agent of a shift from the Torah to the Gospel, from works to faith. The way to become right with God was to commit oneself to Jesus. Thus, for Paul, Jesus represented the kingdom, embodied God's grace. As Paul's vision spread, he saw Jesus' transition from death to life as the climax of salvation history. Jesus the Christ was a new Adam, a new beginning for the human race. All who clung to him, who used him to interpret their lives, became members of his "body." Christ and the Church formed a living entity.

Paul's interpretation of Jesus was the key to early Christianity developing into a universal religion. By dropping the requirements of the Jewish Law and extending membership to all who would base their lives on Jesus, the early Church broke with Judaism irreparably. The Torah had been the cornerstone of covenantal life. Most Jews, understandably, were not willing to throw the Torah over or enter a new covenant. Some who had seen Jesus heal or heard him preach joined his cause; the apostles who began the Church after Jesus' death, for instance, were Jews who journeyed from the Torah to the Gospel. However, most Jews had not heard or seen Jesus, and for historical, psychological, political, and religious reasons they could not accept the claims about him.

The Gentiles who warmed to the Gospel lived in a Hellenistic milieu that was ripe for salvation.[9] Just as Judaism was in turmoil, with Zealots, Pharisees, Sadducees, and Essenes all urging different reactions to Roman rule, so, too, were the belief systems of the Gentiles. Through the mystery religions, Gnosticism, and philosophy, a large number of Gentiles were pursuing salvation avidly. Jesus as a savior figure fit many of their needs. In a short while, Christianity established itself as a new wisdom or gnosis (secret knowledge), too. It offered fulfillment in this life, immortality in a world to come.

A New World View

As a result of the Gospel and Paul's theology, within a generation of Jesus' death Jewish and Greek thought had combined into a powerful new world view.[10] From Judaism came the concepts of prophet and messiah. From Hellenism came the notions of savior and god. In the Church's hands, they all were underscored. Jesus was the successor to Moses, the giver of a new Law, Daniel's Son of man come to inaugurate the messianic age, the conqueror of death and disorder, and the Logos (Word) of eternal divinity come into time. He was alpha and omega—the beginning and the end. All past history, from the first parent Adam, had been but a preparation for his coming. All of the future would unfold his implications, climaxing in a final judgment and a fulfillment in heaven.

At first the Christians expected the future to be short. Jesus would soon return in power and glory to consummate his work. As the years went by, the beliefs shifted. Jesus had accomplished the essentials of salvation through his death and resurrection. However long it took in God's dispensation for Jesus' salvation to work itself out, there was no doubt of the final success. The faithful would just have to endure. Living in faith and hope, they were to preach the good news to all whom they could reach.

In that way—first with a sense that the time was short and then with a sense that Jesus was life's best interpretation—Christianity began its missionary career, preaching the gospel to the ends of the earth. In that, too, it differed from Judaism, which little proselytized. The next chapters in the Christian story concern the effects of moving the gospel into different cultures.[11]

JESUS' PARABLES

One of the main reasons Jesus has remained fresh for each generation of his followers is that the New Testament authors set down some of Jesus' lively teaching stories, his parables. Puzzling, enigmatic, and vivid, these parables have drawn the attention of preachers and audiences through all the Christian centuries. Today the parables have become a favorite topic of scholarly discussion. We can only hint at the main lines of this discussion, but studying one of Jesus' parables, that of the Great Supper (Matt. 22 : 1–10; Luke 14 : 16–24), will take us a few steps into what New Testament scholars are currently conjecturing about Jesus' thought-world.

As a background to our consideration of the parable of the Great Supper, let us first note the tendency of current New Testament scholars to emphasize the parables' underlying conviction of God's monotheism. Believing in their bones that God is an absolute mystery, the sole power responsible for all of creation, the authors of the parables (Jesus and the writers who set them in their New Testament form) instinctively used a paradoxical speech, through which they could hint at God's transcendence—God's overspilling of all our conceptual containers. The parables imply that God cannot be captured in any single set of images. The best way to indicate the divine nature is to juxtapose stories that flash forth now one, now another aspect of what God seems to be like.

Moreover, some of Jesus' parables opposed the assumption of some of his contemporaries that the only way righteous people could experience the rule of God would be through a dramatic, even cosmic overturning of the prevailing patterns, so that the sinners presently in charge would be thrown out. Not so, Jesus' preaching suggested. God does not need earthquakes and revolutions. The reign of God is subtler, and more powerful, than any prevailing political or religious conditions. No matter how bad the times, we can always find something of God in them.

For Jesus, God was always active, always reaching out to people in need. It required no more than common human experience to find the arena of God's actions. There was no need for aggression or technical training. "Even Jesus' way of speaking is nonaggressive and avoids setting up barriers between people. But this way of speaking has a powerful edge; the forgiveness and reconciliation imaged is demanded for everyone's life. The holiness appropriate to the rule of God belongs to all."[12]

Applied to Jesus' liking for parables, this attitude meant a calm "take it or leave it." A parable was an invitation to enter the world of Jesus' Father, to open oneself to Jesus' sense of what God was doing. It was not an oppressive command. The parable of the Great Supper suggests that one could meet Jesus and not even realize that this was the most important encounter of one's life. Jesus would not beat his hearers over the head. God would not flash forth lightning or bellow thunder. The Kingdom of God was in people's midst. To find it they had only to turn around and open themselves to Jesus' good news.

The parable itself tells of a man (or a king) who once gave a great banquet. Deciding to throw this feast, he sent his servants to announce it to those he wanted to invite. The servants told the invitees, "Come, for all is now ready." But the invitees began to make excuses. Not sensing the significance of the invitation, they told the servants such lame tales as "I have bought a field and I must go take a look at it," or "I have bought five yoke of oxen, and I must go examine them," or "I have just gotten married, so I cannot come." (However, Deut. 20 : 5–7 and 24 : 5 suggest that these may traditionally have been considered legitimate excuses.) In each case, they asked to be excused.

The man hosting the banquet got very angry. In Matthew's version, the invitees had treated the man's servants shamefully, even killing them, so the man (who was a king) sent his troops to destroy the murderers and burn their city. In Luke's milder account, the host simply told his servants to go out into the streets and lanes of the city and bring in the most wretched people they could find: the poor, the maimed, the blind, and the lame. When the servants came back to report that they had done this and that there still was room in the banquet hall, the host told them to go out again, this time into the highways and hedges, and make people come in, until the banquet hall was completely full. Those whom he had first invited had shown themselves unworthy of the banquet, but one way or another he would have his house filled.

For Matthew, the story is an occasion to indulge in a bit of allegory. By playing up the theme of the king's punishment of the invitees' bad treatment of the servants, he can allude to the Roman destruction of Jerusalem in 70 C.E., which perhaps he saw as a retribution for the slaying of Jesus. Luke, on the other hand, presents a simpler plot-line, and he is more interested in the redoubling of the host's invitation than in any rejection and punishment. Where Matthew makes an irreparable break between the king and the original guests, Luke passes over this relation, allowing the possibility that it might mend. Accenting the good fortune of the new invitees, he stresses that they are an unlikely group, outcasts and strangers. For Luke, the drama lies in the host's seizing the occasion of the original invitees' refusal or

another story

inability to come and making it a chance to be generous to another class of people. Thus, when most Jews rejected Jesus' message, God offered the Gospel to the Gentiles.

Although they tend to stress the literary structure of the evangelists' different accounts, today's scholars do not neglect the historical or theological dimensions of the parables. For example, they point out that Jewish lore contemporary with Jesus had a story that praised a tax-collector for doing one good deed during his (otherwise hateful) life: inviting some poor people to a banquet when the original guests did not come. Similarly, research into the social customs of Jesus' day has revealed a tendency in sophisticated Jewish circles to invite people twice. Important people, at least, did not take seriously a single invitation but had to have their egos stroked a second time. One of the rabbis used a person dressed and ready to go by the time of a second invitation as an example of wisdom, while a person not ready to go by the time of a second invitation, and so excluded from the good time, became an example of foolishness.

Moreover, by choosing the figure of a banquet, both Jesus and the Gospel writers inevitably conjured up the messianic time. In the messianic time, when Israel's deliverer had come, the people would eat and drink joyously, banqueting together. It may be stretching the original intent of the parable to make it a full symbol of the messianic or heavenly time, as later Christian preachers often have, but the figure itself was bound to suggest inclusion in the occasion of celebrating God's victory or exclusion from it. If one stresses the confrontational side of the invitation and rejection, as Matthew does, one develops a rather harsh, judgmental view of Jesus' messiahship and the invitation to join the Christian community. The understated version of Luke simply hints at what a human situation—a generous host's disappointment that the people he first invited could not come—can reveal about God's ingenuity and goodness. Undaunted, the host finds new outlets for his largess.

Behind Matthew's harsher version probably lie the bitter experiences of the early Christian missionaries, who were confused and hurt that their proclamation of Jesus' good news brought them persecution rather than gratitude.

However, this harsh attitude seems to contradict Jesus' own tendencies, which were to keep contact with people, avoid unnecessary ruptures, and find creative alternatives to strategies that had run into dead ends. Behind Jesus' own mission there seems to have lain a rather constant goodwill. If the members of the establishment were not interested in his message, there were always the crowds on society's margins. If the Jews proved intractable, there were always the Samaritans and the Gentiles. Jesus may not have worked all this out into an explicit theology of his mission, but it seems latent in his regular style. For all that he seems to have been disappointed by the stupidity and hardness of heart he encountered, he kept speaking provocatively of the Kingdom of God, always hoping he would come upon a few people whom God's spirit had prepared to accept his words.

In Luke's version of the parable, the social implications of the Gospel also are important. It is no accident that the outcasts come into the banquet hall. Luke sees the good news of the Kingdom as especially intended for those people who have little other good news in their lives: the poor, the sick, the despised. At the least, his parable implies, those who have received much from God should share it generously with people less fortunate. The host who insists that his banquet not go to waste should be a role model for Christians.

In recent years, excavations at Nag-Hammadi in Egypt have made available to New Testament scholars gnostic versions of the Gospel (see below) that they can compare with the canonical four. The Gospel of Thomas, for example, has a version of the parable of the Great Supper that is quite spare, more like Luke's than Matthew's account. Interestingly, however, the Gospel of Thomas makes several of the original invitees excuse themselves for monetary reasons. Thus one man has some merchants coming the evening of the banquet to pay him money they owe, while another man has bought some property and must go to collect the rent. When the host hears these excuses, he tells his servants to go into the streets and bring back whomever they find. The conclusion of the story is ominous: "The buyers and the merchants shall not come into the places of my Father." Not only does this conclusion make Jesus pass stern judgment on those who reject the invitation, it also castigates business (and by implication all this-worldly affairs) as incompatible with the Kingdom of Heaven.

Overall, the parables remain an absorbing topic for study. Because they stand so close to Jesus' own way of thinking and preaching, they offer some of the best keys to Jesus' intriguing personality. But the parables seldom admit of a clear-cut interpretation, any more than Jesus' other teachings or actions do. They contain so many different levels, possible allusions, and strata of metaphors that one is finally forced to leave off analyzing them and let the parables make a more synthetic, holistic impact. When one does this, it seems clear that Jesus, like many Eastern gurus, was a man filled with lively speech, because he was a man filled with God's presence, pregnant with God's love. The Word of God had burned so deeply into his soul that all his human words sizzled and warmed.

The Apostolic Age

The Gospel writers—Mark, Matthew, Luke, and John—all interpreted the life of Jesus.[13] Even in the most journalistic portions of the New Testament, they have cast Jesus' sayings and doings in terms of their own theologies. Matthew, for instance, works largely with Jewish notions, trying to show that Jesus is the successor to Moses, the Gospel is the successor to the Torah, and so on. The other Gospels, as well as Hebrews and Revelation, are similarly theological. John arranges Jesus' public life around a series of signs giving him a sacramental glow and making him a thaumaturgist (wonder worker). The second half of John's Gospel concentrates on Jesus' "glory": his intimacy with the heavenly Father and his victorious death and resurrection. Hebrews tries to show that Jesus fulfilled Jewish types of sacrifice, while Revelation is a Christian apocalypse (disclosure) designed to shore up faith against Roman persecution.

By the end of the first century, then, the Church had a variety of theologies. The majority were extensions of Jewish religion in the light of Jesus as the Messiah. The "apostolic age" is the period of elaboration of what Jesus meant and how the Church was to organize itself. It embraces roughly the first three centuries, and a central concern was authority. For the early Church, an *apostolos* was a person to whom God delegated Church authority. It depended on the Jewish notion of *saliah*—a Hebrew legal term that meant "the authoritative representation of an individual or group in juridical or legal matters."[14]

During Jesus' ministry, his twelve intimates were the apostles par excellence, since they had received their commission from Jesus himself. Clearly the Twelve formed a collegial group with Peter as their head,[15] and the Church accepted their authority. However, balancing this apostolic, "official" authority was a looser, charismatic leadership expressed through prophecy, teaching, speaking in tongues, and so on.

The earliest Church preaching was intended to show that Jesus fulfilled the promises of Jewish scripture. In their teaching, the apostles relied on oral tradition about Jesus' person and words. The first great problem in the apostolic age, as we saw, was the Pauline (pertaining to Paul) problem of opening the Church to the Gentiles.

During the second century the leadership of the Church passed from those who had seen Jesus themselves to those who had received the gospel from eyewitnesses but had not themselves known the Lord. The "Fathers" who led the second-century Church are therefore apostolic in the sense that they had direct contact with the Twelve. One of the apostolic fathers was Clement of Rome, whom tradition calls the successor to Peter as leader of the Christian community in Rome. Clement wrote an epistle in the style of Paul that called for Church unity. Hermas wrote a pastoral piece that called for tight moral discipline. Ignatius of Antioch wrote several letters about keeping faith in the face of martyrdom. These three apostolic writers and other writers from the early second century[16] reveal something of the young Church's internal and external problems. Internally, keeping discipline was obviously a major difficulty. As Christ's return was delayed, human weaknesses and individualism asserted themselves. Externally, from the time of Nero (54–68), the Church was ever liable to persecution by the Roman authorities.

A celebrated non-Christian source describing the situation early in the second century is a letter written by Pliny the Younger, governor of Bithynia on the Black Sea, to the emperor Trajan about 112. Romans had executed some Christians (their faith seemed incompatible with the pledge of loyalty to Caesar that Rome required), and Pliny described the Christians' religious activities in order to give the emperor the information necessary to ascertain what sort of a threat they really were. According to the letter, the Christians would gather before dawn one day a week, sing hymns to a certain "Chrestus" whom they treated as a god, and take an oath to abstain from crime. Then they would end their meeting with a common meal. Trajan answered that if other Christians would recant and "worship our gods," Pliny might pardon them. Clearly the Roman authorities of the time worried about secret societies that might sow seeds of revolution. Since the Romans looked on religion as the bond of their realm, they were especially sensitive to groups who did not seem to worship the traditional Roman deities.

Christians expanded throughout the Roman Empire during the second and third centuries. By 300 they probably constituted the majority population in Asia Minor and Carthage, and they were at least a noticeable fraction of the population along the northern shore of the Mediterranean. Their major political problem, gaining sufferance from the Roman authorities, was not solved until Constantine came to power early in the fourth century.

Gnosticism

More potentially destructive than Rome were the Gnostic heresies. Their teachings varied considerably, but their common element was heterodox Judaism under the influence of Hellenistic and Iranian thought. In essence most Gnosticism involved a dualistic mythology. Matter, the negative principle, came from a Demiurge—a subordinate divinity whom the Father God begot as Wisdom but who fell from grace. Divinity itself was a *pleroma* (fullness) of times and levels. Gnosticism offered a revelation to certain "elect" persons: If they would hate this lower world of material creation (which was under the fallen Demiurge) and believe in a higher spiritual and divine realm, they might return to glory with God.

To explain their revelation, the Gnostics taught that each of the elect had a hidden spark from God's eternal world. The sparks fell into matter because of a heavenly war between darkness and light (or, in other versions, because of an accident during the production of the divine emanations). The jealous, inferior god who clumsily fashioned the material realm, which is subject to time and fate, was born in the same accidental process. He was the author of carnal humanity, in which the divine spark was a prisoner. Higher beings would one day dissolve this fallen world, but in the meantime they call to our hidden sparks by means of saviours, revelations, and rites of baptism.[17]

Gnosticism blended the Hellenistic notion of divine emanation, mystery religion notions about salvation through sacramental rites, and Jewish notions of sin and redemption. It stressed the division between this world and heaven, the evil of matter and the flesh, and the need for asceticism (celibacy and bodily discipline) to gain freedom from matter. Valentinus is the most celebrated Gnostic teacher, but we know his system largely through the apostolic father Irenaeus, whose influential *Against Heresies* attacked it harshly.

Other threats to Christianity during the early period included the prophecies of Marcion, Montanus, and Mani.[18] Marcion was a Christian excommunicate who maintained that the Christian Gospel is wholly a matter of love rather than a matter of law. On that account, he completely rejected the Old Testament (Jewish scripture), finding the God of Genesis incompatible with the God of Jesus. Montanus led a heretical apocalyptic movement based on the primacy of the Holy Spirit. His followers expected the outpouring of the Holy Spirit on the Church. In its own prophets, Montanism saw the beginnings of the bestowal of the Spirit. Montanism developed an impressive asceticism, and it captured the estimable African thinker Tertullian, who found it more spiritual than Christianity under the discipline of Rome.

Mani lived from about 215 to 275 in Persia and India (to which he fled from Zoroastrian persecution). His system supposed a primeval conflict between light and darkness, and it, too, stressed asceticism. The object of Manichaeanism was to release the particles of light that Satan had stolen and placed in the human brain. Buddha, the Israelite prophets, Jesus, and Mani himself were the messengers whom God had sent to teach human beings the way to salvation. Manichaeanism spread to Egypt, Africa, and even Rome. During the early years of his adult life, the great Christian thinker Augustine was a Manichaean.

The apostolic period, then, was a time of missionary expansion, the development of Christian doctrine (largely through opposition to Gnostic rivals), and persecution. The Roman emperors Decius (249–251) and Diocletian (284–305) made enough martyrs to make professing Christian faith a serious matter. Christians had to meet secretly in catacombs (caves) or private homes, and their organization had to be informal. Their leaders (bishops and elders) were indistinguishable from ordinary people, and their teaching had a *disciplina arcani*—a strict code of secrecy. Those who died giving testimony to their faith (martyrs, etymologically meaning "witnesses") were great heroes, whom heaven would greet with open arms. One of the greatest early controversies, in fact, concerned the status of those who had recanted their faith to avoid martyrdom and then, in a period of calm, asked readmission to the Christian community. Donatus led a party of rigorists who insisted that traitors had no place in the Church and that any sacraments (holy rites) that they administered would be invalid. Augustine successfully opposed Donatus, arguing for greater clemency and for Christ's decisive role in the inner administration of the sacraments.

Only a thin line separates the apostolic fathers from the conciliar fathers and the great theologians of the "patristic" age (age of the Fathers), for the three centuries after the deaths of the Twelve were characterized by a continuity of theological themes. First, there was the task of defending Church discipline and morality against both laxness and rigorism. Second, Church leaders had to walk a middle way between inspiration through charismata and institutional authority. Against Gnostics, the Church had to affirm the goodness of material creation. Against those who denied Jesus' humanity (the Docetists), it had to maintain that he was fully human and had really suffered and died. The Christian Church had little power in the secular world until the conversion of Constantine (312), so even when it was not suffering active persecution, it was not very influential. Church leaders continued to reflect on the relation between Jesus and Judaism, as well as on conceptions of Jesus and God that would make most sense to educated Hellenists.

The apostolic Church developed a rule by local bishops. They became the primary teachers of doctrine, the primary defenders of orthodox (straight) belief. The bishops led the common worship, settled community disputes, and, to the extent that their talents allowed, fought heresies through sermons and writings. They were the main line of Fathers around whom the early Church arranged itself. The great heroes, as we mentioned, were the martyrs, and the life of the community took its liturgical pattern from the Eucharist (communal meal) and baptism (rite of entry into the Church). Forgiving sins raised questions of moral theology, for after baptism all were supposed to keep their faith pure, but gradually the Church allowed sinners to return to the community after they did penance. In the first three centuries, then, the Church established elements of the character that it has borne ever since.

The Conciliar Age

(meetings – establ. discipline + official doctrine dogmas.)

During the fourth and fifth centuries, a number of meetings (councils) of Church leaders were held that formally established the discipline and official doctrine (dogma) that any group in union with the apostolic Church had to adopt.[19] From those meetings came the name for the next period of Christian history. Above all, the meetings dealt with the central issues of the Christian creed, hammering out the dogmas about God, Jesus, salvation, and the like that became the backbone of Christian theology. Various controversies made Church leaders realize that it was imperative to determine which apostolic sources were genuine expressions of faith and which were not. That imperative resulted in the establishment of a Christian scriptural canon.

canon ✗

Three main factors determined the final canon: whether the writing in question came from an apostle or a close associate of an apostle, whether it was accepted by the Church at large, and whether its contents were edifying for faith.[20] As early as 170, leaders in Rome had determined a canon of authoritative books in response to the canon drawn up by the heretic Marcion. Yet for many decades no list was agreed upon by the entire Church because local traditions varied.

For instance, the East long hesitated to accept Revelation, while the West was chary about Hebrews. In the early decades of the fourth century, Bishop Eusebius of Caesarea (perhaps the first significant Church historian) divided candidate books into three categories: acknowledged, disputed, and spurious. The acknowledged and the disputed books constitute the twenty-seven books of today's New Testament. In 367 Athanasius of Alexandria published a "Festal Letter" that listed these twenty-seven books, which earned the approval of Fathers such as Jerome and Augustine and the endorsements of synods (councils) at Hippo (393) and Carthage (397 and 419).

The first great dogmatic council occurred at Nicaea in Bithynia (south of the Black Sea) in 325. It produced the Nicene Creed (statement of belief) that was especially important for clarifying Jesus' divine status as Logos or Son. Prior to Nicaea, most churches had been content to repeat what scripture (Jewish and Christian both) said about God and Jesus. However, Church theologians did not know how to respond to questions that scripture did not address. One such question came from Arius, a priest of Antioch, who proposed that Jesus, as the Logos of God (the divine Son), is subordinate to the Father. In short, Arius' proposition was that if one drew a line between created beings and the uncreated divine substance, the Logos would fall on the side of created beings, because "there was a then when he was not." Arius' principal opponent was Athanasius.

Arius represented the Syrian theological tradition that centered at Antioch, while Athanasius represented the theologians of Alexandria, who descended from Clement of Alexandria (ca. 150–215), one of the first Christian theologians to cast faith as a philosophy that might persuade educated Hellenists, and Origen (ca. 185–254), the first great Christian speculator. Working with Platonic philosophy, Origen wrote immensely influential commentaries on scripture and expositions of Christian doctrine.

Athanasius, drawing on the Alexandrian tradition, assaulted Arius' argument. Speaking for what he held to be orthodoxy, he said that the Logos was of the same sub-

Nicaea agreed v athanasius

107

stance as the Father, possessing the single divine nature. Nicaea agreed with Athanasius, making his position dogma. There were many political machinations, as different factions chose different theological sides, and Arianism thrived among Germanic tribes well into the sixth century. However, the Nicene Creed, which codified Athanasius' position, came into common use, with the result that the divinity of the Logos became common faith.

Trinitarian Doctrine

Athanasius also perceived that the canonical literature gave the Holy Spirit divinity equal to that of the Father and the Son. Therefore, he extended the meaning of his word *homoousion* (of one stuff) to include the Holy Spirit and so set the lines of what would become, at the Council of Constantinople in 381, the doctrine of the Spirit's divinity. That completed the doctrine of the Trinity: one God who is three equal "persons," each of whom fully possesses the single divine nature.

Augustine, bishop of Hippo in Africa, expressed this doctrine in terms of a psychological analogy that shaped Western Christian speculation. He proposed that as memory, understanding, and love are all mind, so (but without human imperfections) are Father, Son, and Holy Spirit all divinity. The Father is as an inexhaustible memory (from which all creation comes), the Logos is as the Father's self-awareness, and the Spirit is as their boundless love.

In the Trinitarian controversies (and perhaps even more in the subsequent Christological controversies [controversies about Jesus Christ]), the terminology that eventually became fixed was still quite fluid.[21] Bernard Lonergan has argued that the Church's decision to respond to Arius and so coin new language for new problems (problems not resolved by scripture) was a decisive advance in its self-understanding.[22] It would have been obscurantism, or anti-intellectualism, to refuse to grapple with questions as serious and legitimate as Arius'. (Indeed, it would have been the sort of "interdict" on the

mind's drive to understand for which Eric Voegelin has severely criticized Karl Marx.)[23] By responding to Arius' challenge, the Church affirmed its ability to determine the meaning of scripture and to develop doctrine as new situations required.

Politics

The conciliar definitions gave Christian faith considerably more precision and at least tacitly encouraged theologians to study and speculate further on the doctrinal tracts that they had laid out. The conciliar age was also fraught with the intrusions of secular leaders, for after Constantine and his successors made Christianity the favored imperial religion, the emperors assumed that they had the right, even the pious duty, to intervene in Church affairs. Thus, the tension between Church and State, as we now call it, started its long and tangled history in the conciliar age. Whether this led to the Caesaropapism (domination of the Church by the emperor) that afflicted the Eastern portions of Christianity before the schism of 1054 is a matter for learned historians to decide. We need only point out here that, because of Christianity's official status, the councils became a matter of imperial interest.

In fact, the councils were the spearhead of the advances that the Church and state made into one another's affairs.[24] No longer were Christians under the constant threat of persecution and martyrdom. They could enter worldly occupations, including government service—a situation that both weakened their faith and made it more realistic. As a result, the original feeling of urgency gave way to the realization that the Lord's return might be far down the road. Thus, Christianity had to become a faith that was viable in the world.

Monasticism

Such worldliness stimulated new religious movements within the Church that opposed the laxness or "accommodation" that worldly success easily begot. The most important reforms generated interest in monasticism and virginity (which overlapped, insofar as monks took vows of celibacy). Both males and females found a monastic life of dedication to prayer and charitable works a way of maintaining their martyrlike intensity of faith. Theirs was a "white" martyrdom, not the red one of blood, and many found that it led them to the desert for solitude and asceticism. The great hero of the day, in fact, was the desert father Antony, who made a great impression on Athanasius. Thomas Merton has gathered a good selection of the desert fathers' sayings.[25] In it one sees both a bare faith and considerable shrewdness about what happens to people when they set out to meet God.

Partly because of the dangers of desert solitude, many monks soon formed communities, and before long these communities admitted women (nuns). In the East, communal (cenobitic) monasticism took form under the guidance of Basil, bishop of Caesarea. His rule (which owed much to Pachomius, the founder of communal monasticism) became the common law. In the West the rule of Benedict predominated. So the dedication that had previously been an informal option (largely in terms of virginity or widowhood) took institutional form. Thenceforth monasteries were powerhouses of Christian faith that laity and clerics alike viewed as centers of holiness. That, too, was an innovation added to New Testament religion, which had no monastic life. The Church's decision that monastic life was truly in keeping with New Testament religion was analogous to the decision to coin new doctrinal concepts. Quite consistently, the Protestant Reformers of the sixteenth century opposed the development of monasticism (as being unbiblical), just as they opposed the development of the Catholic notion of authority.

Christology

The councils not only set the pattern of Trinitarian faith that dominated the following centuries but also dealt with a host of problems that arose when people started to think about Jesus as the divine Word. Nestorius, from Antioch, and Cyril, from Alexandria, squared off in christological controversy, and again Alexandria won. Nestorius stressed the unity of the Christian God, though he affirmed Christ's two natures (human and divine). Cyril thought that Nestorius' affirmation was not strong enough to safeguard the singleness of Jesus Christ the God-man, so he pressed for a "hypostatic" (personal) union of the two natures. Councils of Ephesus (431) and Chalcedon (451) affirmed Cyril's doctrine of one "person" and two "natures." Later christological development affirmed that Jesus had a rational soul, two wills, and two sets of operations. This orthodox Christology resulted from trying to systematize the scriptural teaching about God and Jesus. Orthodoxy cast many groups in the shade, branding their positions as heretical, but it also developed Christ's meaning considerably.

Orthodoxy

Orthodoxy has two principal meanings. It may refer to the Eastern churches that separated from Rome in 1054 or to the "right belief" established by scripture, tradition, and the councils. In this section we address the first concept, describing the growth of Eastern Christianity after the conciliar age (most of the great councils took place in the East). The term *Orthodox* was adopted for two reasons: The Orthodox church thought of itself as keeping the traditional faith, especially regarding the episcopal (pertaining to bishops) focus of Church authority; *orthodoxy* has also meant, especially in the East, "right praise." As "right praise" the term links the Orthodox conception of faith to the glorious Orthodox liturgy (which primarily is a praise of God).

Western theologians, many of whom were monks dedicated to a rich communal worship, coined the expression "Lex orandi, lex credendi"—the law of prayer is the law of faith. Similarly, Eastern theologians felt that the Church expresses itself most fully in the liturgy. This communal worship *(liturgy* means "the work of the people") had developed a sacramental system in which baptism and the Eucharist ("the Lord's Supper") were especially important in the apostolic age. In the early medieval period, when Orthodoxy took form, the liturgy flowered. The result was a calendar of holy days, a full ritual that involved music, art, incense, iconography, and more. Thus, communal worship became the dramatic center of Eastern Church life.

As we have noted, the councils of the fourth and fifth centuries occasioned theological division as well as theological clarification. In the fifth century, during the christological controversies, more deviant versions of faith arose—Nestorian, Monophysite (one nature in Christ), and others—because as the councils established accepted beliefs, they excluded other options. Often the deviant minority party continued a church life, with the result that there were large numbers of heterodox Christians in the East. As Arianism remained robust even after its rejection by the Council of Nicaea, so the christologically heterodox groups did not simply recant or go back into the woodwork. Thus, the major split between East and West that occurred in 1054 was not without Eastern forerunners.[26]

From the ninth to the fifteenth centuries, a complicated, still quite obscure process of alienation between Byzantine (Eastern) Christianity and Roman Christianity resulted in their separation. Each group finally rejected the other, charging it with having broken the traditional faith. Some of the factors in the separation were the fall of the eastern Roman Empire, the failure of the Crusades, the growing antagonism of Islam, the growth of the papacy, the stirrings of Protestant reactions against the papacy, and the rivalry between Russia and western Europe.[27] These factors take us to the beginning of modernity in Eastern Christendom, explaining why East and West have remained divided to the present.

Religious Issues

Thus, the break between Eastern and Western Christianity owed a great deal to political and cultural conflicts. Although separating these conflicts from theological differences is virtually impossible, we can delineate some of the more clearly religious issues. For instance, the patriarch Photius, who presided at Constantinople from 858 to 886, drew up a list of what Byzantines considered to be Latin (Western) errors in faith. This list reveals how the two portions of Christendom had developed different understandings of Orthodoxy. In this list Photius cited irregularities in the observance of Lent (the period of penance before Easter), compulsory celibacy for the clergy, denying priests the power to administer confirmation (the Christian sacrament of adulthood), and false teaching about the Holy Spirit. Clearly, the list concentrates on points of Church discipline and administration. They have serious theological implications (for

Figure 10   Christ in Majesty, fresco from the Church of Santa Maria de Mur, northeast Spain, twelfth century. Courtesy Museum of Fine Arts, Boston, Marie Antoinette Evans Fund.

instance, on the structure of the Church and its authority), but they do not affect the cardinal doctrines of the Christian faith: Trinity, grace, and incarnation, except for Photius' last point on false teaching about the Holy Spirit.

The most acute point of theological difference between the East and the West was what came to be known as the *Filioque*. According to the Nicene Creed, within the life of the Trinity the Holy Spirit proceeds from the Father. The Western Council of Toledo (589) made an addition to the Nicene Creed: The Holy Spirit proceeds not just from the Father but also from the Son (*Filioque* means "And from the Son"). Each tradition became attached to its Trinitarian formula, and so the *Filioque* became a sharp bone of contention. The East claimed that it was heretical; the West claimed it merely articulated a tacit understanding of traditional faith that Nicaea had assumed. The practical significance of the difference is not clear, but it probably shows the East's tendency to appreciate the Father's primal mystery—the Father's status as a fathomless source from which *everything* issues.

In response to Photius, Latin theologians composed their own list. In their view the Eastern discipline that allowed clerics to marry, that baptized by immersion, that celebrated the Eucharist with leavened bread, and that had different rules for fasting deviated from tradition. The debate even descended to such details as whether bishops should wear rings, whether clergy should wear beards, and whether instrumental music was valid at the liturgy. However, the main theological issue continued to be the *Filioque*, while the main political issue emerged as the difference in the churches' understanding of authority. The Eastern church's tradition was a loose federation of bishops, all of whom were considered successors of the apostles. The Eastern church also stressed the rights of individual churches and ethnic groups. The Western tradition was a "monarchical" leadership by the bishop of Rome. As successor to Peter, he claimed primacy over the other churches.

When the Byzantine Empire was about to fall to the Turks, the Eastern and Western factions met for the last time at the Council of Florence (1439). That was long after the mutual anathemas of 1054 (described below), but the East hoped to secure both Church unification and Western help against Islam. On the agenda were only four points (the other disagreements having fallen away as trivial). They were the prerogatives of the bishop of Rome, the *Filioque* clause, the doctrine of purgatory (the teaching that there is an intermediate state between heaven and hell, which the Orthodox condemned as unbiblical), and whether to use leavened or unleavened bread in the Eucharist. In retrospect, theologians have judged the last two items as relatively inconsequential. The first two were interrelated, because the Council of Florence came to focus on the question of whether the pope had the right to alter an ecumenical creed (that is, add *Filioque* to the Nicene Creed). Due to their political problems (the menace of the Turks), the Greeks (Easterners) accepted the *Filioque* and agreed to certain papal prerogatives. The union was confined to paper, though, because back at home Orthodox synods refused to ratify the agreements signed by their delegates.

Separation

The pivotal moment in the East-West division was the mutual excommunications of 1054, which were due more to politics (or to snappish personalities) than to theology. Pope Leo IX had sent a Western delegation to Constantinople headed by one Cardinal Humbert. The Normans were menacing Leo and also the Emperor Constantine Monomachus, so a major goal was to unite the churches to oppose a common foe. Humbert seems to have been a narrow, contentious type, as was his Eastern counterpart, the patriarch Michael Cerularius. When Pope Leo died in 1054, Cerularius held that Humbert's credentials were void. Humbert responded by laying on the altar of St. Sophia in Constantinople a letter that excommunicated the patriarch and all his associates.

The patriarch then assembled his own council, which excommunicated Humbert in return. The emperor dispatched the cardinal back to Rome with presents, hoping that the next pope would appoint a new legate who could heal the breach. But the Normans prevented the popes from resuming negotiations, so the mutual excommunications stood until after the Second Vatican Council in the early 1960s.

Basically, the division between the Eastern and Western branches of the Church was a tragic accident. (Historians now say much the same of the sixteenth-century Reformation split in Europe.) Political circumstances, differences in traditional ways of celebrating faith, and, above all, differences in temperament and cultural backgrounds were more decisive than hard theological differences. What Orthodox and Catholics (and Protestants and Catholics) held in common was far more significant than what they held apart. It took centuries for Christians to realize that millions of people (for example, Asians) knew nothing about their God, let alone their Christ—centuries for them to realize their own solidarity and so begin an "ecumenical (worldwide) movement" for Church unification. The sticking point through those centuries was a main factor in the East-West division—papal authority. Today there are creative approaches by which Protestant and Orthodox churches might acknowledge certain papal powers, but full accord remains quite distant.

Thus, the Orthodox church represents an understanding of Christianity somewhat different than that of Western Christianity.[28] It numbers perhaps 70 million persons, depending on the estimates used for Russia, and within the family of Christian churches it stresses the conciliar tradition, the federation of local churches in geographical families, and a lofty theology of the Trinity, Christology, and grace. As we noted, the liturgy is its center, and it has a rich sacramental life.[29]

At the Orthodox liturgy, one feels a Christian "pneumaticism": The Holy Spirit is dramatically present to effect the sacraments. In the invocation made over the eucharistic gifts (the *epiclesis*), Orthodoxy stresses the Holy Spirit's role in transforming the bread and wine into Christ's substance. In its baptism and confession of sins, Orthodoxy's accent is sharing God's life—beginning divine life in baptism or repairing it in penance. Overall, Orthodoxy places the mystery of the Christian God to the fore. For the East, God is less a lawgiver or a judge than a spiritual power operating through creation. Creation ought to respond to God's power and beauty, so the Divine Liturgy becomes a song of praise, a hymn to the goodness and love that pour forth from the Father of Lights. Orthodoxy especially venerates Mary, the Mother of God, for her share in the "economy" of salvation—her share in the design of grace that raises humans to participate in the divine immortality. Bernhard Schultze offers a full sketch of Orthodox doctrines and a full listing of its different family members.[30] He shows that, through many political troubles, Orthodoxy has kept faith with Jesus and the Christian beginnings.

ORTHODOX SPIRITUAL WISDOM

Both of the major branches of Eastern Orthodoxy, the Greek and the Russian, have fostered a strong monastic life, and from this strong monastic life has come a steady stream of holy persons wise in the ways of the religious spirit. For a fascinating glimpse of such holy persons, one need only pick up *In Search of True Wisdom: Visits to Eastern Spiritual Fathers*,[31] a recent work that beautifully conveys the Eastern Orthodox sense of prayer and asceticism.

This sense of prayer is a major focus in the visit with a Russian recluse of Usui Valamo, a monastery in Finland to which some Russian expatriates retired after the Soviet rise to power. The visit took place in 1954, and it transmits the spiritual advice of Father Michael, a noted holy man of Valamo. Sergius Bolshakoff, the interviewer, was himself an expatriate Russian, who had decided to dedicate his life to the reunion of the Eastern and Western churches, by concentrating on the common monastic life that still kept the two churches quite close in their lives of prayer.

Bolshakoff was sitting with Father Michael at the end of the day in the holy man's little cell. Twilight filled the room, and a little oil lamp flickered in the corner before the holy icons. All was quiet and peaceful. Bolshakoff asked Father Michael to tell him about the tears of grace, one of the signs of advanced prayer. Father Michael replied that the tears of grace express a perfect prayer and the forgiveness of sins, referring to the authority of St. Isaac the Syrian, who had written on this subject. Opening a tome of St. Isaac's writings, he had Bolshakoff read certain passages he had marked off. The passages tell much about the Orthodox tradition of mysticism.

St. Isaac said that when a person is starting to leave obscure prayer, in which things are still confused, the person's heart will begin to burn like fire, and this will grow stronger day by day. No longer will worldly things hold any attraction, not even food or drink. Far more delicious will be the sweet, new, firey thoughts in the person's soul. Then suddenly tears will begin to flow. They will run like a stream while the person reads, prays, eats, drinks, or works. Such tears signal a crucial period, during which a person can make great spiritual advances. Prior to them, the person has not climbed the mountain of God. When they come, the person has arrived, but he must redouble his efforts, so as not to lose a great opportunity.

The tears mean that a person has begun to smell the perfume of a wonderful new air. They announce that the birth of a spiritual child is near. "Our common mother, Grace, wishes to produce in us in her own mysterious way the divine image so that we may see the light of the age to come." After the flow of tears, which must last two years or more, there comes perfect serenity of mind. In this peace of mind, one can begin to contemplate the divine mysteries. The Holy Spirit opens the heavens, and God comes to dwell in the person, to resurrect in her the fruit of the Spirit.

Father Michael admitted that he himself had wept a great deal in his life. When Bolshakoff confessed that a certain book he used to read in the British Museum always moved him deeply, because it spoke so beautifully of a boy growing up in a pious Moscow family prior to the Communists' seizure of power, the monk nodded in understanding. That is not surprising, he said. Our time of unbelief and carnal living has made piety a lovely nostalgia. We think that tears manifest pitiful weakness or something else to be despised. We relegate them to old women. Stony indifference, hardness of heart, and coolness of spirit have become our indices of virility. The truth is, however, that an absence of tenderheartedness is merely a sign of spiritual death. As a Byzantine mystic said long ago, those who attend the Holy Liturgy without tears and a tender heart eat and drink the body and blood of the Lord unworthily. We must cultivate tears and tenderness of heart, because only through them can we purify our thoughts.

The interview passed on to other topics, most of them connected with prayer. At one point, Bolshakoff asked Father Michael to explain to him a puzzling passage from the writings of St. Seraphim. In the passage St. Seraphim says that when the Holy Spirit overshadows us, we must cease to pray. Bolshakoff wasn't sure he understood why. Father Michael said that all mystics have taught as St. Seraphim does, understanding "prayer" to be something we do by our human efforts. In contrast, when the Holy Spirit overshadows us, our efforts cease and there is no "prayer." Rather there is only a sentiment or heartfelt impulse of love that reaches out toward God without words or images. But Father Michael bade Bolshakoff to continue reading, for St. Seraphim also makes it clear that there are different gifts from the divine grace. Some people have the gift of mystical, unceasing prayer. Others are moved to watch their thoughts and pray in the sense of making human efforts. Still other people have the gift to fast, or to gather alms, or to live a virginal life. The point is to find one's own gift, one's own congenial path to God, and use it.

The next passage they discussed was also from St. Seraphim, and it concerned the lightning that one of Seraphim's disciples saw streaming from the saint's eyes, so bright it made the disciple's eyes ache. Seraphim told the disciple that the disciple himself was equally shining, because of God's life in him. The disciple then saw Seraphim's face become like the middle of the sun at its noonday brightest, a blinding light radiating in every direction. This filled the disciple with an inexpressible peace of soul. St. Seraphim explained that this peace is what Jesus meant when he told his disciples, "Peace I leave with you; my peace I give to you; not as the world gives" (John 14 : 27). It proved that the disciple truly had left the world.

When Father Michael commented on this and other writings of the holy fathers about light, he interpreted them as referring to a light like that which the apostles saw emanating from Jesus when they went with him to Mount Tabor and he was transfigured before them (Matt. 17 : 2). Still, such light did not keep the apostles from denying and abandoning Jesus at the time of his arrest, and it did not keep the saints, such as Simeon the New Theologian, from returning to a worldly life for a time. So we should think of it as a temporary strengthening for those who need shoring up, rather than a permanent acquisition or something essential to the state of grace. One can be in the fullest grace and not perceive or externally radiate such light.

The conversation then passed from light to warmth, as though Father Michael and Bolshakoff were exploring all the spiritual dimensions of the inner senses. In this case, however, Father Michael emphasized the supernatural warmth that Seraphim had asked his disciple to describe. "What kind of warmth do you feel, lover of God?" Seraphim asked. The disciple replied that, despite the snow all around them, he felt warmth like that which arises in a Russian bath, when one pours water on the heated stones and steam rises in a column. But the smell was completely different, like no perfume one can find on earth. St. Seraphim smiled in agreement. The consolations of the Holy Spirit are like no perfume on earth. What will the consolations of heaven be like? And, contrary to the warmth of a Russian steam bath, the warmth the disciple was feeling melted none of the snow surrounding the saint's hut. That showed it was warmth of a completely spiritual order, like the warmth the Liturgy asks the Holy Spirit to give. For centuries, Seraphim pointed out, hermits who trekked into the deepest Russian forests did not fear the snows and the cold, because they relied on the inner warmth of the Holy Spirit. The grace of God, God's inner life, filled their hearts and heated their bones.

Again and again Father Michael and the classical authors he was explaining to Bolshakoff returned to the theme of grace, which has always been central in Orthodox theology. As Seraphim put it: "The Lord said, 'The Kingdom of God is within you.' By this Kingdom of God the Lord means the grace of the Holy Spirit. Well, this same Kingdom of God is now within us while the grace of the Holy Spirit shines and warms us, filling the air around us with various perfumes, and sweetens our organs of sensation with heavenly pleasure and our hearts with indescribable joy."

The Orthodox mystical tradition continues, alive and well, in places like Mount Athos in Greece, where monks meditate in the old ways and read the old classics. The center of their lives is something spiritual, something the eye cannot see nor the ear hear nor it enter the hearts of human beings to conceive. Like Hasidim lost in the world of Torah, the Orthodox holy men and women are lost in the world of the Gospel. For them the Gospel words are shining jewels, the Gospel scenes are blazing icons. Contemplating those icons, the Orthodox saints have enjoyed wonderful visions of the life of God that fills the holy soul, the mercy of God that courses through the world. Their meditations have made the scriptural scenes contemporary, much the way Jewish prayer has made the Exodus contemporary.

It is shocking to enter the thought-world of the Orthodox seers, and perhaps equally shocking to realize that that thought-world predominated in the West less than 500 years ago. Less than 500 years ago, even theologians studied the Bible more for its religious feeling than for its literary structure. Even theologians were more interested in feeling compunction than in knowing its definition. Similarly, the terms of reference in Father Michael's world are not the historical or literary aspects of the Bible, but the spiritual experiences and verities the monastic tradition tells him the Bible can promote. What the Holy Spirit did for the apostles, and for the later saints like Seraphim, the Holy Spirit is poised to do today. After all, Jesus, the eternal Son of God, came from God precisely to give us human beings God's life, which the Holy Spirit wants to nurture in us.

God's life, the East always has emphasized, is the perfect community of the Father, Son, and Holy Spirit. It is the Trinity not as the subject of conciliar controversies, or the subject of theologians' dry reflections, but as the spiritual atmosphere in which we can live, move, and have our being, if we will open our souls in faith. What the Eastern Liturgy has always sung, the Eastern holy persons have always stressed: the substantial love of God poured out for the salvation of human beings, humanity's potential elevation to a new, heavenly mode of life.

One will not understand traditional Christianity without an imaginative effort to grasp spiritual convictions like Father Michael's. For the generations who gave their lives to praying over the Gospel scenes, the Spirit offered a light, a warmth, a perfume surpassing anything the world had to offer. With the peace and joy of the Spirit, a person was infinitely blessed. Without the peace and joy of the Spirit, a person was greatly to be pitied.

The Medieval Period

In discussing the medieval period of Christianity, we shift focus from the East, where Orthodox faith took shape, to the European West. Evangelization (missionizing) of Europe progressed steadily from the time of the councils, most of it presuming somewhat vaguely that the bishop of Rome was preeminent among the Church's episcopal leaders. During the fifth and sixth centuries, Christian missionaries made considerable inroads among the Germanic tribes. Frequently they would convert tribal leaders from paganism or Arianism, and then the entire tribe would convert. However, Western state leaders tended to think that the Church was something for them to control. That tendency, plus problems of Church discipline, made the Western situation confusing. From the tenth century, however, there were efforts to reform the Church and increase its spiritual vitality. In the eleventh and twelfth centuries, such efforts —especially those that originated at the Abbey of Cluny in Burgundy—were fairly successful.

As well, individual Church leaders found that they could increase their freedom from local secular rulers by increasing their allegiance to the bishop of Rome. The friction between Church and State therefore shifted to the interaction between the pope and the Germanic emperor. A key issue was who should appoint local bishops. The investiture controversy, as it is called, was solved in a compromise in the Concordat of Worms (1122). Secular rulers had to recognize the independence of the local bishop by virtue of his loyalty to the pope, and the pope had to consult the emperor and appoint bishops acceptable to him.[32]

During the twelfth century the Crusades to the holy sites in Palestine riveted the Christian imagination, but they tended to increase the alienation between Eastern and Western Christendom. When the Fourth Crusade (1204) conquered Constantinople, set up a Western prince, and tried to Latinize the Eastern church, relations deteriorated to their lowest point. By 1453, after the Councils of Lyon and Florence had done little to heal the wounds of division, and after Easterners had suffered centuries of Western domination, a popular slogan circulated stating that Turks would be better rulers than Western Christians.

During the twelfth century, Europe developed strong cities, with a concomitant shift of economic and political power. This development slowly transformed the feudal system of which the Church had been an intimate part. As a result, considerable resistance to the established Church power and faith arose among some groups, such as the Waldenses, who urged a return to apostolic simplicity and poverty. Groups that owed a debt to the East, such as the French Albigensians, pushed Manichaean values in their war on the flesh and their contempt for the material world.

To meet the challenge of such reformers, the Roman church developed new orders of priests and monks, the most important of which were the Dominicans and the Franciscans. Saint Dominic (1170–1221) organized his group to preach against the heretics, and one of the devotions it added was the rosary—a string of beads for counting prayers to the Virgin Mary. The Franciscans stemmed from the charismatic *poverello* (pauper) Francis of Assisi (1181–1226), who dedicated himself to simple living. His angelic love of nature and of the infant Jesus made a deep impression on subsequent generations of Christians. Both Dominicans and Franciscans were innovations on the established (largely Benedictine) model of Western monasticism. Principally, they had more freedom than Benedictines to move out of the cloister and its settled, agricultural rhythms. They were mobile, and therefore quite effective in responding to different religious trouble spots.

Scholasticism

The thirteenth century was the high point of medieval intellectual life, and the movement known as Scholasticism reached its peak then. The Scholastics systematized the conciliar and patristic (the Fathers') theological doctrines.[33] Augustine was their great master, but where Augustine worked with neo-Platonic thought categories (developed by thinkers, such as Plotinus, who developed Plato's ideas), Thomas Aquinas (1225–1274), the greatest of the medievals, worked with Aristotelian categories. Between Augustine and Aquinas lived Anselm (1033–1109), who developed the notion that theology is "faith seeking understanding." That is, on the basis of a firm Christian commitment (rooted in scriptural, conciliar, and patristic doctrine), the theologian ought to learn as much as the divine mysteries allowed.

Anselm's definition was a writ of intellectual emancipation. Though they accepted the disciplines of tradition and the Church's teaching office, the medieval theologians seized the right to develop reason and use it to illumine the realities of faith. Consequently, teachers such as Peter Lombard and Peter Abelard prepared lists of patristic opinions on different theological topics and started to reason them through dialectically. Franciscan theologians, such as Alexander of Hales and Bonaventure, and Dominican theologians, such as Albert the Great and Thomas Aquinas, developed this dialectics, writing voluminously on philosophical and theological topics.

After a great struggle, the position of Aquinas, who most carefully related reason and faith, gained the greatest following. Just as conciliar theology had moved beyond scriptural ideas (in order to illumine scripture), so Aquinas' Scholastic theology moved beyond conciliar theology in order to illumine it through Greek philosophy. For Aquinas, philosophy was the wisdom available to reason. It was a universal basis for discussion, regardless of religious allegiance. Jews, Muslims, Christians, and pagans all had reason, and so all could philosophize. Theology, which rested on divine revelation, perfected philosophy, taking it into realms that it could not penetrate on its own. (For instance, without revelation philosophy would not know of the Trinity or the Incarnation [the Word made flesh].) Aquinas developed a powerful system of philosophical theology, but he was by no means the only impressive medieval thinker. His school, Thomism, trusted in reason, had a hopeful view of the world, thoroughly analyzed the Trinity, Christology, and grace, made a careful analysis of human virtues and vices, and viewed the world as a hierarchy of levels of being, with matter on the bottom, humans in the middle, and God at the top.[34]

Hierarchy

Aquinas' hierarchy had counterparts in the medieval Church structure. The clergy had separated themselves from the laity, and within the clerical order there were numerous ranks: monks, priests, canons, bishops, abbots, archbishops, cardinals, and more. The papacy had a considerable bureaucracy and wielded great secular power. Because the general culture had a Christian world view, heaven and hell had a vivid reality. Thus, the papal power to bar persons from Church membership and so from heaven made people fear the pope greatly. Considerable worldliness entered into the papal use of excommunication, interdict, and the like, because by medieval times the Church had forgotten the *parousia* (second coming of Christ) and was concentrating on shaping daily life.

The unsurpassed literary rendition of medieval Christianity is Dante's *Divine Comedy*. It shows the medievals' hierarchical thinking, their concern with heaven, hell, and purgatory, the venality of many medieval clergy, the infusion of pagan learning into medieval culture, and the sophistication of medieval moral theology, which catalogued virtues and vices quite precisely. Another wonderful source of insight into medieval Christianity is Chaucer's *Canterbury Tales*, which describes the daily habits of representative social types and the unconscious ways in which faith wove through medieval culture. From Dante and Chaucer one gathers that intellectuals of the late medieval period, especially nonclerical intellectuals, found many defects in the hierarchical Church, yet they basically accepted the terms of Christian faith. Their criticism focused on the discrepancy between the values that the Church professed and the all-too-human way in which it conducted itself.

The medieval cathedrals also exhibited hierarchy through their stretching from earth toward heaven. They instruct us about medieval faith, for towns built them to be a means of indoctrination. You can see this today in the Gothic masterpieces of Notre Dame de Chartres and Notre Dame de Paris. The basic architectural thrust is towards heaven, as all commentators point out, yet within the cathedrals are windows and stat-

ues that bring God down into daily life. Most cathedrals were built over centuries, and sometimes the townspeople contributed free labor, as if they wanted the cathedral to praise God doubly. Significantly, Chartres and Notre Dame de Paris both bear Mary's name. As the Virgin Mother of God, Queen of Heaven, and recourse of weak human beings, Mary was a mainstay of medieval faith.

In their battles with the Arians during the fifth and sixth centuries, Church leaders had necessarily stressed Jesus' divinity, which the Arians denied. Consequently, the Roman liturgy had come to place Christ and the action of the Mass apart from the people (as befit Christ-God). The size of the cathedrals, the inability of many people to see the ceremonies, the inability of many people to understand the Latin in which the ceremonies were conducted—all these factors prompted devotion to Mary and the infant Jesus, which brought God closer and made faith more human. Divinity was not fearsome if one could shelter behind a young mother's kindness, a baby's vulnerability. So such devotions balanced the rather stern official cult.

Around the cathedral walls, in wonderful stained glass, were biblical scenes, pictures of saints, and the like that told even the illiterate what faith meant. With the statues of the Virgin and Jesus, they gave comfort to the person who slipped into the cathedral's darkness to pray. In its majestic space, one gained a proper perspective on one's problems. At a time when hard work, early death, and many sufferings were the rule, the cathedrals were for many a great support.

Monastic life progressed during the Middle Ages, though new orders such as the Franciscans and Dominicans neither completely replaced the more stable Benedictines nor completely abandoned their regimes. The great work of the monastic community was to celebrate the divine "office": liturgical prayers throughout the day and a communal Mass. By the thirteenth century, the Eucharist involved a rather complex ceremony, with choral music, gorgeous vestments, and precious vessels for the bread and wine. Gregorian chants best represent the music, which was lively and alert, giving many psalms a joyous lilt. For solemn moments, such as the celebration of Christ's Passion, chant could express deep sorrow, prefiguring, for instance, the music of Johann Sebastian Bach.

As it developed, the Mass increasingly tended to represent Christ's sacrificial death. That did not deny the motif of a common meal, but it shifted emphasis to the consecration of the elements (bread and wine), because in the theologians' interpretations, the separation of the bread and wine stood for the sundering of Jesus' body on the cross. As a prayer (the "sequence") for the feast of Corpus Christi (attributed to Thomas Aquinas) shows, the consecrated host (bread) came to epitomize God's presence and redemptive action. The consecration was a miracle that the liturgy enacted each day. Paradoxically, the host defied the senses and nourished the soul. Because Jesus' body remained in church, the church was indeed God's house. Indeed, in the host, Jesus made himself available for reverence and prayer. Along with the cult of the Virgin (see Figure 11) and the cults of the many medieval saints, the cult of the Eucharist gave people at the bottom of the Church pyramid another source of comfort.

Thus, the average person went through a harsh medieval life in fear and trembling but with many sources of hope that such a life would lead to heaven. The worldliness of much Church life was balanced by the sacramental ceremonies that stressed the primacy of heaven. Rather clearly, the faithful knew that they stood between heaven and earth. They were citizens of two worlds, and the best medieval theology and religious art counseled them to live their dual citizenship gracefully. For instance, the cathedral and monastic schools joined piety to learning. The mystery plays and even the *danse macabre* (dance of death) brought home to the common people that death levels pope and pauper to strict equal-

Figure 11   Madonna with the Child Jesus, late fifteenth century. Nelson Gallery—Atkins Museum (Nelson Fund).

ity. In fact, *"Momento mori"* ("Remember death") was a pietistic watchword. Since death was a gateway to eternal life, *"Momento mori"* had more than negative overtones.

CHRISTIAN ART

As an interlude between the medieval and Reformation periods, let us consider the religious art of two great German painters of the early sixteenth century, Albrecht Dürer (1471–1528) and Matthias Grünewald (ca. 1470–1528). They show an interplay of the humanistic themes that grew out of the Renaissance (but had some forebears in medieval thought) and the emphases on human sinfulness that the Protestant Reformation spotlighted. We may note, however, that both poles of this interplay depend on faith in the Incarnation. Without a strong conviction that God had entered human history, even assuming a body in order to suffer human sin, painters such as Dürer and Grünewald would never have seen the world as they did.

Dürer was born in Nuremberg, the son of a goldsmith. He showed great artistic ability even as a child, so his father apprenticed him to a wood engraver. In 1494–95 he visited Italy and learned about a new technique, called "linear perspective," that made all parallel lines converge at a single vanishing point. He also absorbed the growing Italian interest in human anatomy. Still, perhaps the most important aspect of Dürer's trip to Italy was his exposure to a new conception of the artist's vocation. Whereas the traditional medieval artist had thought of himself as an artisan called to reproduce God's creation, the Italian Renaissance artists were reconceiving the artist as a human genius inspired to create his own personal world.

This new conception of the artist is evident in Dürer's *Self-Portrait*, painted in 1500. The painting suggests "a Christlike figure rather than a prosperous German painter of the turn of the century. The effect is intentional. The lofty gaze of the eyes underlines the solemn, almost religious nature of the artist's vision, while the prominent hand draws attention to his use of the pen and brush to communicate it to us."[35] The long, flowing hair is reminiscent of traditional portraits of Jesus, while the sadness of the eyes indicates the burdens the artistic seer has to carry, his heavy vision of human suffering.

In 1498 Dürer published a famous series of woodcuts illustrating scenes from the Book of Revelation. One of them, *Saint Michael Fighting the Dragon*, shows a warfare proceeding in heaven, while earth is represented by a peaceful German plain with a small town complete with a church steeple. Michael and the other angels look quite human, having long hair like Dürer's own. The demons, however, are gruesome creatures from the swamps of the unconscious, with long snouts and scaly tails. The general impression the woodcut conveys is of a cosmic battle between good and evil, the issue of which is still in doubt. The peace seeming to prevail on the human plain is misleading, since what is going on in heaven cannot fail to affect the human order. Apparently Dürer's sense of foreboding captured the popular imagination, for the fifteen woodcuts of his *Apocalypse* series sold well. The discontents of the period, which were to erupt only twenty years later in Luther's Reform, made apocalyptic visions popular.

Dürer also produced many line engravings, incising his drawings on copper plates, and in this medium he achieved amazingly rich effects. His engraving entitled *The Fall of Man*, produced in 1504, shows an idealized Adam and Eve surrounded by animals representing the sins and diseases that have resulted from the Fall. Whereas Adam and Eve retain some of the splendor of their original creation, the animals emphasize the unideal effects of human beings' having eaten the fruit of the tree of the knowledge of good and evil.

A second trip to Italy in 1505–1507 brought Dürer in contact with the Venice school, which was then producing lavishly colored paintings. Thus his *Adoration of the Trinity*, finished in 1511, shows richly robed cardinals and kings adoring the Trinity. The heavenly host of martyrs and prophets are similarly clothed, while the sublimity of the vision lifts the earthly worshipers right off their feet. In the righthand corner Dürer himself stands in full-length portrait, as though wanting to stress that this glorious scene was his personal creation.

Colorful painting apparently could not hold Dürer's permanent interest, for he went back to engraving. His greatest engravings, produced between 1513 and 1515, included the famous *Knight, Death, and the Devil*. The knight, who may have been inspired by the Dutch humanist Erasmus' *Handbook of the Christian Knight*, published in 1502, represents vigilant Christian faith. He sits astride a magnificent horse, undaunted by either death, who brandishes an hourglass, or the devil, who looks like a mythical beast, complete with long snout and high horn. Beside the knight trots his faithful dog, whom some interpreters see as the tireless devotion that must accompany vigilant faith. The picture projects the great religious demands of the time, the inner warfare that Church corruption and the new humanistic ideals could provoke.

So, on the foundation of the medieval and fourteenth-century preoccupations with death, Dürer erected a new religious vision, equally serious but more appreciative of humanity's inner powers. Human beings are not sure to prevail against such powerful foes as death and sin, but Dürer's human figures say that men and women can fight great fights of faith, aided by the saints, angels, and Jesus, who are always ready to enter the picture.

Grünewald, whose real name was Matthias Gothart Neithart, worked for a while at the court of the cardinal archbishop of Mainz. In the Peasants' War of 1525 he took the side of the peasants against the ruling classes, and his enthusiasm for Luther's ideas lost him the cardinal's favor. Unlike Dürer, Grünewald's paintings show little influence from the new humanistic developments in Italy. Thus, there is little of the Italian Renaissance interest in an idealized human body and little effort to retrieve the humanistic subjects of classical Greek art. Instead, Grünewald turned to the traditional religious themes of medieval German art, suggesting the ferment of his own times through the intensity with which he painted familiar topics.

Two of Grünewald's best-known paintings are the *Crucifixion* and the *Resurrection* from the *Isenheim Altarpiece*, both completed in 1515. The *Crucifixion* depicts the intensity of Christ's anguish through straining hands, thorns stuck in a festering body, and a huge iron spike through the feet. The overall tortured effect is very different from the idealized humanity of Christ one finds in Italian Renaissance art. The figure of Christ so predominates over the other figures in the picture that ordinary humanity is made to seem of little account. At the foot of the cross Mary Magdalene kneels in grief, while to the left John the Apostle comforts Mary the Mother of Jesus. To the right stands a shaggy John the Baptist with an open Bible. He points to Jesus and above his hand are the words, "He must increase, but I must decrease." At John's feet is a small lamb (a traditional symbol of Christ) with a shepherd's crook. The lamb is shedding blood into a liturgical chalice. The power of the death scene comes from the force of the huge cross and strong corpus. This is not a man who died easily. The dark background suggests the brooding melancholy of Good Friday, when the sun was blackened for three hours, and the barren plain takes the picture away from Jerusalem, or any other earthly site, as if to say that history's greatest moment was a unity unto itself.

By contrast, the *Resurrection* shows a Christ of dazzling light. Equally as powerful as the corpus of the *Crucifixion*, the central figure of the *Resurrection* floats in mid-air, as though he has just burst forth from the tomb. The soldiers who were guarding the tomb lie scattered like tenpins. A circular aura of light surrounds the Resurrected One, and his wounds stand out like jewels. The absence of any natural setting and the confused perspective give the painting an unearthly quality. If the *Crucifixion* seems abstracted from history, all the more so does the *Resurrection*. Yet the soldiers and the other physical details make it plain that this unearthly moment is the climax of Jesus' life. Where the great body on the cross droops with heavy defeat, the resurrected body is too light to be kept on earth.

When one realizes that the *Isenheim Altarpiece* was commissioned for the church of a hospital, the juxtaposition of the *Crucifixion* and the *Resurrection* gains further power. The sick people contemplating it could see that none of their sufferings would ever equal the pain of Christ crucified, but also that all of their sufferings would be outweighed by Christ's resurrection, to which faith gave them access.

Thus, traditional Western Christian art took Jesus' humanity deeply to heart. By the eve of the Reformation, the scenes of the Bible had come to illumine the humanity of ordinary people. That Jesus was the Son of God did not mean that he was far from the rest of humanity. It meant that his death and resurrection held the key to all human beings' lives. Thus Albrecht Altdorfer, a contemporary of Dürer and Grünewald, was unusual in painting landscapes that held no human figures. The Dutch painter Hieronymous Bosch, another contemporary of Dürer and Grünewald, was more typical in being fascinated by human concerns, even human depravities. Bosch's *Garden of Earthly Delight*, finished around 1510, crowds into its central panel hundreds of nude human figures engaged in erotic pursuits. The left panel of the tryptich portrays the Garden of Eden (with a naked Adam suspiciously interested in a naked Eve), and the right panel portrays an almost hallucinatory vision of hell, where the pursuit of pleasure has finally received its just deserts. The middle panel, which presumably represents daily human life, is largely hell in anticipation. The final frustration and futility of hell are mainly but human pathos fully revealed.

By the early sixteenth century, Western Christian culture had become so disordered that the German and Dutch artists found little to cheer. Anticipating the pessimistic theologies of the Protestant Reformers, the artists stressed the madness and sordidness that the fourteenth and fifteenth centuries had bequeathed to Europe. After the Black Death and Hundred Years War, even daily peasant life seemed twisted. Whereas the Italian humanists strove to create more optimistic images, the masters in the homeland of the Reformation brooded on folly. However, a generation later the best of them, Pieter Bruegel the Elder (1525–1569), painted human scenes with great compassion. For example, his *Peasant Wedding Feast* (1566–67) takes a kindly view of a small child enjoying some tidbits and a poor, vacant-faced bagpiper waiting to perform. "Let them enjoy a brief time of happiness," the artist seems to say. "Their daily lives are hard enough."

The Period of Reform

In the piety that dominated the period between the high Middle Ages and the sixteenth-century Protestant Reformation, the most influential work was the *Imitation of Christ* by Thomas a Kempis (1380–1471).[36] The book evidences a sober awareness of death and a general view that life is a vale of tears. Both reflect a medieval heritage. Some church historians have called the *Imitation* the second most influential book in Christian history, second only to the New Testament. It breathes a certain air of discontent—the mood of the Netherlands, where it arose. It also breathes a desire to experience religious consolation—the same desire that figured prominently in Martin Luther's spiritual biography.[37] However, the *Imitation* represents only one aspect of the period before the Reformation. Political factors certainly were a dominant influence, as was the fourteenth-century plague, which killed perhaps three-fourths of the population of Europe and Asia,[38] excited a great fear of devils and witches,[39] and made clear humanity's impotence and mortality.

During the late fourteenth and the fifteenth centuries, the papacy was in great disarray. At one point there were two claimants to the chair in Rome, one in Rome and one in Avignon. In the East the Muslims held Asia Minor and Greece, their most dramatic victory being at Constantinople in 1453. Well into the fifteenth century, southern Spain was under Muslim control, while in Italy the spirit of the Renaissance seemed stronger than conciliar attempts to reform the papacy. In addition, there were frictions among local rulers within the Italian, French, and German realms; the middle classes emerged as a result of city life and economic changes; and the pre-Lutheran attacks on Church corruption of the Lollards (followers of John Wycliffe in England) and the Hussites (followers of John Huss in Bohemia) took place.

The spark that set the Reformation

blazing was Martin Luther (1483–1546), an Augustinian monk whose study and spiritual searches had convinced him that the heart of the gospel is the Pauline justification by faith (the belief that only faith makes one right with God). Only by reviving this Pauline theme could Christianity regain its pure beginnings. As John Kent has shown, there is a link between this central Lutheran idea and the themes of religious freedom and religious certainty that preoccupied later Protestants.[40] Justification by faith meant the fall of a whole system of "works" that the Catholic church had developed by late medieval times—the Mass, the sacraments, the rosary, and so forth.

Luther was prompted by the prevailing practice of indulgences (papal remissions of purgatorial punishment due for sins), which one could obtain for various good deeds, including almsgiving. Behind this practice lay some simple economics. The popes had spent lavishly in their Renaissance enthusiasm for art and culture. Leo X, for instance, was perhaps 125,000 ducats in debt at the time that he endorsed the preaching of Johann Tetzel, Luther's first adversary,[41] which endorsed granting an indulgence for a contribution to the building of St. Peter's in Rome. To Luther the whole system—the pope's extravagance, his pretension to control a treasury of merits generated by the saints, out of which he might draw "credits" to cover sinner's debts, and his focusing this economics on the Mass—was blasphemous. On October 31, 1517, Luther nailed his Ninety-five Theses to the door of the castle church at Wittenberg, which amounted to a formal challenge to the system.

Many Germans who for political or religious reasons had grievances against Rome supported Luther. As his thought expanded, he made scripture the sole arbiter of Christian faith, declared the primacy of individual conscience, upgraded the status of the layperson, and urged the use of the vernacular rather than Latin. Luther also stressed the uniqueness of Christ's death on the cross and so taught that the Eucharist principally commemorates the Last Supper, rather than representing Christ's sacrificial death. On the basis of scripture, he judged the doctrine of purgatory unfounded and the practice of monastic life an aberration. Because Luther was a fine preacher, he made these ideas matters for discussion in the marketplace. By translating the Bible into German, he put the central basis for his reform within reach of all literate people (and just about standardized High German in the process). Finally, Luther's departure from monastic life and subsequent marriage led thousands more to leave their monasteries and convents.

The Spread of Reformation

Luther's reform in Germany quickly generated uprisings elsewhere. In Switzerland, Ulrich Zwingli (among the German speaking) and John Calvin (among the French speaking) led movements with similar themes. In England, Henry VIII and Thomas Cranmer separated their church from Rome. Generally, these reformers' writings show the influence of humanistic movements, from the Renaissance on, that had undermined the Scholastic framework.[42] As well, they show a link to the spiritualist movements that were in search of a more emotionally satisfying faith. As the Reformation worked out, Lutheranism took root in countries with a primarily agrarian economy, such as Germany and Scandinavia, while Calvinism took root in countries with a commercial economy, such as French Switzerland, France, Flanders, and the Netherlands.[43]

Calvin had the greatest influence, however, on America, since France and Flanders largely returned to Catholicism, while Dutch Calvinism mixed with both the older piety espoused by the *Imitation of Christ* and the humanism of Desiderius Erasmus. In America, the Puritans from England were inspired by Calvin's desire to honor God by consecrating all of life to his kingship. Consequently, they tried to develop a theocratic state. Calvin's notions of God's sovereignty guided Jonathan Edwards, the first major American theologian,[44] and through Edwards much of the "Great Awakening" (the revivalist movement that Edwards sparked in New England from 1740 to 1743) and subsequent American religious life bore a Calvinist imprint.

From the middle of the sixteenth to the middle of the seventeenth century, religious wars ravaged much of Europe. In France they subserved civil frictions. The Edict of Nantes (1598) preserved the status quo: Protestant areas would remain Protestant, Catholic areas (the majority) would remain Catholic. In the Netherlands the wars had the character of a rebellion against Spain. The northern Netherlands became largely Protestant, while the southern Netherlands remained under Spanish power and so Catholic. Germany was the most furious battlefield. Until the Peace of Münster (1648) there was constant carnage. The upshot in Germany was the famous dictum *"Cujus regio, ejus religio"*: Each area would follow the religion of its prince.

In England, Henry VIII found the Reformation currents useful in his struggle with the papacy to have his marriage to Catherine of Aragon annulled. Henry declared the king supreme in all matters that touched the Church in England, and he eagerly took monastic lands and income to finance his war against France. In 1571, under Henry's daughter Elizabeth I, the English bishops published their Thirty-nine Articles of Faith, which formalized their special blend of Protestantism and Catholicism.

Catholic Reform

The Catholic response to the Protestant Reformation took place at the Council of Trent (1545–1563). Trent affirmed the reliance of the Church on both scripture and tradition, the effective power of the sacraments, the need for humans to cooperate in the work of justification (that is, no justification by faith alone), and the possibility of sin after justification. It also provided for reforms in clerical education and a general

housecleaning to remove the laxness and venality that had made the Reformers' charges more than credible. Probably the most powerful single agent of the Catholic Reformation was the Society of Jesus (the Jesuits), which Pope Paul III approved in 1540. Its founder was Ignatius of Loyola, a Basque.

Ignatius' companions quickly proved themselves the best combination of learning and zealous faith. Therefore, they were assigned many of the tasks of teaching and missionizing that were central to Catholic renewal. Peter Canisius in Germany, Robert Bellarmine in Italy, and Francisco Suárez in Spain were intellectuals and educators (the first two also became prelates) who had a great deal to do with revitalizing Catholicism in their countries. Jesuit missionaries to Asia such as Francis Xavier, Matteo Ricci, and Robert di Nobili, also had great success. Xavier was a charismatic figure of the first order, able to stir crowds without even knowing their language. Ricci and di Nobili took on the customs of the people with whom they worked (Chinese and Indians) and confronted the vast task of forming native versions of Christianity. Jesuits also ministered underground to Catholics in England (several lost their lives in the effort), and they went to the New World to missionize Canada, the American Southwest, and Latin America.[45]

Further Developments

A century after Luther's Ninety-five Theses, Europe washed in waves of Reformation and Counter Reformation (the Catholic Reformation). In England, the alternation of Catholic and Protestant monarchs led to a series of repressive measures, while the Calvinism first of the Scot John Knox and then of the Puritans made great gains. The Spanish and Portuguese were exporting Catholicism through their great trading ventures, while the Dutch and English were exporting Protestantism. Consequently, Christian division became a worldwide affair.

Seventeenth-century America became a refuge for Protestants who opposed what they considered oppressive practices in their native lands and who stressed individual rights of conscience. The Church of England was strong in Virginia, Georgia, and the Carolinas. The Dutch Reformed Church dominated New York and New Jersey. Germans and Dutch flocked to Pennsylvania, while Congregationalists dominated New England. As the Reformation principle of individual conscience worked its influence, more and more groups splintered off to search out places where they could live their convictions in peace. According to Sidney Mead, the unique character of American religion has been that it formed a national culture and law on the basis of its pluralism.[46]

In its Reformation, Catholicism set new standards for its popes and clergy. It also obtained a new spirituality (largely Jesuit) that tried to adapt traditional piety to the new age of individual conscience. Commentators have nominated Loyola's *Spiritual Exercises* as the third most influential Christian book. If we substitute *Catholic* for *Christian*, they are likely correct. The work is in the form of meditations on different gospel scenes, but Ignatius designed them to bring about a "discernment of spirits" and a choice of a way of life. Some commentators point out that the mysticism of the exercises is a shift to the interior in keeping with the shift of the great Spanish mystics Teresa of Avila and John of the Cross, and that the exercises bring the medieval mystical tradition up-to-date by tailoring it to a more active life. Other commentators have shown Ignatius' anticipation of a modern "mystagogy" (exercise in the experience of God) and mystical dialectics.[47] From the *Spiritual Exercises* and other works of the Catholic Reformation, the Roman church learned how persons might work in the world with the hope of finding God in all things. That made it easier for Rome to bless new active orders of priests, brothers, and nuns.

As Robert McAfee Brown has shown,[48] the spirit of Protestantism that has come down from the sixteenth century stresses, first, the notion of reform itself—of always having to renew one's faith because of one's sure distance from God's holy will. Second, it stresses God's sovereignty, the authority of scripture, the priesthood of all believers, and the vocation of the laity to exercise their faith in the midst of the secular world. Ever since Luther and Calvin, the Bible has been the great text for both Protestant worship and Protestant theology, while, as historical sociologists such as Max Weber have suggested,[49] Protestant discipline has been a main ingredient in the rise of capitalistic culture.

The Reformation left Protestants and Catholics at odds, and the conflict has abated only in recent years. Today they seem to agree (despite such throwbacks as Northern Ireland) that the Reformers had legitimate grievances and that the Reformers' return to scripture renewed faith. On the other hand, Protestant and Catholic scholars also agree that many of the defects in modern Christianity result from its lacking the sense of a catholic tradition and common authority. The ecumenical task for the future is for Christians to put their humpty-dumpty together again.

Modernity

In this section we concentrate on the eighteenth and nineteenth centuries, though aspects of modernity clearly are found in the seventeenth century and still persist today. From the myriad events and thinkers who shaped the eighteenth and nineteenth centuries we must select the most crucial. Clearly the Enlightenment was crucial, as were the revolutions in France and America, which were related to it. Of the thinkers, the line from Descartes to Marx that passes through Hume, Kant, and Hegel is perhaps the most significant.

The religious life of the West changed dramatically in the modern period. It had to contend with new political, philosophical, and scientific thought. More profoundly, for the first time it met a passionate counter-faith, for modernity opposed deep commitment to humanity's own powers to reliance on God.

Heribert Raab has written, "The Enlightenment denotes the most revolutionary of all movements which the Occident has undergone in the course of history."[50] He makes reference to Protestant historian Ernst Troeltsch's view that the Enlightenment marks the beginning of the modern period of European culture, ending the previous theological or ecclesiastical culture.

The Enlightenment began in the Netherlands and England in the mid-seventeenth century, but its most outstanding expressions arose in France and Germany. French rationalistic and materialistic philosophy (such as that of Voltaire, Helvétius, and Comte) and French revolutionary political action both derived from the Enlightenment. In Germany, Leibniz, Lessing, and Kant were its first philosophical offspring, while the "enlightened despotism" of Frederick the Great and Joseph II was a political result.

The Enlightenment thinkers saw themselves as part of a movement for progress, the watchword of which was criticism. They took as their enemy ignorance, intolerance, and repression, vowing to attack all their manifestations in national culture. To power this critical warfare they drew on the model of the new physical science (especially that of Newton). That meant setting goals of clarity, precision, and rational order. Thus, the Enlightenment was a tremendous affirmation of humanity's rational capacities. Further, it assumed that both creation and human nature were essentially good, thus producing an expectation of great progress. Things would improve and freedom would increase as trustworthy critical reason expressed trustworthy human nature in a quite trustworthy natural order.

Quite obviously, the Enlightenment view of human nature clashed with that of traditional Christianity. Although reason held an important place in the medieval Scholastic synthesis, the medieval mind never doubted that human nature is only perfectible through divine grace. In Reformation thought, Protestant and Catholic alike, both human reason and human love suffer the effects of sin, with the result that only God can give the fulfillment they seek. The Enlightenment contested the beliefs of both periods.

In fact, Alexander Pope (1688–1744) epitomized his era when he said that the proper concern of man is man. Drawing on Renaissance humanism as well as on Reformation individualism, the Enlightenment thinkers concluded that things outside the province of human experience are of marginal concern. How we define human experience, of course, is a capital question. Enlightenment leaders tended to distrust both mystical experience and systematic reason (Hegel was an exception), preferring empiricism instead. Thus, Hume made a deep impression by limiting human thought to what sensation can verify. In the political sphere, the new thinkers sought to establish empirical laws of human nature that might help provide liberty, fraternity, and equality. Even when such philosophy or political science grew quite abstract (as in the case of the French revolutionary philosophies), there was agreement that theology and revelation were irrelevant.

For Kant and Hegel, the great innovators in the philosophy of consciousness, the reason that was to secure "the system" would not be subordinate to traditional faith. Thus, biblical, conciliar, and even Reformation notions of how things are in the world were rejected during the Enlightenment. By a turn to the thinking subject, reality became the domain that we now call the secular world. The transcendent domain, the holy world that past ages had called the most objective, had no place in the new world view. Only as a manifestation of human self-expression, individual or social, did religion merit attention.

A great many factors were at work in this subjective turn, of course, and not all of them rooted in human pride. A general disgust with religion—well deserved after a century of religious wars—certainly made a new, humanistic beginning attractive. The overbearing weight of ecclesiastical institutions, which regularly stomped on individual rights and opposed free scientific inquiry, made anticlericalism rather healthy. (The Inquisition is a heinous instance of religion used to trample human dignity.)

In the sciences, the excitement of empirical discoveries and the slow differentiation of canons of critical judgment were forces that seemed to oppose faith. Under the banner of religion huddled so much superstition and antiintellectualism that simple integrity drove many educated people away from the Church. The best and the brightest frequently found themselves forced to choose between their love of human culture (intelligence, sober judgment, and compassionate love that represent humanity at its best) and religion, Christianity, or even God.

However, applying Enlightenment beliefs to philosophy and politics did not prove to be an unqualified boon to humanity. Unfettered reason and humanism produced horrors that quite challenged those of the religious witch hunts and inquisitions. For instance, the bloodbaths of the French Revolution differed little from those of the religious wars, showing that not all fanaticism trumpeted about God. The American Constitution, despite its debt to Enlightenment humanism and its expression of democratic freedoms, was the framework of a culture that often considered nonwhites and women less than human.[51] The Marxist-Leninist-Maoist brand of political religion, which is largely indebted to Hegel, produced inhuman totalitarian regimes. Small wonder, then, that Eric Voegelin found the path from Enlightenment to revolution to be a way of self-deification—a vicious way of placing selected human beings in the seat of divine mystery at the expense of others.[52]

Those who defended the pre-Enlightenment order argued that the fallacies in the new order were both subtle and patent. On the subtle side, a thorough critical analysis of experience showed that there is more to reality than what Enlightenment philosophy

acknowledged. For instance, mystical, mythical, poetic, romantic, and even creatively scientific thought all stand outside of Enlightenment epistemology (theory of knowledge). On the patent side, observation of human behavior showed that reason seldom guides public affairs. Putting these objections to Enlightenment together, Christian apologists argued that an experience of God can take one beyond empirical reason and a human irrationality exists that is well labeled "sin." The legacy of modernity is the continuing Western debate over the assets and liabilities of critical reason.

The Contemporary Situation

The principles of Reformation and modernity have worked for more than four and a half centuries since Martin Luther. The reforming spirit continued both within and without Lutheranism and Calvinism, simplifying Christianity to yield a stark biblical faith and worship. Thus, Puritanism, Methodism, and Baptist religion moved Protestantism farther from Catholic dogmatic and sacramental theology. In reacting to this trend, Anglo-Catholicism tried to mediate between the ancient Catholic tradition and the Protestant instinct for the new religious needs of post-Renaissance society. However, the tide of the Protestant sectarians brought waves of individual, enthusiastic experience, which in turn promoted preaching, revivalism, and biblical literalism. Meanwhile, traditional Catholic authority fought modernity tooth and nail, only accepting modern scholarship and modern conceptions of human rights in the twentieth century.

During the nineteenth century, the Enlightenment meant liberalism in religious matters. Christianity was adapted to the needs of the day, which liberals thought were primarily humanistic in character. Adolf Harnack's slogan that the Christian essence is "the fatherhood of God and the brotherhood of man" encapsules much of the liberal spirit.

On occasion, both liberals and evangelicals (people rooted in the Gospel) pressed for social change. The industrial revolution produced some abysmal working conditions, and Christian exponents of the "social gospel" agreed with Karl Marx that such conditions destroyed human dignity. In the "liberation theology" of recent years, this kinship has become explicit, and many liberation theologians are combining Marxist economic analyses with Christian beliefs. The most eloquent are Latin Americans,[53] but thought like theirs has penetrated the counsels of both Geneva and Rome. Recently Latinos, blacks, Asians, and feminists in North America who want to promote social change through radical Christian faith have rallied around liberation theology.[54]

In American religious history, a central theme has been what Martin Marty calls "righteous empire."[55] With this phrase Marty tries to summarize the Protestant experience in the New World. It entailed divine errands in the wilderness, the sacred tasks of making God's new Israel, and a manifest destiny to show the world a truly Christian society. There was some breakup of the empire on the divisions among the many American Christian churches, and so there was a rather reluctant settling for a civic code that granted *all* persons religious liberty, freedom of conscience, and separation of Church and State.

The effort of Enlightenment figures such as Jefferson and Franklin to make a state that was both humanistic and Christian has been a striking experiment. However, American civil religion has been neither fully Christian nor fully human if measured by Christian dogma or post-Enlightenment criticism.[56]

Puritanism, liberalism, and Marxism have all emerged as forms of Gnosticism.[57] Although these three viewpoints relate to the Enlightenment (and contribute to U.S. history) in quite different ways, they all depart from the classical political theory that developed from Greek reason and Jewish-Christian revelation. In other words, the majority movements in modern politics have not been concerned with maintaining a balance between divinity and humanity, faith and reason, transcendent reality and the world at hand. For the most part, they have concentrated on the second terms in these pairings or even tried to convert the first terms into the second.

The result has been an apotheosis (divinization) of humanity, a hearty optimism and faith in human reason, and a nearly mystical commitment to political action—with little feel for the irony involved. In the domain of scholarship, the historian has wielded more power than the theologian. In the domain of popular Christian religion, there has been considerable defense of the secular. Only after Vietnam, Watergate, and a proliferation of crises (ecological, nuclear, and economic), whose interrelationships challenge our cultural values, did Americans begin to suspect that modern Gnosticism had led them far astray. Within Christianity, these crises have become a common challenge. Only people who ignore reality do not feel their impact. They require a thorough rethinking of the faith handed down as well as a thorough critique of the Gospel as lived by Wall Street.[58]

Furthermore, Christians have had to rethink their assumptions about revelation, salvation, the centrality of Christ, and the position of "pagans" as they have learned about other religions. Because of both secular and religious developments, then, the current Christian situation is complex and demanding. Science, technology, politics, and history (in other cultures as well as those that derive from Christianity) all demand reconciliation with traditional faith.

These concerns of current Western theologians press in upon even an introductory text in world religions. First, we cannot separate them from the assumptions with which scholarship approaches any religious tradition today. That is, we cannot cite religious phenomena, separate central ones from peripheral ones, and compose historical or comparative analyses without understanding just what religious phenomena are and why some are central. Even a student or scholar with no express theory about such things has a tacit theory about them.

For instance, some people think of religion in terms of social ceremonies. For them a person who does not attend church or synagogue regularly is not religious. Other people define religion as the urge to know and love that opens onto mystery. For them the irreligious person blocks off contemplative love. We favor the second interpretation.

Second, the concerns that modernity generated often spark a quarrel between scholarship and faith. Persons committed to religious traditions may feel that detached, critical, scientific treatment of their beliefs and worship distorts them. American Indians, for instance, have said that anthropologists' comments on their sacred dances are usually trivial.[59] Without the experience of being lost in communion with the Great Spirit, the anthropologist can only ruminate about group contagion or the therapies of rhythm. There are analogies in every religion. At the heart of the effort to describe the reality of religious experience lie the unavoidable issues of critical reason and experiential faith.

As a result of the Enlightenment, contemporary scholars test every observation, every statement, every memory—they accept nothing uncritically. From traditional faith comes the axiom that one must believe in order to understand, love in order to see. That axiom finally implies that faith is an act greater and more comprehensive than reason.

Third, these interpretational issues are especially acute in contemporary Western culture because they arose due to the effects of Christianity. Indeed, the Christian blend of Israelite revelation and Greek reason may have carried their seeds from the beginning. By the happenstance (or providence) that Christianity became the dominant European world view, and the happenstance that European culture developed science, history, and philosophy into the massive critical apparatus that we possess today, these issues are fundamental to both contemporary Western culture and contemporary Christian faith. The result is a constant, if frequently subtle, interplay.

For instance, religion does not go away just because critical reason argues it off the property. Usually, it simply takes another form—the scientist or historian whose life turns on research becomes "religious" about his or her work. Indeed, the more creative such a historian or scientist is, the more passionate, even lyric and reverent, he or she will be about the commitment to truth and objectivity that the work demands. Similarly, the devoted social activist, whether Marxist or not, tends to survive through a largely unprovable faith that history has a meaningful direction or that giving one's life to improve other people's lot makes sense. Even the typical citizen who goes along without much reflection or passion hears a few whispers of God.[60]

CONVERSION

Emilie Griffin's book *Turning: The Experience of Conversion*[61] sharpens many of the themes of recent Christian religious experience. Seeking the meaning of her own life, Griffin came to the critical point of personal choice: conversion from the secular values of the prevailing culture to an ardent Christian faith. In describing the motives and processes of her conversion, Griffin suggests that the Christian Gospel still has the power to connect some lives to a deep, mysterious source of satisfaction. As we consider her case study of Christian faith, we can note where it challenges the mores of current Western culture and also where the modern critiques of Christian consciousness show it vulnerable to self-deception.

For Griffin, the conversion process began with a great longing, an ache in her heart for something she had never experienced and could not even describe. This is reminiscent of the paradoxical remark of Blaise Pascal (1623–1662) that we would not seek God had we not already found God. Be it world weariness, or the passing of childhood satisfactions, or the strange inability of even great success to satisfy us for long, a disenchantment prompts us to consider a new way of life.

When she began to study the lives of converts, Griffin found that many reported having had intense experiences of nature in their youth, times when the universe stood forth as a fresh and dazzling immensity. A hunger for such experiences surfaced later in their lives, when they found a horizon of "everydayness" cramped and unsatisfying. For example, Thomas Merton, the Roman Catholic convert who became a famous Trappist monk, remembered being five years old and hearing all the birds in the trees start singing when some church bells began to chime. He asked his father why the two of them were not also in church, but his father only said that they would go to church some other Sunday. Similarly, C. S. Lewis, the well-known British convert, reports harkening back to an experience he had when he was six. He could see the Castlereagh Hills from his window, and they filled him with a great longing to touch their beauty.

In Griffin's early life both literature and nature had furnished her great joy. When she left her adolescent world of books and trees, however, and went to New York in search of a career, the joy seemed to drain away from her spirit. This made her brief trips to places like Central Park, or her times free for poetry reading, all the more precious, yet all the more unable to satisfy her growing hunger. Almost accidentally she bought a leather-bound volume of the Book of Common Prayer, which surprised her by the force its words carried, as though something that had informed her distant ancestors was now speaking directly to her own soul.

Before long she became a frequenter of churches. Even when their bad art repelled her, Christian churches hinted at a wisdom about life and death, suffering and joy—the great human experiences she was trying to fathom. While the Christian teaching about immortality seemed to her illogical, she admired the concise statements of faith that rang forth in such venerable Christian formulas as the Apostles' Creed. Her upbringing in Christian Science made the ques-

tion of the relation between flesh and spirit especially engrossing. Slowly she came to suspect that the attraction of Christian churches lay in their materialization of spiritual truths. In their glass and stone, they made faith, hope, and love visible, tangible.

From this suspicion it was but a short step to considering the center of Christian faith, the Incarnation. That Jesus had healed the man born blind (John 9 : 1–40) by spitting on the ground, mixing the spittle with dirt, and applying it to the blind man's eyes seemed utterly human—so human that it must have been orchestrated by God. Similarly, Jesus had turned water into wine, multiplied loaves and fishes, eaten broiled fish and honeycomb after his resurrection. Again and again, Griffin ran into this fusion of matter and spirit, this axis of incarnationalism or sacramentality. The Christian way, she came increasingly to see, was to place divinity in the world, to enflesh the Word of God in human form.

These discoveries only sharpened Griffin's longing to find a spiritual home. When she began to study traditional Christianity more deeply, her study did not spring from an academic interest in Christian religion. It was deeply personal and passionate. Perhaps this life-way held the truth or happiness, the sources of deep satisfaction. Perhaps it could slake the burning thirst of her soul. Reason and dispassion had their place, since she wanted a life-way that was realistic, not a bundle of convenient illusions. But her reasoning was in the service of a heartfelt need for a whole, very human truth. In fact, the closer she came to seeing that she really hungered for God, reality of a more-than-worldly order, the more she feared that affirming God would be an irrational leap spurred by her own needs. Perhaps "God" was only a projection of her great longings.

Yet this familiar argument against God seemed to have an obverse side. Would people long so for God if "God" had no reality? Could nature have made us so vainly, so certain to be frustrated? Back and forth the argument waged within her. Was her desire an unusual neurosis, or an unusual call to health? Before long, though, she decided that her desire for faith was too important to ignore. Better to risk disillusionment than never to test faith's truth. Better to pursue the desire for God to a frustrating conclusion than to hang back and remain divided. So Griffin determined to see the issue through, both intellectually and emotionally.

If we now generalize from Griffin's biography to the question of contemporary Christian faith at large, the intellectual portion of the project of Christian conversion includes accepting the great propositions of the Christian tradition about sin, grace, the Incarnation, and the Trinity. Even if one gets through the door marked "God" and becomes able to affirm the existence of a Creator, Christian faith demands that one accept these further specifications of the Creator's nature and the Creator's actions on human beings' behalf. Finally, on the other side of the room to which the door marked "God" gives access, there are the Christian doctrines about the Church, the scriptures, and the sacraments. If one buys the Christian claims about God and Jesus, these other articles of faith also line up for adoption. Only if they form a coherent system can a responsible person like Griffin judge them an attractive, acceptable package.

Curiously, though, the more Griffin pursued the question of God, the more the entire package became plausible. Having once seriously entertained the possibility that God exists, Griffin found the biblical descriptions of God rather credible. Once again the Incarnation was to be crucial. That God should appear in human form, suffering and rising "for us human beings and our salvation," as the traditional creed put it, was certainly strange, but somehow in keeping with a God as good as the Bible proclaimed God to be.

It was not so strange that the world should have an intelligible source. It was more strange that this source should be as good as the father of the prodigal son described in Luke 15, as willing to sacrifice his eternal Son as Paul insisted in Romans 8. None of this was necessary, automatically entailed in the concept of "God." But all of it somehow was fitting. If God were to choose to make creatures with the spiritual capacities of reason and love, he might well choose to express himself in a human form and solicit their free love by a life of exceptional goodness. At least, this is the way that many converts like Griffin have found themselves starting to reason.

Moreover, this response to the intellectual challenges of accepting Christian faith tends to

supply answers to most of the emotional challenges. Once the option of joining the Christian Church became intellectually respectable, Griffin found the emotional obstacles greatly diminished. The possible ridicule from supposedly sophisticated secular friends paled in comparison to the new meaning that conversion seemed to hold out. And her great longing for coherence, beauty, and a cause worth dedicating herself to seemed on the verge of finding fulfillment. So a certain at-homeness began to overtake Griffin's emotions. More and more the instruction classes she attended, the Church services she took part in, and the circle of new friends she met rang true, outlined a life-style that seemed to fit.

She realized quite well that the Church had many foibles, her new friends were quite imperfect, and much of the attractiveness of Christianity depended on her making a prior commitment of faith. The sacraments were only pregnant with lovely meaning if she believed them to be life-giving actions of God's Spirit. Also, Griffin never forgot that her coming to the threshold of Christian faith and then stepping across into the Christian Church had been powered by her inner needs. She was like a sick person who had come in search of a cure, a puzzled person who had come in search of clarifications. Still, once she decided that this motivation need not discredit the help that Christian faith seemed to provide her, she could convert to Christianity in good conscience.

Griffin's sketch of the conversion process challenges the secular assumption that faith is unreasonable, in the very process of challenging the secular assumption that God is impossible. For Emilie Griffin, both Christian faith and the Christian God became more reasonable than the secular life of many of her friends. Indeed, increasingly she found secular living cramped and unsatisfying. If there was not more to life than good food, interesting work, and clever conversation, life was a cruel hoax. The issue boiled down to whether Christian faith or secularism laid out the richer world view, and for Griffin it finally was no contest. Jesus had words of eternal life and the world mainly spun its wheels.

It does not impugn this honest report on the dynamics of Christian conversion to point out that Christian faith ought to be judged by its fruits. That was Jesus' own criterion (Matt. 7 : 16), and it justifies a certain healthy pragmatism. If Griffin's or any other convert's assumption of a religious world view produces a greater ability to love and to work (Freud's standard for psychic health), an honest observer will account that conversion a good thing. If, on the other hand, a religious world view injures or frustrates love and work, an honest observer will account that world view (or at least the particular convert's version of it) suspect.

What do these standards of "love" and "work" entail? No doubt some subjectivity enters in, but we would have "love" entail an increasing appreciation of the mystery of life, of our fellow human beings, and of ourselves. We would have "work" entail the ability to create, serve, and so make one's time advance the beautification, clarification, and betterment of one's social circles.

Admittedly, these are not precise criteria, but the ground-level question of human or religious authenticity can never be precise. Modern studies of human consciousness show that we are all very complex creatures, with many different motivations and needs. If, overall, we become creatures who are honest and loving, productive and helpful, the world view that forms us to such health deserves high praise. As well, it deserves thoughtful consideration by others, for it might just be the better way that they, too, have been seeking.

STRUCTURAL ANALYSIS

Nature

Theologians who treat the meaning of nature in Christianity show that nature has usually signified human essence.[62] That does not mean that Christianity has denied the reality of the physical world. On the contrary, its Greek and Israelite sources both gave Christianity a realistic orientation toward the world. Moreover, the body of Jesus, insofar as Christian faith made him the Logos incarnate, was an anchor to realism. Against the Gnostics, who were their foremost adversaries, the early Christian writers insisted on the reality and goodness of matter. If God himself had made the world, and God's own Son had assumed flesh, both the world and human flesh had to be good.

Nonetheless, because of the early controversies about the being of God and Christ, the word *physis* (nature) connoted divine and human "whatness" more than it connoted external reality. During the early controversies about free will and sin, Christian speculation finally concluded that the redemption and salvation that Christ had worked were beyond that to which human beings have any right. Thus, they were supernatural gifts that come only by grace. Grace, it followed, is a generosity that God does not owe us. Further, redemption and salvation so transform human nature that it can share in God's own divine nature (2 Pet. 1 : 4). By itself, apart from grace, nature is unredeemed, unsaved, something far from the glory of divinity. These beliefs dominated classical Christian theology (Catholic, Orthodox, and Protestant alike).

In discussing creation we find more extensive Christian considerations of the physical world.[63] God stands to the world as its independent, uncaused source, who made it from nothing by his simple free choice. The first mark of the natural world for the Christian, then, has been its subordination to divine creativity. Considerable time passed before the full conceptualization of creation was developed (from a combination of biblical and philosophical sources), but from the beginning the God of the burning bush was sovereignly free.

Somewhat relatedly, in Western religion the human being has not been the tiny figure found in East Asian landscape painting. In most periods of Christian history, nature was considered mysterious and overpowering, but the Genesis story that God gave human beings dominion over nature shaped a belief that the physical world exists for humanity's sake. Christianity has taught its faithful to husband the physical world and use it. Little in the Christian message proposed that humans should ravage the world, but equally little proposed integrating human life with nature's ecology or preserving nature's gifts through frugality and reverence. In most periods Christians found nature abundant and generous, so conservation was not a major concern.

Further, the biblical fear of nature gods contributed to a semiconscious Christian effort to make nature undivine. In rural places (among European peasants, for instance), this effort succeeded only partially. Overall, though, it was quite central to the Christian theology of creation. Coming from God, the world was good. But since it came from God by his free choice, springing from nothingness, the world was definitely not divine. Thus, the Christian interest in transforming human nature combined with a continuance of the biblical prophets' objection to the nature gods; thus, the physical world was made a subordinate, even somewhat ambivalent, concept.

Nature as Profane

The relative profanity (nonsacredness) that Christians attributed to nature played a rather complex role in the rise of Western science. When the Greek protoscientists, or early natural philosophers, developed a rude demythologizing of nature, they established the principle that the physical world is open to rational investigation. Thus, it was not blasphemous to pry into nature's secrets, and it could be profitable: Nature yields valuable information to those who pry well.

In Christian hands this demythologizing went several steps further. Pre-Renaissance scholars (many of them monks) worked at what we would call physics or biology, although such work was subordinated to theology. In other words, the basically religious culture preceding the Renaissance determined that theology would be the queen of the sciences. At best

philosophy was this queen's handmaid, and natural philosophy (science and philosophy had not yet become clearly separated) was a legitimate but not very pressing task. That the handmaid might pursue this task with enthusiasm was a sign that God has made us by nature Aristotelians (Aristotle said that all persons by nature desire to know), but surely theology was a nobler call.

The phenomenon of Christian alchemy, which scholars do not yet fully understand, suggests an underground resistance to the neat official hierarchy. Psychological studies, such as C. G. Jung's, and studies by historians of religion, such as Mircea Eliade's, suggest that European alchemy was religiously motivated. The Catholic church recognized this, for it associated alchemists with wizards, witches, astrologers, magicians, and sorcerers, tabooing them all as persons who probably were consorting with Satan. In other words, the veneration of nature posed a definite threat to the Church. Church powers thought it incompatible with orthodox faith that Christ had subordinated the psychic or parapsychic powers of "this age" and freed human beings for genuine religion: love of a nature-transcending God and love of fellow humans.

Science

Thus, prior to the Renaissance, the Catholic church kept physical science on a rather short leash. The controversy that the new theories of Galileo Galilei (1564–1642) raised shows the Church attitude that still prevailed in the seventeenth century: Faith had to predominate over the evidence of the senses. Shoring up theological notions (that the earth was the center of the universe was a theological axiom) was more important than allowing intelligence the freedom to investigate nature as it would.

Enlightenment thinkers were reacting to that sort of dogmatism and theological control when they attacked Christian faith. Almost in the name of a higher religion (fidelity to conscience), they attacked theology as dishonest. Since the scientific method, as we now call it, that was disengaging itself from theology (despite the Church's protests) brought tangible results, it drove the ecclesiastical authorities deeper and deeper into their indefensible corner. Still, the passion of their faith made the authorities fly their flag decades after it was in tatters. Long after the Galileo disgrace, when even the Roman Holy Office allowed the sun to be the center of the universe, the Church opposed new scientific theories on theological grounds. Thus, many Christian leaders denounced Darwin and Freud, because evolution and psychoanalysis seemed to refute the image of human nature that religious tradition had developed. The creature who was little less than an angel, the creature for whom Christ had shed his blood, the creature who was the very image of God could not have descended from an ape or have unconscious lust for its parents.

Thus, one can appreciate the modern intellectuals' alienation from the Church. From the Renaissance to the quite recent past, Christian leadership has often opposed free scientific inquiry. As late as 1950, Pope Pius XII blasted polygenism (the anthropological theory that the human race arose from several different protohuman genetic pools) on the grounds that Adam and Eve had to be the original progenitors of all human beings. As well, he blasted existentialism. Even today debates about creation (the Genesis account versus the big bang theory) continue a warfare between theology and science. Literalism, to say nothing of the desire to control other persons' minds and morals, is far from dead in Christian circles.

Regarding the investigation of nature, therefore, the Christian legacy has been mixed. At first Christianity supported reason, the reality and goodness of the world, and the value of scientific contemplation. When investigation seemed to threaten faith, Christian orthodoxy tried to check the scientific mind. In elitist circles today things are much better, for theologians now analyze the implications of scientific findings for ethics and faith. For instance, they discuss genetic engineering, nuclear research, the medical definition of death, and the like from a belief in the Christian concept of human dignity. Some confusion still remains about the line between religion and science, but history has chastened theologians considerably, and they are now slow to condemn scientific research.

On the other side, at least a few scientists doubt that the scientific method alone is a comprehensive way of life. Not only does scientific research tend to ignore ethical questions about the social applications of its findings (for example, its findings about nuclear energy), it also finds itself more and more appreciative of nature's complexity—indeed, of nature's mystery. Every scientific discovery raises many more questions, whether in the realm of atomic particles, the realm of life, or the realm of the stars. Nature itself, we are finding, is a collection of mysteries.[64] Thus, nature commands respect, even awe, that is quite different from the arrogance with which earlier, mechanistic scientists attacked it. In fact, for some philosophers of science, such as Whitehead,[65] nature is the concrete form of divinity.

Sacramentalism and Mysticism

Christian sacramentalism has somewhat closed the gap (between the place of nature in Christian religion and native religion) that was opened by the Western separation of reason from myth. As well, Christian mystics who have sensed a divine presence in woods and birds have been rather naturalist in their style. In its worship and sacramental theology, Christian religion expressed the belief that God called creation good. Often, it applied a mythic and poetic intelligence that made the world mysterious, awesome, and alive. Baptismal water, eucharistic bread and wine, wax, incense, flowers, salt, oil—they have all enriched the liturgy. On the most solemn feast of Easter, the liturgy spoke as though all of creation got into the act, joining in the *Exultet*—the song of great rejoicing. In the liturgy of Good

Friday, which commemorates Christ's death, the tree of the cross (the holy rood) became a new *axis mundi*—a new cosmic pillar linking heaven and earth. Taking over Psalm 150, Christians praised God in his firmament. Taking over other psalms, they made the mountains and the beasts coconspirators to God's praise. All creation, then, should resound to the music of the spheres. All creation should sing as it labors for redemption. Nature was part of a divine drama, part of a cosmic play of sin and grace.

Partly from such liturgical encouragement, Christian mystics have often shown a delight in nature like that of their East Asian counterparts. The accents have been different, since the Christian God is not the impersonal Buddha-nature, but they have not been contradictory. For instance, Francis of Assisi felt free to praise God as manifested in nature. Francis composed famous canticles to brother sun and sister moon, and the

legends about his intimacy with animals are a sort of Christian prefiguring of the messianic age of fulfillment. It recalls Isaiah's figures of the child playing at the asp's hole and the lion lying down with the lamb. In the messianic age men and women will once more be intimate with nature, as they were when God made them "in the beginning."

For the early desert fathers, the wilderness was a place to become sanctified. For many Puritans and early Americans, the wilderness brought to mind Israel's wanderings in the desert—the place where its religion was pure. Thus, a romantic strain of Christian thought kept nature close to God. Sometimes it made the city less desirable for religious life than the country. Often it made solitude close to the elements a privileged place for prayer. As a result, the Christian God was strong as the seas, everlasting as the hills, lovely as the lilies of the field.

CHRISTIAN RITUALS

By means of its sacramental system, the Christian Church has ritualized its members' passage through the life cycle. The system has begun with baptism, the sacrament designed to celebrate a person's birth into divine life and church membership. If the person was an adult, it was usual to require a profession of faith. The questions in the traditional inquiry into the candidate's faith show the transition that the sacrament of baptism was ritualizing.

First, the minister of the sacrament asked the candidate whether she renounced Satan and the spiritual forces of evil that rebel against God. Assuming the answer was yes, the interrogation continued, soliciting affirmative answers to such questions as whether the candidate renounced the evil powers of this world that corrupt and destroy the creatures of God; whether she renounced all sinful desires that drew her away from God's love; whether she turned to Jesus Christ and accepted him as her savior; whether she put her whole trust in Christ's grace and love; and whether she promised to follow and obey Christ as her Lord. Along with a profession of the

traditional creed, this profession of faith set the main lines of what the sacrament of baptism was enacting: a passover from a life of bondage to Satan and the world to a life of freedom in the grace of Jesus Christ.

The celebrant would then pray over the baptismal water, consecrate the oil with which the candidate was to be anointed, and finally baptize (pour water on the forehead of) the candidate in the name of the Father, and of the Son, and of the Holy Spirit. The concluding prayer summarized the effects the action was believed to have: "Heavenly Father, we thank you that by water and the Holy Spirit you have bestowed upon these your servants the forgiveness of sin, and have raised them to the new life of grace. Sustain, them, O Lord, in your Holy Spirit. Give them an inquiring and discerning heart, the courage to will and to persevere, a spirit to know and to love you, and the gift of joy and wonder in all your works. Amen."[66]

The second sacramental rite in the normal life cycle was confirmation, the Christian celebration of coming-of-age. The main motif in this celebration was asking God to give the candidate further strength from the Holy Spirit, in view of the services that adult life would require him to perform.

The Holy Eucharist has been the principal sacrament in the majority of the Christian traditions, and the ritual for the Eucharist began with a Liturgy of the Divine Word. After opening prayers, members of the congregation read several "lessons" from scripture, usually from both the Old and the New Testaments. There followed a sermon, to explain the scripture readings and apply them to daily life, and then a recitation of the Nicene Creed. Next came prayers for various needs, and then the Eucharistic Liturgy proper would begin.

This first offered thanks to God and praise of God's holiness. Then came the main action, a remembrance of the Last Supper that Jesus celebrated with his apostles before his death. The key words of this remembrance were: "For in the night in which he was betrayed, he took bread; and when he had given thanks, he brake it, and gave it to his disciples, saying, 'Take, eat, this is my Body, which is given for you. Do this in remembrance of me.' Likewise, after supper, he took the cup; and when he had given thanks, he gave it to them, saying, 'Drink ye all of this; for this is my Blood of the New Testament, which is shed for you, and for many, for the remission of sins. Do this, as oft as you shall drink it, in remembrance of me.' "

After these prayers of consecration, there would be a recitation of the Lord's Prayer ("Our Father"), more short prayers, and a Communion service, in which worshipers received the consecrated bread and wine. The prayers said when administering the bread and wine summarized the participants' sense of what they were receiving: "The Body of Our Lord Jesus Christ, which was given for thee, preserve thy body and soul unto everlasting life. Take and eat this in remembrance that Christ died for thee, and feed on him in thy heart by faith, with thanksgiving. The Blood of our Lord Jesus Christ, which was shed for thee, preserve thy body and soul unto everlasting life. Drink this in remembrance that Christ's Blood was shed for thee, and be thankful."

Overall, the Church celebrated the Eucharist as both a memorial of Jesus' death and a memorial of his last meal, when he gave himself to his friends under the signs of bread and wine. Since Jesus' death and resurrection were the central events in the Christian reading of history, each Eucharistic memorial laid before the Christian faithful an epitome of their sense of reality. In Jesus' death and resurrection stood revealed the meaning and destiny of each human life.

Moreover, by receiving Jesus' body and blood, the believer was nourished in the divine life that Jesus' death and resurrection had made available. The Eucharist therefore was like the messianic banquet that Jews of Jesus' time had believed would accompany God's definitive victory. Celebrating the good news of Jesus' victory together, Christians renewed their spiritual strength by feeding on Jesus' substance. There was nothing cannibalistic in this. The eating and drinking were simply ways of expressing and strengthening the deep intimacy between Christ and Christians, who, according to St. Paul (1 Cor. 12 : 12), were members of one body, or, according to St. John (John 15 : 5), were united like a vine and its branches.

The person who found baptism, confirmation, and the Holy Eucharist insufficient to keep him from sin could have recourse to sacramental rites of penance, which were designed to reconcile him with God and the rest of the community. Normally the minister of this sacrament offered a prayer over the penitent, and then the penitent confessed his sins: "I confess to Almighty God, to his Church, and to you, that I have sinned by my own fault in thought, word, and deed, in things done and left undone; especially by [here the penitent would mention the specific sins most troubling him]. For these and all other sins which I cannot now remember, I am truly sorry. I pray God to have mercy on me. I firmly intend amendment of life, and I humbly beg forgiveness of God and his Church, and ask you for counsel, direction, and absolution." After whatever counsel and direction he thought appropriate, the minister would absolve the sinner of his sins, in the name of the Father, and of the Son, and of the Holy Spirit.

When it came time to marry, Christians were expected to celebrate their union through a marriage ritual. The theology of marriage likened the conjunction of man and woman in matrimony to the union between Christ and the Church, and it found in the Genesis creation account, in which God gave Eve to Adam, a prototype of the nuptial union. A Christian marriage was meant for both the mutual comfort of the spouses and the procreation of children. It had to be entered into freely by both parties, and usually the minister called upon the assembled community not only to witness the parties' vows but also to support them in their marital venture. The actual marriage took place when the betrothed said to one other, "I take you to be my wife [husband] to have and to hold, from this day forward, for better or worse, for richer or poorer, in sickness and in health, to love and to cherish, until we are parted by death." Then the couple gave one another wedding rings, as a sign of their union.

A sixth sacramental ritual dealt with the ordination of the Church's ministers. In churches with several ranks of ministers, the bishop would preside at the ordination. After satisfying himself that the candidate was qualified, he would solicit the approval and support of the community, pray over the ordinand, and then lay hands on the ordinand's head and pray, "Therefore, Father, through Jesus Christ your Son, give your Holy Spirit to ———; fill him [or her] with grace and power, and make him [or her] a priest in your Church."

Many churches also celebrated sacramental rituals for the healing and consolation of the sick. After prayers and scriptural readings, the sick person usually would go through the penance ritual, and then the minister would lay hands upon the sick person and anoint her with holy oil. The prayers accompanying this anointing would ask God for an inward anointing of the Holy Spirit, to forgive the sick person her sins, release her from suffering, and restore her to wholeness and strength. Often the person then would receive Holy Communion.

The last stage on the Christian's life way was the burial rite, which usually focused the Holy Eucharist for the occasion of death and burial. The Liturgy of the Word would feature psalms and scriptural passages concerned with death and the Christian hopes for resurrection, and the person would be buried in consecrated ground with prayers for forgiveness and the life of the blessed in heaven.

The Christian sacramental system was the basic framework of the traditional Christian's church life. While many churches of the Protestant Reformed tradition came to downplay the sacraments that Catholics and Eastern Orthodox celebrated, Protestants still assembled for baptism, a liturgy of the scriptural Word, and to solemnize such occasions as marriage, ordination, and Christian burial. Whatever reservations they had about the Catholic and Eastern Orthodox development of almost sumptuous rituals, Protestants retained the Christian conviction that God uses material things (if only words and music) to draw human beings to himself in spirit and truth. The churches of the Catholic and Orthodox traditions extended this principle to bread and wine, oil and wax, and various "sacramentals" (signs, such as holy water and ashes, meant to solemnize smaller occasions). The result was a counterbalance to any Christian overemphasis on sin or unbridled condemnation of the world. If God's own Word had taken flesh, the body and the world had to be basically good. All of life, therefore, had "sacramental" possibilities. As the Holy Eucharist showed the deepest potentialities of an ordinary meal, so the union of Christ with the Church showed the deepest potentialities of ordinary sexual intercourse. Not every generation of Christians preached this sacramentalism boldly, but it always lay ready to hand in the mainstream tradition.

The sacramental system epitomized the Christian sense of God's ways with human beings. Where God could have stood apart, in splendid isolation, God freely chose to make covenants, strike bonds, call his people not servants but friends. By enfleshing the eternal Word of his heart, God placed divinity in the very midst of human history. The death and resurrection of Jesus, which was celebrated each Sunday, said that God goes down with human beings in their deepest grief and raises human beings up beyond their wildest hopes. At its most gracious, Christian faith became a dance that partnered time to eternity. God and humanity were joined sacramentally; through the things of matter, space, and time, the timeless Spirit of God touched human beings and quickened them.

Society

Central to the Christian notion of society is the Church. It could oppose the State, standing as the religious collectivity against the secular. It was also the place where Christian life was supposed to show itself as something mysteriously organic— as the "body" of Christ. In the earliest periods of Church history, before Theodosius established Christianity as the official Roman faith, Church leaders led quite unpretentious lives. Meetings of the community tended to be small gatherings in members' homes, and the bishop who led the liturgy might earn his bread as a cobbler or a craftsman. New Testament models suggested that carpentry (the occupation of Jesus) and tentmaking (the occupation of Paul) were more than honorable occupations. To those who waited idly for the *parousia*, the Church said, "Work—or no community support." In fact, most Christians in the beginning were nondescript working people. The *Epistle to Diognetius*[67] portrays a Christian existence in the world whereby faith made one a solid citizen.

Nonetheless, from early times Christians also felt that preaching the Gospel was an especially honorable work and that some community leaders ought to be free to labor at it full-time. The decision to have deacons care for temporal affairs (Acts 6 : 1–6) suggests that Christians quickly established a hierarchy of tasks parallel to the hierarchy of Christian authorities. The work that preoccupied Church leaders and that later theology regarded as the Church's basic duty was a ministry or service in terms of "Word and Sacrament."[68] "Word" was, in the first instance, the scriptures. From the outset, they guided worship, theology, and private reflection. Ministry of the Word included commenting on scripture to edify the assembly and preaching to the outside world (missionizing).

The Word itself was the Gospel, but also the Logos. Thus, it implied reciting the dramatic story of what God, out of his love, had chosen to do for humanity. The decisive episode in that story was Jesus' death and resurrection. And Jesus—the Christ, the Logos—became present in a special way through the preaching of the Gospel. Faith in Jesus was the "entry" to the Gospel view or "economy" of salvation, and faith demanded "hearing."

Developing biblical categories, today's theologians have shown that Jesus himself is the Church's primal sacrament;[69] his flesh is the greatest sign of God's nature and God's love. The Johannine writings contain the richest New Testament sacramental theology, but all the early literature makes clear that sacramental life is a life of union with Jesus. Sacramental life continued the incarnation of divinity; through its cyclical recall of the mysteries of Jesus' life, it led Church members ever deeper into God's love.

Polity

Christian society centered on worship through Word and Sacrament. Its structural organization was rather fluid at first and varied from place to place. In that early arrangement we can discern elements of all three of the later Church polities: the episcopal, presbyterial (of the elders), and congregational. With time, though, came the monarchical structure of Roman Catholicism, the collegial model of Orthodoxy, and the government by elders that characterized much of Protestantism.

In the West before the Reformation, the structure of the Catholic church was pyramidal. At the top was the pope, along the bottom were the laity. In between, in descending order, were cardinals, bishops, and priests. The "religious" (those who had taken vows of poverty, chastity, and obedience, usually in the context of a communal life) were in the middle, though technically most religious groups had both clerical and lay members. Status, naturally and unbiblically enough, was accorded those at the top. Thus, the Council of Trent, reacting against Reformation notions that all Christians are "saints," denounced any diminution of virginity in favor of marriage. As a result, for many Roman Catholics the Church meant the clergy. That was less true for Protestants and Orthodox, because their theologies stressed, respectively, the priesthood of all believers and the mystical union of all believers with Christ as the head. As well, the Protestant churches had a strong theory, if not always a strong practice, that ministry is honorable in the measure that it is a service.

Women's Status

In principle, the Christian Church was democratic in that all persons, regardless of sex, race, or background, were welcome. Each Church member had her or his own gift from God, and each was a unique reflection of God. Thus, there was the Pauline dictum (Gal. 3 : 28) that in Christ there is neither Jew nor Greek, male nor female, slave nor free. In practice, however, women have been second-rate citizens in all branches of Christianity. Neither the Catholic nor the Orthodox churches would ordain women (that remains true today), nor would many Protestant churches. By associating women with Eve, the cause of Adam's fall (1 Tim. 2 : 14), the Church suggested that they were responsible for human misery and sin. Thus, the fulminations of ascetics (usually celibate males) against women's wiles were a staple of the literature on how to avoid sin.

From the New Testament, men could buttress their supremacy by citing Pauline texts (Eph. 5 : 22–23, 1 Tim. 2 : 11–12) stating that wives were subordinate to their husbands and ought to keep silent in church. From the patristic age they could draw on what we can only call the misogyny of Jerome, Chrysostom, Tertullian, and others who portrayed woman as the gateway to hell. Augustine, perhaps from his personal experience of concubinage, made sexual congress the channel of original sin. Medieval theologians, such as the Dominican authors of the *Malleus Maleficarum (Hammer of Witches)* cited witches as being the cause of

much psychological imbalance. In the name of preserving true faith, Church authorities tortured and killed thousands of witches.[70] Moreover, the Reformation did not relieve women's plight. Luther thought that woman's vocation was to "bear herself out" with children, while John Knox trumpeted against "petticoat" power in the Church. Reformation biblicism, then, meant merely a return to the patriarchy of the scriptures.

With a patriarchal God and an ambivalent role model in Mary the Virgin Mother, Christian women for the most part heard and obeyed. They had some measure of religious self-expression in their convents, and some of them gained leadership roles in the Protestant sects, but from the standpoint of today's egalitarian sentiments, their fate through Christian history was uniformly dismal.[71]

Church and State

The Christian view of society outside the Church varied over time. According to the New Testament Revelation, Roman society was a beast that the coming Messiah had to slay if the earth were to be fair. During the persecutions, which some recent scholarship has downplayed, this view was influential. As a result, earthly life was held cheap compared to heavenly life. When the Church gained security with Constantine, it changed its tune. Eusebius, for instance, practically ranked Constantine with the twelve apostles. In reaction to this secularization, as we noted, the monastic movement restored the tension between time and eternity. The Western father Tertullian, for instance, cast doubt on the worth of secular culture, asking what Athens had to do with Jerusalem. However, other patristic figures, such as Clement of Alexandria and Augustine, recognized that Christianity needed an intellectual respectability if it were to prosper, so they started to give their theology an infrastructure of Greek philosophy.

By the medieval period, a certain harmony was obtained, as most of the culture was formed in accordance with Christian ideals (if not practice). There was a balance between reason and revelation, between emperor and pope. In practice, however, the competition between the emperor and the pope was fierce, for each tended to claim ascendancy over the other. Consequently, Church leaders such as Ambrose and Hildebrand, who stood up to kings or even brought them to heel, were great heroes.

The Reformation depended in good measure on the political power plays of its day; through application of the principle that a region would follow the religion of its ruler, a great deal of religious power returned to the local prince. Theologically, Luther tended towards a dualism of powers, religious and secular, while Calvin promoted a theocratic state in which citizens would live under Christian law. Thus, the Reformation did not initially encourage the modern pluralistic state. In America the religious communities of the colonial period had to legalize pluralism if the colonies were to be united. With great reluctance on the part of many, the united colonies disestablished religion, and their act had enormous implications.

Since about the time of Voltaire (1694–1778), American pluralism has become something of a model for world government. Other nations have not formalized that model, with the slight exception of the United Nations, but its spirit has been at least a small counterweight to their nationalism. The model says that to live together well, human beings must find nondogmatic principles that can be common to all and that will generate the basic cooperation necessary for peace.

Through most of Christian history, though, the ideal society has been one that at worst allowed Christians freedom to exercise their religious convictions and at best institutionalized a Christian regimen. For instance, only recently has Roman Catholicism backed off its teaching that it ought to be the established religion in any country with a Catholic majority. By its decree on religious liberty, the Second Vatican Council made an unprecedented acknowledgment of the rights of other religious communities. Orthodoxy has had difficulty with secular rulers through most of its history,[72] in part because of its organization as a cluster of national churches. To this day Russian Orthodoxy, the largest group, is shackled by its country's secular rulers. Protestantism has been more secular than Catholicism or Orthodoxy, so its ideas on the relations between Church and State have been the most advanced.

What the Church ought to do for secular society, in contrast to what it has asked of secular society, has also varied historically. Generally, the Church has thought it should be a city on the hilltop—a witness to the commonweal that comes from mutual support and love. In other words, the Church ought to be the place where society can see human community in action—can see love, cooperation, and mutual support. All human groups seek such community, and they have greater difficulty when they are large or their members have different values. The Church ought to manifest this community. In what Karl Rahner has called today's diaspora situation,[73] in which Christians are losing members, it becomes crucial that this concept of witness replace the ambition to rule over secular society that has dominated many periods of the Christian past. Many contemporary theologians want the Church to be with the poor, the oppressed, the people whom Jesus names in the beatitudes, for that is where its witness would be most vivid.

Self

The conceptions of nature and society that we have sketched above suggest the Christian view of the self. The biblical teaching that God placed human beings over nature has meant to Christians that the human person is of much greater value than the plants and animals.

Furthermore, as Christian social theory interacted with the secular elaboration of human nature through Western history, the individual acquired greater stature than in the East. In the East, as in ancient societies, the group predominated over the individual. One was most importantly a member of a tribe and only secondarily a unique person. As an image of God, the individual was more significant under Christianity. Of course, at times both secular and religious authorities crushed individuals ruthlessly. Nonetheless, because he bore the life of Christ, the individual person commanded respect. In matters of ethics, for instance, the notion of individual conscience counterbalanced the finespun codes of the canon lawyers and the moral theologians. The sacrament of penance epitomized this, for penance was essentially a self-accusation in which the individual, helped by the Church's representative, passed judgment on his or her standing before God.

By standing out from nature and having personal rights, the Christian individual was conscious of being a unique self. Historically, the Church did not lay great emphasis on fulfilling one's unique self by communing with nature, but it did lay great emphasis on fitting into the social body of Christ. In fact, the charity of the community united was to be the primary sign of God's presence. Beyond social fulfillment, however, Christian theology encouraged the self to commune with divinity itself—with the Father, Son, and Holy Spirit. During the biblical period that meant putting on the "mind of Christ." During the patristic age it meant that grace is a share in divine nature and that religion is a process of divinization. Since the Hellenistic divinity was above all immortal, religion was a process of immortalization.

In medieval speculation, the self's fulfillment was the "beatific vision." By directly perceiving God's essence, our human drives to know and love (Augustine's famous "restless heart") would find a restful bliss. For the Thomists, participation in the divine nature through grace meant sharing in the "missions" of the Son and Holy Spirit. Thus, one's contemplation, knowing, and loving flowed into and out from the dynamic relations that characterized God's own inner life. The Reformation returned to biblical

emphases, sending persons to study the Word and to work in the world. For Orthodoxy the Divine Liturgy, with special accents on the Holy Spirit and the Mother of God, nourished one throughout life.[74]

In many periods, Christians never quite found the balance between life in the world and life that looked to heaven as its true home. Prior to the Reformation, Christians probably gave greater emphasis to the latter. Since the Reformation and the Enlightenment, they have emphasized worldliness, for the world has become much more important than heaven.

Religious Development

Stressing communion with God, traditional Christian spiritual masters developed certain models of what happens in the life of the religious person. One of the most influential traditions involved the "three ways" that the self would travel. First, one had to walk the "purgative" way, which meant purging oneself of sin and developing virtuous habits. Then one would enter the long way of "illumination," by which the Christian truths of Word and Sacrament would slowly become one's own. No longer would they be external concepts—in time they would become inner principles of judgment and action. Finally, consummating the spiritual life was the "unitive" way, by which the self would unite with God as in a deep friendship or even a marriage. Occasionally such union would produce experiences of rapture, and one could speak of mysticism strictly so called ("infused contemplation"). Clearly, then, the paradigm of the three ways depended on the notion that final fulfillment is communion with God.

The saints who modeled Christian selfhood tended to be wholeheartedly given to communion with God. They also had to manifest charity for their fellows, but the spotlight was on their love of God. Because solitude or monastic withdrawal seemed to foster love of God, by allowing the freedom for deep, leisurely prayer, most saints went outside of family or civic life to lose themselves in devotion. That was the pattern up to the Reformation, and it took Christian selfhood some distance from the New Testament's view that prayer is important but not dominant.[75] Still, as the world became more important, the concept of saintliness expanded to include the service of other human beings. The Church had always honored certain holy married persons, certain holy civic leaders, but by late medieval times it had to contend with a more dynamic society.

Consequently, the Protestant emphasis on holy worldliness found a ready audience among many postmedievals. This emphasis did not remove the notion that one is a pilgrim trying to make progress through time towards a more lasting city. However, it did upgrade the status of family life, business, and government. Indeed, by the nineteenth century, tracts appeared with the theme that Jesus was the greatest salesman of all time. As well, one could hear Andrew Carnegie defend capitalistic wealth as God's way of keeping the poor from squandering his gifts.

Sin

Related to the capital question of what the self should most value is the complicated Christian teaching about original sin. At its crudest, the teaching said that all persons not baptized were bound to Satan and on the road to hell. Hell was essentially the deprivation of God (the loss of the beatific vision), but because of a gruesome imagery of fire and brimstone, it was popularly conceived of as a place of physical suffering. The ceremony for infant baptism, then, contained an exorcism of Satan—to save the little one from evil and make it pure for God. (Unbaptized babies who died before reaching the age of responsibility, and so before the possibility of personal sin, went to "Limbo," a state of "natural" happiness without beatific vision.)

A key moment in the development of the doctrine of original sin was Augustine's reading of the Fall as a social act. Adam's sin alienated all human beings from God, for Adam was the head of the entire race. Augustine took the seeds of this view from Paul (for instance, Rom. 5:12–14). It suggested that Christ is the head of a now holy race, but those not baptized into Christ belong to an old human nature destined for punishment.

The classical Protestant thinkers owed a great deal to Augustine, whom they much preferred to Aquinas; thus, their reform of theology emphasized original sin. Like Augustine, they interpreted Genesis and Paul rather literally, thinking in terms of corporate sinners and saints. The famous double predestination of Calvinism was an attempt to explain human beings' different fates (going to hell or heaven) as members of Adam or members of Christ without removing the mystery of God's creative vision and providence. Whom God has destined for heaven will surely end up there. Likewise, whom he has set for hell will fall into the flame.

In a fateful development of Calvinistic predestination, the signs of election to heaven became outward decorum and even material prosperity. That meant the double burden of being both poor and damned and the double blessing of being both rich and saved. Eventually more careful Bible readers recognized that this correspondence contradicted the Sermon on the Mount, but a lot of Calvinists thoroughly enjoyed storing up plenty in their barns and letting their souls wax fat.

How inherently wicked or good the self is was an important question in the Reformation debates between Protestants and Catholics. Protestants, following Luther's stress on justification by faith and Calvin's stress on God's sovereignty, tended to emphasize the corruption of human nature through sin. Catholics, partly in reaction to that Protestant position and partly from their own emphasis on the sacraments and the Incarnation, saw an essential goodness in human nature (though they spoke of sin as darkening the mind and weakening the will). Clearly, though, Christianity made the West suspicious of human instincts. Many Christians were indoctrinated with the belief that they were wicked sinners. Often that led them to oscillate between self-punishment and, in compensation, self-indulgence. However, through penance one could experience God's mercy—the almost delicious sense of being loved gratuitously. Then the Johannine promise (1 John 3 : 20) that even when our hearts condemn us God is greater than our hearts could burst into joyous effect.

The Pauline discussion of sin and grace in terms of "flesh" and "spirit" focused Christian discussion of the self as embodied. That Paul's original language did not intend a matter-spirit dualism was almost forgotten after Christianity took up Greek thought. As a result, extremists tended to deprecate the body, marriage, and the world of human affairs as fleshly pursuits. In response to the Manichaean and Albigensian heresies, the Catholic church affirmed the goodness of the body, but the Church's general orientation toward heaven, its introduction of celibacy for holders of high Church offices, and its preference for ascetic saints tended to make the average person regret his or her flesh. For women this caused considerable suffering, because the male Church teachers often projected their sexual problems onto women. In that case, women became wanton, seductive, and dangerous.

On the other hand, a certain realism about worldly life, in which imperfection if not sin was inevitable, tended to soften this rigorism. Christian moral theologians have usually taught that sins of the flesh are less grievous than sins of the spirit (such as pride, anger, or hatred). Although at one point Roman Catholic moralists classified all sexual offenses as serious ("mortal" as opposed to "venial" sins), there were effective if unauthorized counterforces in the bawdiness of Chaucer and Boccaccio and the frequent concubinage of members of the clergy.

Image of God

The self was an image of God, principally because of its reason and free will. The intellectual light that Augustine, in good neo-Platonic style, saw as a participation in eternal light was concrete evidence that God is more intimate to his images than they are to themselves. Most forms of Christianity held the freedom to love or not to love God to be beyond question. How to reconcile this freedom with God's omniscience was a thorny issue, but the idea of freedom was seldom abandoned. Augustine's theories, which tied into his stress on omniscience (as opposed to the Pelagian stress on human freedom), gave ammunition to those who wanted to downplay human works or goodness. Thus, they attracted Luther and others enamored of justification by faith. Aquinas' rather complex position strove for a balance by carefully distinguishing the realms of divine infinitude and human finitude.[76] Jesuits and Dominicans engaged in a tedious debate over this issue at the end of the sixteenth century, and, partly out of exhaustion, most theologians have since been quick to stress the mystery in any relation that involves the incomprehensible divine nature. In practice, then, Christianity has held human beings liable for their acts but has left final judgment to God.

Thus, the Christian concept of self has been complex. Christianity has never had a significant no-self doctrine like Buddhism, but where the self does gravitate—to society, sin, grace, reason, love, God, or something else—has not been clear. The tendency has been to place the self in the mystery of God—to make divinity the beginning and the end of this little consciousness that we carry so fleetingly.

Divinity

God is the heart of Christian religion, as God is the heart of any theistic religion. The first Christian conception of God was Jewish. Jesus himself accepted the God of the Fathers—Abraham, Isaac, and Jacob. This God, as we have seen, interacted with human beings and was personal. His guidance of humanity peaked in his liberation of Israel from Egypt and his covenanting with Israel on Mount Sinai. As numerous theologians have pointed out, it was difficult for Jesus to designate himself as divine, because to do so would have confused his identity with that of his "Father." In other words, the God of Jewish faith was Jesus' Father, his source.

Christians have waged fiery debates about the places of reason and revelation in developing Jesus' notion of God. A generation ago, the Protestant theologians Karl Barth and Paul Tillich presented radically different approaches. Barth insisted on the primacy of revelation, while Tillich began with reason and an existential analysis of the human situation.[77] Barth's position was that we can only know who and what God is through the self-expression that he has made in Jesus Christ. Apart from this primary revelation, Barth said, all reasoning about divinity is a matter of human pride, and the philosophies and religions are enemies of true Christian theology. Tillich argued that no revelation stands apart from human minds and historical circumstances. Jesus himself spoke in the language of his people; the circumstances of his time and place qualified what he could think and say. Indeed, all theology reflects the prevailing understanding. For that reason, we never finally penetrate revelation. The "deposit of faith" that tradition said finished with the death of the last apostle paid such interest through later time that theology kept changing.

Implicit in these two positions is the dialectic between above and below that marks all religion. The conciliar age and the medieval period developed both revelation (considered to be from above) and reason (from below) to interpret the biblical word. One result of this balance was a discussion of God in terms of the (Aristotelian) doctrine of causality, which fascinated the medieval mind. God was the font of being, the prime mover behind the entire creational chain, and the final cause that lures all creation toward its fulfillment. By inference from the contingent (nonnecessary) nature of human experience, the philosophers concluded that God had to be a necessary fullness of existence. According to Etienne Gilson, perhaps the most distinguished Catholic historian of Christian philosophy, this position amounted to a philosophical elaboration of the self-designation God gave in Exodus 3:14—"I am what I am."[78]

In medieval Christian thought, human beings could reason that God exists but not reach what God is. Essentially, God was a mysterious fullness of being too rich or too bright for the human mind to grasp. The less sophisticated thinkers often thought that revelation had removed this mystery. Deeper thinkers, however, realized that, if anything, the Incarnation of the divine Logos (the heart of Christian revelation) compounded the mystery, adding the question of how divinity can express itself in another form—the infinite Son or Holy Spirit, but also, more pressingly, the finite God-man.

What the deep thinkers realized was that they could only propose analogies from human experience. Accepting the fact of revelation in Jesus Christ, which led to the facts of the Incarnation, the Trinity, grace, and creation from nothingness, they had to propose the most astute hypotheses they could. Such hypotheses were precious if they explained at all what the traditional faith, as expressed in the Bible and the councils, said. Nonetheless, no hypothesis gave one a direct vision of God.

God as the Trinity

In dealing with the revealed God's inner nature, the concept of the Trinity was paramount. Orthodox catholic (universal) faith held that Father–Son–Holy Spirit was attested by the scriptures and defined by the councils. As we indicated, the psychological analogy that Augustine and Aquinas developed gained great respect, the West considering it the "purest" (the least material) analogy. Thus, the God of Christian speculation was a fullness of intelligence and love. He was perfection, in need of nothing outside himself. He was the Creator and Redeemer, moved only by his own goodness. The Incarnation was the main instance of his outpouring, but glimpses of God abounded everywhere. Subhuman creatures were his "vestiges" (footprints); human beings were his images. Christians were images of his great image, for they reflected the eternal icon, the Logos-Son.

Regarding the Trinity, Christians stood in the Son's position, receiving their likeness to God from the Father and expressing it through Spirit-carried love. The similitude broke down, however, because the divine persons were only relationally distinct (that is, Son and Father differed only as begotten and begetter), while humans remained creatures distinct from God. Still, the consummation of faith, whether occurring in worldly mystical experience or in the beatific vision,[79] meant knowing with something of divinity's own knowledge, loving with something of divinity's own love.

Biblical Renewal

When Reformation thought returned to biblical conceptions, because it found the medieval synthesis too abstract and unhistorical, it revived the notion that faith is a living interpersonal relation to God. This contrasted somewhat with the position of most Scholasticism, which stressed the propositional knowledge (the information) that faith provides. As well, the Reformers revived the twin notions of God's judgment and his merciful love. By faith, God became one's "rock and salvation"—the one on whom to rely. Between the times of Luther and Kierkegaard, such faith became paradoxical—a leap. In the face of the "impossibility" of the Incarnation, Kierkegaard jumped into the intellectual abyss, proposing that what reason could not fathom divinity could yet do, because it moved by reasons the mind knew not, by reasons of the heart.

The Hebrew notion of *hesed* (steadfast, merciful love), which kept God to his freely chosen covenant, encouraged believers to trust that no situation in their lives was hopeless. If Ezekiel's God could raise dry bone back to fleshly life, Jesus' God could use even suffering and evil to his own inscrutable ends. Was not God's chosen way of salvation, the death of his only begotten Son, the surest sign that no one had ever understood him? As the heavens are above the earth, so were God's ways above the ways of human beings. For that reason, the Reformers wanted only a Pauline faith: God's power and wisdom are Christ crucified.

Did this finally mean a justification of God by surrender? For the deeper theologians, who had frequently wrestled with unbelief personally, the answer was yes. With Job and Paul, they said that the pot cannot tell the potter how to fashion. For the sake of their sanity, they had to affirm that God is wise and just (and even loving) in all his doings. How this worked out, however, they often could not say. Surrender was finally a matter of trust, a matter of unexpectedly feeling God's love. As the mistranslation of Job put it, "Though he slay me, yet will I trust him." The farthest reach of the Christian conception of God was an intimate marriage of lives and fortunes. What the prophet Hosea had written of God's constancy, even his vulnerability, the new biblical theologians found in New Testament *agape* (love).

The Johannine epistles say God is this *agape*. The Pauline epistles say *agape* is the greatest of God's gifts. The biblical theologians translated *agape* as self-sacrificing love. Beyond *eros* (self-fulfilling love) or *philia* (the love of friendship), it worked through God's use of the cross. Thus, it was an attack on evil, on lovelessness. Thus, it broke the circle of tit for tat, of sin and retribution. God the judge finally yielded to God the lover. In Jesus he suffered evil to undo evil, thereby making a new creation. The lamb who was slain for this new creation is worthy of all glory and honor, because his sacrifice shows a divinity greater than one could ever imagine. Only the nursing mother who could never abandon her child, the Lucan (pertaining to Luke) prodigal father, or the lover to whom the beloved is more than another self could glimpse this *mysterion*— this plan of God's love, hidden from all ages.

In contrast to other religions' versions of divinity, Christian theology stressed the personal, loving character of God that Jesus' flesh disclosed. Jesus was God in human

Figure 12   Dead Christ with Angels, by Edouard Manet (1832–1883). Nelson Gallery-Atkins Museum (Nelson Fund).

it was mindful of the continuing election of Israel that Paul had proclaimed (Romans, chapters 9–11). At its worst, Christianity condemned Jews as Christ killers and spoke of their responsibility for his blood. Islam confronted Christianity with claims of a later, perfected revelation and prophecy, and with an adamant insistence on God's unity. For Islam, and for Judaism, the Christian doctrine of the Trinity violated monotheism. Christian claims that God is both one and three seemed to Muslims and Jews incoherent, while Christian allegiance to Jesus clashed with Muslim allegiance to the Qur'an and Jewish allegiance to the Torah. Those clashes remain with us yet.

As the center of the Christian world view, God in Christ dominated Christian conceptions of nature, society, and self. Nature was but God's cloak. It was a lovely gift, but it sprang from nothingness and was wholly under God's control. With each extension of space and time by science, the awe of sophisticated believers increased: A more complex nature only magnified their God all the more.

Similarly, God was the norm and goal of Christian society, because his law was the source of all natural law and because eternal life with God in heaven was the goal of all persons. God wanted human beings to form a community. Christ showed them the love that could bring that about. Thus, the vocation of the self was to obey the great twofold command: to love God with whole mind, heart, soul, and strength and to love neighbor as itself.

terms. (He was also humanity fulfilled by union with divinity.) As a result, Christianity did not appreciate the impersonal divinity of nature so dear to East Asian and Indian thought. This divinity was implicit in Christian theology, but the personalistic emphasis placed it in the shade.

At its better moments, Christianity was grateful to Judaism, since it had adopted most of Judaism's doctrine of God. As well,

Study Questions

1. Why is it easier for a camel to pass through the eye of a needle than for a rich person to enter the Kingdom of God?
2. What is the significance of Jesus' parable of the Great Supper?
3. Elaborate on the following extract: "From Judaism came the concepts of prophet and messiah. From Hellenism came the notions of saviour and god. In the Church's hands, they were all underscored."
4. Why were the Councils of Nicaea and Chalcedon important?
5. How did the Mass summarize medieval Christian symbolism?
6. Describe the spirit of Protestantism.

7. How does the eighteenth-century Enlightenment contrast with faith, mysticism, and symbolism?

8. How has Christianity both spawned physical science and frustrated it?

9. Compose a brief rite for Christian baptism, stressing the Orthodox reliance on the Holy Spirit.

10. Indicate the main issues a contemporary person should consider in converting to Christianity.

11. Why would you like, or not like, to have an interview with the Russian holy man, Father Michael?

12. Give a brief digest of the overall Christian Gospel.

Chapter Four

ISLAM: TWENTY-FIVE KEY DATES

570 C.E.   BIRTH OF MUHAMMAD

609–610   FIRST QUR'ANIC REVELATIONS

622   HEJIRA (FLIGHT TO MEDINA)

630   CONQUEST OF MECCA

632   DEATH OF MUHAMMAD

636–640   CONQUEST OF DAMASCUS, JERUSALEM, EGYPT, PERSIA

CA. 650   ESTABLISHMENT OF THE CANON OF THE QUR'AN

661–750   UMAYYAD CALIPHATE

680   MURDER OF HUSAIN, SHIITE SAINT

711   MUSLIM ENTRY INTO SPAIN

713   MUSLIM ENTRY INTO INDUS VALLEY

750–1258   ABBASID CALIPHATE

Islam

The prophetic religion that began with Israel and took a new turn in Christianity gained a further career in Islam. Islam, which is the world's fastest-growing religion today, arose from the visions of the prophet Muhammad. At its height, Islam stretched from India to western Spain.[1] Today it is a great force in Africa, a middling presence in China and the Soviet Union, a shareholder in the petropolitics of the Middle East, a huge presence in Indonesia, and the religion of more than 6 million North Americans. To study the religion behind the crescent flag, we begin by describing its traces in several different locations.

APPEARANCE

A likely first encounter with Islam is in southern Spain, which has a proud Moorish (Spanish Muslim) heritage. Toledo city walls date back to the Arab conquest, and the art of El Greco reflects a culture that mixed Jews, Muslims, and Christians with few problems. Farther south, the Muslim traces are stronger, as evidenced by the great mosque in Cordoba. Although Christians remade it into a cathedral, Islamic art still shines in the beautiful *mihrab*—the niche in the wall (gilded in blue and gold) that directs the worshiper towards Mecca. At Granada the Alhambra that faces the snow-capped Sierra Nevada mountains demonstrates the architecture that thirteenth- and fourteenth-century Muslim rulers could command. Fernando Diaz-Plaja's study of Spanish character[2] shows that Islam left its effects on the population, too. Something of today's Castilian pride came from Andalusian Moors, who felt that their scimitar contained the courage of Muhammad's original holy warriors and that their mathematics and medicine extended the Greek golden age.

In Cairo all evidence of Islam is current. Though the pyramids and the Nile conjure images of the pharaohs, the dusty main streets feature flowing garments and tapered minarets. In the train terminal, prayer mats come out when the call to prayer sounds. The Westernized businessmen in the air-conditioned, first-class coaches seem to pay the haunting verses little heed, but the verses clearly move the workers outside. On a Friday, the Muslim holy day, what look like middle-class families picnic at the fine Cairo zoo. The university nearby closes on Friday, so students hoist small children to see the lions. In Cairo's back streets, where thousands live five and six to a room, the small children run around in pajamas or run into the streets to play amidst the buses and taxis. The poverty of the back streets suggests a certain fatalism. Just as dozens of children die each year in the traffic, so thousands, perhaps millions, suffer from malnutrition.

In Jerusalem the Islamic presence may seem surprising, if one expects to find only a Jewish capital.[3] But Jerusalem is the third holiest Muslim city, ranking behind only Mecca and Medina. Abraham and Jesus are Muslim prophets, and the Qur'an extols Mary. The mosque at the Dome of the Rock (Figure 13), behind the Western Wall, is a gorgeous tribute to Muhammad's night flight to heaven and to Abraham's faith in being willing to sacrifice Ishmael (in the Muslim version of the story).

The Dome of the Rock is stunning. Its blue, green, red, and gold somehow never clash. The rock itself, around which lushly carpeted corridors wind, is but a mass of stone, but the beauty of its surroundings transforms it into a pillar of faith. In a small chamber under the rock, devout Muslims kneel, lost in obeisance and prayer. Upstairs Israeli guards prod an Arab who has stretched out behind a pillar to enjoy the carpet's softness and steal a mid-morning nap. They are another reminder that the Middle East is very complex.

Northeast of Jerusalem the volatile Shia Islam of Iran presents yet new images. Two-thirds of the women of Tehran are veiled, although they may wear blue jeans under their black draping and their dark eyes may flash contemporary signals. With the ouster of the shah in 1979, Iran became the

Figure 13   Dome of the Rock. Photo by J. T. Carmody.

most visible example of Islam's moves to restore traditional culture. The passions responsible for the headlines showed that submission (the root meaning of *Islam*) was potent indeed. Iran today hardly acknowledges that Zoroaster once inspired its people and little doubts that the Prophet (Muhammad) laid out its way. Everywhere, there is oil, religion, and emotion. How they will mix in the Iranian future will be a prime indicator of what other Muslim states will attempt.

In India, Delhi reveals much more than a Hindu heritage. From 1200 to 1857 Delhi was the center of a Muslim empire. The great mosque of the old city, as well as the Mogul monuments on the outskirts, speak of that empire's splendor. The city of Agra is the most eloquent witness, though, because it is the home of the Taj Mahal. The symmetry of this wonder of the world makes the golden age of Islamic culture appear quite contemporary. Forget that the ruler who built it wanted to memorialize his wife; forget that he was slain before he could build a matching black mausoleum for himself. Simply enjoy the minarets at the corners, the graceful swell of the domes. It is as though the reflecting pool and the gardens mirror the Qur'an's picture of Paradise. Agra's heat is more humid than that of the Arabian desert, and it inspires a longing for cool, shade, and flowing waters.

Behind the Taj Mahal, water buffalo that hulk in the Jumna river flats temper the paradisal daydream, reminding the visitor that this is Indian Islam—Islam that contended with Hinduism, influenced Hindu devotion through its Sufis, begot syncretistic Sikhism, and led, rather inevitably, to partition and the creation of Pakistan. Indian Islam was the faith of conquerors, of outsiders, that gathered millions of disciples but never won the subcontinent's soul. So the water buffalo, though not quite sacred cows, have Hindu rights to life. It would be aesthetically more pleasing were they not squatting behind the Taj Mahal, but Hindu *ahimsa* (noninjury) says let them be.

HISTORY

Muhammad

Islam stems directly from the two precepts contained in the profession of faith: "There is no God but God, and Muhammad is his Prophet." Allah (God) is the ultimate agent of Islamic revelation and religion, but he chose to work through Muhammad. Thus, Muhammad was the spokesman, the medium, of a definitive message and book (the Qur'an). Through it God expressed once and for all the divine mercy and judgment.

Muhammad was born in 570 C.E. in Mecca, which is in present-day Saudi Arabia. Around 610, he began to receive revelations. At that time, the religious milieu of the Arabian Peninsula was "a rather primitive polydemonism and worship of stones, stars, caves and trees."[4] Most of the people identified with one of the nomadic tribes that lived in the area. Mecca was a religious and commercial center, where people came to venerate the Black Stone, set in what is known as the Kaaba. Today scholars surmise that the stone was a meteorite. Whatever its origin, it served as a rallying point for local soothsayers and poets, who dominated the Arab religion that Muhammad witnessed as a youth. The likeliest forerunners of Muhammad's strict monotheism were the *hanifs*, who took offense at the polydemonism and sought a purer faith, although to what extent they inspired Muhammad is not known.

W. Montgomery Watt has stressed the commercial strife that divided the people of Mecca during Muhammad's early years.[5] The conflict between the Byzantine and Persian empires affected Mecca, because traders from those realms passed through it. Among the Arabs there, a difficult social transition

was under way from a nomadic society, in which loyalty was to one's clan, to a mercantile society, in which loyalty was to one's business partners (or simply to profit). The result was considerable upheaval. Before that time persons such as orphans and widows, who fell outside of nuclear families and trading groups, could find support in their larger clans, but the social change destroyed this support. Muhammad grew up as an orphan, so he must have felt some of the suffering experienced by such persons. Indeed, much of the social reform in his early message was to provide a religious basis for a unity extending beyond the clan that would prompt concern for orphans, widows, and the poor.

Muhammad grew up in a branch of the ruling Kuraish family under the care of his uncle, and he probably entered his family's caravan trade as a youth. In adulthood he married a wealthy widow, Khadija, who was some years older than he and who had been his employer. They had six children, of whom four daughters survived. Whether from personal troubles, challenges in the social situation, or a positive desire to understand the world more deeply, Muhammad developed the habit of going off to the hills nearby. There, in a cave, he enjoyed meditative solitude and began to have visions. His first visions, according to the Qur'an (53 : 1–18, 81:15–25) were of someone "terrible in power, very strong."[6] That personage hovered near him on the horizon and imparted a revelation. It and subsequent revelations finally convinced Muhammad that God was choosing him to be a messenger.

At first, he wondered if he was going crazy. However, Khadija encouraged him to believe in the revelations, and as his thought clarified, he attributed them to the angel Gabriel. Muhammad continued to receive revelations for the rest of his life (over twenty years), and these messages, which either he or early disciples wrote down on "pieces of paper, stones, palm-leaves, shoulder-blades, ribs and bits of leather,"[7] formed the basis of the Qur'an.

From what scholars conjecture to be the early revelations, five major themes

5 theme in Qur'an

emerge: God's goodness and power, the need to return to God for judgment, gratitude and worship in response to God's goodness and pending judgment, generosity toward one's fellow human beings, and Muhammad's own vocation of proclaiming the message of goodness and judgment.

Muhammad's proclamation met with considerable resistance, principally because it threatened some powerful vested interests. First, the absoluteness of Allah threatened the traditional polytheism. However, it was much more than a challenge to custom and traditional religion—it was a challenge to the commerce that had grown up around the Kaaba. The livelihoods of the merchants who sold amulets, the soothsayers who sold fortunes, and the semiecstatic poets who lyricized the old gods were all imperiled.[8] Second, Muhammad's call for social justice implied a revolution—if not in contemporary financial arrangements, at least in contemporary attitudes. Third, the message of judgment was hardly welcome, for no age likes to find itself set before divine justice, hell fire, or the sword of retribution. Last, many Meccans ridiculed Muhammad's notion of the resurrection of the body.

Rise to Power

Initially rejected, Muhammad drew consolation from the fate of prophets who had preceded him. Increasingly, it appears, he learned about Judaism and Christianity from believers of those traditions who either lived in the area or traveled it for trade. The first converts to Muhammad's revelations came from within his own family. When he started to preach publicly, around 613, the leaders of the most powerful clans opposed him vigorously. He thus tended to be most successful among the low-ranking clans and those with young leaders ripe for a new order. Also, those who were considered "weak" (without strong clan protection) found the new prophecy attractive. Muhammad was proposing a religious association based on faith in Allah that transcended clan allegiances and so might make the weak stronger.

In 619 Muhammad suffered a personal crisis. His wife and uncle, who had been his foremost supporters, both died. Muslims ("submitters" to his God) were slowly increasing in number, but the future was very uncertain. In 622 he left Mecca and went to Yathrib, to the north, to arbitrate a long-standing dispute between two leading tribes. He settled there, and the town became Medina, the town of the Prophet. Muslims call Muhammad's departure or flight from Mecca the *Hejira,* and they view it as the turning point in the history of early Islam. Annemarie Schimmel interprets the Hejira as the complete breakup of Muhammad's relations with his own tribe—a definitive break with the old order,[9] which was a virtually unheard-of act in the clan-based society of the time.

Al Faruqi emphasizes the positive work that went on in Medina: the "promulgation of a constitution and the launching of the Islamic polity on its universal mission."[10] Muhammad proved to be a good politician, able to organize the Meccan emigrants and the Medina clans into a single group.

One problem for Muhammad in Medina was the local Jewish community, who refused to accept him as a genuine prophet and ridiculed his interpretation of Jewish scripture. Apparently Muhammad either drove them out of Medina or had them killed or sold into slavery.[11] After consolidating his power base and building support among the neighboring bedouin tribes, Muhammad started to challenge the Meccans. He disrupted their trade in an effort to overthrow the city's commercial base, and in 624 his vastly outnumbered troops won a surprising victory at Badr. Finally, after several further skirmishes, Muhammad won a decisive victory at the Battle of the Ditch.

Muhammad's greatest triumphs came through diplomacy among the tribes, however. Mecca finally fell in 630 without the stroke of a single sword. In control, Muhammad cleansed the Kaaba of pagan idols. He then consolidated his victory by a final military triumph over resistant Meccans at Hunayn. This settled the matter for most onlookers, and thenceforth the surrounding tribes were in Muhammad's hands.

In the two remaining years of his life, Muhammad further developed the educational program that he had set up in Medina. "The centre of all his preoccupations was the training, educating, and disciplining of his community. They were to be the leaven to leaven the whole lump—for he had no illusions about the Arab character and realized that any genuine conversion of the majority could only be the end of a long process extending far beyond his own lifetime."[12] Muhammad soon became the focus of Arab solidarity, and just before his death, he apparently contemplated action against the Byzantine powers in the north, perhaps because Muslim nationalism meant a growing hostility toward Greeks and their Christian Arab allies. The quick military victories of his successor Abu Bakr make most sense on the assumption that he simply executed plans that Muhammad himself had formulated.

Personality

Muhammad demonstrated an abundant humanity. In addition to his religious sensitivity and his political and military skills, Muhammad manifested a notable sympathy for the weak, a gentleness, a slowness to anger, some shyness in social relations, and a sense of humor.[13] According to the *Hadith* (tradition), for instance, the Prophet's second in command, Abu Bakr, started to beat a pilgrim for letting a camel stray. Muhammad began to smile and then indicated to Abu Bakr the irony that a pilgrim like Bakr (a pilgrim through life) should beat a pilgrim to Mecca.

In glimpses obtained from the Qur'an and the earliest levels of the tradition, Muhammad seems to have been an ordinary man whom God singled out to receive revelations. Muhammad's virtue was to accept his commission and keep faith with it until death. The emphasis in the Prophet's own preaching on the sovereignty of God and on the divine authority for the Qur'anic message led him to stress his own ordinariness, his liability to error, and the like. He made no claim to miraculous power. The central miracle was the Qur'an itself—a message of such sublimity and eloquence that it testified beyond doubt to a divine source. In keeping with Muhammad's own humility, orthodox Islam has condemned any move to exalt Muhammad above ordinary humanity or worship him.

Nonetheless, popular Muslim religion sometimes seized on hints in the Qur'an and made Muhammad superhuman. The most famous of its images is Muhammad's "night journey" to Jerusalem, after which he ascended to Paradise, talked with the prophets who preceded him, and experienced an ineffable vision of God. This story became so popular that it finally entered orthodox faith. Later religious faith also elaborated on Muhammad's preaching of the coming Last Judgment and tended to think of the Prophet as its shield and intercessor on the Last Day.

Sufis (devotional Muslims) and other mystics elaborated a view of Muhammad as the supreme saint and mystic, while some Muslims given to cosmological speculation gave Muhammad an eternal preexistence, which related to the eternal preexistence of the Qur'an. This belief gave Muhammad a role in creation as the intermediary between God and humanity. The mystic al-Hallaj, whom Islamic authorities killed because he claimed oneness with the deity, saw Muhammad as the first of the prophets—as the Light that was the source of all their lights: "He was before all, his name the first in the Book of Fate; he was known before all things and all being, and will endure after the end of all."[14] In such understandings, the Prophet became the supreme exemplar, the mediator, something close to the Word of creation.

Qur'anic Religion

After Muhammad's death, his followers collected the texts of his revelations and established the orthodox version during the rule of Othman (644–656). "To this day this version remains as the authoritative word of God. But, owing to the fact that the kufic script in which the Koran was originally written contained no indication of vowels or diacritical points, variant readings are recognized by Muslims as of equal authority."[15]

The present version of the collection follows the editorial principle that the chapters (suras) should be ordered in decreasing length. The result is that the present text tells the reader nothing about the chronology of the revelations. While scholars have attempted to distinguish the Meccan utterances from the Medinan, their work is often so tedious (distinguishing separate verses within a sura) that no one theory of the chronology has won universal acceptance. Therefore, it is more expeditious simply to accept the fact that Muhammad's revelations were written down and that he used them as the basis of the program that he urged on his listeners. Among the earliest themes of his preaching were the sovereignty of God, the imminence of judgment, and the need for fraternal charity.

Cragg and other commentators insist on the importance of the Qur'anic Arabic.[16] Muslims consider the Qur'an to be written in the purest Arabic. Its style, as well as its message, prove to them that it must have come directly from God. Jeffrey and al Faruqi have both given thematic presentations of the Qur'an's religious materials.[17] They organize the Qur'an's seemingly repetitious or circular presentations, and by following them we may get a sense of how Islamic revelation developed.

An early Meccan passage (96 : 1–5) emphasizes that Muhammad experienced his call as a command to *recite*, although his recitations only became clear as time passed. Sura 53, lines 1–18, richly symbolizes how Muhammad experienced his call. Because of Muhammad's vision of the angel Gabriel, the Muslim theology of revelation granted Gabriel an important role as the mediator in transmitting the Qur'an. In Sura 81, lines 15–29, are suggestions that Muhammad's early preaching met with disbelief and even

contempt. Indeed, the Prophet seems to have had to defend himself against the charge of jinn (demon) possession.

Suras 73 and 74 buttress the tradition that Muhammad regularly used to go off to a cave to pray. Wrapped in a mantle against the night cold, he would seek God's comfort. This image has been a model for countless Sufis and ascetics as they have sought an experiential knowledge of Allah. Other Qur'anic passages that are considered reflections of Muhammad's early concerns boom forth a praise of God, a sense of God's overwhelming majesty, that suggests Rudolf Otto's classic definition of the holy: the mystery that is both alluring and threatening.

The later passages of the Qur'an, those that likely were written in Medina, concern more practical affairs. As the head of an established political and religious community, Muhammad had to deal with questions of law and order. Thus, we can find the seeds of later Islamic law on inheritance, women, divorce, warfare, and the like. These seeds, plus the *Hadith*, which contain what the Prophet himself taught and judged,[18] are the primary sources of Islamic law. Generally, Muhammad's law and social teaching were advances on the prevailing mores. They improved the lot of the downtrodden and humanized both business and war. For instance, Muhammad made widows and orphans the prime beneficiaries of the *zakat* (almsgiving) required of all the faithful. Two points on which outsiders frequently fault Muhammad and the Qur'an are the doctrines of holy war (jihad) and polygamy. Nevertheless, they were improvements on the pre-Muslim practices and improved treatment of both women and prisoners of war.

On the basis of the Qur'an's prescriptions for a true Islam, a true religion of submission to the will of Allah, Muslims have elaborated five cardinal duties known as the "pillars" of true faith. They are: witnessing to faith (proclaiming the creed), ritual prayer, fasting during the lunar month of Ramadan, almsgiving, and pilgrimage to Mecca. The witness to faith epitomizes the

5 cardinal duties ("pillars" of true faith)

MARY

Sura 19, entitled "Mary," shows some of the connections between Islam and both Judaism and Christianity. The sura begins with an interpretation of the story of the birth of John the Baptist (Luke 1 : 5–80). Zacharias, the father of John the Baptist, approached God and prayed for an heir. He received the answer that he would have a son, to be called John, despite the fact that he and his wife were advanced in years. "It shall be no difficult task for Me, for I brought you into being when you were nothing before."[19] Allah instructed John to observe the scriptures with a firm resolve, bestowing on him wisdom, grace, and purity. John grew up to be a righteous man who honored his father and mother and was neither arrogant nor rebellious. So the Qur'an blesses the day John was born, and blesses the day of his death: "May peace be on him when he is raised to life."

Then Muhammad receives a command to recount the story of Mary, who left her people and betook herself to a solitary place to the east. Allah tells Muhammad that he sent to Mary the divine spirit in the semblance of a grown man. Mary saw the spirit and was seized with fear. But the spirit explained that he was a messenger of Mary's Lord, come to give her a holy son. When she asked how this could be, since she was a virgin, the spirit said that nothing is difficult to God and that this miracle was God's will. The son "shall be a sign to mankind." says the Lord, "and a blessing from Ourself. That is Our decree." Thereupon Mary conceived. When her time of delivery came, she lay down by a palm tree, wishing that she had died and passed into oblivion. But a voice from below her cried out that she should not despair. God had provided her a brook to run at her feet, and if she would shake the trunk of the palm tree it would drop ripe dates in her lap.

Mary took her child to her people, who abused her as a harlot. So she pointed to the baby in the cradle, who spoke up and said: "I am the servant of Allah. He has given me the gospel and ordained me a prophet." The child explained that God had commanded him to be steadfast in prayer, to give alms to the poor, to honor his mother, and to be free of vanity and wickedness.

God had blessed the day of his birth and would bless the day of his death.

The sura then makes a polemical point: This is the whole truth about Jesus, the son of Mary, which "they" (probably the Christians) are unwilling to accept. "God forbid that He Himself should beget a son!" In other words, though Jesus had a marvelous birth, he was in no way the divine Son of God. Only Allah is Muhammad's Lord, and the Lord of Muslims. Therefore only Allah is to be served. That is the right path. Any other path is erroneous. The unbelievers who cling to a different view of Jesus will experience woe on the day they appear before Allah, since they are in the grossest error (idolatry).

Next the sura takes up the story of Abraham. Abraham was a prophet and a saintly man. He asked his father, "How can you serve a worthless idol, a thing that can neither see nor hear?" Further, he told his father that the truth had been revealed to him (Abraham), so that if the father followed Abraham he would follow the even path, away from the worship of Satan, who had rebelled against the Lord of Mercy. But Abraham's father only became angry, banishing him from the house and threatening him with stoning. Abraham prayed that the true Lord would forgive his father, but he departed, since he could not worship idols. God rewarded Abraham with sons called Isaac and Jacob, prophets of high renown.

The next story concerns Moses, who was a prophet, an apostle, and a chosen man. Allah called out to Moses from the right side of a mountain. When Moses came, God communed with him in secret and gave him his brother Aaron, also a prophet. Then there was Ishmael, also an apostle, a seer, and a man of his word. Ishmael enjoined prayer and almsgiving on his people, and thereby he pleased the Lord. Last there was Idris (Enoch), another saint and prophet, whom the Lord honored and exalted.

To all these men, Allah has been gracious. They are the line of prophets, from the descendants of Adam and the people God carried in the ark with Noah. They include Abraham and Israel (Jacob), and they stand out as the line God has guided and chosen. When they received divine revelations, these prophets humbled themselves, falling down on their knees in tears and adoration. In contrast, the generations that succeeded the prophets neglected prayer and succumbed to temptation. Assuredly they shall be lost.

However, those that repent, embrace the faith that Muhammad is preaching, and do what is right will be admitted to Paradise. They shall not be wronged, but shall enter the Gardens of Eden, which the Merciful has promised to his servants as their reward for faith. What God has promised God shall fulfill. In Paradise the just will hear no idle talk, only the voice of peace. Morning and evening they shall receive their sustenance. That is the bliss which the righteous shall inherit.

The sura then interposes a strange transition: "We do not descend from Heaven save at the bidding of your Lord." Muslim commentators tend to interpret this as the voice of the angel Gabriel, answering Muhammad's complaint that the revelations he was receiving sometimes stopped, making for long intervals of silence. Gabriel reminds Muhammad that revelation like this is solely God's affair. To God alone belongs what is before us and what is behind us, and all that lies between.

Gabriel goes on to comfort Muhammad. His Lord does not forget his servants. He is the ruler of the heavens and the earth and all that is between them. Muhammad's task is simple: Worship him and be loyal in his service. After all, what god compares with Allah? To whom else can a sane or devout person go?

But all human flesh is weak, so it finds faith hard to sustain. Thus human beings regularly ask, "When I am once dead, shall I be raised to life again?" God's answer is a call to remembrance. Why do human beings forget that Allah once had to create them from the void? Unless they put their lives in order, God will call them to account, placing them in the company of the devils, setting them on their knees around the fire of hell. Each sect of dissidents will have its stoutest rebels cast down into hellfire. God alone knows who most deserves to burn.

Sternly, the Lord issues a dire warning: Not one of the unbelievers shall not pass through the confines of hell. This is his absolute decree.

God will deliver those who fear him, but wrongdoers will go to their knees to endure the torments of the fire. For the conduct of the unbelievers is wanton. When Allah's clear revelations are laid out before them, they say to Allah's faithful, "Will that way add to your glory or place you in better company than ours?" Such questioning and haggling will bring them speedy destruction. God has destroyed many generations of unbelievers prior to this present one. Faithless people far richer and more splendid than they have been sent on their way to destruction.

Yet, Muhammad is to tell the unbelievers that God is merciful. He will bear with the unbelievers until they witness the fulfillment of his threats, be that a worldly scourge or the hour of doom, when all are called to judgment. At such times of reckoning, the unbelievers will realize the comparative worth of their way and the true way of God. Their worse plight and smaller following will make it clear they have chosen unto their woe.

On the other hand, Allah will more and more guide those that have chosen the right path. Their deeds will bring them lasting merit, a rich reward in God's sight, and an auspicious end. The unbeliever, in contrast, has only empty boasts. He expects wealth and children, as though he had had the future disclosed to him, or the merciful Lord, who alone knows what lies ahead, had made him a solemn promise. The truth is far different. God will record every word of such vain boasts and determine punishments long and terrible. When the unbeliever is brought to judgment, he shall come alone, his expected wealth and children having proven only vain imaginings. The unbelievers have chosen other gods to help them. In the end, these useless gods will reject the unbelievers' worship and turn against them. So the unbelievers will be sent down to the devils that incite their irreligion. True believers like Muhammad should be patient. The days of the unbelievers are numbered.

On the day of reckoning, God will gather the righteous and bring them before him. But the sinful he will drive in great hordes into the fire of hell. Then no one will be able to intercede for the wicked, save the one (Muhammad?) who has received the sanction of the Merciful.

Again the sura lashes out at those who teach that God has begotten a son. That is such a monstrous falsehood that the heavens should crack, the earth should break asunder, the mountains should crumble to dust. Those who ascribe to God a son know nothing of the nature of the Merciful. It does not become him to beget a son. His sovereignty is beyond any such thing. For there is none in the heavens or on earth who shall not return to the Lord in utter submission. God keeps strict count of all his creatures. One by one, they shall all approach him on the Resurrection Day. Those he shall cherish are they who have accepted the true faith Muhammad is preaching and shown charity to their fellows.

Concluding, the sura has God remind Muhammad that he has revealed the Qur'an in Muhammad's own tongue so that Muhammad can proclaim good tidings to the upright and warnings to a contentious nation. How many generations has the Lord not destroyed before this one? Is one of those generations still alive? Does any of them still speak so much as a whisper?

From reading this remarkable bit of the Qur'an, one senses the overwhelming sovereignty of Muhammad's God. Not to believe him, not to accept the way he lays out, is tantamount to blindness or utter corruption of heart. Muhammad finds this way prefigured in the prior prophets of Judaism and Christianity, who deserve high esteem. Jesus, the miraculous child of Mary, the great heroine of faith, was a worthy precursor.[20] But the Christian notion that Jesus was God's son is sheer blasphemy, an effort to diminish God's absolute uniqueness and sovereignty. The Creator is solely responsible for all that happens in the world. Those who confess this will merit good things in the Gardens of Eden. Those who reject it will go to hell, the place of punishing fire and devils. So the choice is very simple: Believe and prosper, or reject belief and perish. The Lord is merciful, so belief is offered to all. The Lord is also just, so unbelief cannot evade due punishment. Those with any wit will open their hearts to God's last Prophet and believe.

Muslim's orientation in the universe: There is no God but God, and Muhammad is his Prophet. Allah is the only fit object of worship, and Muhammad is the last of the prophets—the "seal."

What a comparativist might call the rigorous monotheism of Islam has both negative and positive aspects. Negatively, in what amounts to an attack on false religion, Islam makes idolatry (associating anything with Allah) the capital sin. At the outset, then, Muhammad's revelation implied an attack on the prevailing Arab religion. Later it led to a polemic against Christian Trinitarianism and a check on worldly pride or mammon that might diminish God's sovereignty. Positively, Islamic monotheism generated great praise for the "Lord of the Worlds"[21]—the Creator who guides all things, who is the beauty and power by which the world moves. For the Muslim mystics, the words of the creed swelled with hidden meaning. Like the Cabalists, some

Muslim mystics assigned each letter a numerical value and then composed numerological accounts of how the world hangs together. Many Muslim mystics pushed the concept of divine sovereignty so far that they denied the existence of anything apart from Allah. Not only was there no God beside him, there was no being apart from his Being. While the orthodox Muslims found such pantheism blasphemous, the mystics tended to stress the oneness of the Lord's domain.[22] Last, rigorous monotheism implied that Muhammad himself was not divine. His high status was to be the *rasul*—the prophetic mouthpiece. (In later devotion, as we have seen, there was a tendency to exalt Muhammad, and later theology often viewed the Qur'an as coeternal with God, much as rabbinic theology saw the Torah as coeternal with God.)

The second pillar of faith is prayer, which has worked out as an obligation to pray five times daily. Authoritative authors such as al-Ghazali went to great lengths to specify the postures, words, number of bows, and proper places and times for prayer,[23] but the primary effect of the second pillar on the common people was to pace them through the day in the great Muslim practice of remembrance *(dhikr)*. At each call from the minaret, they were to remember the one God whom they serve—remember his compassion, his mercy, and his justice. Ideally, by praying fervently at the appointed hours, one can forge a chain that links together more and more moments of remembrance, so that God progressively comes to dominate all one's thought, action, and emotion. Experiencing Muslim prayer is impressive. The slow chant of the Qur'anic words becomes haunting, stirring even the non-Arabist. The voice (usually recorded today) is passionate—a lover's near sob, a tremulous witness to God's grandeur.

Third, what the prayer times are to the day, the holy month of Ramadan is to the year. Ramadan is the month of fasting and (interestingly enough) of celebration. Through all the hours of daylight (from the time that one can distinguish a black thread from a white), no food or drink is to pass the lips. Thereby, the Muslim learns discipline, sacrifice, and the price that divine treasures cost.[24] Against the secular succession of months, in which no time is more significant than any other, the religionist erects special times like Ramadan. These times

oppose the flux, fence off a portion of time as sacred.

Fourth, Islam develops a similar paradigm for space by praying toward Mecca and by the obligation to make a pilgrimage to Mecca at least once in one's lifetime. For Muslims, Mecca is the center, the *omphalos* (navel) where the world was born. It is the holy city where Qur'anic revelation was disclosed to the world. Thus, the psychodynamics of the pilgrimage run deep. Without doubt, devout pilgrims feel that they are going to the holiest spot in creation.

On pilgrimage, Muslims dress alike, go through the same traditional actions, and often experience an exhilarating sense of community. The fifth pillar, almsgiving, focuses this sense of community in a practical, economic way. By insisting that all contribute to the support of the poor (often one-fortieth of their wealth annually), Qur'anic religion gives its community *(Ummah)*[25] food and clothing. The Muslim alms, then, is more than a tiny dole or act of charity—it is an act of social, corporate responsibility. Further, it reminds the advantaged that they are one family with the disadvantaged and that the stern Judge will demand a strict account of what they have done with his gifts.

Sura 4, lines 134–137, gathers the pillars together and shows their common foundation: faith in God, in his Word, in his coming judgment:

O believers, be you securers of justice, witnesses for God, even though it be against yourselves, or your parents and kinsmen, whether the man be rich or poor; God stands close to either. Then follow not caprice, so as to swerve. For if you twist or turn, God is aware of the things you do. O Believers, believe in God and His Messenger and the Book He has sent down on His messenger and the Book which He sent down before [the Bible]. Whoso disbelieves in God and His Angels and His Books, and His Messengers, and the Last Day, has surely gone astray into far error. Those who believe, and then disbelieve, and then believe, and then disbelieve, and then increase in unbelief—God is not likely to forgive them, neither to guide them on any way.

That strong commitment to the Prophet and to the Qur'an founded Islam. Muhammad's prophecy became the basis of Islam's external missionizing and internal religious development. Praise belongs only to God. God is the Lord of all beings. He is the all-merciful, the compassionate, the Master of the Day of Judgment and Resurrection. Blessing is to serve God, to pray to God, to have God guide one on the straight path (Qur'an 1:5). Burning with this conviction, Muslims poured out of Mecca to conquer the world.

The Age of Conquest

At Muhammad's death in 632 most of Arabia had accepted Islam, though often the allegiance was superficial. Some tribes took the occasion of the Prophet's death to attempt a revolt. General Khalid al-Walid, who served the first caliph (leader) Abu Bakr, crushed them within a year. Thus, when Abu Bakr died in 636, Arabia was united and poised for adventure. The obvious foes were Byzantium and Persia, which threatened Arabian prosperity and were ripe for religious and military conquest. The Muslim armies were amazingly effective. By 636 they controlled both Damascus and Jerusalem. As important in this lightning conquest as their military skill, though, was the unrest of the peoples they conquered. Those peoples "welcomed the Muslims as kinliberators from Byzantine politics, economic exploitation, Church persecution, and social tyranny."[26] On the eastern frontier, Muslim armies spread into Persian territory, and by 649 all of Persia was in Arab hands.

The quick conquest of Syria released men for further expeditions in the West; by 640 there were conquests in Egypt. Cairo and Alexandria soon fell, and despite resistance from the Roman emperor Constans, the Arabs established themselves as a marine power operating from the southeastern Mediterranean. By 648 they had conquered Cyprus; by 655 they were in charge of the waters around Greece and Sicily. On land in North Africa, the Muslims conquered the Berber region of Tripoli in 643 and then proceeded to Carthage and to the Nubian regions along the Nile, conquering the Nubian capital city of Dongola. When the Umayyad caliphate established itself in 661, the ventures became even more far-reaching. Soon Muslims were as far away as China, India, and western Europe. By 699 Islam occupied Afghanistan, while various campaigns south of the Caspian and Aral seas brought Armenia, Iraq, Iran, and eastern India into the Muslim fold by 800.

At the beginning of the ninth century, Arab rule along the southern Mediterranean stretched from Palestine to the Atlantic. Muslims controlled three-quarters of the Iberian Peninsula, and most Mediterranean traffic had to reckon with Muslim sallies. European campaigns had brought Arab soldiers as far north as Orleans, and they strongly influenced the southern portions of the Frankish kingdom. In 732 Muslims had taken Toulouse and then the whole of Aquitaine, moving into Bordeaux and Tours. Charles Martel stopped them at Poitiers, but in 734 they crossed the Rhone and captured Arles, Saint-Remy, and Avignon. Then they fortified Languedoc and recaptured Lyons and Burgundy. In the ninth century, from their positions in southeastern France, they pushed northeast as far as Switzerland. By daring naval raids, they harassed such ports as Marseilles and even Oye on the coast of Brittany.

Toward the end of the ninth century, Islam controlled most of western Switzerland and ruled many of the Alpine passes. In the mid-tenth century Muslims were at Lake Geneva, taking Neuchâtel and Saint Gall. Only the attacks of the Huns and the Hungarians from the north and northeast and the deterioration of the Spain-based Umayyad caliphate kept them from ruling all of southern Europe. However, Muslim expansion ended after 1050, for the Normans pushed Islam out of southern France, southern Italy, Corsica, Sardinia, and Sicily.

By 1250, Islam's European presence had weakened considerably. Only southernmost Spain and eastern Anatolia held secure.

However, Islam had spread through all of Persia, crossed northern India, and reached the western Chinese border. In East Asia, it had a discernible presence in Sumatra, Borneo, and Java. All of North Africa was securely Muslim, while down the East African coast as far as Madagascar it exerted a strong influence. In many of these regions, of course, substantial portions of the populations remained non-Muslim. For instance, in Egypt many Monophysite and Coptic Christians remained loyal to their own traditions, as did many Christians in Anatolia and Syria. Nestorian Christians in Iraq north of Baghdad held out, while portions of southern Persia remained Zoroastrian strongholds. In India the majority remained Hindu, especially in the central and southern regions.

Motivations

Through this age of conquest and expansion, the basic Muslim strategy revolved around the use of the desert.[27] Just as modern empires, such as the British, made great use of naval power, so the Arabs exploited their experience with the desert, using it for communication, transferring supplies, and retreating safely in time of emergency. In their spread through North Africa, they established main towns at the edge of the desert. In Syria they employed such conquered cities as Damascus to the extent that they lay close to the desert. Through the Umayyad period (to 750), these garrison towns at the edge of the desert were the centers of Arab government. By dominating them and by introducing Arabic as the language of government, the conquerors exerted a disproportionate influence (they usually remained a minority of the total population). The towns served as the chief markets for the agricultural produce of the neighboring areas, and around their markets clusters of artisan quarters developed. By imposing discriminatory taxes on the outlying populations, the Arabs encouraged the citizenry to congregate in the cities, making their control easier.

Historians debate the motivation for all this expansion, and we can safely say that it was complex. The Arabs were likely suffering from population pressures on the Arabian Peninsula, which incited many of them to search for more land. Precedents for such an outflow occurred in the fifth and sixth centuries, prior to Islam, and apparently from even earlier times the land to the northeast, especially the Fertile Crescent, served as a safety valve for overpopulation. Bernard Lewis has suggested that older historians overestimated the role of religion in the Islamic conquests and that more recent historians have underestimated it. In his own view, "its [religion's] importance lies in the temporary psychological change which it wrought in a people who were naturally excitable and temperamental, unaccustomed to any sort of discipline, willing to be persuaded, but never to be commanded. It made them for a time more self-confident and more amenable to control."[28]

Symbolically, religion served as a rallying point for the Arab cause. It stressed common bondage to a single Lord, and it dignified the Arab movement with a sort of manifest destiny. Certainly the generals who dominated the era of conquest were as accomplished in worldly affairs as they were in religious. For Khalid and Amr, two of the most outstanding, the utilitarian values of religion seem to have been clear.

The Islamic administration of the conquered territories was also quite pragmatic. Rather understandably, the interests served were not those of the conquered subjects but those of the aristocracy that conquest created—the interests of the Arab rulers. Thus, the temper of the Arab military commanders and then of the quasi-military Arab governors most determined how Islam treated its new peoples. At the beginning of the conquest in Byzantium and Persia, Muslims kept the old administrative structures. In the 640s, though, they shifted to a new format, through which the caliphs could impress their will more directly.

However, at first there was no unified imperial law. The conquerors struck different bargains with different peoples, and some stipulated that local customs or laws remain in force. The Arabs tended to take only the property of the state (and that of the new regime's enemies); other landowners who were willing to recognize the new regime could keep their holdings provided they paid a sizable tax. Nevertheless, there were opportunities for Muslim "speculators," as we might call them, to gain lands outside the garrison center on which they would have to pay only light levies.

At first, the conquered peoples were allowed to retain most of their traditional civil and religious rights. The Muslims grouped most of the conquered non-Muslims together as *Dhimmis*—members of religions that Arab law tolerated. As "peoples of the book," Jews and Christians had title to special respect. There were nevertheless frictions, especially if subjects were blatantly derogatory of the Prophet and his Book, but usually people were not compelled to convert to Islam. Because Arab rule regularly promised to be more just than Byzantine rule, many Jews and Christians are on record as having welcomed the change. For example, in Palestine the Samaritans actively assisted the invaders. The Arabs were not always sure how to handle such complicity, especially when it developed into a desire to convert to Islam. Islam and Arabism were so synonymous that the first converts had to become *Mawali*—clients of one of the Arab tribes. In fact, converts seldom gained equal status, especially regarding such material benefits as the booty that warriors received after a conquest.

Internal Strife

Despite its enormous outward success in the age of conquest, the Islamic community suffered notable internal divisions. With the exception of Abu Bakr, the first caliphs, known as the *Rashidun* (rightly guided), all left office by murder. (Despite that fact, modern Islam has considered their time the golden age.)[29] Ali, the fourth caliph, was the center of a fierce struggle for control. His main opponent was Muawiya, the head

of a unified stronghold in Syria. Muawiya maneuvered to have the legitimacy of Ali's caliphate called into question. As a result, Ali lost support in his own group, and dissidents called Kharijites appeared who had a hand in many later conflicts. A Kharijite killed Ali in 661, and the caliphate passed to the Umayyad dynasty—the followers of Muawiya.

However, Ali's influence did not end with his assassination. In fact, his assassination became part of Islam's deepest division, the one between the Shia (party), who were loyalists to Ali, and the Sunni (traditionalists). The "party" supporting Ali believed that the successors to Muhammad ought to come from Muhammad's family—in other words, that Islamic leadership should be hereditary. This conviction was supported by certain verses of the Qur'an, in which the Prophet supposedly indicated that Ali would be his successor. The Shia therefore consider the first three caliphs, who preceded Ali, as having been usurpers. After Ali's death, they took up the cause of his sons, Hasan and Husain.

The word that the Shia gave to the power that descended through Muhammad's family line was *imamah* (leadership). Through its history, the Shia has made it a cardinal doctrine that Muhammad's bloodline has an exclusive right to *imamah*. The slaughter of Husain in Iraq in 680 was an especially tragic event, and the Shiites have come to commemorate it as the greatest of their annual festivals. It gives their Islam a strong emphasis on sorrow, suffering, and emotion that quite distinguish it from Sunni piety.[30]

Of course, our brief summary has presented only a slice of the dense military, political, and religious history that shaped the first unfolding of Qur'anic faith. Externally, Islam's quick successes testified as much to the political vacuum within which the conquered peoples lived and to their oppression as it did to Arab military genius. Internally, Islam's great energy made for considerable strife. However, during the following centuries, religion and culture caught up with the military wildfire, consolidating the empire and making it much more than just a far-flung envelopment.

The Golden Civilization

In his history of science, Stephen Mason states that Muslim scientific culture began in the era of the Umayyads.[31] The Umayyads had been auxiliaries of the Romans in Syria, so when they established the caliphate in Damascus in 661, they brought an enthusiasm for Hellenistic culture. In particular, they became patrons of the sciences. For example, in 700 they founded an astronomical observatory at Damascus. However, the Umayyads fell to the Abbasids in 749. The Abbasids set their caliphate in Baghdad and turned to Persian rather than Hellenistic culture, supporting the Persian specialities of medicine and astronomy. Al-Mansur, the second Abbasid caliph, was also devoted to learning, bringing Indian astronomers and doctors to Baghdad and having many Indian scientific treatises translated. Under his successors, translation continued to be a major project. As a result, many Greek treatises (for example, those of Galen and Ptolemy) became available to Muslims. Partly because of Babylonian and Zoroastrian influences, the Baghdad caliphs deemed astronomy especially important. They imported Indian mathematicians to help in astronomical calculations and made Baghdad a center of astronomical learning.

Al-Razi (865–925) collected voluminous lore on medicine from Greek, Indian, and Middle Eastern sources. Indeed, he may even have drawn on Chinese sources, for there is a story that he entertained a Chinese scholar who learned to speak Arabic, and his successors' works include what seems to be the Chinese doctrine of the pulses. A Muslim alchemy arose in the ninth century with Jabir ibn-Hayyar, but in Islam alchemy remained somewhat suspect because the authorities linked it with mystical religion. Some radical Sufis became deeply involved in alchemy, but orthodox Sunni had the works of at least one such group, the "Brethren of Purity," declared heretical and burned. Principally, the orthodox favored the rational geometry and deductive science of the Greeks.

From 970, the Spanish branch of the Muslim Empire had a distinguished scientific center in Cordoba. Similarly, the religious authorities patronized science, especially medicine and astronomy, at Toledo from the early eleventh century. The Spanish Muslims tended to be critical of Ptolemy and to favor Aristotelian doctrines. Averroës (1126–1198) was a great Aristotelian synthesizer who composed a full philosophical corpus.

By conquering the territory between the Muslim East and the kingdom of Sung China, the Mongols expedited trade and the flow of learned information between East and West. Marco Polo (1254–1324) was able to travel to the East because of Mongol rule, which also enabled the Chinese Mar Jaballaha (1244–1317) to come West and become the Nestorian Christian patriarch. When the Mongols conquered China they left its bureaucratic structure intact. They set up an observatory in Peking and staffed it with Muslims. In the West they conquered the Abbasid capital of Baghdad in 1258, where they continued to support astronomical studies.

Albert Moore has shown the effects of Islam's monotheism in the field of art, arguing that it led to a classical concentration on the architecture and ornamentation of the mosque.[32] This art reached its peak in the sixteenth and seventeenth centuries, leaving impressive monuments in Ottoman Turkey, Safavid Persia, and Mughal India. Schuyler Cammann[33] has shown exceptions to the generally nonrepresentational character of Islamic art in Persian works, and Moore indicates that paintings of hunting and of love scenes were permitted in private Muslim homes. Nonetheless, the preponderance of Muslim art during the golden age was nonpictorial, including rugs, vases, lamps, and mosques.

A distinctively Islamic calligraphy developed from the trend to decorate pages from the Qur'an. The Qur'an itself praises the art of writing (96 : 4), and speaks of being written on a heavenly tablet (85 : 21–22). The favorite script was Kufic, which originated in the new Islamic town of Kufa near Babylon, and it was the standard script model from about the seventh to eleventh centuries. It is vertical, massive, and angular, while its prime alternate, the Naskhi script, is horizontal, flowing, and rounded. A favorite subject for embellishment has been the *Bismallah*, the prefix to the Qur'anic suras ("In the name of God"). Through an extension of calligraphic swirls and loops, Muslims developed an ingenious ability to suggest flowers, birds, lions, and so on. The Sufi interest in numerology also encouraged artistic work.

Architecture and Poetry

As we suggested, Islam also influenced architecture. The mosque was a sort of theology in the concrete. Muslim architects tried to embody the faith and conviction that all of life stands subject to Allah, that no great distinction should be made between sacred dwellings and profane. The guiding idea in the construction of a mosque was simply to house a space for prayer and prostration. The *Hadith* reported that the Prophet led his first companions outside the city, so that they could pray together in an open space. At Medina, the usual place for prayer was the open courtyard of Muhammad's own house. For convenience, the architects tried to construct a churchlike building that had the character of an open space where many faithful might go through the same rhythmic motions of bowing, kneeling, prostrating, and praying together.

The representative mosque, such as the great Mosque of Cordoba or the al-Aqsa mosque of Jerusalem, is spacious and beautifully but simply adorned. It has rugs (often very beautiful) on the floors and numerous pillars for support, but no furniture—no pews, chairs, or altars. Often there is a pulpit (in some cases two, one for reading the Qur'an and one for preaching), and the most impressive ornamentation is the tile or gold leaf that decorates the ceiling or the *mihrab*.

THE ALHAMBRA AND SECULAR ARCHITECTURE

Mosque architecture tended not to differ radically from that of Muslim palaces. Most of the renowned Muslim palaces have crumbled, but the Alhambra, in Granada, Spain, still stands, a glorious tribute to the Muslim Golden Age. The Alhambra was built between 1230 and 1354 and served as a great citadel for the Moorish kings. It was mutilated after the expulsion of the Muslims in 1492, but extensively restored from 1828 on. Its beauty suggests the Muslim notion of how religion and secular life ought to interpenetrate.

Physically, the Alhambra is located on a hill overlooking the city of Granada. Although it is surrounded by walls and has the look of a fort, only the lowest parts of the enclosure were actually used for military purposes. According to early Islamic tradition, palaces were supposed to be placed as the Alhambra is: close to the city, yet a little bit apart. Thus the Alhambra strikes us as a country villa, yet also like an urban citadel. One gets the same impression from similar palaces in Aleppo (northwest Syria) and Cairo. There, too, the effort was to retain the amenities of a royal palace while fortifying the ruler's residence against possible incursions. Such military considerations led to architectural innovations in the vaulting, gateways, and towers of the *qal'a* or urban citadel.

The Alhambra goes beyond a simple fusion of the villa and citadel traditions, however, by breaking its sizeable area into a series of separate units. Some of these units are lovely gardens, in the Muslim paradisal tradition. For example, both Iranian and Indian Muslim palaces frequently sought to prefigure Paradise by developing lovely royal gardens. Of the other units of the

Alhambra, the most celebrated is the Court of the Lions. The Court of the Lions has an impressive portico running along several sides, with slim, delicate pillars supporting strong arches. The open space in the center is handsomely tiled, and a small fountain with flowers at the base adds splashes of color. Off the court run complexes of square and rectangular rooms, as though the architect wanted to suggest sumptuousness. This is what one commentator calls the "additive" principle: adding room after room, to imply that the royal resources are limitless. The delicate, filigreed work on some of the wall panelings gives an impression of exquisite lace.

"The most important point is that very few of the halls and courts of the Alhambra had an architecturally definable purpose. A curious dissociation seems to have occurred between building and function, as though individual forms which are definable in architectural terms as courts, porticoes, square or oblong halls, and so forth were merely generalized forms in which a variety of purposes, from traditional audiences to various pastimes, could be performed."[34] This dissociation, or apparent lack of precise function, was a feature of many other Muslim buildings. The masses of kiosks or pavilions in the palaces of Cairo or Istanbul, for example, were similarly "formal" constructions and did not suggest precisely what activities would take place in them. One could relate this Muslim style to recent Western tendencies toward "multipurpose rooms," which are capable of being turned into lecture halls, dining areas, or gymnasiums with little effort.

A third feature of the Alhambra, beyond its fortified and multipurpose aspects, is its extraordinary attention to decoration. When one is inside the Alhambra, the most gripping feature is the careful ornamentation of the pillars, walls, ceilings, and floors. Once again, commentators generalize from the Alhambra to Muslim buildings of Iran, Central Asia, or Turkey. In all these places, the themes and techniques of internal palace decoration were spectacular.

If one asks why Muslims lavished such care on the internal aesthetics of their palaces, the Alhambra provides an important clue to the answer. The impressive stalactite domes, and the thin pillars of the Fountain of the Lions, apparently derived from the medieval Muslim understanding of Solomon, the famed biblical king. In the medieval mythology surrounding Solomon, the jinns made wonderful scenes of beauty for him and his queens. Thus medieval Muslim rulers had a certain stimulus to create scenes of an otherworldly, separate Paradise. Wanting to produce by natural means beauty such as that which Solomon achieved by supernatural power, they came to stress gardens, delicate decorations, and almost tours de force of engineering (thin pillars holding stupendous domes, for instance).

Less spectacularly, the motivations behind architecture like that of the Alhambra led to the "monumentalization" of many ordinary Muslim buildings. Thus in many urban areas, schools, shops, hostels, hospitals, baths, and even warehouses were built with great facades and intricate decorations. The caravanserais (motels, we might say) of thirteenth-century Anatolia (Turkey), for example, employed the latest and most sophisticated techniques of construction. A religion that had a large place for "works"—business, pragmatic affairs, military matters—placed great stress on housing its social activities and secular affairs well. Also, in the medieval period Muslims tended to invest in land or buildings rather than trade or industry. The result was an architecture that little distinguished between the mosque and the secular building. Facades, for instance, seldom gave the external viewer a basis for determining what sort of building he was entering. It was the internal decorations of the buildings, or the activity that occurred within them, that gave them their distinction.

In the history of architecture, the Muslim achievements stand out as the most significant development in the period from Roman times to the Middle Ages. Indeed, the Muslim development of monumental buildings for secular purposes was rivaled only by Roman lavishness. For the most part, this sort of construction seems to have gone forward haphazardly, out of an instinct that daily life ought to be housed well. Exceptions to this general rule stand out: for instance, the organized city planning of Samarqand, Isfahan, and Istanbul.

Curiously, even the specifically religious

architecture of Islam was influenced by Islam secular monumentalism. From the tenth century on, the growth of domes, minarets, and mausoleums was mainly due to a desire to publicize the people who were building the religious constructions, rather than to a desire better to serve the religious activities the constructions would house. Thus Islamic architecture differs from European medieval architecture as consciously more secular.

From the time of the building of the Dome of the Rock (Figure 13) in 691, the *decoration* we stressed in the case of the Alhambra preoccupied Muslim builders. Indeed, increasing the decorative beauty of their buildings seems to have been a prime motivation in the Muslims' development of stucco, in their laying bricks so as to make bold designs, and in their creation of colored tiles. This concern with ornamentation leads to the question of how Muslim construction and decoration relate, a question historians of Islamic architecture debate with some vigor.

A good case to study is the mosque of Cordoba. In the *mihrab* of the Cordoba mosque the domes contain such unusual features as ribs that appear to support the cupola yet form a static mass with the cupola. The squinches (a characteristic support of domes) that accompany the ribs do not really support anything. In other words, the ribs and squinches are present for decorative, rather than constructive reasons. The north dome of the great mosque in Isfahan, Persia, built a century after the *mihrab* of the mosque in Cordoba, has an unusual articulation of supports that also seem more decorative than constructive. The supports correspond to every part of the superstructure and give the impression of being a grid or net filled with decorative masonry. Third, the Muslim use of *muqarnas*, three-dimensional shapes used in many different combinations, seems clearly intended for decorative, rather than constructive purposes. The *muqarnas* draw attention to some principal parts of a building, but they usually have little significance in terms of its engineering.

The debate among scholars of Muslim architecture seems to turn on what value one ought to give these decorative features. Perhaps the best resolution of the debate, for our lay purposes, is the one that stresses that Muslim architects apparently strove, through their engineering and ornamentation alike, to produce a distinctive overall effect. In their great masterpieces, the whole is greater than the sum of its parts. Engineering and ornamentation have so blended that one gets an effect that is more than either brilliant constructive design or artful decoration. The *muqarnas* domes, for example, often give the effect of the revolving heavens. As the source of external light moves around the base of the dome, the complex surface that the *muqarnas* produce on the cupola gives an illumination that is always changing. Like the heavens, the top of the mosque never looks the same yet seems quite motionless.

Due to the secular impact of Muslim faith, Islamic architecture developed such characteristic features as a preponderance of activity (use) over form, a tendency to monumentalize buildings that served quite ordinary functions, and a tendency to fuse construction and decoration into one harmonious entity. However, Islam seldom created its architectural forms entirely from Muslim inspiration. Ordinarily it adapted non-Muslim forms influential in an area it had conquered. Thus in Iran Islamic architects made use of the pre-Islamic *aywan*, a large vaulted hall opening directly onto an open space. This became an axial feature of Iranian mosques, and of Iranian Muslim secular buildings as well. Similarly, in Ottoman Turkey the superb mosques of Istanbul adapted features of the famous Christian cathedral of Hagia Sophia.

Since it conquered so many different areas, Islam had the opportunity, and the need, to graft Muslim ideas onto a variety of different architectural traditions. In India, for example, it tended to experiment with several different Near Eastern Muslim models, trying to adapt them to the local Indian traditions and materials. The result often was a fairly hybrid style, brilliant in such well-planned constructions as the Taj Mahal (Figure 17), but often undistinguished in more commonplace undertakings.

Summarily, then, Muslim architecture suggests that: (1) Islam tended to prize buildings as much for their versatility in being able to serve several functions as for their formal beauty, and (2) it tended to show more originality and brilliance in secular than in strictly religious constructions. Both of these characteristics express the Muslim conviction that religion ought to breathe through all dimensions and activities of life. If one Lord rules all of creation, overseeing each and every human activity, the distinction between sacred functions and profane is quite small.

The basic ornamental motif in much other Islamic art is repetition, seemingly endless patterns, whether representational (roses and leaves), semiabstract (vine tendrils and rosettes), or completely abstract (geometric patterns). This motif is known as the infinite pattern, and some suggest that it has theological significance: It does not want to rival God by creating anything fixed or permanent. Popular art often violates this pattern, suggesting that it most applied to mosques and official constructions. For instance, a Persian manuscript painting of the sixteenth century portrays Muhammad's ascent to Paradise, complete with winged angels, dishes of fruit, showers of pearls, and rubies.

A. J. Arberry has translated a representative collection of Islamic writings,[35] and it suggests a great breadth and lyricism. Poetry always held a place of honor among Arabs, for eloquence had always been considered a trait of a great man, even before the advent of Islam. Much as the Greeks valued military prowess and the ability to persuade others, so the Arabs made their mother tongue a prime object of artistic devotion.

The ancient poetry was born in the desert, so it was replete with desert images and themes. With expansion and conquest, however, Islam became largely an urban culture,[36] so there was need to reshape its poetry. Meter, rhyme, and new imagery became the chief tools. The result was a very complex style: "We have called this poetry arabesque, and indeed it is fully as exquisitely and delicately ornamented as the finest Saracenic architecture."[37] The thirteenth-century poet Ibn al-Khabbaza fashioned an elegy that epitomized Arab eloquence: "Your life was of the order true of Arab elo-

quence; the tale was brief, the words were few, the meaning was immense."[38]

The themes that dominate Arberry's poetic selections are not especially religious: the beauty of a beloved, trees, battle, and, for humor, the flanks and shanks of an ant. Still, some of the religious mystics, such as Junaid, Rumi, and the woman Rabia, gained fame for their poetic skills. Most were Sufis—devotees of religious emotion and feeling. Among the religious poets of Islam, the Persians were most eminent. Their themes and images center on the Sufi goal of self-effacement in the divine immensity. For instance, Rumi often portrayed the soul's sense of abandonment in moments of trial when it could not feel the divine embrace: "Hearken to this Reed forlorn, Breathing ever since 'twas torn from its rushy bed, a strain of impassioned love and pain."[39] In this way, the talented Sufi writers won considerable respect from the cultured. To be able to express their religious vision with eloquence made them seem less eccentric, more representative of traditional Arab cultural ideals.

Law

Within the inner precincts of Islam, neither science nor art constituted the main cultural development. Rather, the most important flowering of Qur'anic faith was the law *(sharia)*.[40] As the opening verses of the Qur'an suggest, a fundamental concern in Islam is guidance, and Islam went to lawyers, not to scientists, poets, or even mystics, for its most trustworthy guidance. In fact, Islam obtained little guidance from philosophical theology, which began a most promising career but foundered on the shoals

Figure 14   Courtyard of Cairo Mosque, with purification fountain. Photo by J. T. Carmody.

of sectarian controversy and debates about the relation of reason to faith. Although numerous schools of law developed, the differences among them were relatively slight, and they usually left little place for innovative reason. Thus, the authorities accounted them more trustworthy than philosophical theology—better cement for Muslim society.

The early theological discussions dealt with the nature of faith. Idolatry and unbelief were the major evils for the Qur'an, so it was important to understand them well. The types of sins were also an important early theological focus. Later debates focused on the unity of God (in the context of discussing the divine attributes) and on the relation of the divine sovereignty to human freedom. While there was a full spectrum of opinions, in Sunni quarters the more moderate positions tended to win favor.

Before long, however, Islam effectively curtailed speculation, favoring instead careful efforts to ascertain what legal precedents any *practical* problem had in the *Hadith* of the Prophet, the Qur'an, community consensus, or analogous situations.

To be sure, Muslims did not view religious law as a human creation. Rather, it was divine guidance, the expression of God's own will. The goal of the lawyers was to offer comprehensive guidance for all of life— much as the rabbis' goal was to apply the Torah to all of life. In practice, the lawyers tended to divide their subject matter into obligations to God (for example, profession of faith and performance of prayer) and obligations to other human beings (for example, individual and social morality, such as not lying and not stealing). The lawyers classified theology under the first set of obligations, for theology was the science of right belief, and right belief was primary among the things that human beings owed to God. As they refined their science, the lawyers also distinguished all human actions according to five headings: obligatory, recommended, permitted, disapproved, and forbidden. Thus, one had to confess the unity of God and the Prophethood of Muhammad, one was counseled to avoid divorce, and one was forbidden to eat pork. Since Muslim society was a theocracy, *sharia* was the code of the land. While that made for a certain unity and order, it also prepared the way for the Sufi emphasis on personal devotion.

Division

A minor source of division within the Muslim community was the differences in law developed by the various schools. The Hanafite school came to dominate Muslim countries north and east of the Arabian Peninsula. Within Arabia itself the dominant school was founded by ibn-Hanbal. Northeast Africa was under Shafite and Hanafite lawyers, while Malikite opinions were the most prestigious in northwestern Africa. In Persia the Shia sect had its own law. On the whole, that distribution still holds today.

Given the four recognized legal codes of Sunni, the large Shia minority, and the division of the Islamic Empire into eastern and western parts centered at Baghdad and Cordoba, respectively, one can see that religious and political unity was less than perfect. Still, Muslims holding to the five pillars and the Qur'an had more in common with one another than they had with any non-Muslim peoples. Thus, legal or creedal differences did not divide Muslim religion severely. In contrast, different devotional styles, such as Sufism, caused considerable hubbub.

Sufism

Opinions about the merits of Sufism differ. Fazlur Rahman, commenting especially on the work of al-Ghazali (1058–

1111), speaks of the "fresh vitality" that al-Ghazali's devotionalism infused into the Muslim community.[41] Isma'il al Faruqi, on the contrary, cites Sufism as the first step in Islam's decline from its golden civilization.[42] It is true that al-Ghazali was not a typical Sufi (he had great learning as well as great piety), and that al Faruqi's sympathies lie with the reforming Wahabis (see below), for whom Sufism was an abomination. Still, a survey of studies shows quite mixed reactions to Sufism. Most commentators agree that its initial centuries (the ninth through thirteenth) were more creative and positive than its later ones.

At the outset, Sufism (the name likely comes from the Arabic word for wool, which Sufis wore as a gesture of simplicity)[43] stood for reform and personal piety. In a time when political and military success tempted Islam to worldliness, and when the rise of the law brought the dangers of legalism, the Sufis looked to the model of Muhammad at prayer, communing with God. For them the heart of Islam was personal submission to Allah, personal guidance along the straight path. In later centuries, through its brotherhoods and saints, Sufism set a great deal of the emotional, anti-intellectual, and anti-progressive tone of an Islam that had lost its status as a world power.

Several cultural streams ran together to form the Sufi movement. First was the ascetic current from traditional desert life, which was basic and simple—a daily call for endurance. Out of a keen sense of the religious values in such a harsh life, Abu Dharr al-Ghifari, a companion of the Prophet, chastised the early leaders who wanted to lead a sumptuous court life after their conquests. Second, many of the Sufi ecstatics, as we mentioned, drew on the Arab love of poetry. Their lyric depictions of the love of God, coupled with the Qur'an's eloquence, drew sensitive persons to the side of a living, personal faith that might realize the beauties of Islam.

Third, the more speculative Sufis drew on Gnostic ideas that floated in from Egypt and the Fertile Crescent. By the ninth century, Sufi contemplatives (especially the Persian Illuminationists) were utilizing those ideas to analyze the relations between divinity and the world. (The Sufis seem to have found the emanational ideas—the theories of how the world flowed out of the divine essence—rather than the dualistic theories of good and evil most attractive.) This kind of understanding, along with the alchemical interests noted previously, was the beginning of the esoteric and sometimes magical lore for which the orthodox theologians and lawyers held Sufis suspect. Lastly, Indian (especially Buddhist) thought apparently influenced the eastern portions of the Muslim realm, and it perhaps was a source of the tendencies toward self-annihilation that became important in Sufi mystical doctrine.

Taken at their own word, the Sufis desired to be faithful followers of Muhammad and the Qur'an. The more honored among them never intended any schismatic or heretical movements. Rather, they resembled spiritual writers of other traditions, such as the Christian Thomas a Kempis, in that they wanted to "feel compunction rather than know its definition." The most famous statement of this desire occurs in al-Ghazali's description of his withdrawal from his prestigious teaching post in Baghdad in order to settle the conflicts in his soul: "I was continuously tossed about between the attractions of worldly desire and the impulses towards eternal life."[44] Upon retiring into solitude to purify his soul, he found the peace he had sought. From being a learned philosopher, theologian, and lawyer, he became a follower of the mystical way, which the Sufis represented: "I learnt with certainty that it is above all the mystics who walk on the road of God; their life is the best life, their method the soundest method, their character the purest character; indeed, were the intellect of the intellectuals and the learning of the learned and the scholarship of the scholars, who are versed in the profundities of revealed truth, brought together in the attempt to improve the life and character of the mystics, they would find no way of doing so."[45]

In Idries Shah's collection of Sufi sayings,[46] one catches overtones of the pedagogical genius that the spiritual masters developed. Much like the Hasidim, they fashioned stories to carry their messages about the paradoxes of the spiritual life, the need for being focused and wholehearted, the way that God comes in the midst of everyday life. In these stories, the poor man turns out to be rich; the fool turns out to be truly wise. Like their counterparts in other traditions, the Sufis left no doubt that riches and prestige tend to be obstacles to spirituality. As well, they questioned the rational, "right-handed" portions of the personality, arguing that the more intuitive, "left-handed" portions must have their due if one is to achieve balance and fullness.

Predictably, this challenge to the expectations of society, of the religious authorities, and of the literally minded won the Sufis no love. Perhaps to intensify their opposition, some Sufis became even more poetic, challenging the establishment and suggesting that its religion was little more than dead convention. For instance, when Hasan of Basra was asked what Islam was and who were Muslims, he replied, "Islam is in the books and Muslims are in the tomb."[47] This oracular reply could mean that the Qur'an holds the secrets to true submission and that the earth holds the bodies of the great exemplars of the past. However, it could also mean that what people take to be Islam (the official version) is actually a dead letter, something buried and forgotten, because no one lives it anymore. Along similar lines is a story of a dervish who meets the devil. The devil is just sitting patiently, so the dervish asks him why he is not out making mischief. The devil replies, "Since the theoreticians and would-be teachers of the Path have appeared in such numbers, there is nothing left for me to do."[48]

Decline

By the beginning of the fourteenth century, the age of some of the greatest Sufi figures was over; Sufism started to decline, and with it much of Islam's religious vitality. The orders continued to multiply, and many princes and sultans continued to patronize them, but abuse, scandal, and superstition became more and more common. In Arberry's view, "It was inevitable, as soon as legends of miracles became attached to the names of the great mystics, that the credulous masses should applaud imposture more than true devotion; the cult of the saints against which orthodox Islam ineffectually protested, promoted ignorance and superstition, and confounded charlatanry with lofty speculation. To live scandalously, to act impudently, to speak unintelligibly—this was the easy highroad to fame, wealth, and power."[49]

Still, the Sufis played a considerable role in the expansion of Islam, largely by serving as models of piety for the common people and giving them hopes of wonder working. For instance, Sufi folk literature played an important role in the expansion of Indian Islam during the fifteenth through seventeenth centuries,[50] while genuine Sufi spirituality aroused strong devotion in North Africa well into the twentieth century.[51] The organizations of Sufi influence were the Sufi orders, or brotherhoods. The first seems to date from the twelfth century. Abd al-Qadir, who began his religious career in Baghdad as a student of Hanbalite law, converted to Sufism and became a preacher on the holy life. The many converts and followers that he gathered came to call themselves Qadiris, and historians often regard their association as the first brotherhood. It has been especially influential in India, where it has a presence even today. Al-Qadir was a traditionalist who called for strict adherence to the Qur'an and condemned any antinomian (lawless) tendencies. No doubt this helped his group become acceptable.

A second great order, also influential in India, derived from al-Suhrawardi (1144–1234), a moderate. Other orders of significant number and influence were the Shadhiliya, who were especially successful in Egypt, North Africa, Arabia, and Syria, and the Turkish order of the Mevleviya, which derived from the renowned Persian poet Rumi.

Typically, at the order's local lodge, a small number of professionals resided to teach and lead worship. Most members were (and are) lay adherents who came for instruction when they could and who supported the lodge by contributing money, manual labor, and so on. Each order tended to have its own distinctive ritual, whose purpose was usually to attain ecstatic experience. The ritual was the group's interpretation of the general virtue of *dhikr* (remembrance) that all Muslims seek. For instance, whirling dances characterized many of the Mevlevi dervish meetings, while Saadeeyeh Sufis developed a ceremony in which the head of the order rode over prone devotees on horseback.

The writings of the theosophist Gurdjieff have introduced a number of Sufi ideas into contemporary American consciousness. Overall, however, Islam has been making its greatest strides among Africans who have found that it suits their traditional tribal structure and their nationalistic mood better than Christianity.[52] The divisions and declines that sundered Islam before this modern resurgence were largely due to a combination of Sufi magic and orthodox rigidity, which undermined the fusion of piety and order that any vital religion has to have.

Islam also suffered from a counterattack by the countries that it had conquered. For instance, the European countries who supported the Crusades sharply contracted the empire that Islam had forged in its golden age. Historians date the point of decline differently. Bernard Lewis, for instance, holds that by the eleventh century Islam was in "manifest decay."[53] In addition to what they suffered at the hands of the Crusaders in the Holy Land and from the Europeans' counterattack in southern Europe, the Arabs found themselves superseded in the East by the Turks, who became Muslims, and by the Mongols, who at first showed no interest in Islam. The latter conquered both Persia and Iraq, causing a breakdown of Muslim power.

The Turkish Mamluks established themselves in Cairo by the mid-thirteenth century, ruling Egypt and Syria until 1517.

When Vasco da Gama circumnavigated Africa in 1498, much of the Muslim economic and political power, which derived from Muslim control of the trade with India, quickly faded. The Ottoman Turks replaced the Mamluks in the early sixteenth century and ruled Middle Eastern Islam for almost 400 years.[54] Only in southern Arabia (Yemen) did Arab speakers remain largely free of foreign domination.

Late Empire and Modernity

During the period of empire (the Ottoman Empire of Turkey and the Middle East, the Safavid dynasty in Persia,[55] and the Mogul dynasty in India),[56] at least three general changes occurred in Muslim society. The first was the transformation of the Islamic Near East from a commercial economy based on money to a feudal economy based on subsistence farming. The second was the replacement in positions of authority of Arabic-speaking peoples by Turks. The Arab tribes retained their independence in the desert regions, where they held out quite well against Turkish rule. In the cities and cultivated valleys (the plains of Iraq, Syria, and Egypt), however, the Arabs became completely subjected, and the glorious language that had been the pride of Islam became the argot of an enslaved population. Psychologically, the Turks grew accustomed to taking the initiative and commanding, and the Arabs grew accustomed to passivity and subjection. The third change was the transfer of the seat of Islam from Iraq to Egypt. Iraq was too remote from Turkey and the Mediterranean to be the base for the eastern wing of Islam, so Egypt—which was on the other principal trade route and which was the most unified area geographically—became the new center.[57]

As a result of this shift, Turkish and to a lesser degree Persian became the languages of Islam. At first many of the subject peoples welcomed the Ottoman takeover from the Mamluks as a return to political order. By the eighteenth century, however, the Ottoman Empire was in decay—corrupt, anarchic, and stagnant. The principal religious form of revolt during this period was Sufism. At first Sufism was mainly an escape for oppressed individuals, but with the organization of more brotherhoods, it became a social movement that was especially powerful among the artisan class. The long centuries of stagnation finally ended, however, with increased contact with the West. From the beginning of the sixteenth century, European expansion brought some of the new learning of the Renaissance and the Reformation. The French in particular had considerable influence in the Middle East, and Napoleon's easy conquest of the Ottoman Turks at the end of the eighteenth century was the final blow to Islamic military glory.

The Wahabis

Also during the time of Napoleon arose an Islamic reform that was designed to check the infection of Sufism.[58] One of the first leaders in this reform was a stern traditionalist named Muhammad ibn Abd al-Wahab, whose followers came to be known as Wahabis. They called for a return to the doctrines and practices of the early generations, of the ancestors whom they venerated.

In law, the Wahabis favored the rigorous interpretations of the Hanbalite school, and they abhorred the veneration of saints, which they considered superstitious. Thus, they inveighed against supposed holy personages, living or dead, and went out of their way to destroy the shrines that had become places of popular piety or pilgrimage. They further objected that the worship of saints presumed "partners" of God and so was idolatrous. The punishment due such idolatry was death. Some of the more rabid Wahabis went so far as to classify the more lenient lawyers and schools as being guilty of idolatry (and so punishable by death). The Wahabis were based in Arabia, whence they waged war on their dissenting neighbors. They went down to military defeat in their 1818 Turco-Egyptian campaign, but their puritanical reform had much ideological success and spread to other parts of the Islamic world.

An immediate effect of the Wahabi movement was great hostility toward the Sufi brotherhoods. In fact, Muslims interested in renovating orthodoxy singled out the Sufis as their great enemies, although they also attacked the scholasticism of such theological centers as al-Azhar in Cairo. One of the leaders of the nineteenth-century reform was the apostle of Pan-Islam, Jamal al-Din al-Afghani, who proposed the political unification of all Muslim countries under the caliphate of the Ottoman sultans. While Pan-Islam has never been realized, it stimulated the widespread search for an effective Muslim response to modernity. In India and Egypt, conservative groups arose that gravitated toward the Wahabi position. Many of the Sufi organizations lost their strength, and those that survived tended to back away from gnosis and return to a more traditional theology.

Even before this conservative threat, however, the Sufis had reformed on their own, sponsoring a number of missions in Africa, India, and Indonesia. For the most part these were peaceful, but occasionally they involved military ventures. In fact, some groups quite consciously took up the Qur'anic tradition of holy war, including the "Indian Wahabis" and the Mahdists in the Sudan. However, even in decline the Sufi brotherhoods kept dear to Islam the notion of bonding together for mutual support in faith.

The organizations that have grown up in recent times, such as the Association for Muslim Youth and the Muslim Brotherhood, seem in good measure an effort to fill the void created by the demise of the brotherhoods. The new groups differ by operating primarily in pluralistic cultures, while the Sufi orders drew on the ardor of a homogeneous culture that was secure in its unchallenged faith.

Western Influence

A characteristic of Islamic modernity was the invasion of Western secular ideas.

These ideas came on the heels of modern Western takeovers in the Middle East, at first through the administrations of the Europeans who governed the newly acquired territories and then through the educational systems, which were Westernized. The new classes of native professionals—doctors, lawyers, and journalists—frequently trained abroad or in native schools run by Westerners. One political effect of such training was to raise Muslim feelings of nationalism and to provoke cries for Westernized systems of government. The new ideas challenged the *madrasas*, or religious schools, too, for it was not immediately apparent that these new ideas could be taught along with traditional theories of revelation and Qur'anic inspiration.

From the nineteenth century on, the economics, politics, education, social habits, and even religion of Muslims were increasingly affected by the upheaval that resulted from the European Renaissance and Enlightenment. Some countries remained largely insulated from Western notions, but they tended to be backward portions of the old empire with little political impact. As we might expect, the cities bore the brunt of the challenge. In theology the outward Muslim reaction was to close ranks. Still, even in the most fiercely traditionalist schools, modern notions—such as the freedom of human beings to shape their own destinies—softened the old propositions about providence and predestination.

Indeed, when it was convenient, theologians incorporated modern science into their argumentation. For instance, some Muslim theologians justified the doctrine that God creates the world continuously by citing atomic theory. The less theologically inclined among the modern educated classes contented themselves by asserting that Islam, as submission to the Master of Truth, in principle cannot conflict with modern science or with any empirically verified truths.

Controversy over societal matters has been more heated than that over theology because the guidance provided by the traditional legal schools diverged more sharply from Western mores than Muslim theology diverged from Western theology. Slowly Islamic countries have developed civil codes and separated civil courts from religious courts. In the mid-nineteenth century, the Turkish Republic breached the wall of tradition when it abolished the authority of the *sharia* in civil matters. In other countries the *sharia* has remained the outer form, but new legislative codes direct the interpretations. The tactic has been to invoke the Qur'an, the Hadith, and the traditions of the schools but to leave the legislators and judges free to choose the authority that is most appropriate. Specifically, the legal reforms have applied primarily to marriage contracts (protecting girls against child marriage), divorce proceedings, and polygamy—central factors in the traditional family structure.

What new theology will emerge from the dynamics of these changes remains to be seen. H. A. R. Gibb has pointed out that by granting jurists freedom to interpret the traditional opinions and by departing from the old norm that there had to be a uniformity of interpretation throughout the Islamic community, the reformers have introduced a "Protestant principle" into the previously "Catholic" social consciousness.[59] Indeed, through its fairly rigid law, Islam had reified (made objective) its community more thoroughly than the other religions had.[60] Whether the demise of the former practice will result in a Protestant splintering of Islam is difficult to predict. On the one hand, it is difficult to recall the critical or independent spirit once it has broken loose. On the other hand, there are signs of a growing Islamic fundamentalism similar to the fundamentalism by which some Protestant Christians are battling the spirit of criticism.

Relatedly, liberal Muslim reformers attracted to Marxist thought seem to bypass the socialist call for a new order and to desire, rather nostalgically, the old ideological uniformity. The traditionalists, such as the Saudis, find Marxism completely repulsive because of its atheism. Whether they can progress satisfactorily by means of a cap-italistic economy and technology, though, is far from certain. Critical-mindedness in the laboratory and simple faith in religion are not impossible, but few people in any faith manage them without a kind of schizophrenia.

Publications of the American Academic Association for Peace in the Middle East suggest that the recent history of such countries ("confrontation states") as Syria and Jordan explains much of the current turmoil in the Middle East.[61] These countries have been trying to adapt their economics, their politics, and their religion to the modern world. On the one hand, their models for this transition have been the Western nations, who produced modernity. On the other hand, Western nationalism has taught them to insist on their right to a nationalistic expression of their ethnicity, their history, and their religious cohesiveness. The current catalysts for this process are Israel and oil.

Finally, Islamic secularism is less advanced than Western secularism. True, fundamentalism attracts a noteworthy number of Christians and Jews, but their cultures more clearly differentiate the civic realm, the realm shared with citizens of other religious convictions (or of none), than Islamic countries do. Conversely, Islam has kept the sacred and the secular more tightly conjoined than Christianity or Judaism has. It professes that there is no secular realm—that everything lives by the will and touch of Allah, who is as near as the pulse at one's throat.

STRUCTURAL ANALYSIS

Nature

The key to the Muslim notion of nature is its concept of creation. As much as the biblical religion on which it built, Islam sees God as the maker of all that is. Several Qur'anic passages establish this doctrine. For instance, Sura 10 describes the Lord as "God, who created the heavens and the earth

LESSONS FROM IRAN

The rest of the Islamic world followed the Iranian upheavals of 1979 with great interest, to say the least, and many interesting commentaries on the meaning of Islam for the late twentieth century arose because of the Iranian events. One such commentary appeared in Cairo, at the instigation of the Islamic Student Association of Cairo University. Studying the reflections of this commentary may open a window on the likely future of Islam's blend of religion and politics.

The commentary begins with a quotation from the Qur'an (3:26) to the effect that God, the possessor of all sovereignty, gives earthly sovereignty to whomever he wishes. Just as freely, God takes earthly sovereignty away. Only God is powerful over all things. If God wishes to raise someone up, he does. If God wishes to debase someone, he does.

From this theological foundation the commentary moves to the recent events in Iran, which have riveted the whole world. This revolution, the violence and restraint of which surpassed the calculations and wildest imaginings of most observers, deserves deep study. Muslims must ponder such marvelous happenings, if they are ever to fulfill their Qur'anic destiny (see 3:110) and "assume the reins of world leadership of mankind once again and place the world under the protection of the esteemed Islamic civilization."[62]

Beginning such study, the first lesson the commentary would underscore is the influence of the creed on the Islamic people. The Iranian people, who had appeared completely submissive to death and tyranny, exploded like a volcano, tossing their fears aside. Their spiritual conquest of the steely forces that opposed them recalls the heroes of earliest Muslim times, and it should remind everyone that faith might muster similar power in many situations. Islam is the religion with the power to redress the injustices of all peoples everywhere. *Overstated?*

Second, the Iranian revolution reminds us that Islam is a comprehensive religion, legislating for both this world and the next. It provides alike for religion and state affairs, education and morals, worship and holy war. In fact, the Iranian revolution magnifies the errors in modern secularism, which would separate religion from state affairs. Clearly, it shows that secularism is the recourse of idolaters, who want to keep religion out of politics, so that they can plunder the wealth of the common people. The only adequate laws and constitutions are those that derive from the Sharia of Islam. When laws and constitutions are man-made, their status is no greater than the idols of the pre-Muslim Arabs. If the pre-Muslim Arabs got hungry, they would eat the Goddess of Pastry. In contrast, the Sharia of Islam, which comes from God, is permanent, just, wise, and perfect.

Third, Iranian affairs show that the true leaders of the Muslim people are the sincere learned men of religion. These men (the *ulama*) have been the guiding lights of all the best modern Muslim liberation movements. The touchstone is justice. For forty years the tyrant shah betrayed his community and brought down on it the most repulsive forms of injustice. God takes his time with the wrongdoer, but when he takes him there is no escaping.

Fourth, shrewd observers will note how the false Iranian leaders had the courage of lions when dealing with their own people but were puppets in the hands of the rulers of the East and the West. Yet the West quickly disowned the shah, abandoning him like a worn-out shoe. To the lesson implied in this one should add the patent effort of Islam's enemies to exploit the sectarian differences between Shiites and Sunnites and tear the Muslim community apart. As well, the enemies of Islam tried to use the Iranian revolution to instigate local governments to strike out at Islamic movements.

Therefore, rulers in other Islamic locales must realize that their true strength lies in the strength of their people, and that the true strength of their people lies in Islam. Wise leaders are those that place their allegiance in God, his apostle Muhammad, and Muslim believers. As the Qur'an (5:49) teaches, only those who rule by what God has revealed can expect to be strengthened. Thus, to those who would instigate strife against Islamic movements, one should reply:

learn X differences

God suffices for us. The Qur'an has said the last word in these matters: "God promised those of you who believe and perform good works that he would make you viceroys on earth as he did with those before you and will make it possible for you to follow the religion which pleases you and will change your fear into safety. You will worship me, associating nothing else with me" (24:55).

Several concerns of the Cairo Students' Association merit special comment, because they are present in the recent resurgence of a passionate Islam in other countries, such as Iran and Pakistan. First, the students obviously long for a return to traditional Muslim law. Chafing under what they think is their recent rulers' secularism, the students believe that returning to the principles of the Qur'an and traditional Muslim law will speedily redress all current wrongs. In its early stages, the revolution in Iran seemed a great vindication of this viewpoint. Even fervent Muslims were amazed that faith was able to bring down so powerful an enemy as the shah. Today, at a greater distance from the events of 1979, and with more experience of what the Ayatullah Khumayni understood the revolution to imply, even zealous students might take pause. The bloody chaos that afflicted the Muslim ranks in Iran after the revolution argues that the Sharia is open to markedly diverse and violent interpretations.

Second, the chauvinism latent in the Islamic students' position paper is not likely to prove the most effective translation of the Sharia for the decades ahead. A great deal of the world does not want to be placed under the protection of Islamic civilization, even when one grants Islamic civilization its great due. Pluralism is a more powerful force than the students seem to realize, and any peaceful assumption of the reins of world leadership will have to handle pluralism quite sympathetically. Any forceful assumption of the reins of world leadership is almost unthinkable, both because Islam is hardly in the position to challenge the West or the East militarily and because military means to power inevitably raise the specter of nuclear war. No nations would profit from a contemporary translation of Islamic "holy war" that led to nuclear confrontations.

Third, students of religion might most profitably focus on the somewhat tacit pleas that run through the Egyptian students' commentary.

For example, there is the tacit plea that the rest of the world take seriously and duly honor a proud religious tradition. Islam came on hard times when the West took charge of modernity. Its pride was wounded, and we can trace much of its strong rhetoric, even its hyperbole, to this wounded pride. Now that Islam is on the march again, more than competitive with the Western religions in Africa and other parts of the Third World, it is trying to recoup some of its emotional losses.

Another tacit plea is for an integral culture, in which religion and daily affairs might fit like hand and glove. Not only is this integration a part of Islam's traditional ideal, as we have seen. It is also a common human desire. Indeed, even the Western cultures play strains of this song. Christian and Jewish fundamentalists, for example, express a passionate desire to bring all of life under the domain of their God. Despite the cultural or religious imperialism to which this desire can lead, it is worth studying sympathetically. The rise of secular cultures in many nations of the world *has* made it more difficult to find transcendent meaning. There *are* many contemporary citizens, East and West, who feel fragmented or schizophrenic.

Probably the most viable solution to this problem is a synthesis at a higher level rather than a fundamentalist reduction to blind faith, but such a synthesis is very demanding. One of the unfortunate features of our late twentieth-century times is the speed that evolution has reached. Whereas in the past people facing demands analogous to today's demand for a resolution of the conflict between a pluralistic secularism and a unified religious faith might have had thousands of years at their disposal, today we cannot be sure we have more than a generation. This should incline us to get on with the task, but also to comfort ourselves with a proper estimate of the task's magnitude. Nothing less than a truly ecumenic, universal humanity will solve our worldwide religiopolitical problems, and achieving a truly ecumenic, universal humanity is almost more than we can imagine.

Still another plea running through the students' manifesto is for simple justice. This plea is not at all tacit; it is quite express and eloquent. Iranians had been suffering injustice. Enough of them had been tortured and abused by the shah to make his regime hated. The popular support for the Iranian revolution is only explainable on the basis of this hatred. Had the shah's innovations, his programs for modernization and economic development, not been perceived as brutally unjust, as well as destructive of the people's cherished religious heritage, the shah would not have become the Iranian Satan. Even when one allows for a considerable emotional excess in the shah's opponents, and their considerable manipulation by religious leaders quite ambitious for power, the political facts seem clear. The clarion call of the religious revolutionaries was for a restoration of justice. A major attraction in the prospect of restoring a Qur'anic government was the possibility of achieving a much greater justice.

As statements by the Ayatullah Khumayni himself suggest, the revolutionaries' ideal was a religious government free of the human caprice that so easily leads to injustice: "The venerable prophet, may God's peace and prayers be upon him, was appointed ruler on earth by God so that he may rule justly and not follow whims." However, things become ominous when Khumayni goes on to say, "The *Shari'a* and reason require us not to let governments have a free hand. The proof of this is evident. The persistence of these governments in their transgressions means obstructing the system and laws of Islam whereas there are numerous provisions that describe every non-Islamic system as a form of idolatry or a ruler or an authority in such a system as a false god."[63] For many Western observers, Khumayni's authoritarianism was exactly a demand for idolatrous obedience, exactly the arbitrary rule of a false god.

in six days, then sat Himself upon the Throne directing the affair." This is the biblical imagery of creation: Genesis spreading God's work over six days. Moreover, the Qur'an finds significance in this creation in that through creation God has given God-fearing people signs of his dominion. By making the sun a radiance and the moon a light, by giving them "stations" so that astronomers can calculate time, and by alternating night and day, God has set over humankind a heaven full of signs. Just as Immanuel Kant spoke of the starry heavens above as a wonder that can incite a true grasp of the human condition, so Muhammad unselfconsciously expressed the sovereignty of his God by referring to the divine guidance of the stars, the heavenly circuits by which the Creator periodizes our time.

Sura 13 repeats this theme, adding earthly phenomena: It is he who stretched out the earth, set firm mountains and rivers, and placed two kinds of every fruit. The abundance of nature testifies to the abundance of nature's source and ought to remind human beings of God's power and provision. Thus, the Creator is not only strong but also admirable in his design of the world and praiseworthy in his concern for human welfare as evidenced by his bounty. In this way the best features of nature become analogies for God in the Qur'an. The "Light-Verse" of Sura 24 gives one of the most famous of these analogies: God is the Light of the heavens and the earth. His light is as a niche where there is a lamp. The lamp is in a glass, the glass is like a glittering star. The lamp is kindled from a Blessed Tree, an olive neither of the East nor of the West, whose oil would shine even if no fire touched it. Light upon light, God guides to the Light whom he will.

Religiously, then, nature is replete with signs in which wise persons discern God's creative presence. However, nature is not itself a divinity or a form of God's presence. Unlike East Asian thought, Islamic thought does not mix divinity with the cosmos. Islam separated from the ancient cosmological myth, in that Allah transcends the world. One may say that the biblical prophets' critique of nature gods combined with Muhammad's negative reaction to the polytheism of his times to correlate transcendence and anti-idolatry. So the signs that nature gives to the God-fearing are not themselves sacraments. They point beyond themselves; the divinity does not come in them. Water, oil, bread, wine—they are not miniature incarnations of divinity. The God of Islam has no incarnation, no personal or material forms by which he becomes present.

Isma'il al Faruqi tries to establish that Islam is rationalistic, meaning that Islam's highest religious certainty *(iman)* is not merely an act of believing, an "act of faith," but "a state in which religious knowledge produces an intuition of its certainty as a result of the consideration and weighing of all possible alternatives."[64] Then, in treating what he considers Islam's second essential quality (that it is "transcendentalist"), al Faruqi argues that Islam rejects all forms of immanentism for the divine. In other words, Creator is Creator, creature is creature, and never the twain shall meet. This transcendentalism provides the context for al Faruqi's discussion of the Muslim view of nature, the lead sentence of which is "Nature is not transcendent and constitutes an autonomous realm."[65] From this it follows that nature contains no divinity in its materials or its forces. It is totally real, wholly created. It is actual and objective, and "it contains no mystery."[66]

Thus, for al Faruqi, Islamic nature is utterly profane, in no way sacred (since nothing is sacred without mystery). That interpretation seems considerably more rationalistic than what most Muslims themselves have thought, for, as we suggested above, most Muslims have not followed Western Enlightenment by separating the sacred from the secular. When al Faruqi says that nature must be unmysterious to be autonomous, regular, and knowable, we are tempted to say that he protests overmuch. The mechanistic scientist of the nineteenth century could write such a description of nature, but few contemporary scientists and few traditional Muslims would do so.

Some Muslim thinkers might have lost contact with nature's mystery, but they were not in the majority, for that would have made Islam a comparative anomaly. For example, Jews and Christians, despite sharing the notion of a transcendent Creator, used psalms that glorified God's provision of food in due season. With Job, they found that the world and its train of strange animals were marvelous indeed. The Hasidim looked to the world for divine sparks, and the Christian poets drew on the sacraments and on the model of saints such as Francis of Assisi to consider the world pregnant with God's power. Both of Islam's sister faiths did develop nature less than the Eastern religions did, and they did fear the forces of fertility, the polytheism, that afflicted the lands of their origin. But in the actual exercise of their faiths, nature was alive with the mystery of God and was neither profane nor autonomous. *Jewish + Xian faiths*

Still, al Faruqi is right in implying that nature never dominated Islam or Arab culture. For instance, the earliest poetry deals more with war and nomadic life than with Father Sky and Mother Earth. Pre-Muslim Arabia worshiped natural and agricultural forces, but Qur'anic monotheism attacked them harshly. In religious art, as we have seen, the prohibition on images was not absolute, although religious art tended to avoid representations of natural scenes, let alone representations of God.

Still, the prime material for worship, the Qur'an itself, contained natural figures and not merely in the context of creation. Thus, it embellished its theme of judgment and recompense with naturalistic imagery. For instance, if one denied God's bounties—did not live the truth that God ever labors creatively for human benefit—then "against you shall be loosed a flame of fire, and molten brass" (55 : 35). Judgment is a day when "heaven is split asunder and turns crimson like red leather" (55 : 37), when sinners will go to Gehenna and hot boiling water. However, those who fear God will enter Paradise. The main image for Paradise is the Garden. There the virtuous will find two fountains running with water, fruits of all kinds, virgin maidens lovely as rubies and coral. Paradise has green pastures, gushing water, fruits, palm trees, pomegranates, and cool pavilions (55 : 50–70).

Thus, the Qur'an considered nature a factor in the mysteries of judgment, punishment, and reward as the images of Fire and Garden clearly show. Moreover, mythological elaboration of these themes in popular religion was quite unrestrained. "Hell, sometimes imagined as a terrible monster, is described as filled with fire and stinking water, and awful trees with poisonous fruits grow there."[67] In the popular conception, angels presided over hell, meting out punishments, while heaven became a place for enjoying fruit, wine, and the charming black-eyed virgins.

Like other religions, Islam maintained that justice would be served in the afterlife through reward for the pious faithful and punishment for the unbelievers. Sex was high on the list of pleasures, so Paradise was rich with sex. Islam depicted sex from the male point of view, with details of "maidens restraining their glances, untouched before them by any man or jinn" (55 : 55). As we shall see below, Islam did not declare the goodness of sex so loudly and clearly for women. In fact, there has been ambiguity, puritanism, and a double standard concerning sex in Muslim society. Still, the basic fact that Islam does not paint heaven as an ethereal, wholly spiritual realm shows that it blesses human nature.

In summary, nature for Islam is one locus of God's signs to humanity. Nature is less prominent than in East Asian or ancient religion. Rather, Islam configures itself socially and theologically, focusing on the community and the sovereign Lord.

Muslim spirituality manifests something of this emphasis, in that one of its interests is to keep nature under control. By fasting, a Muslim tames the nature closest to the self. By confessing that there is no God but God, a Muslim clears the world of competitors to the Creator and Judge. That means that many devout Muslims' ideal is a bare vista. The Sufis manifested this ideal most fully, for many of them saw life as a pilgrimage to union with a God much more valuable than anything worldly. In less deliberate but still consoling ways, the poor merchant or soldier learns from misfortune how precarious a worldly vista is. Although the physical world is definitely real and on occasion quite good, the human's role is to observe it closely enough so that it serves as a guidepost to heaven. A Muslim can be comfortable in the natural world but only as a visitor. Life in the natural world soon passes, and Judgment depends on higher things, such as one's faith, one's prayer, and one's generosity in giving alms. The tradition does not teach people that the Judge will ask them how they treated the environment or whether they tore the bosom of mother earth. Those issues are far less important than whether they remembered Allah and his Prophet.

ISLAMIC RITUALS[68]

Yoruba Muslims of West Africa have ritualized their religion for the life cycle, the religious year, and the ordinary week. By studying these rituals, we may glimpse not only how Muslims have expressed their faith over the centuries, but also how Islam has adapted itself to such new geographic areas as West Africa.

The life cycle of the Yoruba Muslim begins on the day he becomes a member of the worshiping community. This may be the day when, as an adult, he formally converts to Islam, or the eighth day after his birth, when he receives his name. The major action in the adult conversion ceremony is an ablution, to symbolize the pure life the convert is entering upon. The candidates take off their clothes and don loin cloths. The presiding cleric washes their right hand three times, their left hand three times, their right leg three times, and their left leg three times. Then three times he washes their elbows, blows their nose, and washes their ears. Concluding, he pours water on their head and chest. Having been washed and become clean, they are true Muslims.

For the naming ceremony of a newborn child, the presiding cleric receives money in a covered dish. The cleric prays for the child, preaches a solemn sermon (often in Arabic), and then gives the child its name. Some West African Muslims also sacrifice a sheep or cut the infant's hair. (The Yoruba practice circumcision, as well as the drawing of tribal marks on the face or body. Apparently Islam did not introduce these customs but rather gave them a new interpretation.)

The second major stage on the Yoruba Muslim's way is marriage. The presiding cleric must divine that the proposed match is a good one and pray for the marital partners. Before the wedding, the groom has to pay the bride's family several monies and gifts. In modernized West African Muslim rituals the presiding cleric asks the groom: "Do you take Miss _____ as your wedded wife? Will you love her, honor her, feed her, clothe her, and lodge her in proper lodging?" Then he quotes the Qur'an (4 : 34), to the effect that one of the signs God has given human beings is creating mates for them, that they may find quiet of mind. Putting love and compassion between these mates, God gives reflective people a sign of his goodness and care. The presiding cleric also asks the bride similar questions, including whether she will love, honor, and obey her husband. He repeats most of the quotation from the Qur'an, and reminds the bride that "the good women are therefore obedient, guarding the unseen as Allah has guarded." The ceremony concludes with prayers to Allah that he bless this wedding. (Most of the West African Muslim community supports the traditional polygyny.)

Funeral rites complete Islam's ritual impact on the Yoruba life cycle. When a person has died the neighbors come together and dig a grave. Then they wash the corpse, repeating the ablutions of the conversion ceremony. They dress the corpse in a white cap, loin cloth, and sewn sheet, and then put it into the grave and cover it with earth. The presiding cleric prays for the deceased person, that God may forgive her sins. The dead person's family is expected to pay the cleric hand-

somely, with food as well as money. Some modernized sects hold a second ceremony, on the eighth day after the burial, with readings from the Qur'an, a sermon, and a eulogy of the deceased.

In addition to these three major ceremonies for the life cycle, Yoruba Islam has an annual cycle of feasting and fasting. The cycle begins with the Muslim New Year, which is a day for hearty eating in most sects and for orgiastic nude bathing and mock battles in a few. The New Year festival recalls Noah, who disembarked from the ark very hungry.

The next festivals in the annual cycle are two celebrations of Muhammad, his birthday and the night of his heavenly journey to Jerusalem and Paradise. The more conservative Yoruba Muslims have made much of the Prophet's birthday, using it as an occasion to display their learning. In their circles children act out scenes from the Prophet's life, and those who teach the Qur'an receive special stipends. The Yoruba do not understand the Prophet's heavenly journey well, so they tend to make little of it.

The month of Ramadan is the great time of fasting, but many of the Yoruba elderly fast during the month of Rajab as well. The last Friday of Ramadan is especially important, because then one may ask forgiveness for one's laxities in worship during the past year. Among the modernizing Yoruba Muslims the Ramadan ceremonies include the prayer, "O Allah! whom our obedience does not benefit and our disobedience does not harm, please accept from us what does not benefit you, and forgive us what does not harm you."

The two greatest feasts in the Yoruba Muslim calendar are the Feast of the Breaking of the Fast and the Feast of the Immolation. Each entails two days of public holidays in Nigeria. For the Feast of the Breaking of the Fast, worshipers dress elaborately and bring expensive prayer rugs. The ceremony includes an almsgiving, to solemnize gratitude for a successful conclusion to Ramadan, a visit to the ruler of the Yoruba, and a visit to the graves of the first two imams (religious leaders) of the community. The Feast of the Immolation reminds the Yoruba that their fellow Muslims in Arabia are performing this sacrifice in Mecca, as part of their *hajj*. The immolation itself usually is the sacrifice of a small goat. After the communal ceremony many individuals also sacrifice goats or rams at the entrances to their own houses.

The last feast of the annual cycle is the *hajj*, the pilgrimage to Mecca. Since Nigerian independence, the government has supported the pilgrimage, making the *hajj* available to the prosperous farmer, shopkeeper, or local leader. If the individual can make an initial outlay of money, he or she usually will receive supplementary gifts from friends. Once the pilgrims return to their local communities, they enjoy great status, since they have been to the center of the Muslim world. Usually the experience of Islam as a worldwide fellowship greatly broadens the Yoruba pilgrim's horizons. Not all Yoruba Muslims have the opportunity to travel to Mecca, but each year at the time of the *hajj* all turn their imaginations to the holy city and picture what is taking place there.

In the weekly religious cycle of Yoruba Muslims, Friday is the crowning day, but Wednesday and Thursday also have special significance. The last Wednesday of each lunar month is esteemed as a day of special blessings. All are encouraged to increase their prayers, that they may protect themselves from the evil every month contains. The darkness of the moon at the end of the month is probably the spark for this attitude. A prayer of modernizing Muslims expresses the last Wednesday mood: "In the name of God, the Merciful, the Compassionate: O God, O Terrible in power, O Terrible in cunning, O Strong One, O Thou Who guidest by Thy might everything in Thy Creation, shield me from the evil of everything Thou has created."

In folk Islam, Wednesday is considered replete with blessings, as is Thursday. Most Yoruba groups have adopted this folk attitude. Thus, most marriages, celebrations of a student's completion of the Qur'an, and groundbreakings occur on Wednesdays or Thursdays. One of the many functions of the Yoruba *alfa* (presiding cleric) is to divine an auspicious date for these celebrations. Conservative Muslims, who tend to be better educated, downplay such divinations, and do not attribute any special significance to particular days of the week.

However, Thursday evening has a special significance, because it is the threshold to Friday, the Muslim Sabbath. Indeed, most Yoruba Muslims offer prayers for the dead on Thursday night. A popular tradition says that on Thursday evening God allows the dead to come back to the world and see what is going on. This ties into a Yoruba tradition of leaving gifts for the deceased. If a dead person does not have gifts left for him, he loses prestige among his group of age-peers.

A certain conflict between traditional, pre-Muslim notions about the dead and Muslim ideas confuses many Yoruba Muslims. The traditional pictures show the dead existing in a shadowy heaven *(orun)*, where they need the care of those they have left behind. The Muslim beliefs in judgment and resurrection do not square with these pictures, so the status of the dead is rather murky. Some Yoruba Muslims translate resurrection so that it becomes a state much like *orun*, but others accept the more orthodox Muslim notion that resurrection is a wonderous event that will occur in the future.

Friday is the center of the weekly cycle, when all good Muslims are supposed to gather at noon in the main mosque for communal worship. In the large towns the mosques are crowded with male worshipers. (A smaller number of women are allowed to worship, segregated from the males, at the back of the mosque.) The service begins with the call to prayer and then has a sermon in the vernacular. Often this "sermon" turns out to be more like a group session of petitionary prayer. People come up to the prayer-leaders and whisper their intentions, which "megaphonists" then repeat in a loud voice, so that God and the community at large can hear them. The sermon sometimes amounts to no more than a few moral exhortations tossed in as editorial comments on the prayers people have offered. The people also contribute money.

After the sermon comes the heart of the Friday service, the communal *salat* or ritual prayer. Together the group go through the actions of the fivefold daily prayer—bowing, kneeling, and touching their foreheads to the ground. Muslim prayer is essentially this doing, this performative act. So "a mosque in the last resort is not a building: It is a place of prostration and any patch of ground in ritual purity suffices where a human frame may stretch itself—a fact about Islam which accounts in large measure for the naturalness of its occasions and the contagion in its expansion. A faith that does not need to house its worshipers has no walls to hide its creed."[69]

Through the life cycle, the annual cycle, and the weekly cycle, the great lesson the Yoruba or any other Muslims are learning is the lesson of prostration. Bowing before God, the Almighty, the Muslim deepens her sense that only one power is in charge of the world. To be at peace with God is life's greatest accomplishment; to be at war with God is life's greatest tragedy.

Society

Estimates of the social innovations that Islam introduced and the degree of social perfection that it achieved vary considerably. In this section we present a positive opinion, a negative opinion, a view on Islamic ethics, and a short essay on women under Islam.

A Positive View

The proponent of Islam, Isma'il al Faruqi, begins with the thesis that Muslim society existed so that human beings might realize the "divine pattern." Elemental in that pattern was the family. Marriage was a civil contract, not a sacrament, and a man could marry more than one wife so long as he provided justice, equity, and loving care. Private property and the pursuit of wealth were inviolate rights, but wealth brought the obligation to care for the deprived. Concerning the right to life: "The life of one's fellowman is inviolate, except by due process of law. Nothing may henceforth be decided by force or violence. Such recourse is legitimate only in self-defense and in the safeguarding of the security of missionaries. For the Muslim is duty-bound to bring his faith to the knowledge of mankind with sound preaching and wise counsel, to convey with warning and command of his Lord."[70]

The Muslim political unit was the *Ummah*, which was as comprehensive as the broadest notions of church or synagogue. Tradition says that the Qur'an teaches that the Prophet and his successors bore a theocratic power. That is, they had authority in both the religious and the secular spheres, because Islam does not distinguish the two. Due to the concept of the Ummah, Muslims had to fight for brethren in other places who suffered tyranny (Qur'an 4 : 75). For Muslim leaders, the consensus of the community was an important goal, for they wanted a single divine rope to bind the Ummah together. Strong faith was to create an equality among all believers, and God would reward every man and woman who was faithful through difficulties and trials. Muslims were to bring their disputes to the Prophet or his successors, and they all had a common duty to worship God, to obey God's commands, and to do good and avoid evil.

Members were to be to one another as brothers and mutual guardians (9 : 71), respecting life and enjoying its good things. Woman came from the soul of man (4 : 1). Both men and women had the right to what they had earned, and both could enter Paradise, although "men have priority over women, by virtue of what God has endowed to them and by what they spend on women of their wealth" (4 : 34). Men were to provide their women tenderness and affluence if they could. Marriage was the usual state, and Islam did not support celibacy. Almsgiving was a primary obligation, and one was to go beyond justice to charity and forgiveness. From the call that God gave the Prophet, ideally all human beings would come to reason and felicity. Since God clearly did not compel non-Muslims to believe, Muslims themselves had no right to force others to believe (10 : 99, 108). However, the Qur'an regards balefully non-Muslims who contract with Islam and renege: "Lesser than the beasts in the eye of God are the unbelievers for they have covenanted with you and violated their covenant shamelessly in every case. If you lay hold of them in war, make of them a lesson to the others" (8 : 55).

The covenant of Medina that Muhammad composed gave Jews explicit rights: "To the Jews who follow us belong assistance and equal treatment from us without either injustice or discrimination."[71] The basic status of non-Muslims within the state that Muhammad envisioned was what might be called "colleagueship"—peaceful cooperation. The democratic principles applying to Muslim citizenship were individual responsibility, equality, the leaders' responsibility to run the government, and the mutual security of all citizens. In its law the state was to regard itself as a replica of the cosmic state that God runs by strict and unalterable laws. In effect, this meant buttressing Islamic convictions with a sure faith in divine justice on Judgment Day. The imam, or leader, led the community in upholding the law. This was the basis for his quasi-contractual relationship with the Ummah.

The Islamic state made a threefold division of humanity: Muslims, covenanters, and enemies. The Muslim peoples who constituted the *Dar al-Islam* (House of Islam) could not legitimately resort to war against one another. Covenanters were non-Muslims who had made compacts of peace, and their rights and duties were the same as those of Muslims. Al Faruqi does not specify the fate of enemies, although he notes the Qur'anic teaching that Muslims are to preach to them but not force them to convert. Presumably, holy war only resulted when enemies rejected both conversion and covenant. If an enemy responded with hostility, Muslim security necessitated war. What happened when the enemy simply wanted to be left alone or considered a Muslim takeover of its area unacceptable is not clear. However, it was clearly not blameworthy for Islam "to combat with the sword the sword which stands between it and man, preventing Islam from conveying its call and man from listening to or receiving it."[72]

A Negative View

Evaluating Muhammad and Islam in the context of the ecumenic age, Eric Voegelin enters a more critical opinion: "Islam was primarily an ecumenic religion and only secondarily an empire. Hence it reveals in its extreme form the danger which beset all of the religions of the Ecumenic Age, the danger of impairing their universality by letting their ecumenic mission slide over into the acquisition of world-immanent, pragmatic power."[73]

On occasion, the Arab militancy of Muhammad's ancestors shaped the Qur'anic conception of religious mission itself (for example, 21 : 16–18). In Sura 8, this leads to counsel that is easily abused: "The infidels must desist from their unbelief or the tension between truth and falsehood in the world will be removed by energetic action (VIII, 40–41). . . . For 'surely the worst beasts in the sight of God are the ingrate who will not believe' (VIII, 57)."[74] Although Voegelin does not consider the Qur'anic precepts on respecting non-Muslims' consciences, al Faruqi does not mention the counsel to slaughter (8 : 68).

Ethics

Annemarie Schimmel has sketched Muslim ethics, which presumably directed Muslim actions.[75] The guiding principle was to serve God as though you saw him in front of you. In other words, belief in Allah, Judgment, and the necessity of right deeds were the bases of Islamic ethics. Religious bonds rather than blood bonds, pure faith rather than idolatry, and sexual restraint rather than indecency—these were notable advances made by the Qur'an over Arab paganism. In addition to the exhortations to justice and charity found in the Meccan suras and the detailed legislation of the Medinan suras, those who survived Muhammad looked back on the Prophet's own life as the key to how a Muslim ought to live.

The early disputes about the fate of a sinner and the place of good works, which divided the theological and legal schools, suggest that human beings were considered free and responsible. As we noted, the law distinguishes five kinds of actions, from the commanded to the forbidden. The Qur'an deals with adultery, murder, and theft, prescribing stern punishments for them. Women had the right to refuse a proposed marriage, but men had greater rights than women in divorce. The wife had to obey her husband, who could punish her, and she always had to be at his disposal. "If a husband kills his wife and her lover *in flagrante delicto* [in the act of adultery itself] he is not punishable. Sodomy is likewise forbidden (though often practised in a society which excluded women largely from daily life. The object of Persian and Turkish love poetry is generally masculine).[76]

The Qur'an takes slavery for granted, but it recommends humane treatment and commends freeing slaves. Only non-Muslim prisoners of war could legally become slaves. Discrimination because of color and race was unlawful, though some racial prejudice mars Islamic history. When the law reached its final stage of development around 1000, its detailed specifications tended to become mechanical. The mystics therefore tried to make ethics spring from a deeper relationship with God. The first virtue they taught was *wara*—abstention from everything unlawful or dubious. In other words, one was not to nitpick but to act from the heart and turn away from anything that might displease God. Masters such as al-Ghazali developed a shrewd psychology of virtue and vice, which they deployed in order to bring about the highest perfection. That perfection was living every moment in the presence of God. Finally, the general effect of Muslim ethics was to heighten awareness of one's distance from the divine purity and so lead one to beg God's mercy and forgiveness.

Women's Status

The status of women in Islam says a great deal about Muslim society.[77] In the Qur'an there is some basis for sexual equality: Reward and punishment in the afterlife depend on deeds, not gender; marriage and conjugal life are precious; women have dowry rights in some divorces, inheritance rights, rights to remarry, and rights to protection in time of pregnancy and nursing. However, women's rights were not equal to those that the Qur'an gave males in either divorce or inheritance. Moreover, the Qur'an does not even consider the possibility that women might assume leadership roles in the community, receive an education equal to that of males, teach law or theology, or engage in polygamy (as males could).

Further, the misogyny latent in most patriarchal religions had dark effects in Muslim society. As late as 1970, an Arab sheik offered the opinion that "educated or not a woman is a woman and the Prophet—God's prayers and peace on him—had said that women are lacking in mind and religion."[78] The tradition placed more women in the Fire than in the Garden, and the prime determinant of their destiny was their treatment of their husbands. In legend Muhammad virtually despised female nature as stupid and irreligious. Its specific defects were menstruation, which interfered with prayer and fasting, and unreliability, which made a woman's witness worth only half a man's in court. Obedience to her husband was the woman's first duty; failure to do so can still get her killed today.[79]

The Muslim woman was considered erotic and empty-headed. Thus she was subject to purdah (seclusion and veiling), polygyny, concubinage, and the harem. Women were not to be taught to read and write ("a great calamity"), and they were morally "bent" because they came from Adam's bent rib. Thus, in many men's eyes, they had a dismal existence: "It were best for a girl not to come into existence, but being born she had better be married or buried."[80] Recent Muslims, especially Africans, have defended clitoridectomy and kindred operations, frequently with the following sort of rationale: "Circumcision of women releases them from their bondage to sex, and enables them to fulfill their real destiny as mother."[81] As she has done in the cases of Indian suttee, Chinese foot binding, and Christian witch burning, Mary Daly has vividly described African genital mutilation, eschewing defused scholarly speech.[82]

Another revealing view of women in Islamic society comes from the imagery of the Garden.[83] For many men, the best part of the heavenly Garden was the *hur:* dark-eyed, buxom virgins. In addition to his earthly wife, each male in heaven could expect to have seventy *hur.* They would never be sick, menstruating, pregnant (unless he wished), bad-tempered, or jealous. He would be able to deflower a thousand each month and find them all intact when he returned to them. In descriptions of the Judgment scene, one sees the reverse of this fantasy: Women are in charge of men, which is a sure sign of disorder.

In fairness, Islam improved the lot of Arab women considerably, and certain parts of the community allowed women a function in the Hadith,[84] in scholarship, and in saintliness.[85] Also, many modern Muslims deplore the injustices that women have suffered in the past, interpret Qur'anic religion in a way that gives women great dignity, and bitterly oppose the drive of fundamentalists to return to such traditions as marrying girls off when they reach thirteen.

Divisions

The different Islamic cultures were bonded by the Qur'an despite their geographical, linguistic, ethnic, and even theological differences. The principal theological division, as we noted, has been between the Shiites and the Sunnites. However, as W. Montgomery Watt has shown, the formative period of Islamic thought saw a variety of controversies and then "heterodoxies."[86]

In India Islamic elements fused with Hindu elements to create Sikhism, and Islam was also the inspiration behind Baha'i. Baha'i is a universalist religion that stresses the unity of all traditions and the basic oneness of the human race. It arose in nineteenth-century Persia when a Shiite Muslim, Sayyid Ali Muhammad, declared that he was the twelfth imam—the last, messianic leader whom the Shia awaits. Sayyid took the designation *Bab* ("gate"), and his follower Baha Ullah produced writings that became classic works of Baha'i faith. Today Baha'i has about 5 million adherents. Its world center is on Mount Carmel in Haifa, Israel, where there is a lovely garden and shrine to the Bab (Figure 15).[87]

Self

The strong control of the Ummah by religious law had two primary effects on the individual or self. First, the common code that governed external behavior shaped and constrained the majority. In other words, most Muslims accepted the ethics sketched above. Second, the Sufis and mystics drew a substantial minority to a more internal doctrine of the self shaped by personal devotion. Such devotion sought to unite the individual with God experientially. Thus, the first lesson that it taught was that the human person has a spiritual substance or capacity that can unite with God.

These two effects on selfhood produced a balance in Muslim religion: The self learned that membership in the House of Islam depended on observing the common law, which led to merit and the Garden, and that it could anticipate the Garden and taste God's joy in the present life.

The orthodox conception of the self began with the notion of creation. In Sura 96 the self is described essentially as a small thing that God made from a blood clot or a drop of sperm. The essence of Islam and of being a Muslim was to recognize the creator-creature relation: a sovereign God who is completely the Lord of a very insignificant vassal. The basic scriptural message of Islamic anthropology is submission, even a certain holy slavery.

This attitude was no false humility. Rather, it was the bare truth of the human condition. Human beings came from God, and their destiny depended on living out the pattern that God had in making them. Thus, they had no basis for self-glorification. Thus, the exclamations of an al-Hallaj, who

Figure 15   Shrine to the Bab, Haifa. Photo by J. T. Carmody.

claimed identification with God (through mystical union), could only sound blasphemous to the majority, who were immersed in the literal text. Between the divine Lord and the human vassal there stretched an impassable gulf. However much genuine love might have drawn the spirit up to God, however much God's intimate mercy might have descended toward human flesh, the essential difference in their states remained.

From other Qur'anic accounts of creation one can gather the impression that, despite their lowliness, human beings have a special status among all creatures. Al Faruqi calls this status being God's "vicegerent" on earth.[88] The word *lakum* ("for you") appears in the stories of how God made the earth to produce herbs, crops, and animals and of how God made the sea to carry ships and the

camels and sheep to bring forth their offspring.[89] In the stories of Adam's creation (for instance, 2 : 28, 15 : 29, 32 : 8), the angels object to God's making human beings, but God forms this first man from clay and water, gives him a most beautiful form, and breathes his spirit into him. Then he makes the angels bow before Adam, for Adam is to be the *khalifa* (vicegerent) on earth, having in this capacity the right and duty to carry out God's orders. Echoing Genesis, Sura 2 : 31 speaks of God's teaching Adam the names of all things, which means giving him power over all things, since to control a being's name was to have power over it. The end God had in mind for such a creature, the recompense that He expected, was adoration: "We have created men and jinn only for adoration" (51 : 51).

We can see, therefore, the basis for

the Islamic view that God made the earth subject to human control. Along with the doctrine of God's transcendence, this anthropocentricity in creation helped to deemphasize nature. As we argued above, naming and ruling the world did not remove nature's mystery. Even with nature's mystery, however, the Muslim felt that the earth had been given into his (and to a lesser extent her) control. Nonetheless, Muslim teachings about human nature honored its ties with the earth, its creation from clay and water.

Anthropology

In traditional Muslim anthropology (view of human nature) the spiritual faculties had several names. The *nafs* was essentially the animal soul, the source of concupiscence (desire). It had the connotation of belonging to the lower part of the personality—to the flesh that incites evil. (Sometimes, though, it just means "self.") The *ruh* was the spirit, come from Allah, that animates the human body. Muslims often pictured it as a subtle matter that permeates the human body. Reason *(aql)* was the spiritual faculty by which human beings discern right and wrong. Finally, the mystics spoke of the *qalb*—the heart that is the faculty by which one obtains direct knowledge of God.

For some of the Sufis, the doctrine of creation in God's image was crucial. On occasion, neo-Platonic or Gnostic notions colored this doctrine to mean that the soul wanders in exile. It can return to its home, though, if it appropriates secret teaching or learns certain meditative techniques. From the notion of creation in God's image, the Sufis also developed their concept of the *insan kamil*, the perfect man. Usually they applied it to Muhammad, who contained all the divine attributes and who served as a microcosm of divinity.

The destiny of the human being, as we have seen, was either the Fire or the Garden. Islam did not consider man and woman to be laboring under a "fallen" human nature, for Muslims did not regard the sin of Adam and Eve as being contagious or passed on to their offspring. Thus, Islam did not speak of redemption. The Prophet was a revealer or a medium of revelation; he was not a ransom, a victim, or a suffering servant. Instead of sin (in the deep sense of alienation from God by irrational actions), Islam tended to stress human forgetfulness (of God's goodness). Human nature was weak—prone to a kind of religious amnesia. In the Prophet's own conception of human destiny, men and women have a common responsibility to remember God's goodness and to respond by fulfilling his will. Originally, both men and women were to offer prayer and alms; however, in later times women's status deteriorated, and they did not have this obligation.

The self that was faithful to the identity set by the community could expect to gain Paradise. God would forgive sins (violations of religious law), so they did not mean a loss of community membership. (However, the dissident Kharijites said that every Muslim who committed a grave sin was an unbeliever.) What separated one from the Ummah in the orthodox view was to deny that the injunctions of the Qur'an came from God and thus were eternally binding. Among the Shia, who predominate in Iran, faith also included acknowledging the mystical imam of the time—the hidden successor to Ali whom the Shiites expect to come as the Messiah. By uniting with this hidden imam, one partook of salvation.

Historically, the major theoretical question concerning the self was the relation of human freedom to divine will. At least in the Meccan sections, the Qur'an takes human freedom for granted. Muhammad's call and his preaching make no sense without a capacity to respond. Similarly, the scenes of Judgment Day assume that human beings have been responsible for their actions—that they could have done otherwise than they did. However, later Qur'anic passages emphasize God's omnipotence. As a result, the question arises, Does God lead some persons astray—or at least leave them in error?

In the Umayyad period a group of

Figure 16   The Meeting of the Theologians, by 'Abd Allah Musawwir (mid-sixteenth century). Nelson Gallery-Atkins Museum (Nelson Fund).

satisfied many people with the following formula: "God creates in man the will to act and the act, and man acquires the act by performing it." To say the least, the issue vexed Islam. In later times the common person frequently felt that life was fated—that it was out of his or her hands. Among the few monistic mystics, human freedom was lost in the divine nature.

In summary, Islam has given the self rather complex directives. The core message is that membership in the Prophet's community and submission to God fulfill the human duties. The way to realize oneself is to follow the community law. In the present, such self-realization means spiritual security; in the future, it will mean Paradise. While waiting for Paradise, one can work the earth, trade, fight, or enjoy the pleasures of the senses, so long as the chosen activity does not divert one from the ultimate reality of God. If one is submissive to God, most things are licit. More things are licit for men than for women, as we have seen, but the Qur'an did improve the Arab woman's lot considerably.

Still, the popular image of Muhammad as a man who could satisfy nine wives and still receive revelations greater than those of Jesus inculcated a certain bravado in all but the most ascetic males. Since Islamic education deals primarily with religious lore, it does not necessarily demythologize Muhammad's popular image. As well, education is largely denied women. Therefore, tradition tends to describe sexuality mainly from a male point of view. That point of view tends to meld with the patterns set forth in the eternal Qur'an. Following these patterns, one lets God more and more dominate the entire self.

strict predestinarians (the Jabriya) stressed God's complete control. Opposing them were the Qasriya, who defended human responsibility. The Mutazilites defended both human freedom and God's perfect justice. Still another position, that of al-Ashari,

MUSLIM SAINTS[90]

When we considered the life cycle rituals, the annual rituals, and the weekly rituals of Yoruba Muslims, we glimpsed Islam's accommodation to the West African religious traditions that predated it. We get another glimpse of such cross-

cultural accommodation by studying the different ways the different Muslim ethnic groups have conceived sainthood, the peak of the Muslim life. For example, the Indonesian Muslims, who have been greatly influenced by Indian culture, have focused their religious imagination on saints whose style is markedly quieter than the style of the saints Moroccan Muslims have venerated. Since "Islam" only starts to come into focus when one begins to find the unity underlying such differences, let us attempt a comparative study of the Indonesian and Moroccan Muslim saints.

In Indonesian Muslim lore, Sunan Kalidjaga is the most important of the group of nine "apostles" considered to be the founders of Indonesian Islam. Legend has it that he was born the son of a high royal official of Madjapahit, one of the greatest and last of the Indonesian Hindu-Buddhist kingdoms, which dominated most of Eastern Java during the fourteenth and fifteenth centuries. In the sixteenth century Madjapahit declined, caught between the old Hindu-Buddhist order and the new Muslim order that was emerging. Pressured by this change, Kalidjaga moved to the new harbor state of Djapara, where he met another of the early apostles, Sunan Bonang, and was converted to Islam. Later Kalidjaga so greatly influenced Javanese politics that he is credited with Java's having become solidly Muslim. Symbolically, therefore, Kalidjaga serves as a bridge between the old Indic world of god-kings, ritual priests, and Indian shrines and the new Islamic world of pious sultans, Qur'anic scholars, and austere mosques. Indonesians love to contemplate the story of his conversion, for it recapitulates their good fortune in having gained access to the world of Allah, and it drives home the conviction that Islam is the best flower of the new phase of their history.

When Kalidjaga arrived in Djapara, he was a ne'er-do-well, accomplished in stealing, drinking, whoring, and gambling. So deep were his vices, he stole all his own mother's money, and when he had dissipated this he set out to steal from the public at large. Eventually he became a highwayman of such renown that people were afraid to go to the Djapara market lest they encounter him and lose all their goods.

Into this scene strolled Sunan Bonang, a Muslim (probably an Arab) dressed in gorgeous clothes and expensive jewels, and carrying a cane of solid gold. Naturally he attracted the attention of Kalidjaga, who put a knife to his throat and demanded all his finery. But, to Kalidjaga's amazement, Bonang laughed in his face. Calling Kalidjaga by his name (though he had never met Kalidjaga before), Bonang chided him as though he were a little boy: "Don't always be wanting this thing and that thing. Such material desires are pointless. We live but a moment. It is foolish to be attached to worldly goods. Look: there is a whole tree full of money."

Kalidjaga turned and saw a banyan tree transformed to gold and hung with jewels. At a stroke, he realized that material things were nothing compared with Bonang's power. What sort of a man must Bonang be, to be able to turn trees into gold and jewels and yet not care about gold and jewels at all? With this thought, Kalidjaga's life of vice repulsed him, and he begged Bonang to teach him spiritual power. Bonang agreed, but he warned Kalidjaga that such teaching was very difficult. Kalidjaga vowed he would persist until death, but Bonang merely told him, "Wait here, by the side of the river, until I return." Then he took his leave.

Kalidjaga waited by the side of the river for forty years, lost in thought. Great trees grew up around him, floods arose and receded, crowds jostled him back and forth, buildings went up and were torn down. Still he waited, lost in thought. Finally Bonang returned, and he saw that Kalidjaga had indeed been steadfast. So instead of teaching Kalidjaga the doctrines of Islam, Bonang simply told him that he had been a good pupil—indeed, that he had come to surpass Bonang himself. To prove this, Bonang asked Kalidjaga difficult questions about religious matters, and Kalidjaga answered them all correctly. Then Bonang told him to go forth and spread the truths of Islam, which Kalidjaga did with unsurpassed effectiveness.

What a remarkable story! The master apostle of Javanese Islam becomes a great saint without ever having seen the Qur'an, entered a mosque, or prayed a Muslim prayer. His conversion comes directly from a change of heart deepened by yoga-like meditation. It is not so much a change in belief (taking that word to refer mainly to matters of thought) as a change in will.

Because he had reformed his life, and penetrated the implications of his reform, Kalidjaga had become a Muslim. When he walked the meditative way that Indian culture had been impressing on Indonesia for centuries, he came out a Muslim—the new holy man forged in the fires of Indonesia's cultural transformation. So the message that was trumpeted whenever the legend of Java's greatest saint was told was that Islam is the obvious expression of the reformed, converted, highly developed religious personality. If one finds the depths of human authenticity, one eventually realizes that the Qur'an, the mosques, and the Muslim scholars are human authenticity's best expressions.

The Moroccan saint Sidi Lahsen Lyusi is quite a contrast to Kalidjaga. Lyusi was born into an obscure tribe of shepherds in the Middle Atlas Mountains of Morocco in 1631. Although he probably was of Berber descent, he claimed to be a *sherif* or direct descendant of Muhammad. Lyusi died in 1691, so the sixty years of his life coincided with the rise of the Alawite dynasty (which still rules today in Rabat, the capital of Morocco) from the chaos of a preceding sectarian strife. Like Kalidjaga's, therefore, Lyusi's sainthood was intimately tied to a difficult time of transition, when people were looking for models of a new order. However, where Kalidjaga functioned as a miniature of the new harmony that Indonesia sought, Lyusi directly opposed the power he saw rising in his times. Thus Clifford Geertz, whose description of these two saints we are following, characterizes Lyusi's approach as moralistic, in contrast to the aesthetic approach of Kalidjaga.

The chaos of Lyusi's life is sometimes called the Maraboutic Crisis, and it arose after the collapse of the last of the Berber dynasties, the Merinid. A *marabout* is a holy man, and during the Maraboutic Crisis Morocco splintered into different political groups clustered around different holy men. Lyusi wandered from political center to political center, always restless and on the move. When he arrived in Tamgrut, a desert oasis, he encountered the famous Muslim saint Ahmed ben Nasir. Ben Nasir was sick with smallpox, and so he asked his disciples, one by one, to wash out his loathsome nightshirt. Each disciple refused, repelled by the disgusting garment and afraid for his health. Lyusi, who had just arrived and was not known to ben Nasir, approached the saint and volunteered for the job. He took the shirt to a spring, rinsed it, wrung it out, and then drank the

foul water it produced. When he returned to the master his eyes were aflame, not with sickness but with what Moroccans call *baraka*: the supernatural power that makes a marabout.

The story summarizes the Moroccan notion of sainthood. The main forces at work in Lyusi's transformation into a man of *baraka* were his extraordinary physical courage, his absolute personal loyalty to his "teacher," his moral intensity, and an almost physical passage of sainthood from teacher to disciple. Thus the Moroccan notion of Muslim sainthood seems more energetic than the Indonesian. Whereas Kalidjaga was transformed by forty years of meditation near a river, Lyusi was transformed by a single act of heroic courage.

Thirty years after this event, Lyusi had a momentous confrontation with Sultan Mulay Ismail, the great consolidator of the Alawite dynasty. In 1668 the Alawites had put an end to the Maraboutic Crisis and gained power in Morocco. The confrontation took place in the Sultan's new capital of Meknes, and it reveals the delicate relation between strongman politics and Maraboutism that has dominated Moroccan history. The warrior and the saint have been the two basic forms of heroism in Morocco, and this epic confrontation pitted a great warrior against a greater saint.

When Lyusi arrived in Meknes, Mulay Ismail received him as an honored guest. Indeed, he brought Lyusi to the court and made him his spiritual advisor. The sultan was building a large wall around the city and treating the men working on the wall cruelly. When one of the workmen fell from exhaustion and was sealed into the wall, some of the other workers came to Lyusi secretly to complain. Lyusi said nothing, but that night, when his supper was brought to his chamber, he broke all the dishes. He continued to do this, night after night, until all the dishes in the palace were broken.

Eventually the sultan learned what was happening and ordered Lyusi brought to him. When he asked the saint why he was acting so outrageously, the saint asked in return whether it was better to break pottery of clay or the pottery of Allah (human beings). Then he proceeded to upbraid the sultan for his cruelty to the workers.

The sultan was not moved. Lyusi had abused his hospitality (a high crime in Moroccan culture), so he ordered Lyusi out of the city.

Lyusi left the palace and pitched his tent near the wall that was being built. When the sultan asked why the saint had not obeyed the royal order, Lyusi said that he had left the sultan's city and taken up residence in God's city. At this answer the sultan was so enraged that he charged out on horseback. Interrupting the saint's prayers (another high crime), he again asked why the royal order had been disobeyed. Again he received the answer that Lyusi was now in the city of God. Wild with fury, the sultan advanced to kill the saint. But the saint drew a line on the ground and

when the sultan's horse crossed the line the horse's legs began to sink into the earth. Terrified, the sultan begged mercy and promised that he would reform. Lyusi said he only wanted a decree acknowledging that he was a *sherif*, entitled to the honors of a direct descendant of the Prophet. The sultan gave him this decree and Lyusi left Meknes (fearing for his life) to preach to the Berbers in the Middle Atlas forests. After his death a great cult developed at his tomb, and he has since been revered as a most powerful marabout. In Lyusi, Moroccan Islam has found an ideal embodiment of its moral passion, just as in Kalidjaga, Indonesian Islam has found an ideal embodiment of its meditative passion.

Divinity

Islam is perhaps the most theocentric of the major religions.[91] In Muhammad's revelation, Allah emerged to become the sovereign Lord. Before Muhammad, some Arabs had spoken of a high god "Allah" who was above the numerous idols. The divine name itself seems to fuse two words: al-Ilah ("the God"). It was an attempt to designate an ultimate divinity, a God who was beyond all demigods. From his visionary experience, Muhammad recognized that Allah is the only divinity, and that his primary designations are "Creator" and "Judge." As such, Allah leaves no place for other deities to function in either the world's creation or in the destiny of humankind.

Islam polished its theocentricity through controversy with polytheistic Arabs and then with Christians committed to the Incarnation and the Trinity. Sura 112, which Schimmel calls the logical end of the Qur'an,[92] puts the matter succinctly: "Say: He is Allah, One; Allah, the Eternal; He brought not forth nor hath He been brought forth; Coequal with Him there hath never been anyone."

The Creator made the world in six days (or in a single moment, according to

Sura 54 : 50). Muslims trusted that he guides the world wisely and unfailingly. God's knowledge of all creatures is total, and his mercy extends to all who acknowledge him. It is God in whose name every work is being begun and upon whose will every future action depends. Thus, one had to add "insha Allah" ("if God wills") to every sentence that refers to a future act or a new direction of thought. To try to indicate God's fullness, the Qur'an encircles him with "most beautiful names." He is the First and the Last, the Inward and the Outward. Above all, he is Merciful and Compassionate. He is the All-Holy, the Peace, the Light of Heaven and Earth. Transcendent though he be, he is also as near as the jugular pulse. Wherever one turns, there is his Face (the Qur'anic expression for God's essence).

Many scholars find the negative portion of the creed ("no God but Allah") very important, since it unequivocally rejects other peoples' gods. As well, it determined that the greatest sin in the Muslim code would be *shirk*—idolatry or "association" (of other objects of worship with God). The mystics sometimes took this to mean that nothing but God exists—that God alone is real. Among modern Muslims, anti-idolatry on occasion has worked against ideologies such as Marxism, capitalism, and nationalism, which some orthodox Muslims find incompatible with pure monotheism. Insofar as such ideologies enlist the ultimate concern of many human beings, they amount to new kinds of paganism.

However, the theology of the Qur'an itself is not without ambiguity. After Muhammad's death, debates arose about God's nature. At the beginning, the orthodox clung to the letter and imagery of the received text. That meant accepting descriptions of God that gave him a face, hands, and the like. The Mutazilites, who had contact with Hellenistic rationalism, pointed out the dangers latent in such anthropomorphism: When we think of God in human terms, we think of him as finite.[93] Thus, the Mutazilites clung to the absolute unity of God, accepting as a consequence that God cannot be imagined. In other words, they prized God's difference—the gulf that lies between the Creator and everything created. In Western terms, that made them "negative" theologians. Indeed, to safeguard God's unity, the Mutazilites even questioned the doctrine of the divine attributes (that God has speech, sight, and so on). For that reason, the orthodox described the Mutazilites as "those who deny the attributes," a charge of heresy.

In these debates, Muslims shared with Jews and Christians the consequences of an exposure to Greek reason. They had to ask whether their descriptions of God could be reconciled with what they could infer from the divine transcendence. For instance, they could infer that a Creator would be independent of the world, unlimited, unimaginable in created terms. From that it followed that any picture of God would be at best a happy convenience—a more or less useful fiction that might help some people's faith. As a further extension of such rationalism, the Mutazilites denied that the Qur'an is God's uncreated word. To them that would have made it a coeternal attribute, something ever existent with God. However, calling the Qur'an "created" deeply offended the orthodox, for whom the Arabic text expressed a heavenly prototype. The human Qur'an was unalterable (which led the orthodox to resist all attempts to translate it from Arabic), because it derived from eternity. Thus, the Mutazilites and the orthodox clashed in their theologies of revelation.

Further, the Mutazilites insisted that God has to be just and true. For the divine will to be arbitrary would violate God's own inner consistency. Consequently, God has to reward the just with heaven and punish the evil with hell. As well, God cannot be the author of sin, so human beings must have free will. To the less intellectual Muslim majority, this logic seemed rarefied, and they could not follow its deductive chain. "Limiting" God's freedom jarred with their sense of the divine sovereignty. Indeed, popular orthodoxy never fully accepted either human freedom or the notion that God had to obey rules for creation, even if they were his own. Popular orthodoxy preferred to leave all things in God's hands and saw little reason to puzzle over human freedom, God's noncontradiction, or the other problems that vexed the Mutazilites.

Al-Ashari, who had mediated the debate on the question of divine providence and human freedom, also mediated the question of the divine attributes. To the Mutazilites, he insisted that God has attributes (thereby saving the picture in the Qur'an). To the traditionalists, he insisted that we cannot say precisely how God has his attributes. In al-Ashari's eyes, both anthropomorphism and the denial of attributes were grave sins.

Among the Arab philosophers,[94] such as Avicenna, Greek doctrines stimulated the conception of God as a first cause whose being is pure existence. In contrast, the Sufis forwent philosophical speculation, favoring instead a personal experience of the divine. For them the profitable way was not reasoning but intuition. Further, the Sufis opposed Qur'anic fundamentalists by proposing that we should obey God out of love. To the fundamentalists, such a personal relationship seemed novel, for they admitted only a relationship of obedience: The Creator commanded and the creature obeyed. Because the Sufis were more ecstatic than either the fundamentalists or the philosophers, they are a richer source for ascertaining the beauty of the Islamic God—the allure of Allah's mystery and its fearsomeness.

The basic Islamic program for worshiping God has always been the five pillars. In the daily prayer *(salat)*, one expressed one's submission to God and so one's faith in God's Lordship. Historically, men attended the Friday common worship in the mosque, while women prayed at home. Sufi circles developed unstructured prayer, which frequently involved a repetition of God's holy names. On the folk level, magical practices mixed with worship. The Qur'an gives them some foundation by saying that the (bad) angels Harut and Marut taught the Babylonians magic (2 : 96). Ordinarily, the magician knew formulas that could conjure the jinns or the angels. This has led to an expansion of the ways in which one can imagine the spirits and call them to one's aid. Amulets, reproductions of verses from the Qur'an, reproductions of God's names, and so on, are popular expressions of Muslim (magical) interest in attaining good luck. Similarly, Muslims continue to dread the "evil eye." To ward off its malignant influence, people constantly intersperse their conversation with "as God wills." As well, they wear amulets or give their children ugly names to keep the evil ones away.

Popular religion also retains a considerable interest in astrology, prophecy, and fortune-telling. A favorite technique for divining the future is to open the Qur'an at random and take the first verse that one's eye falls on as a cipher for what is to come. Other popular methods are reading palms or coffee grounds.

Sacrifice also has a place in Muslim worship. Those who can afford it immolate a sheep on the Day of Slaughtering during the annual pilgrimage to Mecca. This sacrifice is in memory of Abraham, who was willing to sacrifice his son Ishmael. People also make votive offerings—cocks, sheep, and so on— at holy places such as the tombs of saints.

The animal should be slaughtered ritually, by cutting its jugular and trachea in one stroke; tradition recommends giving it to the poor. Finally, sacrifice is appropriate on almost any important occasion, such as starting construction of a house, celebrating a child's birthday, or expiating an offense.

Although Islam places no mediators between God and human beings, it has made both Muhammad and many saints quite important objects of devotion. The members of Muhammad's family enjoyed special privileges, and Ali, his cousin and son-in-law, became a cult figure while still alive to those who considered him to be Muhammad's legitimate heir. The Shia expanded the creed to include the words "Ali is the Friend of God." The Shia also venerated the line of imams, with special emphasis upon the currently hidden imam. He is the ruler of the age, and he will return at the end of the world to fill the world with justice. In Iran this imam's name accompanies the promulgation of laws, and he is for true Shiites an object of intense personal devotion.[95] Ali's son Husain also plays an important role, for the celebration of his assassination is a day of deep mourning.[96] Among the Sufis, the leaders of the orders were venerated, as were holy persons who gained a reputation for miracles. The latter often received special tombs to which the faithful would go for cures and favors.[97]

Angels are also essential objects of Muslim faith. According to tradition, God created them from light. The Qur'an stresses that they are neither children of Allah nor female beings. They are intelligent and can become visible. From the Qur'an, Muslims know Gabriel as the angel of revelation. Israfil will blow the trumpet at Doomsday, and Azrael is the angel of death. Iblis is the fallen angel. Like Harut and Marut, he is a source of evil. Harut and Marut taught humankind witchcraft, but a beautiful woman seduced them and then imprisoned them in a well in Babylonia.[98] Thus, the sacred space between the creature and the Creator has been abuzz with personages of interest.

The Islamic divinity is similar to that

of the other theistic religions. Though its official doctrine insists on God's uniqueness, the comparativist finds that its popular practice deviates from its doctrine. Muslims perhaps have read the Qur'an more literally than other religionists have read their respective scriptures, since Islamic orthodoxy reified it into God's eternal Word, but there are analogies in Judaism, Christianity, and Hinduism. Clearly, though, Muslim faith aspired to make things simple: a black-and-white doctrine of God, Muhammad, and Judgment; a program of genius (the five pillars) for reducing this faith to practice; a single community of believers dedicated to filling the earth with true religion—with submission to the Grand Lord of the Worlds.

As events in Iran and Afghanistan in early 1980 showed, this aspiration toward simplicity has often had quite complicated effects. The condition of human beings—their space, time, and imperfection—renders pure submission to the Lord of the Worlds more an ideal than a fact.

Study Questions

1. Contrast Muhammad with Jesus.
2. In what sense is Islam the preeminent religion of the book?
3. Why do the five pillars make a comprehensive, fully adequate religious program?
4. Explain briefly how Qur'anic religion could inspire the golden age of Arabic civilization.
5. What does Sufism contribute to the family of Islam?
6. Compare the position of women in Islam, Judaism, and Christianity.
7. How well does submission describe the relation between the Muslim and Allah?
8. Contrast the sainthood of Lyusi and Kalidjaga.
9. Why is Islam so fervently opposed to God's having a son?
10. What are the assets and liabilities in the Muslim idea of a theocracy with no separation between religion and politics?

Conclusion

AMERICAN RELIGIOUS HISTORY: TWENTY-FIVE KEY DATES

1492	ABOUT 10 MILLION AMERICAN INDIANS LIVING NORTH OF RIO GRANDE
1565	ROMAN CATHOLIC COLONY AT ST. AUGUSTINE
1619	BEGINNING OF BLACK SLAVERY
1620	MAYFLOWER COMPACT
1654	FIRST JEWISH SETTLEMENT IN NEW AMSTERDAM
1683	WILLIAM PENN FOUNDS PHILADELPHIA
1734	GREAT AWAKENING IN NEW ENGLAND
1776	DECLARATION OF INDEPENDENCE EXPRESSES NONCONFORMIST, ENLIGHTENMENT-INFLUENCED RELIGIOUS OUTLOOK
1784	DEATH OF SHAKER LEADER ANNE LEE
1799	CREATION OF RUSSIAN ORTHODOX DIOCESE IN ALASKA
1801	BEGINNINGS OF WESTERN REVIVALISM
1836	FOUNDING OF TRANSCENDENTALIST CLUB IN CONCORD, MASS.

Summary Reflections

t the outset, we postulated that the religious life of humanity is a vast and diversified spectacle. Perhaps you now find that postulate only too well verified. The ancient religious mind, the wisdom religions of the East, the prophetic religions of the West all combine to make a tapestry of unmanageable proportions. We have tried to discern some of this tapestry's principal patterns. We have tried to present the information and the themes that might make such terms as *Judaism* or *Islam* intelligible. Our final task is to review the whole and suggest its implications.

UNITY AND DIVERSITY

The unity of the phenomena we have studied is religion—the common quest for a way to the center. The diversity of the phenomena makes the religions—the distinctive traditional ways in which sizable numbers of people have worked at this quest together.

The quests are all deeply humanistic. For instance, according to C. G. Jung,[1] the American Indian or African who greets the sun as a daily miracle performs deep psychic work. The Hindu who makes *puja* (worship) or whom prayer carries to Krishna constructs a world that makes sense and provides emotional comfort. The same is true of Hasidic Jews who learn diamond cutting to preserve what they can of the old *shtetl* life. In most times and places, the religions have supported or developed meaning unpretentiously, unobtrusively. For most people the traditions have worked subtly as sets of largely unquestioned assumptions.

Still, the traditions have varied in their subtleness. People who ate bean curd sensed the world differently than people who ate roasted lamb. The Prophet who recited, "There is no God but God," oriented Arabs away from the world that the Greek philosopher Thales saw ("The world is full of gods"). The recent introduction of social scientific and critical historical methods has made religious studies more empirically minded and so more sensitive to such variety. Thus, the differences among the religions have been in the spotlight. Increasingly scholars debate whether there is a common quality among all the traditions, a common religion at the traditions' cores.

We believe that there is such a common quality or unity, and at various points we have described it as a common attraction toward mystery. Relatedly, we believe that the empiricism that misses such unity and mystery is at least an unwitting reductionism—an insistence that humanity is no more than as it behaves. Usually, that insistence indicates an impoverished imagination and interiority—an inability to intuit how two different behaviors (for example, shamanic ecstasy and mystical prayer) might be directed toward the same goal: sacredness, the really real.[2]

The tricky thing about meaning, which extroverted observers tend to miss, is that ultimacy or mystery is always but a step away. Still, distraction and lack of reflection on the part of either the people under scrutiny or the scholars who are scrutinizing are defenses that mystery easily breaks down. As Wakan Tanka, the Torah, God, and Allah, ultimacy broke down the defenses against deep meaning in the peoples we have studied. Whether they wanted it or not (and usually they did), sacred mystery defined their world.

If one can see the sacred, it breaks through the Iron, Bamboo, and other curtains that divide our world today. Perhaps the only traces of the sacred we can see are the anxieties on which the aspirin industry trades. Or perhaps we are able to appreciate it in the Nobel Prize–winning efforts of outstanding scientists and writers. Either way, with or without overt theology, ultimacy is always at hand. We may choose not to embrace it, not to call mystery our inmost vocation. However, as surely as we suffer and die, it will embrace us. All people by nature desire to know, Aristotle declared. Our mortal condition makes Aristotle's dogma existential: All people by nature desire to know the mystery from which they come

Figure 17   Taj Mahal: Islam on Hindu soil. Photo by J. T. Carmody.

and to which they go. All people are by nature set for religion.

Religion

The word *religion* refers to the inmost human vocation. By empirical fact as well as theoretical interpretation, *religion* pertains to all life that is reflective, that heads into mystery. Largely for that reason, the word *religion* was seldom uttered by the great teachers.[3] They rather spoke of meaning, the way to "walk," the traditional wisdom, the balance called justice, and the fire called love. Because they were embodied spirits speaking to other embodied spirits, they used familiar figures: mountains, rivers, widows giving alms. Further, their speech led to common action: rhythmic prostrations, gutsy resistance to the emperor, danc-

ing with the Torah, helping a friend. All of these actions, though, were religious.

People organized communities around the great teachers' speech and actions. The communities expressed their religion (their venture after meaning into mystery) in ways that Joachim Wach has labeled theoretical, social, and active.[4] That is, they made theologies, brotherhoods and sisterhoods, and liturgies and laws. Regularly, the communities lost the spirit of their founders, as succeeding generations regularly prized order more than charisma, control more than inspiration, and orthodoxy more than creativity. Just as regularly, reformers tried to find their way back to the original vision. In China it was "Back to the ancients." In the West it was "Back to the Word."

The various traditions have shaped

their peoples in endless ways. Some have spoken rather simply—Judaism and Islam, for instance. Others have made strange bedfellows and cultures more complex, such as the religions of China and Japan. Still, all traditions have used the past to decipher the present and to prepare for the future. All have received and handed on.

That handing on is what we mean by *tradition*.[5] None of us fashions meaning free of external influences. All of us receive a cultural inheritance, meager or rich, to which we add. We do this willy-nilly—by having children, teaching students, working with colleagues, supporting friends. Original sin is the dark side of such a sense of tradition. According to this concept, we all take our first breath in air that is polluted, in a game that is tilted against us. How polluted or tilted the world is has been a matter of vigorous debate. The only consensus seems to be that evil is a sad fact and that there is sufficient good to justify hope. The handing on therefore leads all the religions to revile evil and to buttress hope—a process that can be called a concern for salvation.

For instance, ancient peoples banded together for evolutionary salvation—against the evil of extinction and in hope that the race would go on. Close to the earth, they thought in concrete terms, undifferentiatingly, telling stories of life and death. Life came from the fatherly sky and the motherly earth. Life was as possible, as renewable, as heavenly water and productive dirt. Death was breathtakingly near, but perhaps the dead were as seed falling in the ground. Perhaps they were but a link in the chain of generations. Or, maybe they passed to a new form of life. As smoke passes from burning wood, so perhaps the subtle part of a human, the part that thinks and travels in dreams, could pass to a new state. In those ways, perhaps, ancient peoples fought for hope, tried to block out absurdity.

To suffer, lose, rejoice, or trust—such acts know no religious, ethnic, or national bounds. We all walk a way (if only a way to death) that we cannot name. We all seek (if only covertly) a path that is straight, a path

that mystery blesses. If some of our predecessors have been Nordic berserks, who heated up to feel mystery boil, others have been Eastern yogis, who so slowed themselves that they could be buried alive. If some of our predecessors have been erotics, convinced that the force of the way is sexual power, others have been lonely ascetics, convinced that meat clouds the spirit. There are few roads that no one has taken, few options that no one has tried. Though the options make all the difference for the individual, we can see from others where we might have gone. Indeed, that is a major reason why we study the humanities. There would be no basis for studying the humanities were there no unity called human nature. Likewise, there would be no religious studies were there no unity called religion.

Contending with nature, society, the self, and whatever ultimacy they have known, all human beings have mused about their sunrise and sunset. For all of them, the cosmos and the group have had effects, the self and ultimacy have beguiled. Without and within each person, the world has taken shape, changed, occasionally threatened to slip away. Since we are "synthetic" beings, whose incarnate spirits include the lowest matter and the heights of thought, we cannot escape religion's full span. Madness comes when the span tilts and the synthesis comes unglued. Boredom comes when we lose the span's tension, when imagination goes stale. In health, we find nature, society, and the self fascinating. In health, science, politics, and art are all essential, all deeply humanistic. If they become so specialized, so arcane, that their essential humanity is not apparent, we must speak of disease—of dysfunction, pathology, alienation.

Though disease has terrible power in our time, as the arms race and the prison systems show, it has always written arguments for despair. Parents who wept over dead children heard despair at Stonehenge, Gettysburg, and My Lai. Every woman raped, every man tortured, has heard counsel to abandon hope. Amazingly, though, human beings will not live by despair alone. Their very sense that the times are out of joint is a cry that there ought to be health.

Until we give up completely, we label health as normal. Disease, we say, is the lack of health. Evil, we say, is the lack of good— of proper order, right being, justice, and love. Indeed, so deep is our drive toward health that we cannot think of nonbeing and evil directly. They are irrational, absurd, and void. In their hope, then, the religions uncover more religion. In their hope, Marxists and Christians can dialogue.

Meaning and Idiosyncrasy

The themes above are some of the constants that all the traditions carry. If they are general, it is because they pertain to all of humanity. In religious perspective, our human characteristics comprise a common condemnation (or consecration) to meaning. Thus, the differences among traditions are simply *how* their peoples have sought, conceived, and enacted meaning. That affirms, of course, that differences do differentiate.[6] It affirms that a Buddhist is not a Hindu and a Christian is not a Jew.

Because he or she is always dealing both with religion as a whole and with the individual religions, the student of religion must develop a peculiar balance. If she or he is blind to the unity behind all religions, the student will miss the deep humanity that the traditions can offer us. On the other hand, if the student sweeps all the information together, making all Buddhists anonymous Christians or all Christians renegade Jews, he or she will miss the texture that religion always has in people's lives. As is often the case, the ideal involves a duality: *both* cutting to the heart of the matter, where all humans are siblings, *and* respecting the idiosyncrasies that differentiate people as nations, tribes, sexes, individuals, and traditional religionists.

The idiosyncrasies are mysterious. Why should the Buddha have proposed that there is no-self? A first answer might be because no-self answered the question of suf-

fering that Buddha's personal life and the life of his Indian culture posed. Fine, but this is hardly an end to the matter. Why should death, disease, and putrefaction have troubled this particular prince so deeply? Presumably many other princes saw corpses without deciding to leave their palaces, wives, and children to adopt a life of asceticism; similarly, many other cultures experienced suffering. Why, then, did the Indians penetrate the psychology of suffering so profoundly? Why not the Babylonians, Chinese, Aztecs, or Mayans?

As those questions show, there is a limit to historical analysis. It can explain some of the differences among individuals or cultures, but their real origin lies beyond it. For the real origin of differences is the incomprehensible world order[7]–Paul's *mysterion*. We did not set the cosmic dust spinning. We don't know why it wove the combinations it did. Therefore, when we respect differences, we respect the totality of history and its mystery. We respect the ultimacy behind the facts, the often very brutal facts, that just this universal drama has played and no other.

Let us again try to be concrete. The Australian dream world, as scholars imperfectly reconstruct it from artifacts and interviews, reflects the peculiar landscape of the Australian continent. The aboriginal myths are similar to those of other areas that explain how the ancestors or demiurges fashioned the world, yet the aboriginal world is unique. The Australian use of the *tjurunga*, the sacred wooden boards, for instance, is distinctive. Other ancient peoples painted and carved, but none (that we know) with just the Australian concern for totemic ancestors. Or consider African peoples' use of masks. That, too, has analogies—with the American Indian use of *kachinas* and even the Greek use of theater masks. Yet in Africa masks relate to thought that speaks of man and woman, fox and anthill, smithy and granary as the people of no other continent do. Again, the Chinese divination practice of *feng-shui* (geomancy) is like the complex basket divination of the Africans, yet they differ greatly. The two types of divination have the same purpose (to determine what will happen in nature and time), but they express it differently. *Feng-shui* would not seem appropriate in the Congo.

Differences also appear among religions about which we have more historical information. For instance, Judaism memorialized the Exodus (flight from Egypt) in a Passover ritual. Something happened to get the people out of Egypt, and Jewish religious memory attributed it to God and Moses. In time the happening became a paradigm for interpreting Jewish history. Because of what happened in the past, faithful Jews endured their trials with hope. God would deliver them again somehow. That sort of historical memory, that "anamnesis," gave Jews an identity different than that of the Canaanites, Egyptians, Romans, or Germans. Indeed, without their religious memory, Jews today would have little identity crisis. It is the Exodus that makes the Holocaust so shattering. It is the Exodus and the Holocaust together that make the current state of Israel so tense.

For Christians, the Exodus was a prefiguration of the liberation that Jesus' death and resurrection worked. In their eyes, Jesus' "passover" made a new creation, Jesus' spirit formed a new Israel, Jesus' teaching established a new covenant. The lamb of the old Passover was a figure of Jesus the victim and conqueror. In the heavenly Jerusalem, Jesus the lamb receives all power, glory, and honor. In fact, the lamb has married the heavenly Jerusalem. Further, the heavenly Jerusalem has no temple, because "the Lord God Almighty and the Lamb were themselves the temple, and the city did not need the sun or the moon for light, since it was lit by the radiant glory of God and the Lamb was a lighted torch for it" (Rev. 21 : 22–23). This imagery—this radical interpretation of Exodus and Passover—developed within a century of Jesus' death. By then Christians and Jews had irrevocably separated. For nineteen centuries, they have identified themselves through mutual opposition.

For Muslims, Muhammad makes a reality different from the reality that Moses makes for Jews or Jesus for Christians. The difference is rooted in pre-Islamic Arab culture and took form in Muhammad's own psyche, where he received visions not of a burning bush or a dove descending from heaven but of the angel Gabriel. This difference flowered in Islamic conquest, which made the Prophet's people imperial in ways that Jews and Christians never were. Muslims swept across the Mediterranean world as Jews never thought to do, and they rejected priests, monks, and sacraments. Even their abuse of women was distinctive: a blend of polygyny, purdah, the harem, clitoridectomy, and *hur*.

A mosque, a synagogue, and a church all show likenesses to a Hindu or a Buddhist temple. All five enclose sacred space. But the first three have a family likeness that separates them from the latter two. Principally their space reverberates with the Word of a creator God. Still, one is not likely to confuse a mosque with a church or a synagogue. The Word takes a different form in St. Peter's than it does in a synagogue in Skokie, Illinois, or a mosque in Cairo.

Differences, then, are real. We could develop that theme for Hinduism contrasted with Jainism or Buddhism, for Catholics contrasted with Orthodox or Protestants. How great differences are, how divergent they make their adherents' realities, is difficult to determine. Often it seems as much a matter of the analyst's temperament as of the adherents' realities. In the terms of a recent debate,[8] the analyst who has an "esoteric" (inner) personality tends to stress the unity in the traditions, while the "exoteric" (outer) personality tends to stress the diversity.

Esoteric types respond to innermost notions and innermost realities. For them, a common mystery is as real as distinctive facts, even more real. Therefore, esoteric types tend to the negative way—the Hindu *"neti, neti"* ("not this, not that"). They may downplay or even disparage the diverse ways that people have chosen to pursue the supreme value. In contrast, exoteric types respond to outer phenomena—to the actual births, hungers, murders, orgasms, and deaths that make people's lives colorful, intense, palpably real. They fear that moving away from such realities ignores the way things are.

Beside exoteric blood, sweat, and tears, God does seem esoteric, pale and abstract. Looking closely, though, we find that esoterica have given religions most of their life. For instance, what would American Indian ceremonies—the Sun Dance, the vision quest, the potlatch (gift-giving feast)—have been without Wakan Tanka,

without the Great Spirit? What would the Egyptian pyramids have been without Osiris and Re? Those pale gods gave the ceremonies and massive stones their meaning. Apart from such meaning, exoterica are mute. The same applies in other traditions. In the West, circumcision, the Eucharist, and the Muslim *hajj* (pilgrimage to Mecca) depend on the convenant, the redemption, and the external Word. In the lives of religious people, the exoteric is a body for the esoteric. It should be the same in the writings of religion scholars.

METHODOLOGICAL ISSUES

In this book we have tried to present the exoteric and esoteric sides of the Western religions by stressing history and structural analysis. Our historical sections have tended to report on the events, personalities, and ideas that shaped the "outside" of the tradition in question, its "body," while our structural analyses have tended to reflect on the "inside" of the tradition in question, probing for its "soul." If we have succeeded at all, you now have a beginning sense of both how "Islam" evolved and what "Islam" connotes as a world view, a perspective on reality.

There are other ways of presenting the Western religions, of course, and it would be well for you to be aware of them. Although we have not followed these other ways, except as brief detours from our main approaches, other scholars have shed considerable light on Western religions by employing them. W. Richard Comstock once offered beginning students a list of five basic methodological perspectives,[9] and our describing these five should fill out your map.

First, there is the *psychological* perspective. Since the time of Freud (1856–1939), who was quite interested in religion's parallels with neurosis, Western scholars have been sensitive to the inner drives that set people to work, parenting, religion, and the many other aspects of human culture. For example, sexual satisfaction, acceptance by our peers, and a sense of control all play a part in our development of human culture. C. G. Jung (1875–1961) broke with Freud over the interpretation of sexual and religious drives. For Jung

the second half of life tends to be a pursuit of meaning (giving one's time and experience coherence). Often the symbols that people use in pursuing meaning are religious, so even today the psychoanalyst probing his patients' dreams can come upon archetypal symbols reminiscent of ancient religious mythologies.

If we generalize the sensitivity that recent psychological studies sharpen, the main point seems to be that we must stay alert to the complexity of human motivation. For example, in studying a holy man such as Mahatma Gandhi, we should realize that his asceticism had a basis in his adolescent sexual traumas, and that his political ambitions were forged by his experiences of racial discrimination in young adulthood. At these formative times in his life cycle, Gandhi was tested to an unusual degree. He found himself unready for the erotic aspects of marriage, and his experience as a "colored" person in South Africa told him he had to champion India's oppressed.

If we so focus on psychological issues such as these that we neglect the history, sociology, economics, politics, and other aspects of Gandhi's life and times, we become reductionists, trying to squeeze all of reality onto the psychoanlyst's couch. On the other hand, if we neglect such inner demons and angels, we divorce ourselves from a powerful tool of understanding (probably because we don't want to face the similar demons and angels warring in our own souls). As usual, a balanced use is the ideal.

Just as scientific psychology is a fairly recent development, not available to scholars of religion a century ago, so is scientific *sociology*. And just as the pioneer psychologists were quite interested in religion, so were pioneer sociologists such as Max Weber (1864–1920) and Emile Durkheim (1858–1917). In both cases, their interest was religion's role in making a group cohesive. The religious ideas of a tribe, or even a large culture, are always in part a projection of the tribe's or the culture's sense of its own identity. For example, Jews have been people especially "chosen" by God. Christians have been people making one "body" with Christ. Americans have been high-minded refugees come to make a place of justice and freedom in a new world. Thus neither Jewish sexism, nor Christian anti-Semitism, nor American racism could be the patent inhumanity an outside observer might think it. Sacralizing the way they talked about themselves, all three peoples wrote their customs heavenly approbations.

Recently cultural anthropologists such as Clifford Geertz and Victor Turner have tuned the interests of the classical sociologists more finely. Living in the midst of the societies they would interpret, they have sought the deep structures and threshold moments through which a people reveals how it constructs its world view. Geertz's study of the Balinese cockfight,[10] for example, is a marvel of sophisticated participant-observation. Sensitive to the drama of what he calls "deep play," Geertz makes the cockfight a microcosm of the Balinese thought-world.

A third methodological orientation popular in recent religious studies is the *historical*. One of the drawbacks of the psychological and sociological approaches is that they can seem to bracket time past (and time future), as though their analyses were moved by an Archimedean lever standing outside the flowing stories of either their subjects or themselves. But such ahistoricism obviously is fallacious. The self always enacts a story, a unique version of the common life cycle, and a society is always being pushed by its past and lured by its future. Since the modern discovery of evolution and the rise of modern retrieval techniques such as archeology, the study of religion has become more historical, and so more faithful to the traditions' ongoing changes. Even the most conservative tradition alters in at least small ways, generation by generation. Though they perform the same rituals and tell the same myths, a people of any era understand themselves somewhat differently than their forebears did or their children will.

The good historian's goal is telling the story of these changes. Representing the past as most likely it was, the good historian brings her reader from point alpha to point omega. In the beginning, at the earliest point we can reconstruct, Buddhists understood Gautama in such and such a way. A thousand years later, when controversies inside the community had caused much debate, there were the three following major interpretations. Today, in Japanese Buddhism, the third of these interpretations prevails, due to such and such factors.

One thinks, then, of a continuum or a map. In the image of the continuum, the historian grants all centuries a certain equality, showing how Buddhism changed century by century. In the image of a map, the historian plots the journey from the Buddha's India to modern Japan, showing the geographic and cultural routes the teaching traveled. The result should be a sense of perspective and interrelationship. Alpha led on to beta, because of factor alpha prime, just as today omega seems to be leading on to omega-plus-one, because of factor omega prime.

Comstock's fourth methodological perspective is *phenomenological*. Referring to the work of scholars such as Geradus van der Leeuw (1890–1950), who have concentrated on the different *forms* that many religious traditions seem to share, we can emphasize the concern many phenomenologists have to find *typical* patterns that show up repeatedly across the full range of religious data. So, for example, sacred persons appear in most traditions. East and West, monks or ascetics or yogins have generated great veneration. One can distinguish among these three categories of holy persons, but they share an orientation away from worldly affairs, toward contemplation and self-discipline. The typical Hindu holy man fits this pattern of withdrawal, as does the typical Buddhist monk. In China and Japan, both Buddhism and Taoism prized withdrawal from worldly affairs, seclusion in order to grow better attuned to the teaching or the Way.

Phenomenological studies therefore tend to stress the sameness of certain structural features, providing a basis for discussing how Hindu yogins differ from Buddhist monks, or how Eastern ascetics differ from Western ascetics. By grouping them together in general terms, we are stimulated to ask how they differ in particulars. The results of such inquiries can seldom be ironclad, since there are usually exceptions to general trends, but the inquiries are very stimulating. (They are also very useful for orienting beginning students, so long as they remain flexible and open to exceptions. Our own categories of nature, society, self, and divinity owe more to a philosophical analysis of the constants in human experience than to a phenomenological description of how the religious traditions present themselves, but in part we have used these structural categories because they facilitate comparisons.)

Comstock's fifth methodological perspective is *hermeneutical.* If anything, this perspective has increased in importance since the time he made his survey. Hermeneutics is the study of interpretation. It concerns processes such as that by which a teacher from Massachusetts tries to explain to a student from Kansas what it was like to live in medieval Europe or Arabia. In one sense, hermeneutics applies to all parts of this communication. Even the gap between Massachusetts and Kansas can be significant. But the gap between twentieth-century America and medieval Europe or Arabia is enormous. Thus, hermeneutics tends to be more concerned with how we can tease reliable interpretations of past or foreign cultures. The cultural anthropologists we mentioned have come to the forefront of the hermeneutical debates, but historians, psychologists, sociologists, and philosophers of language have also been prominent. These debates tend to get very technical, generating schools such as structuralism and subdisciplines such as semiotics, as well as a lot of bad writing. The scholarly end of the hermeneutical "turn" is not yet in sight; its overall significance is still emerging.

For undergraduates, though, the gist of the hermeneutical perspective is clear enough: Try to be quite sensitive to the sources and ranges of the meanings you are studying. Above all, realize that in studying a text, or any other cultural artifact, you are involved in a two-way conversation. A text is not a brute object whose meanings are obvious to any beholder. Physically, a text is simply some marks on a piece of paper or some impressions in clay. To convey meaning, these marks have to "speak" from the mind of the person who set them down to the mind of people like you who are trying to pick them up. Thus, the languages and assumptions of both minds come into play, your own as much as the author's. You can assume that you and the author share a great deal, since you are both human, but you must be careful about how you deploy this assumption. The death of a child in seventh-century Mecca was both very like the death of a child in contemporary America, and very different. Thus, you are back to balancing the esoteric and the exoteric. Boiled down, hermeneutics is but walking the tightrope between sameness and difference.

THE USES OF RELIGION

Our discussion so far suggests that religion has served several uses. Historically, most people have groped after meaning through a religious tradition. Even when they came to conclusions that differed from those of fellow traditionists (fellow Jews or fellow Christians, for instance), a tradition set before them their major questions. For example, Maimonides and Halevi evaluated reason differently, but their common Jewish tradition set them the question, How does reason relate to faith? Similarly, Aquinas and Bonaventure evaluated love differently, but their common Christian tradition set them Paul's dictum that love is the greatest of God's gifts. In those cases, unity probably predominated over difference, though when partisanship flamed, the difference generated great heat.

Jews, Christians, Hindus, and Buddhists also tried to be faithful to the unity that they glimpsed in diverse peoples. They all met peoples who did not accept their tradition—did not accept the Torah, Jesus, the Vedas, or Buddha. Such peoples sought a living, wept when they were in pain, and hoped for a happy future. They might have had funny customs, but they, too, worried about doing what was right. Sometimes they even came through with a surprising act of kindness. Even when they did not—when they were abrupt traders or harsh rulers—they expressed qualities one already knew from home: Fellow Hindus profiteered, fellow Christians kicked the dog.

Thus, the fact that people were members of particular religions and members of the human race made people aware that their cultures were both many and one. The notion of a universal humanity[11] may only have come to consciousness clearly in the ecumenical age, but people knew it instinctively long before that time. When sexual relations with a foreign slave begot a half-breed, people instinctively knew the falsity of racist biology. When a foreigner performed an act of kindness, prejudice had to loosen.

Because religion has been at the historical center of people's meaning systems, religion has played a key role in this dialectic of unity and difference, and this dialectic has played a key role in religion. When Francis Xavier met the Japanese, he thought that they were the most moral people in the world. As a result, his notions of sin, grace, paganism, and hell were challenged. Centuries later, his fellow Jesuit Karl Rahner, building on experiences such as Xavier's, developed a theory he called the "supernatural existential."[12] Simply, it meant that no people live apart from grace.

A first value of religion, then, is that it prompts people to broaden their horizons. When it deals with a genuinely mysterious ultimate, religion makes all fellow humans brothers and sisters. (When it does not deal with a genuinely mysterious ultimate, we may infer, religion makes fellow humans slaves, victims, and enemies.)

A second value of religion is education. From its station at the core of people's quests for meaning, religion can teach students of human behavior that reality can be both/and. For instance, religious wars have shown that faith can be *both* demonic *and* sanctifying. In Jewish, Christian, and Muslim faith, it has made for demonic faith a special symbol: holy war. Thus, Psalm 137 told Israelite soldiers to smash the heads of enemy babies against the wall. Thus, the Qur'an (8 : 68) instructed Muslim soldiers to slaughter and reap booty. Thus, American "Christian" soldiers found it fitting to destroy Vietnamese towns in order to save them. Muhammad, David, Saint Louis—they are all ambiguous warrior saints.

To be sure, religious battle is not monochromatic. In its time, the theory of a just war made much sense. There is an ambiguity about war, as there is an ambiguity about pacifism. Sensing the latter, Gandhi gave the opinion that it was better to fight than to choose pacifism out of cowardice. Films of British and Indian soldiers felling Gandhi's followers with clubs and rifle butts show that his opinion came from experience.

A similar both/and attends marriage, celibacy, the treatment of women, and the treatment of slaves. For instance, though slavery is almost wholly a stigma, some Muslim and Christian owners treated their slaves compassionately. The same is true of polygamous husbands—traditional African, Muslim, and Mormon alike. For example, as Islam improved the lot of slaves at its outset, so it improved the general lot of wives.

Thus, a knowledge of religion stimulates a respect for human variety—for the wide spectrum between good and evil. As the religious philosophers who reflect on ultimate mystery find human beings quite alike, so the religious historians find that religious peoples are nearly equal in their diversity and complexity.

The utility of a religious venerable such as Black Elk is a case in point. Clearly, his vision that the Sioux nation's hoop would be restored did not come to reality in his lifetime, but that did not make his vision without value. The core of religion is mystery-held meaning. Black Elk's vision illumined the Sioux condition and nursed the Sioux with meaning. Just by occurring, then, it was beneficial. To be sure, it would have been better had mundane improvements in the Sioux condition been made. To be sure, the tribe ought to have regained its freedom to revere its holy land. Core meaning, in Black Elk's vision or any other religious benefaction, does not take care of all worldly needs. Nonetheless, shamanism is finally useful because of meanings we cannot touch or see. It is finally useful because of its spiritual intuition, its "faith."

Were shamanistic dance only a choreography, not a matter of faith, we could reproduce it off Broadway. Because it makes sacred the four compass directions, giving them mystery-held meaning, shamanistic dance is more than entertainment. The four directions are symbols of the one force of creation; they are points at which the Great Spirit can enter the world. Because the human spirit has, in Aquinas' term, a quasi-infinity, it can reach up to the Great Spirit. Because it has, in Augustine's term, a restless heart, fair maidens, fair lads, precious metals, and abundant crops all fail to satisfy it. The human spirit must intend the All.

Still, our reflection turns again. The All must touch fair maidens and rich crops. It must shine and blow in a world of particulars, a world firm under moccasined feet. Thus, north, south, east, and west are the gates of heaven. By another of the endless paradoxes that make religion useful, heaven enters our gates to become heaven-for-us. The Great Spirit descends through the east, where the sun rises. It comes from the west, where the sun beds down. We can feel it when we face north, where the quickening breeze stirs. It is lovely to the south, where summer sun retreats.

When Gandhi went looking to buttress *satyagraha*, his politics of truth-force, he settled on the fourth of the *Bhagavad Gita's* yogas. Most useful to him was karma-yoga discipline—grasping ultimacy through selfless labor. He found it a high art, a trick hard to master. Can we engage in politics today as though spinning thread carelessly? Can an

effective action not be concerned with the fruits of success? To Western ears, those are strange questions. On the other hand, is there any effective action that is attached, that is concerned with success? Don't we see again and again in the West that success mottles our work, that ego corrodes our politicians?

Thus, Gandhi's work dialectic sharpened his religion, honing it to a paradox. To become an instrument of truth, he saw, he had to lose self, ambition, concern. Bone weary with service, he had to count all his service as nothing. Yet, marvel of marvels, self-loss was energizing. It sent him on long marches to the sea, on long terms in prison. In his depths it evoked love for his enemies, help for those who persecuted him. Indeed, in his depths it did away with enemies and made his persecutors brethren.

If Gandhi had not freed a modern nation, we would count his *satyagraha* as so much hot air, but India used *satyagraha* to gain home rule (and then abused it to produce the Hindu-Muslim partition). Thus, we have to consider *satyagraha* quite real. In fact, we have to be humble enough to see in *satyagraha* one of Western religion's own truths about action: Work as though everything depended on God, and pray as though everything depended on yourself.

In the past few pages, we have taxed your patience, getting more than a little oracular in order to conjure how living religions actually speak. Such language perhaps shows a final utility that shamans, sages, and prophets have offered humankind—their capacity to shock sleepy humanity awake. The paramount religious figures have forced humanity to be more than animal by insisting that life is more than food and the body more than clothing. They above all have underscored the strange play of life and death that prompts deep reflection.

What is genuine living? What riches are valuable? Such questions can be cultural dynamite. For instance, if it is easier for a camel to pass through the eye of a needle than for a rich person to enter the kingdom

COMPARING THE WESTERN TRADITIONS

This deep reflection offers a first handle for comparing the Western traditions. American Indians, Egyptians, Iranians, Greeks, Jews, Christians, and Muslims have all had priests, shamans, or sages who deeply pondered the meaning of their people's lives.

For the nonliterate traditions of the West, the main meaning of the people's life was to live harmoniously with nature. Nature was virtually coextensive with reality, and what was sacred, worthy of supreme veneration, was more nature's depth than something standing apart from the cosmos, the world of space and time. To be sure, the Great Spirit was something that fleshly thoughts could never fathom. But the tribal peoples' many efforts to reach the Great Spirit almost always came to fruition as a vision or sense of communion that brought harmony with the natural world.

The Egyptian concern with life and death somewhat extended this tribal sense of reality. Although they enjoyed the pleasures of their life in the sun and their good fortune to live by the Nile, the Egyptians pondered the afterlife so intensely that they left the pyramids as massive memos. As the pyramid texts suggest, the Egyptians sensed that the afterlife would only be fortunate if one could pass the test of a strict judgment on one's days of earthly life. Unless the soul were light and clean, it would gain no good immortality. The brief Egyptian flirtation with "monotheism" proved less powerful than an instinct that all the forces of nature, all the vectors of life and death, have to be represented, written large as divinities, if we are to understand the tensions of earthly life to the depth that our imaginative spirit wishes.

Iranians who flocked to Zoroaster heard a different message about our imaginative spirit's wishes. To their great seer, the primal forces were Truth and the Lie, the human spirit as open to the light or the human spirit as closed. Thus Zoroaster seems to have meditated with his "topmost" mind, while his naturalistic predecessors in Egypt and among the Western tribes burrowed toward the roots of the unconscious. Zoroaster's concern with light, ideas, and images of heavenly forces all suggest a person aware of the human spirit's "transcendent" inclinations, its drive to rise higher and higher, go farther and farther beyond what it has conceived in the past.

The Greeks are remarkable for the fullness of their religious life, which spanned from the deepest roots of the unconscious to the most transcendent inclinations of the topmost mind. The riches of Greek mythology are a remarkable treasury, full of experiences of nature, family relations, and the struggles of the unconscious mind. The great tragedians used this treasury most artfully, leaving the West unsurpassed renditions of humanity's most basic conflicts. The philosophers seem to have taken the dazzling physical light of the Greek islands as a challenge to find dazzling mental counterparts. Building on the work of the early philosophers of nature, Socrates, Plato, and Aristotle finally accomplished the monumental feat of differentiating human reason. Following the light of the mind, the logos that made human beings a unique species, they saw that this light is the inreach of divinity, whose Light is coincident with any creature's reason-to-be. Although Hellenistic religion largely lost the classical philosophers' great achievement, enought of their differentiation remained to turn Western culture in a distinctively rational direction.

Along with Greek reason, biblical revelation also pushed Western culture to find its reason-to-be in God. However, where the Greek accent was the Divine Light, the biblical accent was the Divine Love. Thus Judaism formed a people around the free overtures of a God who wanted to make a people uniquely covenanted to himself. As biblical Jews understood this relationship, it was not the product of any special merit on their part. It was completely the product of God's own love. From his own goodness God decided to reveal himself over time, walking with the Jews as a fellow-traveler. The Exodus was the warrant for Jewish faith that God could make the walk a liberation, while the covenant was the codification of the traveling relationship. Through the permutations of biblical history, biblical prophecy, biblical wisdom literature, rabbinic reflection, cabalistic lore, and Hasidic piety, Judaism retained this sense of being bonded to

God. The Master of the Universe had shown the people a personal face. He had pledged them his mercy and steadfast love. This revelation and pledge held the deepest mystery of time.

Christianity accepted Judaism's stress on God's love, but by the fourth century it had added more of Greece's stress on God's Light. Jesus himself preached and taught as a Jew, quite aware of the biblical traditions. For him the deepest mystery of time was on the verge of a definitive self-expression. The Kingdom of God, in which God's love and mercy would become dominant in many people's hearts, was as near as his intimate heavenly Father. When Christians reflected on Jesus' life and death, they moved the Kingdom into his person. This singular man, they said, himself embodied what God's love and mercy could do. Indeed, his resurrection was the pledge and first fruits of the Kingdom's cosmic import. Whoever clung to Jesus as Jesus had clung to the Father could hope to rise with Jesus to the Father's right hand. There Father, Son, and Spirit, the fullness of the Christian God, would give one a full understanding of time's mysteries, a full experience of love's beatitude.

The Jewish and Christian experiences of God's revelation somewhat shaped Islam, but the visions of Muhammad really determined Islam's world view. For Muhammad, God was Light and Love, but more powerfully God was the sole Creator, the omnipotent Lord of the Worlds. Thus Islam has accented human beings' need to submit completely to God. When God speaks, every creature ought to bow low, as in the daily prayer. When any creature considers the world, she ought to revere the many signs the world gives of God's great wisdom and power. Allah is a stern judge, demanding a full recognition of these truths. People who will not listen to Muhammad's recital are surely marked for the Fire. So for Islam the great disaster is unbelief. Sin and error play their woeful parts, but the core ruin to which human beings are prey is unbelief, which usually shows itself as idolatry. In all aspects of life, from Friday worship in the mosque to daily business in the street, the One God has set the standards. The devout Muslim prays each day to stay on the sole path that is straight, the path of Allah's guidance.

There are other strands in the history of Western religion, of course, but these traditions certainly account for most of the Western configurations. In modernity they ran up against a powerful atheistic revolt, so we "postmodern" Westerners tend to experience these religious traditions as somewhat strange. For example, the changes in Western consciousness that the Enlightenment and Marxist philosophies have worked suggest to many of our contemporaries that traditional religion is at best a curio, at worse an impediment to human growth. For the Enlightenment philosophers, the crux was our human capacity to make "reality." They saw that much that we think is "out there" comes from "in here," our own minds. For the Marxist philosophers, such speculative matters have been less important than the practical business of overthrowing current injustices. Understanding an imperfect reality, they have said, is only half the job. The full job includes building a new, better reality.

The traditional Western religions could agree with one part of the Enlightenment/Marxist program, but they would have to disagree with another part. Accepting the Greek understanding of humanity's vocation to follow the light of reason, the Western religious traditions could listen to the modern antireligionists quite sympathetically, marveling at how the moderns' rejection of traditional faith has helped them to make many splendid discoveries in physical science, epistemology, psychology, biological science, and sociology. These are all further disclosures of the inreaching Divine Light, so what is true and noble in them deserves religious veneration.

Accepting the biblical understanding of humanity's vocation to follow the love of covenantal sharing, the Western traditions could also listen quite sympathetically to the modern pragmatists. There is a biblical imperative to do justice and make a world fit for human beings to live in. There is a Qur'anic call to fellowship that transcends all boundaries of nations and races. Therefore, much in the modern Enlightenment/Marxist program preaches in terms almost identical with the Western religious traditions' own sacred scriptures.

On the other hand, the Western religious traditions could not agree with the modern anti-religionists' hatred of God, nor with their murky view of human nature. For the religious traditions, only God gives human beings prosperity. Islam has driven this home like a stake in the heart: Idolatry is utter ruin. Unless the Creative Love and Power that makes the world afresh every day dominates human consciousness, human consciousness errs grievously and strews cruel wreckage left and right. Thus a clear view of human nature balances on a thin edge. It is neither optimistic nor pessimistic. It is hopeful, because open to God. Human beings have a limited capacity to follow the Light and understand. They have a limited capacity to give and receive love and so build peaceful communities. When they open themselves to God's help, human beings can do justice, make beauty, prosper in truth. When they close themselves to God, they truncate and warp their limited powers, and so produce trash, injustice, and great suffering. As the religious forms of arrogant closure to God have given the West many dreadful "holy" wars, so the irreligious forms of arrogant closure to God have given the West Gulag Archipelagos, Nazi concentration camps, Latin American butchery, and North American greed. To be human, our species needs the Light that Plato saw, the Love that Jeremiah hoped would make a new covenant. Without these, we treat one another worse than wolves. Without these, it does not matter whether we call ourselves religious or irreligious, for our true names are simply "Ruined."

When confronted by godless modernity, the Western traditions tend to pull together. For Judaism, Christianity, and Islam, the Creator is the creature's inmost definer. For the other Western traditions we have studied, the case is a little more complicated, but the upshot is much the same: Human beings are not the measure of reality. As we shall further discuss the samenesses and differences of the Western traditions, let us conclude here by summarizing the current, postmodern situation. In the eighteenth and nineteenth centuries, the Western religious traditions were thrown on the defensive, forced to grow beyond their insular, and in many ways self-serving, understandings of revelation. In the second half of the twentieth century, the irreligious humanisms have been thrown on the defensive, shown by their totalitarian tyrannies and nuclear horrors to be precipitous paths to hell. The question for the twenty-first century will be whether these two strains of current Western humanity can grow enought to cooperate with one another and make the full circle of checks and balances survival will demand.

THE PROPHET AS WESTERN ARCHETYPE

For the Asian traditions, it is relatively clear that the dominant personality, the religious ideal, has been the sage. Buddha, Confucius, Lao Tzu, and the various Hindu holy men have all been philosophic contemplatives, concerned with ordering or saving human life by penetrating the structures of the cosmos. For the Western religious traditions, the case is not so clear. The prophet seems the strongest personality, but often the sage and the mystic run a close second and third.

Among the nonliterate Western tribes, the dominant personality has been the shaman. Specializing in ecstatic techniques, the shaman has gone out of himself (less frequently, herself), to make contact with the sacred forces running the world. Thus the Eskimo shaman might go into trance in order to travel to Sedna, the goddess of the undersea who had fenced in the seals.

For Egypt, the priest, officiating at religious ceremonies, and the king, mediating *maat*, were highly visible personalities. Egypt also produced an interesting wisdom literature, most of it rather stoical. The message of Egyptian wisdom usually was that human experience teaches the value of prudence. The person who wants to prosper should keep her mouth shut and her eyes open.

For Iran, the Zoroastrian prophecies placed a high premium on the inner spirit of light. As the fire burned in the Zoroastrian rituals, so the truth should blaze in the human heart. The magi who later spoke for Zoroastrian wisdom earned a handsome reputation in the Middle East, much of it for their astrological learning. True to the continued immersion of the tradition in the cosmological myth, they set human affairs under the influence of the stars.

In Greece the philosopher, the lover of wisdom, ruled the psychological stage. Shamanist types and priests played strong roles in the days of Olympian religion, but after historians, natural scientists, political thinkers, and dramatists had come to the fore, the philosopher's search for the unseen measure prepared to take the place of honor. When Socrates, Plato, and Aristotle assumed this place, philosophy was a way of life, not an academic discipline. Speaking of their illuminations in religious terms, they would have dismissed any strong distinction between philosophy and revelation. In their experience, when the soul took wing and rose toward the idea of the good, God was the prime mover and drawer.

In both Judaism and Islam, prophets dominated the first stages of the tradition. Moses struck the covenant because he had received the Word of the Lord, while Muhammad was simply the *rasul*, the messenger commanded to recite God's Qur'an. In later periods both religions developed a less prophetic, more jurisprudential understanding of God's guiding Word (Torah or Sharia). Then the rabbis and lawyers dealt with an ethics both more complex and less explosive than the original prophetic Word. As well, both the Jewish rabbis and the Muslim lawyers assumed something of the philosopher's mantle, and both of their cultures opened to Greek rationalism, though seldom to the point where prophetic revelation was endangered. For when rabbinical theology or Muslim Sharia seemed in danger of running dry, the Hasidim, Cabalists, and Sufis rose up to water it with devotion. Thus Sufi teaching lore enlivened the Muslim lawyers' codes, while Haggadah enlivened the Talmudists' halakah.

Overall, the biblical prophets and Muhammad *the* Prophet kept the notion of the Divine Word central. If both Judaism and Islam strike the comparativist as more ethical than metaphysical, it is because both thought of the Divine Word as more an imperative than an indicative. Revelation of God commanded that the people be holy, since they were to consort with the Holy One. In both traditions' understanding

of this holiness, what one thought was less important than what one did. Such "doing" included worship as well as morality, but it had a distinct priority over speculative or purely contemplative theology. Speculation and contemplative theology had their places, but their potential for division was large. For the community to hold together, the people had first of all to keep the same Sabbath and kosher laws, to depend upon the same five pillars.

In the case of Christianity, Jesus, also, seems more a prophet than a sage, despite the fact that the New Testament occasionally casts Jesus in the lines of Old Testament wisdom. Jesus teaches the crowds, but what he teaches is mainly a view of God leading to a new mode of living. The centrality of love in Jesus' preaching somewhat distinguishes his prophecy from that of the Hebrew prophets, and even more from that of Muhammad, but we should not exaggerate this distinction. The love of God and love of neighbor that epitomize Jesus' program have at least analogues in both Judaism and Islam.

Where Christianity departs from the prophetic typology of Judaism and Islam is in divinizing its main prophet. Neither Moses nor Muhammad became sons of God, sharers in the divine creative nature. Moreover, an infusion of Greek philosophy made Christianity quite ontological about Jesus and the Trinity. True, the conciliar controversies of the fourth and fifth centuries were passionate, rather than detached, bouts of speculation, but they determined that the Logos related intimately with the world's reason-to-be. The Christian God expressed his being in both an ongoing act of creation and the Incarnation of the Logos. Picking up hints from Col. 1 : 15–20, the Christian theologians came to think that creation occurred in the Divine Word, whom God had planned to incarnate from eternity.

The Incarnation made Christianity a prophetic religion instinctively sacramental. Where Judaism and Islam prohibited the representation of God, Christianity was fundamentally iconographic. Since God had made an icon of himself, uttering his Word into human flesh, all material things were open to the inspiration of God's Spirit. When the Spirit moved over the waters, the waters became baptismal. When the Spirit moved over the bread and wine, the bread and wine became the body and blood of the Lord. Above all, human affairs became the primary arena of God's action. Accepting the Jewish notion of covenant, Christianity said that Jesus and his people were bonded like a groom and bride. The story of the Church therefore was like the saga of an extended family, relating the increases and diminishments the original marriage had produced. To be sure, the marital compact would only come to full fruition in heaven, where the glory of the lamb (Rev. 5 : 12) would blaze forth, but even the days of earthly time could bring touches of conjugal union.

Although they rejected Christian incarnationalism and sacramentality, Judaism and Islam developed their own equivalents. Both became this-worldly religions, Judaism in large part by adding marriage and good deeds to Torah to make a trinity of holy blessings. As a result, Jews have influenced Western culture, literary and scientific alike, out of proportion to their small numbers. Since Adonai had made history his chosen field of interest, temporal things ranked high on the Jewish agenda. Islam largely agreed, sponsoring a splendid, fullbodied culture during its golden age. The Islamic stress on Judgment and afterlife probably made it more eschatological than Judaism, more preoccupied with heaven and hell, but the Muslim theocratic ideal assured that politics, business, and war would all seem inseparable from religious practice.

Further, neither Judaism nor Islam approved of celibacy, so neither had a corps of monks testifying to the rights of eternity. While the rabbis and Sufis hardly were robust in their encouragement of sexuality, they felt that God's command to increase and multiply, as well as ordinary human psychology, made marriage the healthiest estate. So, unlike their counterparts in much of Christianity, the prophetic and legal masters of Judaism and Islam felt a constant pressure to provide for wives and children. While this did not promote women to equal status with men, it did assure that family life received a thorough consideration. Thus the rabbis saw that the Genesis account of creation made humanity male-female, and that it suggested the Fall was in part a sexual awakening. Thus the Cabalists spoke of redemption in sexual terms, hoping that

one day the fragmented world would return to God's full embrace.

In hindsight, neither Judaism, Christianity, nor Islam gave physical nature the appreciation it deserved. Although the trail from the beginnings of these religions to today's ecological crises is tangled, there is little doubt that the biblical and Qur'anic subordination of nature to human beings helped the prophetic religious cultures to ravish the earth. Neither the Bible nor the Qur'an said to ravish the earth, but both so feared fertility religion and idolatry that they downplayed nature's divinity. They knew the Creator had to be present to rocks and trees, if rocks and trees were to exist at all, but the prophetic religions shied away from the implications of creation, not wanting to say that whatever exists is inviolable.

So only at their most confident times did the prophetic religions make sacraments and humanisms that welcomed nature kindly. No doubt rural peoples of these traditions always sensed God's coming through the seasons, but the main Word of the prophets stressed God's transcendence of the world, implying that God cared little for the seasons. (Therefore, high on the agenda of East-West religious dialogue should be discussing the East's greater appreciation of nature, and its greater appreciation of the impersonal side of God with which nature is allied.) The Western prophetic religions all experienced God as fiercely personal, a Word and Will impressing themselves mightily. Although the mystics in these traditions (especially the Christian mystics) went beyond words and feelings to the naked divine immensity, the mainstreams in these traditions (especially the Christian mainstream) pictured God as a human person.

Today the most important legacy of the prophetic religions probably is their cry for justice. The Word of God the West has trumpeted is a shout for honesty and love. Through the Israelite prophets, Jesus, and Muhammad, God demanded that human beings treat one another well. Even though Judaism, Christianity, and Islam often have narrowed this demand, becoming ethnocentric and insular like other tribes, the demand itself is virtually their constitution. "If you would worship the true God," they all have heard, "you must do justice to your neighbors."

So all the prophetic religions stand against the exploitation or oppression—capitalist, Marxist, or other—that denies the sanctity of human beings. So the racism, sexism, and religious bigotry in the prophetic religions themselves denounce them before their God. In evolutionary terms, this may be the prophetic religions' great significance. Imperfect though all their peoples have been, the prophetic religions have still nursed an ideal of just, genuine living.

---

of God, what happens to Judaism's blessing for wealth, the Mormon Tabernacle, and St. Peter's in Rome? Seers, founders, and saints all qualify our instinctive values. Instinctively we all tell the mirror, "Prosper, fill your barn, appease your loins." The saints answer, "You fool! This night God may require your soul." Because of saints, we have been prompted to think that money, sex, and fame are not all.

But is this shock really useful? Does it do anything more than upset the slothful majority and tempt the upsetters to pride? Our answers to that question say a great deal about our own values. If there is nothing but cradle to grave, religious persons are of all the most to be pitied. The merit in teasing the mind over paradoxes, in disciplining the heart to search out reasons, stands or falls by whether the examined life is more than sound and fury. At bottom, there are just the two ways that Deuteronomy foresaw. One is death to humanity—to reflection, making a self, freedom, and love. It is the way that denies the examined life, that denies faith. The other way—reflection, freedom, love—makes real life.

The choice between the two ways, between death and life, is inalienable: No one can make it for you. Even not to choose is a choice—a choice to drift. There is a time to drift, as there is a time to come ashore. To drift too long, though, is to choose against the deeper spirit, against the deeper life. Religion has the (painful) utility of forcing us to hear that we are not what we eat. We are what we choose to be. In Augustine's terms, we can choose love of self unto contempt of divine mystery, or love of divine mystery unto contempt of self.

The contempt in the second half of

Augustine's dichotomy is not self-hatred. It is not tearing the psyche to keep the ego important. Rather, it is letting go, opening up, saying yes to a world one did not make and does not finally control. At the end of the life cycle, Erik Erikson says, the "virtue" (power) we most need is wisdom. Wisdom, then, is the ability to love life in the face of death, to say yes in the face of nature's no. Before old age, wisdom often is the ability to say yes in the face of the senses' no. Accordingly, we are hardly wise if the senses have been our only tutors.

The religions say that the senses are splendid—when they serve the spirit, the mind, and the heart. Then, a tree is just a tree in a quite different way. In enlightenment, all trees are sacramentals. In the illuminative way, basic human acts (eating, intercourse, washing, anointing) are sacraments. They make life good enough to merit a profound love in the face of death. They make the golden mean, the Aryan middle way. The final utility of religion is that it can teach us how to die and how to live. For Plato, the love of wisdom was the art of dying. Plato was everything we require a religious sage to be.

ON BEING AN AMERICAN CITIZEN OF THE RELIGIOUS WORLD

We have not paid special attention to America in this book, because in the full history of religion, America has only occupied a small fraction. In general handbooks such as the *Historical Atlas of the Religions of the World, Historia Religionum,* and *The Concise Encyclopedia of Living Faiths,* American religion does not receive 2 percent of the space. The first lesson that the world religions offer Americans, then, is that America is not as important as Americans tend to think. Our 400 years of religious experience are not much beside India's 5,000. If our 6 percent of the world's population and almost 40 percent of the consumption of the world's raw materials are disproportionate, we need all the help we can get to help us become less important.

We are not advocating the suppression of patriotism. Few existing cultures are very old. Europeans or Asians who sniff because their cultures go back more centuries than ours are hardly less ridiculous than we. All nations need a perspective on world history. All nations need to see things "under the aspect of eternity."

For most Americans, religion has been Christianity, and Christianity has often pivoted on Jesus and the founder of one's own sect. In some cases the dark ages between those two personages stretch 1,800 years. For such sects, Catholics are not considered Christians, and Orthodox are beyond the pale. True, Americans modified this intolerance by coexisting with their neighbors. Almost all Americans, though, need a deep breath of cosmopolitan air.

The root of provincialism is what Erik Erikson calls "pseudospeciation"—pretending that we are the only true human beings. In the past, that "we" has been Chinese, Japanese, and Eskimos. It has been Boston Brahmins and Oklahoma dirt farmers. It has been Catholics who would never darken a Protestant church door, Orthodox who would never visit a synagogue. Fortunately, we now know enough about the psychodynamics of pseudospeciation, largely through analyses of prejudice, to show that it has little to do with religion as such. In fact, we now know that genuine religion directly opposes pseudospeciation.

In most cases, pseudospeciation stems from a combination of fear and self-interest. We fear the universal humanity, the radical equality, that a pluralistic world implies. It would force us to shed our shells; it would snatch away our platform for boast-ing. Similarly, we fail to grasp notions such as the Christian Church because it is to our advantage that "in Christ" there be male and female (Gal. 3 : 28). We fail to enact the notion of a union of all nations, because it is to our advantage to dictate prices to the world. Few of us are magnanimous willingly, textbook writers included.

If we Americans are to gain stature in religion's golden eye, we will have to become more realistic about time and space than we have tended to be. Throughout all time, most people have not been Americans, Christians, or whites, and any true God has blessed more lands than just ours. By today's standards, the colonial Puritans' "errand in the wilderness" was terribly naive. Those who launched it simply did not have our facts about human prehistory and human diversity. It was largely ignorance, then, that led them to locate salvation in New England. The same is true of those who proposed that America be God's new Israel. Sober students of American history wonder to what extent such notions were used to justify ravaging the Indians. Historians of religion stumble over the obvious fact that God's old Israel was perfectly well.[13]

If we deflate our egos, we may see things in better perspective. From the vantage point of an astronaut or the sun-god Re, Americans have never been *the* holy people. Long before the whites, reds revered every striking American locale. Shortly after the whites, blacks became America's suffering servants. Unbeknownst to our pioneers, peoples in Asia were living lives of grace under pressure.

The only holy people, in religious perspective, are of the single race, the single species. All divisions make but partial stories. There is a dictum in religious studies that he or she who knows just one religion knows no religion. By that dictum Americans urgently need to study world religions; if only to determine our own identity, we need to know what others have been, what alternatives there were.

In addition, the world religions can suggest what in American religious experi-

Figure 18   The Underground Railroad, by Charles T. Webber. Courtesy of the Cincinnati Art Museum.

ence has been distinctive. This topic is immense, so we can only offer a few leads. First, the Reformation and Enlightenment had a marked effect on American religion. Together, they led to a peculiar blend of pietism and rationalism. Of course, pietism and rationalism have been present in other cultures. For instance, Islam embraced both Sufism and the law *(sharia)*. In America, the mixture tended to set the Bible against the brain. Evolution and the Scopes trial of 1925 brought this tension to the fore. In colonial times, Calvinists made syntheses that pleased at least themselves. During the drafting of the Constitution, it appears that reason ousted piety—unless we should call the founding fathers pietistic.

One way of looking at American pietism and rationalism is aesthetic. William Clebsch has recently elaborated that point of view.[14] In his opinion, thinkers such as Jonathan Edwards, Ralph Waldo Emerson, and William James tried to envision the world's beauty. Another approach to American religion is to emphasize American religious liberty. Sidney Mead has argued that the American experiment in religious pluralism has proven as momentous as the establishment of Christianity in imperial Rome.[15]

Both of these views owe much to the Enlightenment's advances on the Reformation. The Reformation set the principles of individual conscience and individual interpretation of scripture. The Enlightenment proposed that reason—nondogmatic thought common to all—should be judge when individual interpretations shattered civic peace. In this new land, where individual opportunity was rich, reason sat in the driver's seat.

In the matter of religious liberty through law, Americans made quantum leaps over their European forebears. There was much less than full political equality, as generations of blacks and women have underscored, but something novel was present that we have come to call pluralism. In religious terms, it was an attempt to live together as equals despite differences in creed. In secular terms, it was a search for a common sense to ensure economic and political cooperation. In theological terms, it conjured natural theology—speculation about God apart from scripture or dogma. For Roman Catholics, the implications of American pluralism only hit Europe in the "Decree on Religious Liberty" of Vatican II.

Despite its faults, America has done much that is commendable. In a world where the majority still seek basic human rights, including the right to religious liberty, America looks quite good. Even in the perspective of the world religions, our civic tolerance is remarkable.

At its most tepid, American religion has tolerated civic piety—mouthings on Memorial Day and the Fourth of July. However, it has also sponsored ecumenical debate, academic freedom, and political and religious dissent. The question now is whether pluralism is so inseparable from secularism that it condemns us to religious superficiality.[16]

Has our agreement to disagree about fundamentals relegated them to the private sphere? If religion is absent from the public places where we forge our national culture, our center may not hold. But if religion is only pursued by the pious, genuine traditionalists will not want it to hold. Eric Voegelin has said that a crucial mark of a culture is whether it enlists the best of its youth or alienates them. For both United States government and United States religion, that is now a hard saying.

We have become used to speeches telling us that our government has only to be as good as its citizens for America to prosper. In too many political assemblies, churches, and synagogues, that is a palliative. It brings no health or distinction to the speaker or the audience. To a religious guru, it shows that the speaker ignores the human condition—the beginner's mind, the nature of enlightenment. Unreflective, unmeditative, the speaker cannot be terse, poetic, evocative; he or she can only pour forth the old, stale, placating language. Ignorant of ignorance and sin, the speaker sees no tragedy. Lacking rigor, stupid in the reasons of the heart, the speaker thinks hope is found in good cheer.

Much the same is true of the audience, of ourselves. Not having gone down in spiritual death, we do not fly to the gods. Not set for spiritual combat, we do not resent that the seats are plush, the rhetoric easy. In part, that is because our culture tells us that only eggheads knit their brows and ponder. In part, it is because we are too lazy to live. It is a major accomplishment for us to endure ten minutes of silence.

From a religious perspective, the economics of American popular culture—the money we pay entertainers, athletes, and business executives—is obscene. Compared to what we pay the people who shape our nation's soul—the artists, scientists, nurses, teachers, and mothers—it is what Aeschylus called *nosos*—spiritual madness. Compared to how we treat the world's starving, it is beyond expression. Two thousand years ago, the Chinese *Book of Mencious* began by condemning profit. Wise persons would have taken that lesson and banked it. We, however, have built a culture on profit. It is what makes our Sammy and Sally run. When will we see that they are running in circles?

People who say things that others do not want to hear, no matter how true such things may be, will suffer for their indiscretion. Socrates stands as the paradigm of their fate, and Socrates shows that in the political realm, prophets and sages are one. He also shows that prophets and sages cannot live for audience applause. They must do what they have to do, say what they have to say, because it is their truth, their good, their charge. Shamans, for instance, must sing—because it relieves their sadness, because it makes them whole. Plato's "Seventh Letter" says that the philosophical soul must live by a love of the Good, that it can only deny the Good by denying its self. Religious people, creative people, humanity's benefactors—they have all found something more precious than human praise. Better, they have all been found by something more precious.

That something is the sacred, the numinous, the holy, the really real. It is Wakan Tanka, the Tao, Buddha-nature, God. Commonly, it is the essence of any conviction significant in the ultimate order, in the world as it finally is. The world as it finally is is the one place where you get what you are. It is where someone may finally tell you, "If you do not believe in mystery, God, or the Tao, be honest about it." By doing so you will reap two benefits. First, you will not bring those realities into further disrepute. Second, you will take the first step in the pilgrimage toward wisdom—simple honesty.

A second step is no less simple or heroic. It is to love the truth that you see. That may be the truth that mystery is beautiful or the truth that the religions often cant. It may move you to sound the ram's horn or to void at the flag. The point is not so much the content as the act. The dynamic of human consciousness, on which any genuine wisdom takes its stand, is a movement from one's present light to wherever that light leads. "Lead kindly light," Cardinal Newman and others have prayed. Go to your light's source, Augustine and others have counseled. Your light shines in the darkness, and the darkness cannot overcome it—so long as you want to be human, so long as samsara is not your all.

Whatever is noble, whatever is good, whatever is honest—think on it, Paul said. Whatever is your current belief about American religion, face it and start to love it. If it

is a solid truth, your personality will ripen, your social circle will take fire. If it is a rotten pseudotruth, you will hear a call to turn and change your heart. In the spiritual life, the only disaster is avoidance. Because they will not face their own beliefs, whether solid or rotten, many stay half-asleep.

Thus, human consciousness becomes intrinsically religious by pursuing the light to where it is love. Worthy religious traditions and patriotism have nothing to fear from this pursuit. The pursuer does have some things to fear, but they pale in comparison with what there is to gain. In Eastern terms, the pursuer learns about ignorance: how much is illusory in his or her starting "truth." In Western terms, the pursuer learns about sin: how difficult it is to follow only the light. Why we do not know the good we should know, why we do not do the good we should do—they are among our deepest mysteries. Only when you ponder them can you call yourself mature, let alone wise. Still, understanding these mysteries is the major therapy that any self needs. Understanding them is the heart of traditional political science.

However, the religions' dharma and prophecy illumine more than ignorance and sin. Ultimately they lead to enlightenment and grace. Enlightenment happens: It is an empirical fact. Light floods some people, bringing them inexpressible joy. Similarly, grace happens: There are marvelous saints. They love God with whole mind, heart, soul, and strength. They serve sisters and brothers more than themselves.

In a dark and troubled time (that is, in any historical time), saints and enlightened people save our beleaguered hope. Just one of them is stronger than all the rubbish, all the valid ground for cynicism. For a single really holy, really religious, really humane person says that what we want and need is possible. We want and need light and love. Light and love are possible. By definition, light and love are Buddha-nature and God, our center.

Study Questions

1. To what extent do the religions share a common attraction toward mystery?

2. Explain the following: "The final utility of religion is that it can teach us how to die and how to live."

3. What have been the principal strengths and weaknesses of American religion?

4. Write a brief definition of *religion* that takes into account the traditions' unity and the traditions' diversity.

5. How does being seized by the Word of God make one a religious prophet?

6. What truth does the protest of Judaism and Islam against Christ's divinity protect?

p.199-200

Appendix A

One Hundred Key Dates
in World Religious History

4.6 billion years ago	Formation of the earth	800–400	Upanishads
		750	Homer and Hesiod written down
500,000 years ago	Homo erectus using fire	750–550	Hebrew Prophets
		ca. 628–551	Zoroaster
100,000 years ago	Homo sapiens: ritual burial	599–527	Mahavira, founder of Jainism
		586	Fall of southern kingdom (Judah)
50,000 years ago	Homo sapiens in Australia	551–479	Confucius
		536–476	Buddha
30,000 years ago	Prehistoric painting and sculpture; Mongoloid peoples cross Bering Strait	525	Persian conquest of Egypt
		525–406	Aeschylus, Sophocles, Euripides
8,000–6,000 B.C.E.	Agriculture, domestication of animals, rise of towns	500–200	*Mahabhrata, Ramayana, Bhagavad Gita*
4500	Early Jomon period of hunting and gathering in Japan	427–347	Plato
		350	*Tao Te Ching*
4000	Casting of bronze	331	Alexander conquers Palestine
3500	Invention of wheel; Megalith cultures in Britain and Iberia	273–236	Asoka
		200	Rise of religious Taoism
3100	Unification of Egypt; Invention of writing in Sumer	80	Buddhist decline in India
		50	Formation of Buddhist canon
3000	Farming in central Africa	5 C.E.	Building of Japanese National Shrine at Ise
2750	Growth of civilization in Indus Valley		
		30	Death of Jesus of Nazareth
1600	Shang Bronze Culture in China	50–95	New Testament writings
1570–1165	New Kingdom in Egypt	70	Romans destroy Jerusalem
1500	Vedas, Rise of Iranian-speaking peoples	80–110	Canonization of Hebrew Bible
1200	Exodus of Hebrews from Egypt	220–552	Buddhist missions to China and Japan
1000	Colonization of Arctic		
900	Nubian kingdom of Kush	304–589	Huns fragment China

325	First Ecumenical Council at Nicaea	1526–1707	Islamic Mogul Dynasty in India
400	Fall of Indian Gupta dynasty	1549	Francis Xavier in Japan
451	Council of Chalcedon	1565	Roman Catholic colony at St. Augustine
500	Compilation of Babylonian Talmud	1585	Matteo Ricci in China
570–632	Muhammad	1619	Beginning of black slavery in colonial America
637	Islamic invasion of Persia	1620	Mayflower Compact
645	Taika reform—Japan takes Chinese model	1654	Jewish settlement at New Amsterdam
650	Canonization of Qur'an	1734	First Great Awakening in New England
700	Golden Age of Chinese poetry	1801	Beginnings of revivalism in western United States
712–720	Shinto Chronicles	1809–1882	Charles Darwin
749	First Buddhist monastery in Tibet	1818–1883	Karl Marx
750–1258	Abbasid caliphate	1856–1939	Sigmund Freud
762	Foundation of Baghdad	1868–1871	Meiji persecution of Buddhism
787	Second Council of Nicaea	1869–1948	Mahatma Gandhi
788–820	Shankara	1879–1955	Albert Einstein
800–900	Rise of Hindu orthodoxy	1880–1913	Partition of Africa by Western powers
845	Persecution of Chinese Buddhists	1893	World Parliament of Religions in Chicago
966	Foundation of Cairo	1893–1977	Mao Tse-tung
1054	Mutual anathemas of Rome and Constantinople	1894–1905	Japanese victorious in wars with China and Russia
1058–1111	Al-Ghazali	1910	Beginning of Protestant ecumenical movement
1130–1200	Chu Hsi, leading Neo-Confucian	1933–1945	Nazi persecution of Jews
ca. 1135	Maimonides	1945	Japanese surrender; Disestablishment of Shinto
1175	First Muslim empire in India	1947	Partition of Pakistan from India
1175–1253	Introduction of Pure Land, Zen, and Nichiren schools in Japan	1948	Creation of state of Israel
1225–1274	Thomas Aquinas	1954–1956	Sixth Buddhist Council, Rangoon
1453	Ottoman Turks capture Constantinople	1962–1965	Second Vatican Council
1469–1539	Nanak, founder of Sikhism	1964	Civil Rights Act in United States
1473–1543	Nicolaus Copernicus		
1492	Expulsion of Jews from Spain		
1517	Luther's ninety-five theses		

Appendix B

Membership Data on Major American Religious Groups (1979)

Adventists, Seventh Day	525,000
Baptists	26,000,000
Buddhists	60,000
Christian Church (Disciples of Christ)	1,260,000
Christian Churches and Churches of Christ	1,050,000
Church of the Nazarene	455,000
Churches of Christ	2,500,000
Eastern Churches (Orthodox)	4,050,000
Episcopal Church	2,820,000
Friends United Meeting (Quakers)	65,000
Jehovah's Witnesses	555,000
Jewish Congregations	5,775,000
Latter Day Saints (Mormons)	2,670,000
Lutherans	8,500,000
Mennonites	100,000
Methodists	13,500,000
Pentecostals	3,300,000
Presbyterians	3,600,000
Roman Catholics	50,000,000
Salvation Army	400,000
Unitarian Universalist Association	200,000
United Churches of Christ	1,800,000

Notes

Introduction

[1]This story is adapted from the Dutch Catholic bishops' work, *A New Catechism* (New York: Herder and Herder, 1967), p. 3.

[2]See Michael Polanyi, *Personal Knowledge* (New York: Harper Torchbooks, 1964); Stephen Toulmin, *Human Understanding* (Princeton, N.J.: Princeton University Press, 1977). For a discussion of Western religion and the distinctive rise of Western science, see Stanley L. Jaki, *The Road of Science and the Ways to God* (Chicago: University of Chicago Press, 1978).

[3]Philip Kapleau, *The Three Pillars of Zen* (Boston: Beacon Press, 1967), pp. 189–291.

[4]For example, Heinz Robert Schlette, *Toward a Theology of Religions* (New York: Herder and Herder, 1966).

[5]Another view of theology, geared to its easier practice in the university, is Shubert Ogden's "Theology and Religious Studies: Their Difference and the Difference It Makes," *JAAR*, 1978, 46(1):3–17.

[6]John Carmody, "Faith in Religious Studies," *Communio*, 1976, 3(1):39–49.

[7]Mircea Eliade, *Cosmos and History* (New York: Harper & Row, 1959), pp. 8–16.

[8]Rudolf Otto, *The Idea of the Holy* (New York: Oxford University Press, 1958), pp. 12–40.

[9]G. Van der Leeuw, *Religion in Essence and Manifestation, I* (New York: Harper & Row, 1963), p. 23.

[10]Bruce Lincoln, "Treatment of Hair and Fingernails among the Indo-Europeans," *HR*, 1977, 16(4):351–362.

[11]Manabu Waida, "Symbolisms of the Moon and the Waters of Immortality," *HR*, 1977, 16(4)407–423.

[12]Mircea Eliade, *From Primitives to Zen* (New York: Harper & Row, 1967).

[13]Hartley Burr Alexander, *The World's Rim* (Lincoln: University of Nebraska Press, 1953), pp. 63–99.

[14]Joseph Campbell, *The Masks of God, I: Primitive Mythology* (New York: Viking, 1970), p. 151.

[15]Durango Mendoza, "Summer Water and Shirley," in *American Indian Authors*, ed. Natachee Scott Momaday (Boston: Houghton Mifflin, 1972), pp. 96–105.

[16]Clyde Kluckhohn, *Navaho Witchcraft* (Boston: Beacon Press, 1967), pp. 13–61.

[17]Ruth Underhill, *Red Man's Religion* (Chicago: University of Chicago Press, 1965), p. 51.

[18]Carlos Castaneda, *Tales of Power* (New York: Simon & Schuster, 1974), pp. 118–162.

[19]Annie Dillard, *Pilgrim at Tinker Creek* (New York: Harper's Magazine Press, 1974), pp. 163–164.

[20]Some of the usual methods of structural analysis are surveyed in Frederick J. Streng, *Understanding Religious Life*, 2nd ed. (Encino, Calif.: Dickenson, 1976). More directly influential on this work is Eric Voegelin, *Anamnesis* (Notre Dame, Ind.: University of Notre Dame Press, 1978).

[21]This cognitional theory is most fully elaborated in Bernard J. F. Lonergan, *Insight: A Study of Human Understanding* (New York: Philosophical Library, 1958).

Chapter One

[1]Mircea Eliade, *A History of Religious Ideas*, vol. 1, *From the Stone Age to the Eleusinian Mysteries* (Chicago: University of Chicago Press, 1978).

[2]Ibid., p. 4.

[3]See Joseph Campbell, *The Masks of God I: Primitive Mythology* (New York: Viking, 1970), pp. 173–176; Adolf E. Jensen, *Myth and Cult among Primitive Peoples* (Chicago: University of Chicago Press, 1963), pp. 107–112.

[4]Eliade, *History of Religious Ideas*, vol. 1, pp. 38–39.

[5]Ibid., p. 115.

[6]See Eric Voegelin, *Order and History, I: Israel and Revelation* (Baton Rouge: Louisiana State University Press, 1956), pp. 1–15.

[7]Helmut Ringgren, *Religions of the Ancient Near East* (Philadelphia: Westminster Press, 1973), pp. 1–123; W. H. P. Romer, "The Religion of Ancient Mesopotamia," in *Historia Religionum, I*, ed. C. J. Bleeker and G. Widengren (Leiden: E. J. Brill, 1969), pp. 115–194.

[8]R. Schilling, "The Roman Religion," in *Historia Religionum, I*, ed. C. J. Bleeker and G. Widengren (Leiden: E. J. Brill, 1969), pp. 442–494.

[9]Robert N. Bellah, *The Broken Covenant: American Civil Religion in Time of Trial* (New York: Seabury, 1975).

[10]H. R. Ellis Davidson, "Germanic Religion," in *Historia Religionum, I*, ed. C. J. Bleeker and G. Widengren (Leiden: E. J. Brill, 1969), pp. 611–628; Maartje Draak, "The Religion of the Celts," in *Historia Religionum, I*, ed. C. J. Bleeker and G. Widengren (Leiden: E. J. Brill, 1969), pp. 629–646; Fr. Vyncke, "The Religion of the Slavs," in *Historia Religionum, I*, ed. C. J. Bleeker and G. Widengren (Leiden: E. J. Brill, 1969), pp. 647–666.

[11]Laurette Séjourné, "Ancient Mexican Religion," in *Historia Religionum, I*, ed. C. J. Bleeker and G. Widengren (Leiden: E. J. Brill, 1969), pp. 667–679; Antje Kelm, "The Religion of Ancient Peru," in *Historia Religionum, I*, ed. C. J. Bleeker and G. Widengren (Leiden: E. J. Brill, 1969), pp. 680–691.

[12]See John Fowles, *Daniel Martin* (Boston: Little, Brown, 1977), pp. 493–494.

[13]Henri Frankfort, *Kingship and the Gods* (Chicago: University of Chicago Press, 1978), pp. 15–214.

[14]See Voegelin, *Order and History, I*, pp. 88–95; John A. Wilson, *The Culture of Ancient Egypt* (Chicago: University of Chicago Press, 1956), pp. 58–60.

[15]Voegelin, *Order and History, I*, p. 99.

[16]C. J. Bleeker, "The Religion of Ancient Egypt," in *Historia Religionum, I*, ed. C. J. Bleeker and G. Widengren (Leiden: E. J. Brill, 1969), pp. 47–49.

[17]Voegelin, *Order and History, I*, p. 108.

[18.]James B. Pritchard, ed., *Ancient Near Eastern Texts* (Princeton, N.J.: Princeton University Press, 1969), p. 370.

[19]Voegelin, *Order and History, I*, p. 86.

[20]Hans J. Klimkeit, "Spatial Orientation in Mythical Thinking as Exemplified in Ancient Egypt: Considerations toward a Geography of Religions," *HR*, 1975, 14(4):266–281.

[21]Frankfort, *Kingship and the Gods*, pp. 148–212.

[22]C. J. Bleeker, *Egyptian Festivals* (Leiden: E. J. Brill, 1967), pp. 91–123.

[23]C. J. Bleeker, *The Rainbow: A Collection of Studies in the Science of Religion* (Leiden: E. J. Brill, 1975), pp. 167–173.

[24]Pierre Montet, *Everyday Life In Egypt*

(Westport, Conn.: Greenwood Press, 1974), p. 51.

[25]Vern L. Bullough, *The Subordinate Sex* (Baltimore: Penguin, 1974), pp. 32–33.

[26]Ibid., p. 39.

[27]John A. Wilson, *Culture of Ancient Egypt*, p. 78.

[28]James B. Pritchard, *Ancient Near Eastern Texts*, p. 34.

[29]Ibid., p. 35.

[30]Jacques Duchesne-Gullemin, *The Hymns of Zarathustra*, trans. M. Henning (Boston: Beacon Press, 1963), p. 1.

[31]R. Ghirshman, *Iran* (Baltimore: Penguin, 1954), p. 27.

[32]Arnold Toynbee, *Mankind and Mother Earth* (New York: Oxford University Press, 1976), pp. 91–116.

[33]Richard Frye, *The Heritage of Persia* (New York: World, 1963), pp. 19–20.

[34]R. C. Zaehner, *The Dawn and Twilight of Zoroastrianism* (New York: Putnam's, 1961), pp. 60–61.

[35]Duchesne-Gullemin, *Hymns of Zarathustra*, p. 135.

[36]Ibid., p. 137.

[37]Isma'il R. al Faruqi, "Zoroastrianism," in *Historical Atlas of the Religions of the World*, ed. I. al Faruqi and D. Sopher (New York: Macmillan, 1974), pp. 133–134.

[38]Eric Voegelin, *Order and History, IV: The Ecumenic Age* (Baton Rouge: Louisiana State University Press, 1974), p. 149.

[39]Ibid., p. 151.

[40]Ibid., p. 152.

[41]Zaehner, *Dawn and Twilight*, p. 99.

[42]Frye, *Heritage of Persia*, p. 190.

[43]Ghirshman, *Iran*, p. 269.

[44]On Manichaeanism, see J. P. Asmussen, "Manicheanism," in *Historia Religionum, I*, ed. C. J. Bleeker and G. Widengren (Leiden: E. J. Brill, 1969), pp. 580–610.

[45]Jacques Duchesne-Gullemin, "The Religion of Ancient Iran," in *Historia Religionum, I*, ed. C. J. Bleeker and G. Widengren (Leiden: E. J. Brill, 1969), pp. 366–367.

[46]Ibid., pp. 358–363.

[47]Emily E. Culpepper, "Zoroastrian Menstruation Taboos," in *Women and Religion*, rev. ed., ed. J. Plaskow and J. A. Romero (Missoula, Mont.: Scholars Press, 1974), pp. 199–210.

[48]Mary Boyce, "Zoroastrianism," in *Historia Religionum, II*, ed. C. J. Bleeker and G. Widengren (Leiden: E. J. Brill, 1971), pp. 228–229.

[49]Eric Voegelin, *Anamnesis* (Notre Dame, Ind.: University of Notre Dame Press, 1978), p. 92.

[50]John Fowles, *The Magus: A Revised Version* (New York: Dell, 1978), p. 69.

[51]Toynbee, *Mankind and Mother Earth*, pp. 77–78.

[52]Phillipe Borgeaud, "The Open Entrance to the Closed Palace of the King: The Greek Labyrinth in Context," *HR*, 1974, *14*(1):1–27; Raymond Christinger, "The Hidden Significance of the 'Cretan' Labyrinth," *HR*, 1975, *15*(2): 183–191.

[53]Eliade, *History of Religious Ideas*, vol. 1, p. 136; K. Kerenyi, "Voraussentzungen in der Einweihung in Eleusis," in *Initiation*, ed. C. J. Bleeker (Leiden: E. J. Brill, 1965), pp. 59–64; M. Mehauden, "Le secret central de l'initiation aux mystères d'Eleusis," in *Initiation*, ed. C. J. Bleeker (Leiden: E. J. Brill, 1965), pp. 65–70.

[54]B. C. Dietrich, *The Origins of Greek Religion* (New York: de Gruyter, 1974), pp. 191–289.

[55]Eliade, *History of Religious Ideas*, vol. 1, pp. 247–250.

[56]W. K. C. Guthrie, *The Greeks and Their Gods* (Boston: Beacon Press, 1955), pp. 73–87.

[57]E. R. Dodds, *The Greeks and the Irrational* (Berkeley: University of California Press, 1966), pp. 76–82.

[58]Ibid., pp. 270–282.

[59]Eliade, *History of Religious Ideas*, vol. 1, p. 360.

[60]Dodds, *Greeks and the Irrational*, pp. 6–8.

[61]H. J. Rose, *A Handbook of Greek Mythology* (New York: Dutton, 1959), pp. 91–94.

[62]Edith Hamilton, *Mythology* (New York: New American Library, 1942), pp. 103–105.

[63]Guthrie, *Greeks and Their Gods*, p. 318.

[64]Ibid., pp. 217–253.

[65]Ibid., pp. 254–306.

[66]See A. W. H. Adkins, "Greek Religion," in *Historia Religionum, I*, ed. C. J. Bleeker and G. Widengren (Leiden: E. J. Brill, 1969), pp. 402–406, 411–422.

[67]Gilbert Murray, *Five Stages of Greek Religion* (New York: Doubleday Anchor, 1955), p. v.

[68]See Eric Voegelin, *Order and History, II: The World of the Polis* (Baton Rouge: Louisiana State University Press, 1957), pp. 203–331.

[69]Ibid., pp. 332–373; Eric Voegelin, *Order and History, IV: The Ecumenic Age* (Baton Rouge: Louisiana State University Press, 1974), pp. 178–183.

[70]John Carmody, "Plato's Religious Horizon," *Philosophy Today*, 1971, *15*(1):52–68.

[71]Voegelin, *Order and History, IV*, pp. 187–192; Werner Jaeger, *Aristotle* (New York: Oxford University Press, 1962), pp. 366–406.

[72]Bernard Lonergan, *Verbum* (Notre Dame, Ind.: University of Notre Dame Press, 1967).

[73]Jaeger, *Aristotle*, pp. 426–461.

[74]Murray, *Greek Religion*, pp. 119–165; Dodds, *Greeks and the Irrational*, pp. 236–269.

[75]M. J. Vermaseren, "Hellenistic Religions," in *Historia Religionum, I*, ed. C. J. Bleeker and G. Widengren (Leiden: E. J. Brill, 1969), p. 495.

[76]Sharon Kelly Heyob, *The Cult of Isis among Women in the Graeco-Roman World* (Leiden: E. J. Brill, 1975), pp. 111–127.

[77]See Vermaseren, "Hellenistic Religions," pp. 522–533.

[78]Ibid., pp. 523–528.

[79]See Mircea Eliade, *From Primitives to Zen* (New York: Harper & Row, 1967), p. 55.

[80]See Eliade, *History of Religious Ideas*, vol. 1, p. 256.

[81]See Bullough, *Subordinate Sex*, p. 59.

[82]Eliade, *From Primitives to Zen*, p. 540.

Chapter Two

[1]Michael Avi-Yonah et al., *Jerusalem* (Jerusalem: Keter, 1973); Robert L. Cohn, "Jerusalem: The Senses of a Center," *JAAR*, 1978, *46*(1), Supplement F; Giora Shamis and Diane Shalem, *The Jerusalem Guide* (Jerusalem: Abraham Marcus, 1973).

[2]Gerhard Kressel et al., *Zionism* (Jerusalem: Keter, 1973).

[3]Jacob A. Argus, "Judaism," in *Historical Atlas of the Religions of the World*, ed. I. al Faruqi and D. Sopher (New York: Macmillan, 1974), p. 156.

[4]R. J. Zwi Werblowsky, "Judaism," in *Historia Religionum, II*, ed. C. J. Bleeker and G. Widengren (Leiden: E. J. Brill, 1971), p. 1.

[5]Herbert May, ed., *Oxford Bible Atlas*, 2nd ed. (New York: Oxford University Press, 1974), p. 57; G. Widengren, "Israelite-Jewish Religion," in *Historia Religionum, I*, ed. C. J. Bleeker and G. Widengren (Leiden: E. J. Brill, 1969), p. 226.

[6]Isadore Epstein, *Judaism* (London: Penguin, 1959), pp. 12–14; Eric Voegelin, *Order and History*, vol. 1 (Baton Rouge: Louisiana State University Press, 1956), pp. 188–195.

[7]I. al Faruqi and D. Sopher, eds., *Historical Atlas of the Religions of the World* (New York: Macmillan, 1974), p. 286.

[8]John L. McKenzie, S. J., *Dictionary of the Bible* (Milwaukee, Wis.: Bruce, 1965), pp. 153–157.

[9]William Foxwell Albright, "The Biblical Period," in *The Jews: Their History*, ed. Louis Finkelstein (New York: Schocken, 1970), pp. 15–19.

[10]See Samuel Sandmel, *The Enjoyment of Scripture* (New York: Oxford University Press, 1972), pp. 164–175.

[11]For example, Roland Murphy, "Introduction to Wisdom Literature," *The Jerome Biblical Commentary*, vol. 1, ed. R. Brown, J. Fitzmyer, and R. Murphy (Englewood Cliffs, N.J.: Prentice-Hall, 1968), p. 487.

[12]John J. Collins, "The Jewish Apocalypse," in *Apocalypse: The Morphology of a Genre*, ed.

John J. Collins (Missoula, Mont.: Scholars Press, 1979), pp. 21–59.

[13]Eric Voegelin, *Order and History*, vol. 4 (Baton Rouge: Louisiana State University Press, 1974), pp. 117–133, 153–165.

[14]Victor Tcherikover, *Hellenistic Civilization and the Jews* (New York: Atheneum, 1974), pp. 152–234.

[15]Joseph Fitzmyer, "A History of Israel," in *The Jerome Biblical Commentary*, vol. 2, ed. R. Brown, J. Fitzmyer, and R. Murphy (Englewood Cliffs, N.J.: Prentice-Hall, 1968), p. 692; Judah Goldin, "The Period of the Talmud," in *The Jews: Their History*, ed. Louis Finkelstein (New York: Schocken, 1970), pp. 121–129.

[16]*Encyclopedia Judaica*, s.v. "Talmud, Babylonian."

[17]See Jacob Neusner, "Form and Meaning in Mishnah," *JAAR*, 1977, *45*(1):27–54; "History and Structure: The Case of the Mishnah," *JAAR*, 1977, *45*(2):161–192.

[18]R. Travers Herford, *Pirke Aboth: The Ethics of the Talmud* (New York: Schocken, 1962).

[19]Renée Bloch, "Midrash," in *Approaches to Ancient Judaism*, ed. William Scott Green (Missoula, Mont.: Scholars Press, 1978), pp. 19–50; Nahum N. Glatzer, ed., *Hammer on the Rock* (New York: Schocken, 1962).

[20]Epstein, *Judaism*, pp. 121–194. On the Talmud's view of prophecy (which its law was somewhat trying to replace), see Nahum N. Glatzer, "A Study of the Talmudic-Midrashic Interpretation of Prophecy," in his *Essays in Jewish Thought* (University, Ala.: University of Alabama Press, 1978), pp. 16–35.

[21]See Jacob Neusner, *The Life of Torah* (Encino, Calif.: Dickenson, 1974), pp. 17–24.

[22]Epstein, *Judaism*, p. 140.

[23]See Robert Goldenberg, *The Sabbath Law of Rabbi Meir* (Missoula, Mont.: Scholars Press, 1978), pp. 159–264.

[24]For a contemporary view of the Sabbath, see Richard Siegel et al., *The Jewish Catalogue* (Philadelphia: Jewish Publication Society of America, 1973), pp. 103–116.

[25]For an overview of the medieval period, see Jacob B. Argus, *The Meaning of Jewish History*, vol. 2 (New York: Abelard-Schuman, 1963), pp. 232–297.

[26]Epstein, *Judaism*, p. 180.

[27]On this whole question, see S. D. Goitein, *Jews and Arabs* (New York: Schocken, 1955).

[28]Epstein, *Judaism*, p. 191.

[29]See Julius Gutmann, *Philosophies of Judaism* (New York: Holt, Rinehart and Winston, 1964).

[30]Moses Maimonides, *The Guide for the Perplexed*, 2nd ed., trans. M. Friedlander (New York: Dover, 1956), p. 11.

[31]R. J. Zwi Werblowsky, "Judaism, or the Religion of Israel," in *The Concise Encyclopedia of Living Faiths*, ed. R. C. Zaehner (Boston: Beacon Press, 1967), pp. 45–48.

[32]Gershom G. Scholem, *Major Trends in Jewish Mysticism* (New York: Schocken, 1961).

[33]See J. Doresse, "Gnosticism," in *Historia Religionum, I*, ed. C. J. Bleeker and G. Widengren (Leiden: E. J. Brill, 1969), pp. 536–537.

[34]Werblowsky, "Judaism," p. 24.

[35]See Gershom G. Scholem, ed., *Zohar: The Book of Splendor* (New York: Schocken, 1963), pp. 12–21.

[36]Argus, *Jewish History*, pp. 300–485; Cecil Roth, *A History of the Jews* (New York: Schocken, 1961), pp. 235–424.

[37]Roth, *History of the Jews*, pp. 180–294.

[38]Leon Poliakov, *The History of Anti-Semitism* (New York: Schocken, 1974).

[39]See Elie Wiesel, *Souls on Fire* (New York: Vintage, 1973).

[40]Mark Zborowski and Elizabeth Herzog, *Life Is with People* (New York: Schocken, 1962).

[41]Meyer Levin, *Classic Hasidic Tales* (New York: Penguin Books, 1975), p. 125. We have adapted Levin's version of the story, found on pp. 125–131.

[42]Martin Buber, *Hasidism and Modern Man* (New York: Harper Torchbooks, 1966).

[43]Abraham J. Heschel, *Man's Quest for God* (New York: Scribner's, 1954); *God in Search of Man* (New York: Farrar, Straus & Giroux, 1955).

[44]Argus, "Judaism," p. 152.

[45]Jacob Neusner, *The Way of Torah*, 2nd ed. (Encino, Calif.: Dickenson, 1974), pp. 68–71.

[46]Arthur Green, "The *Zaddiq* as *Axis Mundi* in Later Judaism," *JAAR*, 1977, 45(3): 327–347.

[47]Martin Buber, *Tales of the Hasidim*, 2 vols. (New York: Schocken, 1947–48).

[48]Elie Wiesel, *The Gates of the Forest* (New York: Avon, 1966), pp. 6–10.

[49]On this conflict in the United States, see Sydney Ahlstrom, *A Religious History of the American People* (New Haven, Conn.: Yale University Press, 1972), pp. 969–984; also Neusner, *Life of Torah*, pp. 156–203.

[50]Argus, "Judaism," p. 154.

[51]Eva Fleischner, "A Select Annotated Bibliography on the Holocaust," *Horizons*, 1977, 4(1):61–83.

[52]See, for example, Rosemary Ruether, *Faith and Fratricide* (New York: Seabury, 1974).

[53]See McKenzie, *Dictionary of the Bible*.

[54]Werblowsky, "Judaism, or the Religion of Israel."

[55]Geoffrey Wigoder et al., *Jewish Values* (Jerusalem: Keter, 1974).

[56]Voegelin, *Order and History*, vol. 4, chaps. 1, 3, 7.

[57]Salo Wittmayer Baron, *A Social and Religious History of the Jews*, vol. 1, *Ancient Times*, 2nd ed. (New York: Columbia University Press, 1952), pp. 4–16.

[58]Sherry B. Ortner, "Is Female to Male as Nature Is to Culture?" in *Woman, Culture and Society*, ed. M. Z. Rosaldo and L. Lamphere (Stanford, Calif.: Stanford University Press, 1974), pp. 67–88.

[59]Phyllis Bird, "Images of Women in the Old Testament," in *Religion and Sexism*, ed. Rosemary Radford Ruether (New York: Simon & Schuster, 1974), pp. 41–88.

[60]Judith Hauptmann, "Images of Women in the Talmud," in *Religion and Sexism*, ed. Rosemary Radford Ruether (New York: Simon & Schuster, 1974), pp. 184–212. On Mishnaic menstrual taboos, see Jacob Neusner, *A History of the Mishnaic Law of Purities* (Leiden: E. J. Brill, 1977), pt. 22.

[61]I. Epstein, "The Jewish Woman in the Responsa: 900 C.E.–1500 C.E.," *Response*, Summer 1973, no. 16, pp. 23–31.

[62]For an overview of women in Judaism, see Denise Lardner Carmody, *Women and World Religions* (Nashville: Abingdon, 1979), pp. 92–112. For current issues, see Carol P. Christ and Judith Plaskow, eds., *Womanspirit Rising* (New York: Harper & Row, 1979); Elizabeth Koltun, ed., *The Jewish Woman: New Perspectives* (New York: Schocken, 1976).

[63]See his contributions to *The Life of Torah: Readings in the Jewish Religious Experience*, ed. Jacob Neusner (Belmont, Calif.: Dickenson, 1974), p. 104.

[64]Judith Plaskow, "Bringing a Daughter into the Covenant," in *Womanspirit Rising*, ed. Carol P. Christ and Judith Plaskow (San Francisco: Harper & Row, 1980), p. 181.

[65]See *The Jewish Catalogue*, ed. Richard Siegel et al. (Philadelphia: The Jewish Publication Society of America, 1973), p. 158.

[66]On this point, Robert L. Cohn reminded us of Hillel's saying, "Sever not thyself from the congregation" (*Pirke Avot*, 2:5).

[67]Richard L. Rubenstein, *After Auschwitz* (Indianapolis, Ind.: Bobbs-Merrill, 1966).

[68]Emil Fackenheim, *God's Presence in History* (New York: New York University Press, 1970).

[69]Hanna Arendt, *Eichmann in Jerusalem* (New York: Viking, 1965).

[70]See Elie Wiesel, *The Oath* (New York: Random House, 1973).

[71]See, for example, Joel Blocker, ed., *Israeli Stories* (New York: Schocken, 1965).

[72]Michael Polanyi and Harry Prosch, *Meaning* (Chicago: University of Chicago Press, 1975). That does not mean, however, that the Talmud did not meditate deeply on Jewish divinity. See A. Cohen, *Everyman's Talmud* (New York: Schocken, 1975), pp. 1–26. For a contemporary view, see Leo Baeck, *The Essence of Judaism* (New York: Schocken, 1961), pp. 83–150.

[73]See Neusner, *The Life of Torah*, pp. 17–24.

[74]See Lewis S. Ford, *The Lure of God* (Philadelphia: Fortress, 1978).

[75]Friedrich Heiler, *Prayer* (New York: Oxford University Press, 1932).

Chapter Three

[1]For a brief study of Christianity that includes fine maps of its spread, see Gerald Sloyan, "Christianity," in *Historical Atlas of the Religions of the World*, ed. I. al Faruqi and D. Sopher (New York: Macmillan, 1974), pp. 201–236.

[2]One of the most thorough recent treatments of the critical and theological issues concerning Jesus is Edward Schillebeeckx, *Jesus* (New York: Seabury, 1979).

[3]See Raymond E. Brown, *The Birth of the Messiah* (New York: Doubleday, 1977).

[4]Geza Vermes, *Jesus the Jew* (London: Fontana, 1976), pp. 18–82.

[5]Joachim Jeremias, *New Testament Theology: The Proclamation of Jesus* (New York: Scribner's, 1971), pp. 29–36.

[6]Karl Rahner and Herbert Vorgrimler, *Theological Dictionary* (New York: Herder and Herder, 1965), pp. 236–241.

[7]A succinct discussion of New Testament ethics is J. L. Houden, *Ethics and the New Testament* (New York: Oxford University Press, 1977).

[8]Jeremias, *New Testament Theology*, pp. 250–257.

[9]See Eric Voegelin, "The Gospel and Culture," in *Jesus and Man's Hope*, vol. 2, ed. D. Miller and D. Hadidian (Pittsburgh: Pittsburgh Theological Seminary, 1971), pp. 59–101.

[10]Joseph A. Fitzmyer, "Pauline Theology," in *The Jerome Biblical Commentary*, vol. 2, ed. R. Brown, J. Fitzmyer, and R. Murphy (Englewood Cliffs, N.J.: Prentice-Hall, 1968), pp. 810–827.

[11]On the problems of writing the history of the realities of Christian faith, see Van A. Harvey, *The Historian and the Believer* (New York: Macmillan, 1966).

[12]Pheme Perkins, *Hearing the Parables of Jesus* (Ramsey, N.J.: Paulist Press, 1981), p. 94. Our treatment adapts pp. 94–98.

[13]Recent and readable is Stephen Neill, *Jesus through Many Eyes* (Philadelphia: Fortress, 1976). For a literary stress, see Leonard L. Thompson, *Introducing Biblical Literature* (Englewood Cliffs, N.J.: Prentice-Hall, 1978), pp. 213–307.

[14]Antonio Javierre, "Apostle," in *Sacramentum Mundi*, vol. 1, ed. Karl Rahner et al. (New York: Herder and Herder, 1968), p. 77.

[15]Raymond E. Brown et al., eds., *Peter in the New Testament* (Minneapolis, Minn.: Augsburg, 1973).

[16]See Maxwell Staniforth, trans., *Early Christian Writings* (Baltimore: Penguin, 1968).

[17]J. Doresse, "Gnosticism," in *Historia Religionum*, I, ed. C. J. Bleeker and G. Widengren (Leiden: E. J. Brill, 1969), pp. 536–537.

[18]Succinct information on personages such as these is available in F. L. Cross, ed., *The Oxford Dictionary of the Christian Church* (New York: Oxford University Press, 1966).

[19]See Jaroslav Pelikan, *The Christian Tradition, 1: The Emergence of the Catholic Tradition* (Chicago: University of Chicago Press, 1971).

[20]J. G. Davies, "Christianity: The Early Church," in *The Concise Encyclopedia of Living Faiths*, ed. R. C. Zaehner (Boston: Beacon Press, 1967), pp. 60–69.

[21]On patristic terminology, see G. L. Prestige, *God in Patristic Thought* (London: Society for the Promotion of Christian Knowledge, 1959).

[22]Bernard Lonergan, *The Way to Nicaea* (Philadelphia: Westminster, 1976).

[23]Eric Voegelin, *Science, Politics and Gnosticism* (Chicago: Gateway, 1968), pp. 22–28.

[24]William A. Clebsch, *Christianity in European History* (New York: Oxford University Press, 1979), pp. 29–84; Stephen Reynolds, *The Christian Religious Tradition* (Encino, Calif.: Dickenson, 1977), pp. 35–77.

[25]Thomas Merton, *The Wisdom of the Desert* (New York: New Directions, 1960).

[26]Nicholas Zernov, "Christianity: The Eastern Schism and the Eastern Orthodox Church," in *The Concise Encyclopedia of Living Faiths*, ed. R. C. Zaehner (Boston: Beacon Press, 1967), p. 86.

[27]Donald W. Treadgold, *The West in Russia*

and China, vol. 1 (Cambridge: University Press, 1973), pp. 1–23.

28On classical Eastern theology, see Jaroslav Pelikan, *The Christian Tradition, 2: The Spirit of Eastern Christendom* (Chicago: University of Chicago Press, 1974); see also G. P. Fedotov, *The Russian Religious Mind* (Cambridge, Mass.: Harvard University Press, 1966).

29See Timothy Ware, *The Orthodox Church* (Baltimore: Penguin, 1964).

30Bernhard Schultze, "Eastern Churches," in *Sacramentum Mundi*, vol. 2, ed. Karl Rahner et al. (New York: Herder and Herder, 1968), pp. 120–133.

31Sergius Bolshakoff and M. Basil Pennington, *In Search of True Wisdom: Visits to Eastern Spiritual Fathers* (Garden City, N.Y.: Doubleday, 1979).

32C. W. Monnich, "Christianity," in *Historia Religionum, II*, ed. C. J. Bleeker and G. Widengren (Leiden: E. J. Brill, 1971), p. 65.

33Jaroslav Pelikan, *The Christian Tradition, 3: The Growth of Medieval Theology* (Chicago: University of Chicago Press, 1978), pp. 268–307.

34Anthony Kenney, ed., *Aquinas* (New York: Doubleday, 1969); see also H. Francis Davis, "St. Thomas and Medieval Theology," in *The Concise Encyclopedia of Living Faiths*, ed. R. C. Zaehner (Boston: Beacon Press, 1967), pp. 108–112.

35Lawrence Cunningham and John Reich, *Culture and Values: A Survey of the Western Humanities*, vol. 2 (New York: Holt, Rinehart and Winston, 1982), p. 99. Our treatment adapts pp. 99–103.

36On the history of the notion of reform, see Gerhart B. Ladner, *The Idea of Reform* (Cambridge, Mass.: Harvard University Press, 1959).

37Erik H. Erikson, *Young Man Luther* (New York: Norton, 1962).

38*The New Columbia Encyclopedia*, s.v. "plague."

39See Pennethorne Hughes, *Witchcraft* (Baltimore: Penguin, 1965).

40John Kent, "Christianity: Protestantism," in *The Concise Encyclopedia of Living Faiths*, ed. R. C. Zaehner (Boston: Beacon Press, 1967), pp. 117–149.

41Owen Chadwick, *The Reformation* (Baltimore: Penguin, 1964), p. 41.

42See Lewis Spitz, ed., *The Protestant Reformation* (Englewood Cliffs, N.J.: Prentice-Hall, 1966).

43C. W. Monnich, "Christianity," p. 72.

44See William A. Clebsch, *American Religious Thought* (Chicago: University of Chicago Press, 1973), pp. 11–56.

45James Brodrick, *The Origin of the Jesuits* (London: Longmans, 1940); *The Progress of the Jesuits* (London: Longmans, 1946).

46Sidney E. Mead, *The Lively Experiment* (New York: Harper & Row, 1976); *The Nation with the Soul of a Church* (New York: Harper & Row, 1975); see also Sydney E. Ahlstrom, *A Religious History of the American People* (New Haven, Conn.: Yale University Press, 1972), pp. 121–229.

47Harvey D. Egan, *The Spiritual Exercises and the Ignatian Mystical Horizon* (St. Louis: Institute of Jesuit Sources, 1976); Gaston Fessard, *La dialectique des exercices spirituels de saint ignace de loyola* (Paris: Aubier, 1956).

48Robert McAfee Brown, *The Spirit of Protestantism* (New York: Oxford University Press, 1965).

49Max Weber, *The Protestant Ethic and the Spirit of Capitalism* (New York: Scribner's, 1958).

50Heribert Raab, "Enlightenment," in *Sacramentum Mundi*, vol. 2, ed. Karl Rahner et al. (New York: Herder and Herder, 1968), p. 230; see also Crane Brinton, "Enlightenment," in *The Encyclopedia of Philosophy*, vol. 2, ed. Paul Edwards (New York: Macmillan, 1967), pp. 519–525.

51See the articles by Sidney E. Mead, Sydney E. Ahlstrom, Vincent Harding, and Robert Bellah in *Soundings*, 1978, 61(3):303–371.

52Eric Voegelin, *From Enlightenment to Revolution* (Durham, N.C.: Duke University Press, 1975).

53The breakthrough work was Gustavo Gutierrez, *A Theology of Liberation* (Maryknoll, N.Y.: Orbis, 1973). Especially provocative is Jose Miranda, *Marx and the Bible* (Maryknoll, N.Y.: Orbis, 1974). A fine survey that brings liberation thought to the United States is Robert McAfee Brown, *Theology in a New Key* (Philadelphia: Westminster, 1978).

⁵⁴See Sergio Torres and John Eagleson, eds., *Theology in the Americas* (Maryknoll, N.Y.: Orbis, 1976).

⁵⁵Martin E. Marty, *Righteous Empire* (New York: Dial Press, 1970).

⁵⁶Robert Bellah, *The Broken Covenant* (New York: Seabury, 1975).

⁵⁷See Voegelin, *Science, Politics and Gnosticism;* see also his *The New Science of Politics* (Chicago: University of Chicago Press, 1952).

⁵⁸Carnegie Samuel Calian, *The Gospel According to the "Wall Street Journal"* (Atlanta: John Knox, 1975).

⁵⁹See Sam D. Gill, "Native American Religions," *The Council on the Study of Religion Bulletin,* 1978, 9(5):125–128.

⁶⁰Peter L. Berger, *A Rumor of Angels* (Garden City, N.Y.: Doubleday, 1969).

⁶¹Emilie Griffin, *Turning: The Experience of Conversion* (Garden City, N.Y.: Doubleday, 1980). We especially draw on pp. 31–49.

⁶²Jorg Splett et al., "Nature," in *Sacramentum Mundi,* vol. 4, ed. Karl Rahner et al. (New York: Herder and Herder, 1969), pp. 171–181.

⁶³Pieter Smulders et al., "Creation," in *Sacramentum Mundi,* vol. 2, ed. Karl Rahner et al. (New York: Herder and Herder, 1968), pp. 23–37.

⁶⁴See Harold K. Schilling, *The New Consciousness in Science and Religion* (Philadelphia: United Church Press, 1973).

⁶⁵Alfred North Whitehead, *Process and Reality* (New York: Harper Torchbooks, 1960).

⁶⁶*The Book of Common Prayer* (New York: Seabury Press, 1977), p. 308. Our description of the sacramental rituals depends on the *Book of Common Prayer.*

⁶⁷See Staniforth, *Early Christian Writings,* pp. 171–185.

⁶⁸See Bernard Cooke, *Ministry to Word and Sacrament* (Philadelphia: Fortress, 1976).

⁶⁹Edward Schillebeeckx, *Christ: The Sacrament of Encounter with God* (New York: Sheed & Ward, 1963).

⁷⁰Mary Daly, *Gyn/Ecology* (Boston: Beacon Press, 1979), chap. 6.

⁷¹Denise Lardner Carmody, *Women and World Religions* (Nashville: Abingdon, 1979), pp. 113–136; Carol P. Christ and Judith Plaskow, eds., *Womanspirit Rising* (New York: Harper & Row, 1979); Elizabeth Clark and Herbert Richardon, eds., *Women and Religion* (New York: Harper & Row, 1977); Rosemary Radford Ruether, ed., *Religion and Sexism* (New York: Simon & Schuster, 1974); Mary Daly, *The Church and the Second Sex* (New York: Harper Colophon, 1975).

⁷²Steven Runciman, *The Orthodox Churches and the Secular State* (Auckland: Auckland University Press, 1971).

⁷³Karl Rahner, *The Shape of the Church to Come* (New York: Seabury, 1974).

⁷⁴See Vladimir Lossky, *The Mystical Theology of the Eastern Church* (Crestwood, N.Y.: St. Vladimir's Seminary Press, 1976); Alexander Schmemann, ed., *Ultimate Questions* (Crestwood, N.Y.: St. Vladimir's Seminary Press, 1977).

⁷⁵John L. McKenzie, *The Power and the Wisdom* (Milwaukee, Wisc.: Bruce, 1965), pp. 252–255.

⁷⁶See Bernard Lonergan, *Grace and Freedom* (New York: Herder and Herder, 1971).

⁷⁷A handy collection of relevant texts on Barth is Karl Barth, *Church Dogmatics: A Selection* (New York: Harper Torchbooks, 1962), pp. 29–86. On Tillich, see his *Systematic Theology,* vol. 1 (Chicago: University of Chicago Press, 1967), pp. 71–159.

⁷⁸Etienne Gilson, *The Elements of Christian Philosophy* (New York: Mentor-Omega, 1963), pp. 135–145.

⁷⁹A profound interpretation is Karl Rahner's "Thomas Aquinas on the Incomprehensibility of God," *Journal of Religion,* 1978, 58, supp.:107–125; see also Paul Ricoeur, " 'Response' to Karl Rahner's Lecture on the Incomprehensibility of God," *Journal of Religion,* 1978, 58, supp.: 126–131.

Chapter Four

¹There are good maps on the spread of Islam in Geoffrey Barraclough, ed., *The Times*

Atlas of World History (Maplewood, N.J.: Hammond, 1979), pp. 104–105, 134–135, 138–139; see also I. al Faruqi and D. Sopher, eds., *Historical Atlas of the Religions of the World* (New York: Macmillan, 1974), pp. 237–281.

[2]Fernando Diaz-Plaja, *El espanol y los siete pecados capitales* (Madrid: Alianza Editorial, 1966), esp. pp. 17–122.

[3]On the Muslim quarter of Jerusalem, see Giora Shamis and Diane Shalem, *The Jerusalem Guide* (Jerusalem: Abraham Marcus, 1973), pp. 93–105. On Muslim history in Jerusalem, see Michael Avi-Yonah et al., *Jerusalem* (Jerusalem: Keter, 1973), pp. 48–142.

[4]Annemarie Schimmel, "Islam," in *Historia Religionum, II*, ed. C. J. Bleeker and G. Widengren (Leiden: E. J. Brill, 1971), p. 127.

[5]W. Montgomery Watt, *Muhammad: Prophet and Statesman* (New York: Oxford University Galaxy Books, 1974), pp. 45–55.

[6]We have used the translation by A. J. Arberry, *The Koran Interpreted* (New York: Macmillan, 1973).

[7]Watt, *Muhammad*, p. 7.

[8]On the pre-Islamic background, see Ignaz Goldziher, *Muslim Studies*, vol. 1 (Chicago: Aldine, 1967), pp. 11–44; Marshall G. S. Hodgson, *The Venture of Islam*, vol. 1 (Chicago: University of Chicago Press, 1974), pp. 103–145; M. M. Bravmann, *The Spiritual Background of Early Islam* (Leiden: E. J. Brill, 1972).

[9]Schimmel, "Islam," p. 129.

[10]Isma'il al Faruqi, "Islam," in *Historical Atlas of the Religions of the World*, ed. I. al Faruqi and D. Sopher (New York: Macmillan, 1974), p. 241.

[11]Charles J. Adams, "The Islamic Religious Tradition," in *Judaism, Christianity and Islam*, ed. J. O'Dea, T. O'Dea, and C. Adams (New York: Harper & Row, 1972), p. 166.

[12]H. A. R. Gibb, *Mohammedanism*, 2nd ed. (New York: Oxford University Press, 1962), p. 30.

[13]See Watt, *Muhammad*, pp. 229–231.

[14]H. A. R. Gibb, "Islam," in *The Concise Encyclopedia of Living Faiths*, ed. R. C. Zaehner (Boston: Beacon Press, 1967), p. 179.

[15]N. J. Dawood, trans., *The Koran* (Baltimore: Penguin, 1968), p. 10.

[16]Kenneth Cragg, *The House of Islam*, 2nd ed. (Encino, Calif.: Dickenson, 1975), pp. 30–34; Arberry, *Koran Interpreted*, p. 28.

[17]Arthur Jeffrey, ed., *Islam: Muhammad and His Religion* (New York: Bobbs-Merrill, 1975); Isma'il al Faruqi, "Islam," in *The Great Asian Religions*, ed. W. T. Chan et al. (New York: Macmillan, 1969), pp. 307–395.

[18]On the development of the *Hadith*, see Ignaz Goldziher, *Muslim Studies*, vol. 2 (Chicago: Aldine, 1975), pp. 17–251.

[19]N. J. Dawood, trans., *The Koran* (Baltimore: Penguin, 1968), p. 32. Our treatment of this sura draws on pp. 32–37.

[20]See Geoffrey Parrinder, *Jesus in the Qur'an* (New York: Oxford University Press, 1977).

[21]Cragg, *House of Islam*, pp. 5–18.

[22]See Martin Lings, *A Sufi Saint of the Twentieth Century*, 2nd ed. (Berkeley: University of California Press, 1973), pp. 121–130; R. C. Zaehner, *Hindu and Muslim Mysticism* (New York: Schocken, 1969), pp. 86–109.

[23]W. Montgomery Watt, *The Faith and Practice of al-Ghazali* (London: Allen & Unwin, 1953), pp. 90–130.

[24]See Cheikh Hamidou Kane, *Ambiguous Adventure* (New York: Collier, 1969).

[25]Cragg, *House of Islam*, pp. 73–108; Frederick Mathewson Denny, "The Meaning of *Ummah* in the Qur'an," *HR*, 1975, *15*:34–70.

[26]al Faruqi, "Islam," in *Historical Atlas*, p. 248.

[27]Bernard Lewis, *The Arabs in History*, rev. ed. (New York: Harper Torchbooks, 1966), p. 55; see also Edmund Bosworth, "Armies of the Prophet," in *Islam and the Arab World*, ed. Bernard Lewis (New York: Knopf, 1976), pp. 201–224; V. J. Parry, "Warfare," in *The Cambridge History of Islam*, vol. 2, ed. P. M. Holt et al. (Cambridge: University Press, 1970), pp. 824–850.

[28]Lewis, *Arabs in History*, p. 56.

[29]See Hodgson, *Venture of Islam*, pp. 187–217.

[30]See W. Montgomery Watt, *The Formative Period of Islamic Thought* (Edinburgh: University Press, 1973), pp. 253–278.

[31]Stephen F. Mason, *A History of the Sciences*, rev. ed. (New York: Collier, 1962), p. 95; see also A. I. Sabra, "The Scientific Enterprise," in *Islam and the Arab World*, ed. Bernard Lewis (New York: Knopf, 1976), pp. 181–200; G. Anawati, "Science," in *The Cambridge History of Islam*, vol. 2, ed. P. M. Holt et al. (Cambridge: University Press, 1970), pp. 741–779.

[32]Albert C. Moore, *Iconography of the Religions: An Introduction* (Philadelphia: Fortress, 1977), pp. 213–226; see also Richard Ettinghausen, "The Man-Made Setting," in *Islam and the Arab World*, ed. Bernard Lewis (New York: Knopf, 1976), pp. 57–88; G. Fehervari, "Art and Architecture," in *The Cambridge History of Islam*, vol. 2, ed. P. M. Holt et al. (Cambridge: University Press, 1970), pp. 702–740.

[33]Schuyler V. R. Cammann, "Religious Symbolism in Persian Art," *HR*, 1976, *15:* 193–205.

[34]Oleg Grabar, "Architecture," in *The Legacy of Islam*, 2nd ed., ed. Joseph Schacht and C. E. Bosworth (New York: Oxford University Press, 1979), p. 263.

[35]A. J. Arberry, *Aspects of Islamic Civilization* (Ann Arbor: University of Michigan Press, 1967); see also Charles Pellah, "Jewellers with Words," in *Islam and the Arab World*, ed. Bernard Lewis (New York: Knopf, 1976), pp. 141–160; Irfan Shahid et al., "Literature," in *The Cambridge History of Islam*, vol. 2, ed. P. M. Holt et al. (Cambridge: University Press, 1970), pp. 657–701.

[36]Oleg Grabar, "Cities and Citizens," in *Islam and the Arab World*, pp. 89–116.

[37]Arberry, *Aspects of Islamic Civilization*, p. 257.

[38]Ibid.

[39]Ibid., p. 111.

[40]See J. Schacht, "Laws and Justice," in *The Cambridge History of Islam*, vol. 2, ed. P. M. Holt et al. (Cambridge: University Press, 1970), pp. 539–568.

[41]Fazlur Rahman, *Islam* (Garden City, N.Y.: Doubleday, 1968), p. xxii.

[42]al Faruqi, "Islam," in *Historical Atlas*, p. 267.

[43]Martin Lings, *What Is Sufism?* (Berkeley: University of California Press, 1977), pp. 45–46; A. J. Arberry, *Sufism* (New York: Harper Torchbooks, 1970), p. 35.

[44]Watt, *Al-Ghazali*, p. 57.

[45]Ibid., p. 60.

[46]Idries Shah, *The Way of the Sufi* (New York: Dutton, 1970).

[47]Ibid., p. 162.

[48]Ibid., p. 169.

[49]Arberry, *Sufism*, p. 119.

[50]Richard M. Eaton, "Sufi Folk Literature and the Expansion of Indian Islam," *HR*, 1974, *14:*117–127.

[51]Lings, *Sufi Saint*; see also Clifford Geertz, *Islam Observed* (Chicago: University of Chicago Press, 1971).

[52]See Roger Le Tourneau et al., "Africa and the Muslim West," in *The Cambridge History of Islam*, vol. 2, ed. P. M. Holt et al. (Cambridge: University Press, 1970), pp. 209–405; Benjamin Ray, *African Religions* (Englewood Cliffs, N.J.: Prentice-Hall, 1976), pp. 174–191.

[53]Lewis, *Arabs in History*, p. 144.

[54]See Norman Itzkowitz, "The Ottoman Empire," in *Islam and the Arab World*, ed. Bernard Lewis (New York: Knopf, 1976), pp. 273–300.

[55]Roger M. Savory, "Land of the Lion and the Sun," in *Islam and the Arab World*, ed. Bernard Lewis (New York: Knopf, 1976), pp. 245–272.

[56]S. A. A. Rizi, "Muslim India," in *Islam and the Arab World*, ed. Bernard Lewis (New York: Knopf, 1976), pp. 301–320; see also I. H. Qureshi et al., "The Indian Sub-Continent," in *The Cambridge History of Islam*, vol. 2, ed. P. M. Holt et al. (Cambridge: University Press, 1970), pp. 1–120.

[57]Lewis, *Arabs in History*, pp. 158–159.

[58]See Rahman, *Islam*, pp. 237–260.

[59]Gibb, "Islam," p. 207.

[60]See Wilfred Cantwell Smith, *The Meaning*

and *End of Religion* (New York: Mentor, 1964), p. 79.

[61] Anne Sinai and Allen Pollack, *The Syrian Arab Republic* (New York: American Academic Association for Peace in the Middle East, 1976); *The Hashemite Kingdom of Jordan and the West Bank* (New York: American Academic Association for Peace in the Middle East, 1977).

[62] The Islamic (Student) Association of Cairo University, "Lessons from Iran," in *Islam in Transition*, ed. John J. Donohue and John L. Esposito (New York: Oxford University Press, 1982), p. 246.

[63] Ayatullah Ruhullah Khumayni, "Islamic Government," *Islam in Transition*, p. 318 (both quotations).

[64] al Faruqi, "Islam," in *Great Asian Religions*, p. 308.

[65] Ibid., p. 310.

[66] Ibid.

[67] Schimmel, "Islam," p. 186.

[68] This section adapts Patrick J. Ryan's *Imale: Yoruba Participation in the Muslim Tradition* (Missoula, Mont.: Scholars Press, 1978), pp. 249–270.

[69] Kenneth Cragg, *The House of Islam* (Belmont, Calif.: Dickenson, 1969), p. 60.

[70] al Faruqi, "Islam," in *Great Asian Religions*, p. 359.

[71] Ibid., p. 366.

[72] Ibid., p. 374.

[73] Eric Voegelin, *Order and History*, IV (Baton Rouge: Louisiana State University Press, 1974), pp. 142–143.

[74] Ibid., pp. 144–145.

[75] See Schimmel, "Islam," pp. 160–166.

[76] Ibid., p. 163.

[77] For an overview, see Denise Lardner Carmody, *Women and World Religions* (Nashville: Abingdon, 1979), pp. 137–155. On current attitudes, see Elizabeth Warnock Fernea and Basima Qattan Bezirgan, *Middle Eastern Muslim Women Speak* (Austin: University of Texas Press, 1977).

[78] Joseph Graziani, "The Status of Women in the Contemporary Muslim Arab Family," *Middle East Review*, 1976–77, 9:48.

[79] *Ms.*, March 1977, p. 112.

[80] Kari Ka'us Iskander, *A Mirror for Princes* (London: Cresset, 1951), p. 125.

[81] George Allgrove, *Love in the East* (London: Gibbs and Phillips, 1962), p. 128.

[82] Mary Daly, *Gyn/Ecology* (Boston: Beacon Press, 1979), chap. 5.

[83] Jane I. Smith and Yvonne Haddad, "Women in the Afterlife: The Islamic View as Seen from the Qur'an and Tradition," *JAAR*, 1975, 43:39–50.

[84] See Goldziher, *Muslim Studies*, vol. 2, pp. 366–368.

[85] On scholarship and saintliness, the Sufis somewhat sponsored women, though their overall view of women was ambivalent; see Annemarie Schimmel, *Mystical Dimensions of Islam* (Chapel Hill: University of North Carolina Press, 1975), pp. 426–435.

[86] Watt, *Formative Period of Islamic Thought*.

[87] See J. E. Esslemont, *Bahaa'u'llah and the New Era: An Introduction to the Baha'i Faith* (Wilmette, Ill.: Baha'i Books, 1970).

[88] al Faruqi, "Islam," in *Great Asian Religions*, p. 347.

[89] Schimmel, "Islam," p. 179.

[90] This section draws on Clifford Geertz, *Islam Observed* (Chicago: University of Chicago Press, 1971), pp. 25–35.

[91] For a sensitive study of the meaning of *Islam*, more suitable for the end of our survey than the beginning, see Jane I. Smith, *An Historical and Semantic Study of the Term Islam as Seen in a Sequence of Quran Commentaries* (Missoula, Mont.: Scholars Press, 1975).

[92] Schimmel, "Islam," p. 142.

[93] On the Mutazila, see Watt, *Formative Period of Islamic Thought*, pp. 209–250.

[94] See S. Pines, "Philosophy," in *The Cambridge History of Islam*, vol. 2, ed. P. M. Holt et al. (Cambridge: University Press, 1970), pp. 780–823.

[95]Earle Waugh, "En Islam Iranien," *HR*, 1975, *14*:322–323.

[96]See Gustave Thaiss, "Religious Symbolism and Social Change: The Drama of Husain," in *Scholars, Saints, and Sufis*, ed. Nikki R. Kiddie (Berkeley: University of California Press, 1972), pp. 349–366.

[97]Fatima Mernissi, "Women, Saints, and Sanctuaries," *Signs*, 1977, *3*(1):101–112.

[98]Schimmel, "Islam," p. 168.

Conclusion

[1]C. G. Jung, *Memories, Dreams, Reflections* (New York: Vintage, 1963), p. 235.

[2]In our view, Mircea Eliade shows that persuasively; see his *Shamanism* (Princeton, N.J.: Princeton University Press/Bollingen, 1972); *Yoga* (Princeton, N.J.: Princeton University Press/Bollingen, 1970).

[3]See Wilfred Cantwell Smith, *The Meaning and End of Religion* (New York: Mentor, 1964); on the rise of the term *religio* with Cicero, see Eric Voegelin, *Order and History, IV* (Baton Rouge: Louisiana State University Press, 1974), pp. 43–48.

[4]See Joachim Wach, *The Comparative Study of Religions* (New York: Columbia University Press, 1961).

[5]Three recent works that illumine tradition are Huston Smith, *Forgotten Truth: The Primordial Tradition* (New York: Harper & Row, 1976); E. F. Schumacher, *A Guide for the Perplexed* (New York: Harper & Row, 1977); Peter Slater, *The Dynamics of Religion* (New York: Harper & Row, 1978).

[6]This is a theme in John Bowker, *The Sense of God* (Oxford: Clarendon Press, 1973).

[7]See Voegelin, *Order and History*, pp. 330–335.

[8]Huston Smith, "Frithjof Schuon's *The Transcendent Unity of Religion:* Pro," and Richard C. Bush, "Frithjof Schuon's *The Transcendent Unity of Religion:* Con," *JAAR*, 1976, *44*:715–719, 721–724.

[9]W. Richard Comstock, *The Study of Religion and Primitive Religions* (New York: Harper & Row, 1971), pp. 13–17.

[10]See Clifford Geertz, *The Interpretation of Cultures* (New York: Basic Books, 1973), pp. 412–453.

[11]Voegelin, *Order and History*, pp. 300–335.

[12]See Karl Rahner and Herbert Vorgrimler, *Theological Dictionary* (New York: Herder and Herder, 1965), pp. 308–309.

[13]On religious interpretations of American destiny, see Conrad Cherry, ed., *God's New Israel* (Englewood Cliffs, N.J.: Prentice-Hall, 1971).

[14]William A. Clebsch, *American Religious Thought* (Chicago: University of Chicago Press, 1973).

[15]Sidney Mead, *The Lively Experiment* (New York: Harper & Row, 1976).

[16]On American pluralism, see *Soundings*, 1978, *61*(3), entire issue.

Annotated Bibliography

The following books ought to appeal to undergraduates, and we recommend them for further reading. Adventurous students may pursue the other, often more specialized resources given in the chapter notes.

Introduction

Carmody, Denise Lardner. *The Oldest God: Archaic Religion Yesterday and Today.* Nashville: Abingdon, 1981. A study of the ancient religious mentality from prehistoric times to the present.

Carmody, Denise Lardner. *Women and World Religions.* Nashville: Abingdon, 1979. A survey of female images and roles in the major religious traditions that describes what being religious as a female has meant in the past and means today.

Carmody, John. *The Progressive Pilgrim.* Notre Dame, Ind.: Fides/Claretian, 1980. An extended essay on the religious life, stressing its expression in education, prayer, play, marriage, and other primary zones.

Comstock, W. Richard. *The Study of Religion and Primitive Religions.* New York: Harper & Row, 1971. A somewhat dry introduction that surveys recent approaches to the world religions and then treats religious symbol systems.

Dunne, John S. *A Search for God in Time and Memory.* New York: Macmillan, 1969. A meditation on the autobiographical aspects of religion, stressing insights of Sören Kierkegaard, Bernard Lonergan, and C. G. Jung.

Eliade, Mircea. *The Sacred and the Profane.* New York: Harcourt, Brace & World, 1959. A concise statement of Eliade's view that human beings try to find meaning by making sacred the primary realities of their lives.

Ellwood, Robert S., Jr. *Introducing Religion: From Inside and Outside.* Englewood Cliffs, N.J.: Prentice-Hall, 1978. A readable introduction that stresses social scientific approaches to the world religions and tries to relate them to contemporary Western life.

Lewis, I. M. *Ecstatic Religion.* Baltimore: Penguin, 1971. An anthropological study of spirit possession and shamanism that shows their function in modern people's social lives.

Novak, Michael. *Ascent of the Mountain, Flight of the Dove.* New York: Harper & Row, 1971. An exposition of religious studies as a personal exploration of the self, society, culture, and religious organizations.

Chapter One: Religions of Ancient Civilizations

Frankfort, Henri. *Kingship and the Gods.* Chicago: University of Chicago Press, 1978. A detailed study of the meaning of sacred kingship in the ancient Near East.

Frankfort, Henri, et al. *Before Philosophy.* Baltimore: Penguin, 1949. A popular classic presentation of the mythical thought of Egypt and Mesopotamia.

Frye, Richard. *The Heritage of Persia.* New York: World, 1963. An informative if rather fact-laden history of ancient Iran.

Guthrie, W. K. C. *The Greeks and Their Gods.* Boston: Beacon Press, 1955. A thorough commentary on the religion of classical Greece.

Hammond, Mason. *The City of the Ancient World.* Cambridge: Harvard University Press, 1972. Useful background on the urbanization that arose with early civilizations.

Renault, Mary. *The Last of the Wine.* New York: Pocket Books, 1964. One of her several historical novels that absorbingly reconstruct the classical Greek world—in this case, that of Socrates and Plato.

Snell, Bruno. *The Discovery of Mind.* New York: Harper & Row, 1960. A difficult but fascinating study of how the Greeks clarified the notion of human reason.

Voegelin, Eric. *Plato.* Baton Rouge: Louisiana State University Press, 1966. A difficult but immensely rewarding study of the father of Western philosophy.

Wilson, John A. *The Culture of Ancient Egypt.* Chicago: University of Chicago Press, 1956. A general history, not too difficult and good on the principal ideas.

Zaehner, R. C. *The Teachings of the Magi.* New York: Oxford University Press, 1976. A brief compendium of Zoroastrian beliefs.

Chapter Two: Judaism

Cohen, A. *Everyman's Talmud.* New York: Schocken, 1975. A topical presentation of rabbinic Judaism's main teachings, rich in quotations and details.

Heilman, Samuel C. *Synagogue Life: A Study in Symbolic Interaction.* Chicago: University of Chicago Press, 1976. A description and analysis of the dynamics of a Jewish congregation that illustrates, often almost in passing, how the Torah has been translated into recent Jewish community life.

Heschel, Abraham Joshua. *God in Search of Man: A Philosophy of Judaism.* New York: Farrar, Straus and Giroux, 1955. A profound meditation on Judaism, by one of the foremost Jewish thinkers of the past generation.

Levin, Meyer. *Classic Hasidic Tales.* New York: Penguin Books, 1975. A good collection of tales about the Baal-Shem-Tov and his grandson, Rabbi Nachman, that show the Hasidic imagination in full flower.

Neusner, Jacob. *The Life of Torah.* Encino, Calif.: Dickenson, 1974. A selection of readings that illustrate basic aspects of Jewish faith, both traditional and modern.

Neunser, Jacob. *The Way of Torah.* 2nd ed. Encino, Calif.: Dickenson, 1974. A readable introduction to Judaism that delineates its classical structure, the Torah, and the modern situation.

Roth, Cecil. *History of the Jews.* New York: Schocken, 1961. A lucid presentation of Jewish experience from biblical times to World War II.

Siegel, Richard, et al. *The Jewish Catalogue.* Philadelphia: Jewish Publication Society of America, 1973. A mine of information about recent Jewish adaptations and retrievals of traditional prayers, ceremonies, customs, and arts.

Tullock, John H. *The Old Testament Story.* Englewood Cliffs, N.J.: Prentice-Hall, 1981. An up-to-date and readable text that surveys the entire Old Testament.

Zborowski, Mark, and Elizabeth Herzog. *Life Is with People.* New York: Schocken, 1962. An absorbing portrait of *shtetl* life prior to World War II, based on interviews and personal reminiscences.

Chapter Three: Christianity

Bolshakoff, Sergius, and M. Basil Pennington. *In*

Search of True Wisdom. Garden City, N.Y.: Doubleday, 1979. Visits to Eastern spiritual fathers that beautifully convey the Eastern monastic viewpoint.

Booty, John E. *The Church in History*. New York: Seabury, 1979. A readable overview, from a Western and Anglican viewpoint.

Brown, Robert McAfee. *The Spirit of Protestantism*. New York: Oxford University Press, 1965. A lucid analysis of the major emphases in Protestant theology and faith.

Carmody, John Tully, and Denise Lardner Carmody. *Contemporary Catholic Theology: An Introduction*. New York: Harper & Row, 1980. A layperson's guide to the current state of Roman Catholic theology.

Clebsch, William A. *Christianity in European History*. New York: Oxford University Press, 1979. A somewhat demanding but stimulating view, set in terms of religious studies rather than Church history.

Griffin, Emilie. *Turning: Reflections on the Experience of Conversion.* Garden City, N.J.: Doubleday, 1980. A lucid and sincere treatment that throws light on contemporary religious experience.

Neill, Stephen. *Jesus through Many Eyes*. Philadelphia: Fortress, 1976. A good presentation of recent New Testament scholarship that shows the distinctive theologies of the different New Testament writers.

Schmemann, Alexander. *The Historical Road of Eastern Orthodoxy*. Crestwood, N.Y.: St. Vladimir's Seminary Press, 1977. A view of the development of Orthodoxy from New Testament times, originally written for Russian Christians.

Shinn, Roger L., ed. *Faith and Science in an Unjust World, Vol. 1: Plenary Presentations*. Philadelphia: Fortress, 1980. Papers from the 1979 World Council of Churches' Conference at the Massachusetts Institute of Technology on "Faith, Science, and the Future."

Wilmore, Gayraud S., and James H. Cone, eds., *Black Theology*. Maryknoll, N.Y.: Orbis, 1979. A documentary history of recent black theology showing the primacy of biblical and political themes.

Chapter Four: Islam

Arberry, A. J. *Aspects of Islamic Civilization*. Ann Arbor: University of Michigan Press, 1971. Selections that illumine major themes of Muslim culture, including science, law, poetry, and mysticism.

Cragg, Kenneth, *The House of Islam*. 2nd ed. Encino, Calif.: Dickenson, 1975. An analysis of major topics in Islam, such as its view of God, the role of Muhammad, liturgy, and Sufism.

Cragg, Kenneth, and Marston Speight, eds. *Islam from Within*. Belmont, Calif.: Wadsworth, 1980. A fine anthology of readings on Islam, covering most of the major headings.

Donohue, John J., and John L. Esposito, eds. *Islam in Transition*. New York: Oxford University Press, 1982. An anthology of recent Muslim opinion, especially focused on recent social change.

Geertz, Clifford. *Islam Observed*. Chicago: University of Chicago Press, 1968. A brief, somewhat difficult but rewarding analysis of religious development in Morocco and Indonesia by a leading cultural anthropologist.

Lings, Martin. *A Sufi Saint of the Twentieth Century*. 2nd ed. Berkeley: University of California Press, 1973. A somewhat cumbersome analysis of the impact and teaching of a leading North African sheik.

Rahman, Fazlur. *Islam*. Garden City, N.Y.: Doubleday, 1968. A solid, fact-filled history of Islam from Muhammad to the present.

Rodinson, Maxime. *The Arabs*. Chicago: University of Chicago Press, 1979. A simple and readable overview of the dominant Muslim people.

Schacht, Joseph, and C. E. Bosworth, eds. *The Legacy of Islam*. 2nd ed. New York: Oxford University Press, 1979. Somewhat specialized studies covering most aspects of Muslim history and culture.

Swartz, Melvin L., ed. *Studies on Islam*. New York: Oxford University Press, 1981. A wide-ranging collection of rather scholarly studies by Islamic specialists.

Conclusion: Summary Reflections

Ahlstrom, Sydney. *A Religious History of the American People.* New Haven, Conn.: Yale University Press, 1972. A massive, authoritative treatment of American religion from precolonial times to the end of the 1960s.

Bowker, John. *The Religious Imagination and the Sense of God.* Oxford: Clarendon Press, 1978. A stimulating study of several religious traditions that shows the great yield sympathetic and imaginative scholarship can produce.

Carmody, John. *Theology for the 1980s.* Philadelphia: Westminster, 1980. Recent trends and prospects for Christian theology, set in an ecumenical horizon that includes the non-Christian religions.

Foy, Witfield, ed. *Man's Religious Quest.* New York: St. Martin's Press, 1978. A good general sourcebook on the world religions, offering many primary texts.

Gremillion, Joseph, and William Ryan, eds. *World Faiths and the New World Order.* Washington, D.C.: The Interreligious Peace Colloquium, 1978. Papers from a Muslim, Jewish, Christian symposium of 1977.

Johnston, William. *The Inner Eye of Love.* New York: Harper & Row, 1978. Shows the contemplative foundations of religion, with special reference to Christianity and Buddhism.

Krim, Keith, ed. *Abingdon Dictionary of Living Religions.* Nashville: Abingdon, 1981. The best single volume resource for the main concepts, people, and events of the world religions.

Schimmel, Annemarie, and Abdoldjavad Falaturi, eds. *We Believe in One God.* New York: Seabury, 1979. Somewhat specialized papers by Muslim and Christian scholars on topics related to the monotheistic experience of God.

Slater, Peter. *The Dynamics of Religion.* New York: Harper & Row, 1978. A rather conceptual but rich theory of how the religions configure and can best be analyzed.

Streng, Frederick. *Understanding Religious Life.* 2nd ed. Encino, Calif.: Dickenson, 1976. An analysis of methodology in religious studies, traditional ways of being religious, and the varieties of religious expression.

Glossary

aesthetic: concerning the beautiful or artistic

Allah: Muslim God

animism: ancient tendency to assume spirits in all things

anthropomorphism: personification; treating something nonhuman as though it were human

apostle: one sent forth; original Christian witness

archaic: old; premodern and prescientific

asceticism: discipline; abstinence from self-indulgence

Ashkenazim: Jews of German origin.

baptism: Christian sacrament of initiation with water

Cabala: Jewish mystical tradition

cosmos: the universe conceived as an orderly system

***dhikr* ("zicker"):** Muslim term for recollection or remembrance (of God)

Diaspora: Jewish term for dispersion or exile from Israel

divination: art of discerning future events

ecumenism: largely Christian term for movement toward worldwide or transdenominational unity

empiricism: philosophical outlook that stresses sense experience and limits speculation

Enlightenment: eighteenth-century European movement that stressed the untrammeled use of reason

eschatology: Christian doctrine regarding the final things, such as the end of the world, judgment, heaven, and hell

ethics: study or teaching concerned with morality or right and wrong

Eucharist: Christian sacramental meal of thanksgiving, based on Jesus' Last Supper

faith: belief; commitment or assent beyond factual surety or proof

fetish: object believed to have protective powers

Gemara: comments on and discussion of the Mishnah

Gnosticism: religious movement based on secret knowledge *(gnosis)* that contested with early Christianity

God: the Supreme Being; usually considered personal in the West

god: a being of more than human power

Gospel: the Christian glad tidings or joyous message of salvation

239

grace: divine favor or free help

hadith: Muslim traditions about Muhammad

haggadah: Jewish stories or lore

hajj: Muslim pilgrimage to Mecca

halakah: Jewish legal tradition

Hejira: Muhammad's flight from Mecca to Medina in 622

holy: set apart and dedicated to the worship or service of the divine

imam: spiritual guide of Shiite Muslims

Incarnation: Christian doctrine that the divine Word was made flesh in Jesus of Nazareth

Islam: the faith, obedience, and practice of Muslims

jihad: Muslim holy war

jinn: Arabic term for demon or spirit

Karaism: movement among Middle Eastern Jews of the eighth to twelfth centuries who rejected oral Torah

kibbutz: collective, often agricultural settlement in Israel

kosher: fit, proper, suitable according to Jewish law

maat: Egyptian notion of cosmic order

magi: ancient Persian and Zoroastrian priests

magic: attempts to control divinities for one's own use

metaphysics: philosophical study of underlying causes

midrash: Jewish exegesis of scripture

mikvah: Jewish ritual bath

minyan: quorum of ten needed for Jewish worship

Mishnah: code of Jewish law formally promulgated around 200 C.E.

mitzvah: Jewish commandment; scriptural or rabbinical injunction

Muslim: submitter to Allah; follower of Islam and Muhammad

mystery: something that has not been explained or cannot be explained

mysticism: experience of direct communion with ultimate reality

myth: explanatory story, usually traditional

nature: physical reality in its totality; whatness or character

ontology: the study of being or existence

oral peoples: those peoples whose cultures had or have no writing

orthodox: straight, correct, or approved in belief or worship

Pharisees: ancient Jews who defended oral Torah

prehistoric: prior to written history

priest: religious functionary who performs sacrifices, rites, interpretations, and so on

primitive: original or underived; undeveloped

prophet: spokesperson for God or a divinity

rabbi: Jewish title for teacher of oral Torah

Ramadan: Muslim lunar month for fasting

rasul: Muslim prophet or messenger

redemption: retrieval ("buying back"); deliverance from sin

religion: communion with, service of, or concern for ultimate reality

revelation: disclosure (of sacred truth)

ritual: prescribed, formalized religious action or ceremony

sacrament: sacred, empowering action, such as Christian baptism or Eucharist

sacrifice: an offering that "makes holy"; oblation of something of value (such as an animal) to God or sacred powers

Sadducees: ancient Jewish priests who stressed written Torah

salvation: saving from sin; making whole and healthy

secularism: worldly view of life that tends to depreciate religion

Sephardim: Jews of Spanish origin

shaman: ancient specialist in techniques of ecstasy

Shema: Jewish proclamation of God's unity (based on Deut. 6:4–9)

Shia: sectarian Islam that opposes the Sunni orthodoxy

sin: offense against God; moral (culpable) error or misdeed

Sufism: devotional, ascetic, or mystical Muslim tradition whose adherents are often members of a lodge or brotherhood

Sunni: majority sect of Islam

synagogue: Jewish house of assembly, study, and prayer

Talmud: primary source of Jewish law and rabbinic learning; Mishnah plus Gemara

theology: study or teaching about God or the gods

Torah: Jewish revelation or law

totem: animal, plant, or other object that serves as a clan emblem

tradition: teaching and practice that has been handed down

transcendence: going beyond the usual limits, often out to the divine

Trinity: the Christian God as Father-Son-Spirit

Ummah: the community of Islam

witch: one who performs sorcery or magic with evil intent; a wise woman in some feminist circles today

Yom Kippur: solemn Jewish holiday, Day of Atonement

zakat: Muslim almsgiving

Zionism: Jewish movement to secure a state in Palestine

Zohar: prime text of Jewish Cabalists

Index of Names and Places

Index of Subjects

Abba (Father), 99
afterlife, 17, 24, 28, 37, 40, 41, 46, 62, 66, 89–90, 184
agriculture, 50
Albigensians, 115–16, 142
alchemy, 18, 132, 163, 170
allegorical exegesis, 69, 70, 71–72
allegory, 102, 103
almsgiving. *See zakat*
American religion, 127, 214–17
anathemas, 111–12
anawim, 71
ancestors, 17, 18, 20
angels, 193
animism, 30
anthropocentricity, 187
anthropomorphism, 42, 43, 70, 94, 192
anti-Semitism, 65, 73–75, 76, 78, 80
apocalypse, 62–63, 104, 106, 119
apostolic age, 104–107
apostolos, 104, 111
apotheosis (divinization), 127
architecture, Islamic, 164–67
arete (excellence), 39, 47
Arianism, 108, 110, 115, 117
art, Christian, 119–21; Islamic, 163–67
Aryans, 30
asceticism, Christian, 105, 106, 109, 112, 142;
    Hasidic, 71; Islamic, 155, 159, 179
authority, Christian, 104, 109, 111–12, 124
Avesta, 30, 32

baals (Canaanite), 57, 58, 80, 87
Babylonian Talmud. *See* Talmud

Baha'i, 185
baptism, 107, 110, 112, 134, 141
bar mitzva(h), 68, 83–84
bas mitzva(h), 84
Battle of the Ditch, 153
beatific vision, 140, 141
Bhagavad Gita, 6
biblical exegesis, 69–70. *See also* allegorical exegesis
bishops, 106–107, 109, 111, 115, 137
Bismallah, 164
Black Death, 121
Booths (Sukkoth), 68
Byzantine Christianity. *See* Eastern Orthodoxy

Cabalism, 71–72, 79, 90
Caesaropapism, 108
caliph (leader), 160, 161, 162
Canaanite religion, 57, 61, 80
cannibalism, 18
canon, Christian, 107
Canterbury Tales, 117
caste system, 33, 34
cathedrals, Gothic, 117–18
cave paintings, 17
celibacy (virginity), 109, 110, 137–38, 142
Chalcedon, Council of (451), 109
Christian Church, 99, 100–101, 106–107, 137; and
    State, 108, 115, 138–39
Christianity, 6, 42, 54, 98–146, 156–58; conciliar age,
    107–108; medieval age, 115–21; as universal,
    100, 143
Christology, 109, 112
chthonioi (spirits), 41, 42